Economics of Monetary Union

more land move money to your family?

why CAP: self sufficiency environmental defend farmers.

How does CAP work:

China is a range importen
agriculture.

If stop subsidy, fewer farmers.

For 3% of agriculture, 40% EU budget gives to the subsidy.

EU budget also subsidizes Chinese import.

zone that you have to protect

Economics of Monetary Union

ELEVENTH EDITION

Paul De Grauwe

John Paulson Chair in European Political Economy

London School of Economics

OXFORD

UNIVERSITY PRESS

OXFORD
UNIVERSITY PRESS

Great Clarendon Street, Oxford, OX2 6DP,
United Kingdom

Oxford University Press is a department of the University of Oxford.
It furthers the University's objective of excellence in research, scholarship,
and education by publishing worldwide. Oxford is a registered trade mark of
Oxford University Press in the UK and in certain other countries

Eighth edition 2009
Ninth edition 2012
Tenth edition 2014

Impression: 1

Published in the United States of America by Oxford University Press
198 Madison Avenue, New York, NY 10016, United States of America

British Library Cataloguing in Publication Data

Data available

Library of Congress Control Number: 2015947357

ISBN 978-0-19-873987-6

Printed in Great Britain by
Bell & Bain Ltd., Glasgow

Contents

PART 2 **Monetary union**

Introduction

Economists are often criticized because they are very bad at predicting crises and very good at explaining afterwards why these crises were inevitable. However, if there is one area where this criticism does not apply, it is in the economics of monetary union. In the 1980s and early 1990s, when the European leaders were discussing the plans for a monetary union in Europe, economists, including the present author, warned that this would be a risky undertaking, mainly because it would be a monetary union lacking a budgetary union. The European leaders, who were driven by political motives in pushing for monetary union, brushed this criticism aside and created an incomplete monetary union that, because of its incompleteness, would be fragile. The economists' prediction has now turned out to be vindicated. This has been especially true since the emergence of the second Greek debt crisis in 2015 when the possibility of a Greek exit from the Eurozone was openly discussed.

As in the previous editions of this book, the focus in the first part is on the costs and benefits of a monetary union. As in the previous edition, emphasis is placed on an analysis of why the incompleteness of the Eurozone creates additional costs, and why it leads to problems of sustainability. This will lead us to study different ways to 'complete' a monetary union. Inevitably this will bring us to the question of how a monetary union can be embedded in a political union, and what the implications are of such a union.

The analysis of the costs and benefits of a monetary union also leads us to the question of whether the UK, Denmark, Sweden, and new EU member countries are likely to benefit from being members of the Eurozone. In addition, we will have a few things to say about whether other parts of the world—East Asia, Latin America, and Africa—would benefit from monetary unification.

The start of EMU (Economic and Monetary Union) on 1 January 1999 was a historic event. There have been few attempts ever to introduce a monetary union without the force of arms. Monetary union in Europe has created problems that are exciting to analyse. The second part of this book deals with these problems of running a monetary union in Europe. We will analyse how the European Central Bank (ECB) was designed to conduct a single monetary policy. We will also discuss some of the shortcomings of this design. The issues of the political independence and accountability of the ECB will loom large in this discussion.

Many of the issues with which the ECB is confronted today are practical ones. How does the ECB make a choice between the different targets a central bank should pursue? What are the most appropriate instruments to achieve these targets? Is the ECB attaching too much importance to the money stock? How can it improve its credibility? How should the ECB react to different business cycle developments in the Eurozone and what are the relations between monetary and budgetary policies?

Since the dramatic eruption of the financial crisis in 2007, new issues and questions have arisen. How should the ECB deal with the financial crisis? Has its response been sufficient and does it have the right instruments to face this crisis? These questions will also lead us to formulate reforms that are needed to prevent the emergence of future crises. In this connection we will criticize the singular focus of the ECB on inflation targeting, and we will argue that modern central banks need to enlarge the list of objectives they pursue. We will also stress the need for the ECB to be a lender of last resort both in the banking sector and in the markets of government bonds. Since 2012, the ECB has accepted the principle of being a lender of last resort in the government bond markets. This principle, however, is still very much contested. We will discuss why.

The present edition of the book also adds discussions about recent institutional changes. An important one is the decision to create a banking union in the Eurozone. We will analyse the ingredients of this banking union. We will ask whether it is sufficient to deal with new banking crises and what it implies for the future of the Eurozone.

The study of the workings of a monetary union is fascinating. So many new ideas are still to be discovered. My first hope is that this book can contribute to the discovery of these ideas. My second hope is that I can convey to the reader the same sense of excitement that I have when I study the subject.

This book would not have come about without the intense discussions and debates with colleagues and students in which I have been involved over many years. Many of them were kind enough to read parts of the manuscript and to formulate their comments and criticism. In particular, I am grateful to Filip Abraham, Michael Artis, Richard Baldwin, Juan José Calaza, Bernard Delbecque, Harris Dellas, Casper de Vries, Hans Dewachter, Sylvester Eijffinger, Michele Fratianni, Vitor Gaspar, Wolfgang Gebauer, Francesco Giavazzi, Daniel Gros, Søren Harck, Romain Houssa, Gerhard Illing, Henk Jager, Catrinus Jepma, Lars Jonung, Georgios Karras, Clemens Kool, Ivo Maes, Ugo Marani, Carlos Marinheiro, Jacques Mélitz, Stefano Micossi, Wim Moesen, Francesco Mongelli, Franco Praussello, Waltraud Schelkle, Marc-Alexandre Sénégas, Hans-Werner Sinn, George Tavlas, Niels Thygesen, Francisco Torres, Alfred Tovias, Jürgen von Hagen, Frank Westermann, and Charles Wyplosz. During the years leading to the tenth edition of this book I was very much helped by the competent research assistance of Yunus Aksoy, Cláudia Costa Storti, Marianna Grimaldi, Yuemei Ji, Pablo Rovira Kaltwasser, Vivien Lewis, Magdalena Polan, Frauke Skudelny, and Nancy Verret. My gratitude goes especially to Yuemei Ji, who patiently checked this eleventh version of the manuscript.

For further information visit the Online Resource Centre:
www.oxfordtextbooks.co.uk/orc/degrauwe11e/

Part 1

Costs and benefits of monetary union

The <u>costs</u> of a common currency

Introduction

The costs of a monetary union derive from the fact that when a country relinquishes its national currency, it also relinquishes an instrument of economic policy, i.e. it loses the ability to conduct a national monetary policy. In other words, in a full monetary union the national central bank either ceases to exist or will have no real power. This implies that a nation joining a monetary union will no longer be able to change the price of its currency (by devaluations and revaluations), to determine the quantity of the national money in circulation, or to change the short-term interest rate.

One may raise the issue here of what good it does for a nation to be able to conduct an independent monetary policy (including changing the price of its currency). There are many situations in which these policies can be very useful for an individual nation. The exchange rate is useful as a policy instrument, for example, because nations are different in some important senses, requiring changes in the exchange rate to occur. In Section 1.1 we analyse some of the differences that may require exchange rate adjustments. In later sections we analyse how the loss of monetary independence may be costly in some other ways for an individual nation, in particular in the way government budget deficits can be financed.

The analysis that follows in this chapter is known as the 'theory of optimum currency areas'. This theory, which was pioneered by Mundell (1961), McKinnon (1963), and Kenen (1969), has concentrated on the cost side of the cost–benefit analysis of a monetary union.[1]

1.1 Shifts in demand (Mundell)

Consider the case of a demand shift developed by Mundell (1961) in his celebrated article on optimum currency areas. Let us suppose first that two countries, which we call France and Germany, form a monetary union. By that we mean that they have abandoned their national currencies and use a common currency, the euro, which is managed by a common central bank, the European Central Bank (ECB). Let us assume further that for some reason

---

[1] For surveys of this literature, see Ishiyama (1975); Tower and Willett (1976); and Mongelli (2002).

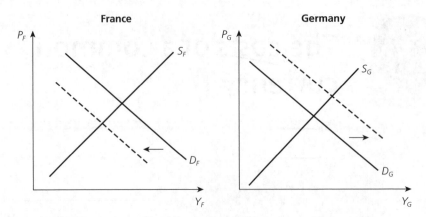

Figure 1.1 Aggregate demand and supply in France and Germany.

consumers shift their preferences away from French-made to German-made products. We present the effects of this asymmetric shock in aggregate demand in Fig. 1.1.

The curves in Fig. 1.1 are the standard aggregate demand and supply curves in an open economy seen in most macroeconomics textbooks.[2] The demand curve is the negatively sloped line indicating that when the domestic price level increases the demand for the domestic output declines.[3]

The supply curve expresses the idea that when the price of the domestic output increases, domestic firms, in a competitive environment, will increase their supply in order to profit from the higher price. In addition, each supply curve is drawn under the assumption that the nominal wage rate and the prices of other inputs (e.g. energy, imported inputs) remain constant. Changes in the prices of these inputs will shift these supply curves.

The demand shift is represented by an upward movement of the demand curve in Germany, and a downward movement in France. As will be discussed later, it will be important to know whether these demand shifts are permanent or temporary. For the moment we assume that these shifts are permanent, e.g. due to a change in consumer preferences. The result of these demand shifts, then, is that output declines in France and increases in Germany. This is most likely to lead to additional unemployment in France and a decline in unemployment in Germany.

Both countries will have an adjustment problem. France is plagued with reduced output and higher unemployment. Germany experiences a boom, which also leads to upward pressures on its price level. The question that arises is whether there is a mechanism that leads to automatic equilibration.

The answer is positive. There are two mechanisms that will automatically bring back equilibrium in the two countries. One is based on wage flexibility, the other on the mobility of labour.

1. *Wage flexibility*. If wages in France and Germany are flexible the following will happen. French workers who are unemployed will reduce their wage claims. In Germany, the excess

---

[2] See Krugman and Wells (2005); Mankiw (2006); or Blanchard (2008).
[3] This is the substitution effect of a price increase. In the standard aggregate demand analysis, there is also a monetary effect: when the domestic price level increases, the stock of real cash balances declines, leading to an upward movement in the domestic real interest rate. This in turn reduces aggregate demand (see De Grauwe (1983)). Here we disregard the monetary effect and concentrate on the substitution effect.

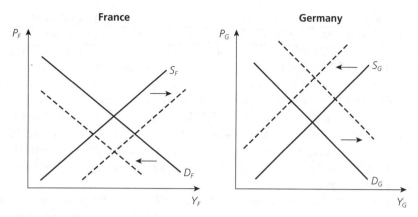

Figure 1.2 The automatic adjustment process.

demand for labour will push up the wage rate. The effect of this adjustment mechanism is shown in Fig. 1.2. The reduction of the wage rate in France shifts the aggregate supply curve downwards, whereas the wage increases in Germany shift the aggregate supply curve upwards. These shifts lead to a new equilibrium. In France, the price of output declines, making French products more competitive, and stimulating demand. The opposite occurs in Germany.

Note also that the second-order effects on aggregate demand will reinforce the equilibrating mechanism. The wage and price increases in Germany make French products more competitive. This leads to an upward shift in the French aggregate demand curve. Similarly, the decline in French costs and prices makes German products less competitive and shifts the German aggregate demand curve downwards.

2. *Mobility of labour.* A second mechanism that will lead to a new equilibrium involves mobility of labour. The French unemployed workers move to Germany where there is excess demand for labour. This movement of labour eliminates the need to let wages decline in France and increase in Germany. Thus, the French unemployment problem disappears, whereas the inflationary wage pressures in Germany vanish.

Thus, in principle the adjustment problem for France and Germany will disappear automatically if wages are flexible, and/or if the mobility of labour between the two countries is sufficiently high. If these conditions are not satisfied, however, the adjustment problem will not vanish. Suppose, for example, that wages in France do not decline despite the unemployment situation, and that French workers do not move to Germany. In that case France is stuck in the disequilibrium situation depicted in Fig. 1.1. In Germany, the excess demand for labour puts upward pressure on the wage rate, producing an upward shift of the supply curve. The adjustment to the disequilibrium must now come exclusively through price increases in Germany. These German price increases make French goods more competitive again, leading to an upward shift in the aggregate demand curve in France. Thus, if wages do not decline in France the adjustment to the disequilibrium will take the form of inflation in Germany.

What would have happened if the two countries had not been in a monetary union? In that case they would have been free to use their national monetary policy tools to adjust to the asymmetric shocks. There are several ways in which countries that maintain their monetary independence can use their monetary policy instruments. We distinguish two methods here that are related to the exchange rate regime that countries use. In a first regime, these countries keep their exchange rates flexible, very much as the US, the UK, and Japan are doing. In that case, they can change their monetary policies (through changes in the domestic interest rate and/or the money supply) to achieve a particular objective. In a second regime, countries peg their exchange rates to another currency, e.g. Denmark to the euro, or several Latin American countries to the dollar. In this case they can devalue or revalue their currencies.

Suppose first that France and Germany had chosen a flexible exchange rate regime. In that case, France could have lowered its interest rate, thereby stimulating aggregate demand, while Germany could have raised its interest rate, thereby reducing aggregate demand. These monetary policies conducted by France and Germany would likely have led to a depreciation of the French franc and an appreciation of the German mark, thereby making the French products sold in Germany cheaper. Both the interest rate and exchange rate changes would have tended to boost aggregate demand in France and to lower aggregate demand in Germany.

If France and Germany had chosen to peg their exchange rate, France would have been able to devalue the franc against the mark, thereby achieving similar effects on aggregate demand. The devaluation of the franc would have increased the competitiveness of the French products, thereby stimulating the demand coming from Germany.

The effects of these national monetary policies are shown in Fig. 1.3. The expansionary monetary policy in France (or in the second regime, the devaluation of the French franc) shifts the French aggregate demand curve upwards. In Germany, the opposite occurs. The restrictive monetary policy in Germany (the appreciation of the mark) reduces aggregate demand in Germany, so that the demand curve shifts back to the left.

The effects of these demand shifts are that France solves its unemployment problem and Germany avoids having to accept inflationary pressures. This remarkable feat is achieved using just one instrument. (The reader may sense that this is too good to be true. And indeed

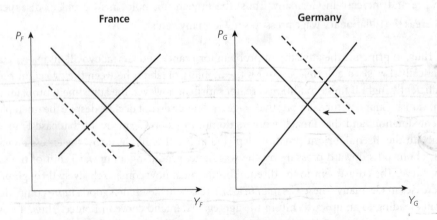

Figure 1.3 Effects of monetary expansion in France and monetary restriction in Germany.

it is. However, for the moment we just present Mundell's theory. We come back with criticism in Chapter 2.)

In contrast, when France is part of a monetary union with Germany it relinquishes control over its monetary policy. If it is saddled with a sustained unemployment problem, that can only disappear as a result of deflation (a price decline) in France. In this sense, we can say that a monetary union has a cost for France when it is faced with a negative demand shock. Similarly, Germany will find it costly to be in a monetary union with France, because it will have to accept more inflation than it would like.

Let us recapitulate the main points developed in this section. If wages are rigid and if labour mobility is limited, countries that form a monetary union will find it harder to adjust to asymmetric demand shifts than countries that have maintained their own national money and that can devalue (revalue) their currency. (In Box 1.1, we analyse whether this

---

BOX 1.1 Symmetric and asymmetric shocks compared

We have seen that the occurrence of asymmetric shocks creates costs of adjustment in a monetary union if there is a lack of flexibility in the labour markets. Things are very different when symmetric shocks occur. We illustrate this using the same two-country model of aggregate demand and supply as in Fig. 1.1. We now assume that the demand shocks are symmetric. More specifically, we assume that in both France and Germany the demand curve shifts to the left in equal amounts. The result is shown in Fig. 1.4.

Can France and Germany deal with this negative demand shock when they are in a monetary union? The answer is yes, at least in principle. In a monetary union, monetary policy is centralized in the hands of the union central bank. Call it the European Central Bank (ECB). In addition, in a monetary union there is only one interest rate as the money markets are perfectly integrated. The ECB can now lower the interest rate, thereby stimulating aggregate demand in both countries. This contrasts markedly with the case of asymmetric shocks. There the ECB will be pretty much paralysed, because it has only one instrument to deal with two problems. If it reduces the interest rate so as to stimulate aggregate demand in France, it increases inflationary pressure in Germany. If, on the other hand, it increases the interest rate so as to deal with the inflationary pressure in Germany, it reduces aggregate demand in France, and intensifies that country's problem.

It is also interesting to analyse what would happen if the two countries that face a symmetric shock were not in a monetary union. Would devaluation then be an attractive policy option? The answer is no. Suppose that France were to devalue. This would stimulate aggregate demand in France, at the expense of Germany. In France, the aggregate demand curve would shift to the right. The French devaluation would, however, shift the German aggregate demand curve further to the left. The French would essentially solve their problem by exporting it to Germany. It is likely that the latter would react. The danger of a spiral of devaluations and counter-devaluations would be real. In the end the effectiveness of changing the exchange rate would be greatly reduced. In order to avoid such a spiral the two countries would have to coordinate their actions, which is difficult among independent nations. In a monetary union, by contrast, this monetary cooperation is institutionalized. We conclude that a monetary union is a more attractive monetary regime than a regime of independent monetary authorities if shocks that hit the countries are symmetric. When shocks are asymmetric, however, this advantage of a monetary union disappears.

It should be noted that we have assumed that the ECB can manipulate aggregate demand in the union. There are reasons to believe that the effectiveness of monetary policy in raising aggregate demand is limited. The same criticism, however, applies as far as the effectiveness of devaluations is concerned. When countries are independent and they use the exchange rate as an instrument to deal with asymmetric shocks, they face similar limitations on the effectiveness of exchange rate policies. We return to these issues in Chapter 2.

(Continued...)

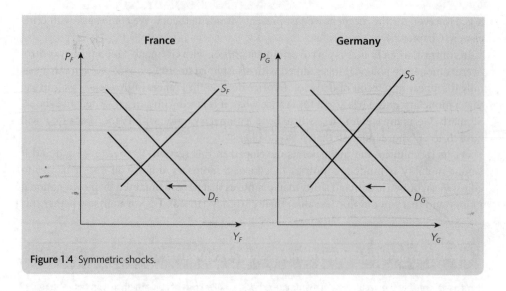

Figure 1.4 Symmetric shocks.

conclusion holds when demand shocks are symmetric.) In the case of countries that have kept their own money, national monetary policies, including the exchange rate, add some flexibility to a system that is overly rigid. Put differently, a monetary union between two or more countries is optimal if one of the following conditions is satisfied: (*a*) there is sufficient wage flexibility; (*b*) there is sufficient mobility of labour.

1.2 Monetary independence and government budgets

When countries join a monetary union they lose their monetary independence. As argued in Section 1.1, that affects their capacity to deal with asymmetric shocks. This is the essence of the traditional theory of optimal currency areas as developed by Mundell (1961). This theory, however, is incomplete. It overlooks another major implication of the loss of monetary independence: the entry into a monetary union fundamentally changes the capacity of governments to finance their budget deficits. This is important, but surprisingly it was overlooked until the sovereign debt crisis in the Eurozone emerged in 2010. Let us develop this point further.[4]

Members of a monetary union issue debt in a currency over which they have no control. For example, when France, Germany, and Spain entered the Eurozone they ceased to issue their debt in their national currencies (the French franc, the German mark, and the Spanish peseta) over which they had full control. Instead, they now issue their debt in euros, a currency that none of these governments control. This has a profound implication. It implies that these governments cannot give an ironclad guarantee to the holders of government bonds that they will have enough cash to pay them (the bondholders) out when the bonds come to maturity. This contrasts with a standalone country like the UK. The UK government

---

[4] The following sections are based on De Grauwe (2011).

can give a full guarantee to holders of UK government bonds that they will be paid out when the bonds mature. The reason is that there is a central bank, the Bank of England, that will be ready (or be forced) to provide liquidity to the UK government if the latter were to face a liquidity shortage, which would prevent it from paying out bondholders. Governments of member countries of a monetary union have no central bank that can be forced to provide liquidity in times of crisis.

As will be shown in the next paragraphs, the fact that governments of a monetary union cannot give a guarantee to the holders of the government bonds that they will always be paid out at maturity, implies that financial markets acquire the power to force default on these countries. This is not the case in countries that are not part of a monetary union, and that have kept control over the currency in which they issue debt. These countries cannot easily be forced into default by financial markets.

In order to show why this is so, we analyse in detail what happens when investors start having doubts about the solvency of these two types of countries. We will use the UK as a prototype monetary 'stand-alone' country and Spain as a prototype member country of a monetary union.[5]

The UK scenario

Let's first trace what would happen if investors were to fear that the UK government might be defaulting on its debt. In that case, they would sell their UK government bonds, driving up the interest rate. After selling these bonds, these investors would have pounds that most probably they would want to get rid of by selling them in the foreign exchange market. The price of the pound would drop until somebody else was willing to buy these pounds. The effect of this mechanism is that the pounds would remain bottled up in the UK money market to be invested in UK assets. Put differently, the UK money stock would remain unchanged. Part of that stock of money would probably be re-invested in UK government securities. But even if that were not the case so that the UK government could not find the funds to roll over its debt at reasonable interest rates, it would certainly force the Bank of England to provide it with the cash to pay out bondholders. Thus the UK government is ensured that the liquidity is around to fund its debt. This means that investors cannot precipitate a liquidity crisis in the UK that could force the UK government into default. There is a superior force of last resort, the Bank of England.

The Spanish scenario

Things are dramatically different for a member of a monetary union such as Spain. Suppose investors fear a default by the Spanish government. As a result, they sell Spanish government bonds, raising the interest rate. So far, we have the same effects as in the case of the UK. The rest is very different. The investors who have acquired euros are likely to decide to invest these euros elsewhere, say in German government bonds. As a result, the euros leave the Spanish banking system. There is no foreign exchange market and flexible exchange rate

---

[5] See Kopf (2011) for an insightful analysis and Winkler (2011) for an interesting comparison with the US banking system of the nineteenth century.

to stop this. Thus, the total amount of liquidity (money supply) in Spain shrinks. The Spanish government experiences a liquidity crisis, i.e. it cannot obtain funds to roll over its debt at reasonable interest rates. In addition, the Spanish government cannot force the Bank of Spain to provide the cash. The common central bank (the ECB in the Eurozone) can provide all the liquidity in the world, but the Spanish government does not control that institution. The liquidity crisis, if strong enough, can force the Spanish government into default because it cannot find the cash to pay out the bondholders. Financial markets know this and will test the Spanish government when budget deficits deteriorate. Thus, in a monetary union, financial markets acquire tremendous power and can force any member country onto its knees.

The situation of Spain is reminiscent of the situation of emerging economies that have to borrow in a foreign currency. These emerging economies face the same problem, i.e. they can be confronted with a 'sudden stop' when capital inflows suddenly stop, leading to a liquidity crisis (see Calvo 1988 and Eichengreen et al. 2005).

The previous analysis stresses the fragility of a monetary union. When investors distrust a particular member government they will sell the bonds, thereby raising the interest rate and triggering a *liquidity* crisis. This may in turn set in motion a *solvency* problem, i.e. with a higher interest rate the government debt burden increases, forcing the government to reduce spending and increase taxation. Such forced budgetary austerity is politically costly, and in turn may lead the government to stop servicing the debt, and to declare a default. Thus, by entering a monetary union, member countries become vulnerable to movements of distrust by investors. Note that there is a self-fulfilling prophecy in these dynamics. When financial markets start distrusting a particular government's ability (or willingness) to service its debt, investors sell the government bonds, making it more likely that the government will stop servicing the debt. We come back to this feature of government debt crises in Chapter 5.

Note also that these dynamics are absent in countries that have kept their monetary independence. The reason is that these 'stand-alone' countries issue their debt in their own currencies. These countries, therefore, can always create the liquidity to pay out the bondholders. This does not mean, of course, that these countries may not have problems of their own. One could be that the too-easy capacity to finance debt by money creation leads to inflation. But it remains true that these countries cannot be forced against their will into default by financial markets. The fact that this is possible in a monetary union makes such a union fragile and costly.

There is an important interaction between the fragility of a monetary union and asymmetric shocks. We discuss this interaction in Section 1.3.

1.3 Asymmetric shocks and debt dynamics

Let us return to the two-country model presented in Section 1.1. We discussed the adjustment problem France and Germany face in a monetary union when they are hit by an asymmetric demand shock. How is this adjustment affected when we take into account the budgetary implications? Let us first concentrate on France. As a result of the negative demand shock, output and employment decline in France. The effects on the French government budget are the following. First, the decline of French GDP leads to a decline of government tax receipts. This decline is probably more than proportional to the decline in GDP because income taxes are progressive. Second, because unemployment increases, the French government expenditures increase. When adding up these two effects we conclude that the French government budget deficit increases. This increase follows automatically from the decline in GDP. It is inherent in the government budget.

If the decline in aggregate demand is strong enough, the ensuing automatic increase in the French government budget deficit can become so large that investors start having doubts about the solvency of the French government. Let us go through the scenario that we developed for Spain in Section 1.2 and apply it to France. Distrust in the French government will lead investors to sell French government bonds, leading in turn to an increase in the interest rate and a liquidity crisis. The macroeconomic implications of this crisis are that the aggregate demand curve in France shifts further to the left, i.e. with a higher interest rate in France, French residents will spend less on consumption and investment goods. We show this effect in Fig. 1.5. The asymmetric demand shock shifts the demand curve from D_F to D'_F. This was the effect analysed in Fig. 1.1. The debt crisis now adds to the negative demand shock by further shifting the demand curve to D''_F. Thus, the debt crisis amplifies the initial negative demand shock.

What is the effect of the French government debt crisis on Germany? In order to analyse this we go back to the moment that investors sell French government bonds. After these sales, investors acquire cash (call them euros) that they will want to invest. Presumably since they were holding (French) government bonds they will want to acquire other government bonds that they trust. In the present circumstances, these are likely to be German government bonds. So, let us assume that these investors buy German government bonds. The effect of these purchases is that the price of German government bonds increases. This in turn reduces the yield on these bonds. The effect of this liquidity flow (out of French bonds into German bonds) is that the interest rate in Germany declines. This will then in turn increase aggregate demand in Germany. We show this effect in Fig. 1.5. The initial positive demand shock is now reinforced by an additional shift in the demand curve.

We conclude from this analysis that the debt crisis in France leads to an amplification of the asymmetric demand shock, amplifying the negative effects in France and amplifying the positive effects in Germany. This amplification effect occurs because the interest rate increases in France and declines in Germany. Thus, these interest rate changes, instead of

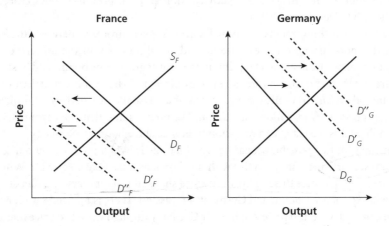

Figure 1.5 Amplification of asymmetric shocks.

stabilizing the system, tend to destabilize it. All this intensifies the adjustment problems of both countries.

The reader may be surprised that in this monetary union between France and Germany, interest rates can diverge. Isn't it a characteristic of a monetary union that the interest rates are the same everywhere? The answer is that this is the case for the short-term interest rate that is under the control of the common central bank. The long-term interest rates, however, can diverge. These are the interest rates on long-term government bonds. The latter will diverge if the investors attach different risks of holding the different government bonds. Thus, in the example of France and Germany developed here, investors perceive a higher risk of default on French government bonds than on German government bonds and will therefore want a higher interest rate (yield) on French bonds. Note also that it is the long-term interest rate that affects aggregate demand.

1.4 Booms and busts in a monetary union

The asymmetric shock discussed in the previous paragraphs is an exogenous event with permanent effects, produced by a change in consumer preferences. Many asymmetric shocks, however, are of a different nature.

Capitalism is a wonderful human invention that manages to steer individual initiative and creativity towards capital accumulation and ever more material progress. It is also inherently unstable, however. Periods of optimism and pessimism alternate, creating booms and busts in economic activity. The booms are wonderful; the busts create great hardship for many people.

Booms and busts are endemic in capitalism because many economic decisions are forward-looking. Investors and consumers look into the future to decide to invest or to consume. But the future is dark. Nobody knows it. As a result, when making forecasts, consumers and investors look at each other. This makes it possible for the optimism of one individual to be transmitted to others, creating a self-fulfilling movement in optimism. Optimism induces consumers to consume more and investors to invest more, thereby validating their optimism. The reverse is also true. When pessimism sets in, the same herding mechanism leads to a self-fulfilling decline in economic activity. Animal spirits prevail (Keynes 1936, Akerlof and Shiller 2009, De Grauwe 2012).

As long as these movements in animal spirits are synchronized between the member states of the monetary union, they pose no additional problem for the union, i.e. the fact that these countries are in a monetary union does not aggravate the booms and busts. Things are different if these movements are not synchronized, i.e. when some countries experience booms and others an economic downturn. Let us analyse the case of desynchronized business cycle movements in a monetary union. We now assume that the asymmetric shock shown in Fig. 1.1 is the result of a recession in France and a boom in Germany.

We distinguish two possible scenarios. The first one is benign; the second one is not. In the benign scenario the union can live with the desynchronized business cycle. Why is this?

First we note that since this is a business cycle shock, it is temporary, i.e. after some time France will experience a boom and Germany a recession. There is no need for France to try to adjust through wage and price declines, or Germany through wage and price increases, or through emigration of French workers to Germany.

Second, the automatic stabilizers in the budget can be used to do their job of stabilizing the business cycle. In France, the recession leads to a budget deficit; in Germany, the boom leads to a budget surplus. This mechanism will tend to reduce the intensity of the recession in France, because by running a budget deficit the French government injects purchasing power in the economy. It also reduces the intensity of the boom in Germany because the budget surpluses reduce purchasing power in that country.

This scenario, however, can only operate when investors keep their trust in the French government's capacity to service its debt (which in a recession inevitably increases). When investors trust the French government they are willing to buy the extra government bonds without requiring a higher interest rate. In this scenario of trust the French interest rate can indeed be kept unchanged. The reason is that in Germany the government has a budget surplus. When a government has a budget surplus it retires government bonds from the market. Put differently, the supply of German government bonds declines. In France the supply of government bonds increases. If markets trust the French government as much as they do the German government, they will be willing to compensate the reduced holdings of German government bonds in their portfolio by higher holdings of French government bonds. They consider German and French government bonds to be perfect substitutes. It follows that the French government can easily finance its budget deficit because bondholders (mainly German ones in this case) are willing to buy these French bonds.

Thus, in this benign scenario, we observe that capital markets in the monetary union play a stabilizing role: when France is in trouble because of a downturn in economic activity, capital markets will make it possible to transfer revenues from the booming country to the country in recession, thereby alleviating the pain of the recession.

The previous scenario was based on the assumption of trust. Let us now introduce the other scenario, in which the increased budget deficit and debt level in France lead investors to lose their trust in the French government. (This was the assumption we made implicitly in Section 1.3). This may happen if the recession is particularly deep, and a lot of uncertainty arises about the length of this recession. In this case, investors will start selling French government bonds and buying German government bonds. This leads to a liquidity flow from France to Germany (the opposite of what happened in the previous scenario) and an increase in the long-term interest rate in France coupled with a decline in Germany. The aggregate demand curve in France is pushed further down, thereby making the recession more intense and prolonging it. In Germany the opposite occurs. Note again the self-fulfilling nature of expectations. If the investors expect trouble with the French government deficits and debt because they fear a prolonged recession, their actions prolong the recession. Fear of problems makes these problems more likely to occur.

Thus, in this scenario of distrust the business cycle movements are amplified: the recession is deeper in France and the boom is more intense in Germany. Being in a monetary union then leads to more volatility of output and employment; not a very attractive feature.

Note also that in this scenario, the capital markets of the monetary union cease to be a stabilizing force. On the contrary, countries in a recession experience an outflow of capital, making the recession deeper, while countries experiencing a boom attract capital, making the boom more intense. Desynchronized business cycles in a monetary union make these business cycles more intense.

If France and Germany had chosen not to be in a monetary union, they could have mitigated these destabilizing dynamics. Take the case of France, and assume now that France has kept its monetary independence, issuing its own currency. When, during a recession, investors start selling French government bonds and switch to German bonds, they necessarily have to go through the foreign exchange market. Thus, they will sell French francs and buy German marks. The effect of this is that the French franc depreciates and the German mark appreciates. The French franc depreciation in turn tends to boost aggregate demand in France, while the appreciation of the German mark tends to reduce aggregate demand in Germany. There is a stabilizing effect from exchange rate changes, which is absent when France and Germany belong to a monetary union. Thus, in a monetary union business cycle movements will be amplified if the financial markets are not fully confident in the solvency of one or more of the member governments. In Box 1.2 we present a case study of the Eurozone during the recent 'Great Recession' and illustrate how asymmetric shocks were amplified by large divergent movements in the long-term interest rates.

Handwritten margin note: How exactly monetary union work? using the same currency?

BOX 1.2 Asymmetric shocks and debt accumulation in the Eurozone (2008–15)

The industrialized world was hit by a major financial crisis in 2007–8. This led to what has been called the 'Great Recession' of 2008–9, during which GDP declined significantly. From 2010, GDP growth resumed in most countries but at a very unequal pace. The divergence in the movements of GDP is particularly strong in the Eurozone. We show this in Fig. 1.6. This presents the cumulative growth of GDP from 2008 to 2015 in the Eurozone. We observe very large differences. Five northern Eurozone countries succeeded in overcoming the recession of 2008–9 and lifting their GDP above the level of 2008. This was not the case with Finland, the Netherlands, and the southern Eurozone countries, in which GDP remained significantly below the level of 2008. Thus, one can say that large asymmetric shocks (desynchronized business cycles) occurred in the Eurozone during 2008–15.

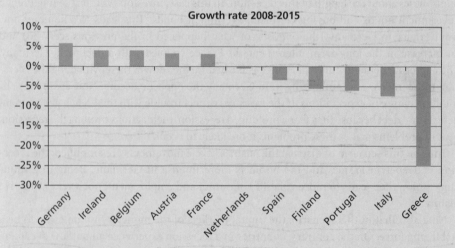

Figure 1.6 Cumulative growth of GDP (2008–15).

Source: European Commission, AMECO databank.

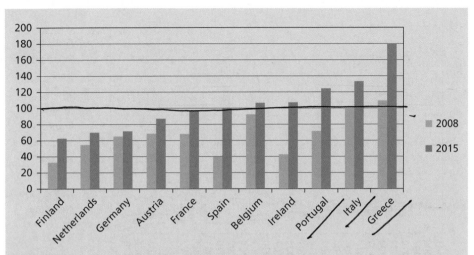

Figure 1.7 Government debt as a percentage of GDP.

Source: European Commission, AMECO databank.

These asymmetric shocks had important implications for government finances within the Eurozone. We show this in Fig. 1.7, which presents the government debt ratios (the ratios of government debt to GDP) in the Eurozone in 2008 and 2015. We observe everywhere significant increases in these government debt ratios, but also large differences in this increase. Belgium, Austria, Germany, and the Netherlands experienced relatively small increases, while most southern countries and Ireland experienced very large surges in their government debt ratios. This suggests that there is a strong correlation between the cumulative growth experiences of the Eurozone countries and the increase in their government debt ratios. We show this in Fig. 1.8. There is indeed a strong negative correlation. Countries that managed to grow during the period 2008–15 experienced weak increases in their government debt ratios. Countries that experienced sharp declines in GDP also saw their government debt ratios surge.

How did financial markets respond to these widely divergent movements in growth and budgetary performance within the Eurozone? We show the answer in Fig. 1.9. This presents the 10-year government

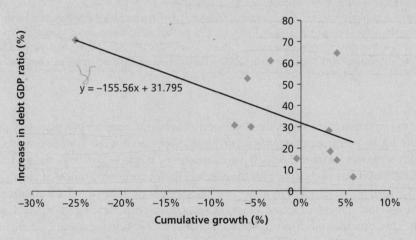

Figure 1.8 Cumulative growth and increase in debt ratios (2008–15).

Source: European Commission, AMECO databank.

(Continued...)

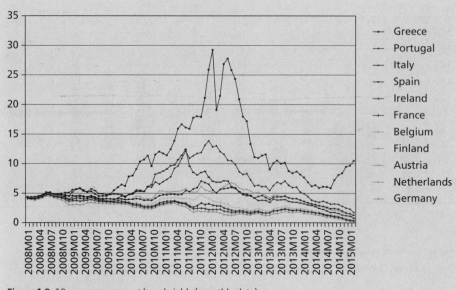

Figure 1.9 10-year government bond yields (monthly data)

Source: Eurostat.

If investors don't want to buy a country's loan. then. this country will try to raise the interest to attract

bond rates in the Eurozone. While at the start of 2008 these bond rates were practically the same in all the Eurozone countries, by the end of 2008 large divergences had occurred. Financial markets lost confidence in the capacity of southern Eurozone countries and Ireland to continue to service an exploding government debt. As a result, they sold the government bonds of these countries, thereby raising the interest rates. The mirror images of these selling activities were the purchases of the government bonds of northern Eurozone countries. As a result, the long-term interest rates in these countries declined significantly. Note how in 2012 the bond rates of Southern Eurozone countries declined sharply. We will analyse this phenomenon when we discuss the role of the European Central Bank as a lender of last resort in Chapter 6.

Thus, the asymmetric shocks (desynchronized business cycles) that occurred in the Eurozone led to divergences in the long-term bond rates. These had the effect of making the adjustment problems of the countries hit by negative shocks more severe. These countries faced very high interest rates that further reduced economic activity. The opposite occurred in the countries experiencing positive shocks.

We can summarize the preceding discussion as follows. Countries in a monetary union that are hit by permanent asymmetric demand shocks need wage flexibility and labour mobility to correct for these shocks. If these asymmetric shocks lead to large budget deficits, financial markets are likely to amplify the effects of these asymmetric shocks, increasing the need for (painful) adjustment in wages and labour mobility. It helps to have an insurance mechanism that allows for income transfers to the country experiencing a negative demand shock. This insurance mechanism, however, does not substitute for adjustment when the demand shock is permanent. What it does is to give countries more time to effect the needed adjustment. To the extent that countries face rigidities and have poorly organized insurance systems, the costs of the monetary union may be substantial.

When asymmetric shocks are temporary, i.e. the results of unsynchronized booms and busts, the issue is not so much flexibility but stability. The fact that member countries of a monetary union are vulnerable to changing market sentiments can lead to more volatility in the business cycle. Thus, a country experiencing a recession and an increase in the budget deficit may be hit by large-scale sales of its government bonds, leading to a liquidity crisis and higher interest rates. This is likely to force the government of that country to introduce budgetary austerity, i.e. to increase taxes and reduce spending, thereby exacerbating the recession. Governments then find out that their capacity to stabilize their economies is severely curtailed, worse that they are forced to implement fiscal policies that destabilize the economy.

1.5 Monetary union and budgetary union

In Section 1.4 we saw that a monetary union can be very fragile. When it is hit by large asymmetric shocks, the member states of the union face difficult adjustment problems. Since asymmetric demand shocks will typically lead to increasing budget deficits in some countries, financial markets may force a liquidity crisis on these countries, thereby amplifying the asymmetric shocks. Can one design a mechanism that will alleviate these problems and thereby reduce the costs of a monetary union?

In principle, it is possible to design such a mechanism in two parts. The first one concerns the role of the common central bank in making it possible to avoid liquidity crises. The second one consists of centralizing a significant part of the national budgets into a common union budget. Here we concentrate on the second part. We will come back to the role of the common central bank in Chapter 6.

The centralization of national budgets amounts to having a monetary union together with a budgetary union. Such a budgetary union achieves two things. First, it creates an insurance mechanism triggering income transfers from the country experiencing good times to the countries hit by bad luck. In doing so, it reduces the pain in the countries hit by a negative shock. Second, a budgetary union allows consolidation of a significant part of national government debts, thereby protecting its members from liquidity crises and forced defaults. Let us analyse these two mechanisms.

A budgetary union as an insurance mechanism

Let us return to the two-country model of France and Germany and let us assume that a large part of the government budgets of France and Germany is centralized at the European level. Thus, let us suppose that a European government exists that directly levies taxes (including social security taxes) and directly transfers revenues (e.g. pensions, unemployment benefits) to residents in France and Germany. As a result of such budgetary centralization, a decline in output in France leads to a reduction in the tax revenues of the European government from France, while the tax revenues from Germany increase because German output has increased. At the same time, however, the European government increases its spending (unemployment benefits) in France and reduces these in Germany. The net result of all this is that the central budget automatically redistributes income from Germany where output has increased to France where output has declined.[6] Put differently, this budgetary centralization allows French citizens to smooth consumption following a negative output shock. Note that there is also consumption smoothing in Germany, but in the other direction. As a result, the cost of the monetary union is reduced, i.e. French and German citizens can stabilize their consumption over time despite asymmetric shocks in output. The reason for Germany's interest in such a scheme is that it can profit from it when it suffers a negative shock.

Like in many insurance systems, the main problem of this insurance scheme is that it often leads to moral hazard. This is made clear by its operation within countries. In many countries (e.g. Belgium, Germany, Italy) the national budget automatically transfers income from regions with high output growth to regions with low growth. These transfers tend to reduce the pressure on regions to adjust. As a result they become permanent. The use of such schemes at the European level would certainly be problematic. It could lead to a situation in which the centralized budget induces large and permanent transfers from some countries to others. This would certainly create a lot of resistance in countries whose incomes are transferred to other countries.

A budgetary union as a protection mechanism

We have seen that a monetary union in which each country keeps its own budgetary independence is very fragile. In such a union, national governments issue debt in a currency they have no control over. This makes these governments vulnerable to movements of distrust that can lead to liquidity crises and forced defaults. It is now immediately evident that, in principle, a budgetary union can solve this problem. The reason is that in a budgetary union, national government debts are also centralized into a union government debt (or at least a significant part of national government debts are). As a result, the union government acquires the characteristics of a 'stand-alone' government, i.e. it issues debt in a currency over which it has full control. Thus, the union government cannot be confronted with a liquidity crisis (at least if the union maintains a flexible exchange rate with the rest of the world, as in our example of the United Kingdom). This budgetary union also implies that there is a strong union government capable of forcing the common central bank into providing for liquidity in moments of crisis.[7] In such a regime, national governments, which would have lost much of their sovereignty, would also be protected by the union government.

Is there any prospect that Europe could move into such a budgetary union? The European Union's budget amounts to only 1% of European Union GDP, while national budgets typically absorb 40% to 50% of GDP. There is very little prospect for the centralization of national budgets at the European level in the foreseeable future. Such centralization would require a far-reaching degree of political unification. It would require a large transfer of national sovereignty in the field of taxation and spending to a European government and parliament. There is simply no willingness in Europe to go in this direction. As a result the

---

[6] In some federal states there also exist explicit regional redistribution schemes. The most well-known of these is the German system of *Finanzausgleich*, in which *Länder* (states) whose tax revenues fall below some predetermined range receive compensation from *Länder* whose tax revenues exceed that range

[7] In Chapter 6 we analyse the role of the common central bank in a monetary union. to avoid the moral hazard problem.

insurance mechanism and the protection mechanism through budgetary centralization are simply not available in the European monetary union.

From the previous discussion, it follows that a monetary union without a budgetary union is likely to function in a very different way from a monetary union that is coupled with a budgetary union. The former can be labelled an 'incomplete monetary union', and the latter a 'full monetary union'. We will come back to this distinction in Chapter 5, where we will analyse different types of incomplete monetary union. We will analyse the fragility of incomplete monetary unions, and in particular of the Eurozone, which is an incomplete monetary union. In Chapter 6, we will analyse whether institutions can be created that, although they fall short of full budgetary and political union, may nevertheless provide some insurance and protection for the member states of an incomplete monetary union, such as the Eurozone. We will discuss how these institutions can be designed in such a way as to avoid the moral hazard problem.

1.6 Private insurance schemes

A budgetary union provides for an insurance mechanism in a monetary union. There is another way to organize an insurance scheme in a monetary union.[8] This scheme operates through the financial markets. We assume, as before, an asymmetric shock hitting France negatively and Germany positively. Suppose (and this is a crucial assumption) that the financial markets of France and Germany are completely integrated.

Let us concentrate here on how integrated bond and equity markets facilitate the adjustment.[9] As a result of the negative shock, French firms make losses, pushing down French stock prices. Since the equity market is fully integrated, French stocks are also held by German residents. Thus, the latter pay part of the price of the drop in economic activity in France. Conversely, the boom in Germany raises the stock prices of German firms. Since these are also held by French residents, the latter find some compensation for the hard economic times in France. Put differently, an integrated stock market works as an insurance system. The risk of a negative shock in one country is shared by all countries. As a result, the impact of the negative output shock in one country on the income of the residents of that country is mitigated.

A similar mechanism works through the integrated bond market. As a result of the negative shock, firms in France make losses, and some also go bankrupt. This lowers the value of the outstanding French bonds. Some of these French bonds are held by German residents, so that they also pay the price of the economic duress in France.

The advantage of this insurance scheme based on private financial markets is that it reduces the danger of moral hazard. However, there is also a large drawback. The poor unemployed in France who do not hold financial assets issued in Germany will obtain little compensation from this private insurance scheme. Instead the well-to-do French citizens with large portfolios of assets are more likely to obtain most of the transfers. As a result, such a private insurance scheme without a public one is certainly going to provide insufficient coverage for a large majority of French citizens.

---

[8] The importance of financial market integration in order for a monetary union to function well was first stressed by Ingram (1959).

[9] In Chapter 11, we go into more detail and also analyse the banking sector. Thus, we will assume there is one bond market and one equity market, and the banking sector is also completely integrated.

1.7 Differences in labour market institutions

Up to now, when discussing asymmetric shocks we have concentrated on demand shocks. There are, however, other asymmetries that may force member countries of a monetary union to institute difficult adjustment processes. We discuss some of these asymmetries in this and in the following section.

There is no doubt that there are important institutional differences in the labour markets of European countries. Some labour markets are dominated by highly centralized labour unions (e.g. Germany). In other countries, labour unions are decentralized (e.g. the UK). These differences may introduce significant costs for a monetary union. The main reason is that these institutional differences can lead to divergent wage and price developments, even if countries face the same disturbances. For example, when two countries are subjected to the same oil price increase, the effect this has on domestic wages and prices very much depends on how labour unions react to these shocks.

Macroeconomic theories have been developed that shed some light on the importance of labour market institutions. The most popular one was developed by Bruno and Sachs (1985). The idea can be formulated as follows. Supply shocks, such as an oil price increase, have very different macroeconomic effects depending upon the degree of centralization of wage bargaining. When wage bargaining is centralized (Bruno and Sachs call countries with centralized wage bargaining 'corporatist'), labour unions take into account the inflationary effect of wage increases. In other words, they know that excessive wage claims will lead to more inflation, so that real wages will not increase. They will have no incentive to make these excessive wage claims. Thus, when a supply shock occurs, they realize that the loss in real wages due to the supply shock cannot be compensated by nominal wage increases.

Things are quite different in countries with less centralized wage bargaining. In these countries, individual unions that bargain for higher nominal wages know that the effect of these nominal wage increases on the aggregate price level is small, because these unions only represent a small fraction of the labour force. There is a free-riding problem. Each union has an interest in increasing the nominal wage of its members. If it does not do so, the real wage of its members would decline, given that all the other unions are likely to increase the nominal wage for their members. In equilibrium this non-cooperative game will produce a higher nominal wage level than the cooperative (centralized) game. In countries with decentralized wage bargaining, therefore, it is structurally more difficult to arrive at wage moderation after a supply shock. In such a non-cooperative set-up no individual union has an incentive to take the first step in reducing its nominal wage claim, for it risks having the others not follow, so that the real wage level of its members will decline.

The analogy with the spectators in a football stadium is well known. When they are all seated, the individual spectator has an incentive to stand up so as to have a better view of the game. The dynamics of this game is that they all stand up, see no better, and are more uncomfortable. Once they stand up, it is equally difficult to induce them to sit down. The individual who takes the first step and sits down will see nothing, as long as the others do not follow their example. Since that individual is sitting, most spectators in the stadium will not even notice this good example.

This cooperation story has been extended by Calmfors and Driffill (1988), who noted that the relationship between centralization of wage bargaining and outcomes is not a linear process. In particular, the more we move towards the decentralized spectrum, the more another externality comes to play a role. For in a very decentralized system (e.g. wage bargaining at the firm level), the wage claims will have a direct effect on the competitiveness of the firm, and therefore on the employment prospects of individual union members. Excessive wage claims by an individual union will lead to a strong reduction in employment. Thus, when faced with a supply shock, unions in such a decentralized system may exhibit a considerable degree of wage restraint.

This insight then leads to the conclusion that countries with either strong centralization or strong decentralization of wage bargaining are better equipped to face supply shocks, such as oil price increases, than countries with an intermediate degree of centralization. In these 'extreme' countries there will be a greater wage moderation than in the intermediate countries. As a result, the countries with extreme centralization or decentralization tend to fare better following supply shocks, in terms of inflation and unemployment, than the others. (For empirical evidence, see Calmfors and Driffill (1988); for an in-depth analysis of the importance of different labour market institutions in a monetary union see Hancke (2014)).

It follows that a country might find itself in a situation where wages and prices increase faster than in other countries even when the shock that triggered it all is the same. In terms of the two-country model that we used in Section 1.1, the supply curve shifts upwards more in one country than in the other country. This will lead to macroeconomic adjustment problems of the same nature as the ones we analysed in the previous sections.

We conclude that countries with very different labour market institutions may find it costly to form a monetary union. With each supply shock, wages and prices in these countries may be affected differently, making it difficult to correct for these differences when the exchange rate is irrevocably fixed.

1.8 Differences in legal systems

Despite decades of integration in the European Union (EU), legal systems continue to be very different in the member states. These differences run deep and sometimes have profound effects on the way markets function. We concentrate on just a few examples.

The mortgage markets operate very differently in the EU countries. The main reason is that legal systems differ. The law protects the banks extending mortgage loans better in some countries than in others. As a result, mortgages are very different products, with different degrees of risk, from one country to another. For example, the value of the loan (the mortgage) is typically below the value of the house (the collateral). Thus, the loan-to-value ratio is generally less than 100%. However, the loan-to-value ratio applied by banks in different countries can vary a great deal. Legal differences also lead to differences in the frequency with which interest rates are adjusted. Thus, there are countries where banks offer mortgage loans with a floating/changing interest, and others where mortgage rates are fixed for the whole maturity of the loan. As a result of these differences, the same shocks (e.g. an increase of the interest rate by the European Central Bank) are transmitted very differently across the member states of the monetary union. Several empirical studies confirm that these differences in the transmission of the same shocks can be substantial (see Dornbusch et al. 1998; Cecchetti 1999; Maclennan et al. 1999; Peersman and Smets 2001; Mojon 2000).

The ways in which companies finance themselves are very different across the EU. In countries with an Anglo-Saxon legal tradition, firms tend to go directly to the capital market (bond and equity markets) to finance investment projects. As a result, these markets are well developed, sophisticated, and very liquid. In countries with a continental legal tradition, firms attract financial resources mainly through the banking system. As a result, capital markets are less developed. Here again, these differences lead to the result that the same interest rate disturbances are transmitted very differently. To give an example, take an increase in the interest rate. In countries with an Anglo-Saxon type of financial system, this is likely to lead to large wealth effects for consumers. The reason is that consumers hold a lot of bonds and stocks. An interest rate increase lowers bond and stock prices, so that the wealth of consumers is likely to decline. Wealth effects will be less pronounced in countries with continental-type financial markets. In these countries, the interest rate increase will affect consumer spending mainly through the bank-lending channel. A sufficiently high increase in the interest rate will induce banks to start rationing credit.[10] We conclude that the way in which the same interest rate increase is transmitted into consumption and investment spending will be very different across Union members.

1.9 Conclusion

In this chapter we discussed why countries that join a monetary union face important costs. These costs arise from the fact that countries are different in many ways. We observed that countries can use national monetary policies, including exchange rate changes, to correct for these differences. We found that in most cases there is an alternative to using national monetary policy as an instrument. For example, when confronted with a loss of domestic competitiveness, countries can try to regain competitiveness by reducing wages and prices. However, these alternatives are often more painful for a member of a monetary union than for a 'stand-alone' country that has kept its monetary independence (including the capacity to change the exchange rate).

Another source of costs arises from the fact that when entering a monetary union, governments have to issue debt in a 'foreign' currency over which they no longer have control. This makes these governments fragile, i.e. vulnerable to movements of distrust in financial markets. These movements can push governments into default against their will. They also have the effect of amplifying the movements in the business cycles.

We concluded that countries may find it costly to relinquish their national moneys and join a currency union, especially when that union is incomplete, i.e. does not include a fiscal union. (Note, however, that we have still not introduced the benefit side of the analysis. It is still possible that even if there are costs associated with relinquishing one's national money, the benefits outweigh these costs.)

The analysis discussed in this chapter, which is based on the theory of optimum currency areas, has been subjected to much criticism. This has led to new and important insights. In Chapter 2 we turn our attention to this criticism.

[10] For a classic analysis of credit rationing, see Stiglitz and Weiss (1981). For an analysis of the implications for monetary union, see Cecchetti (1999).

2

The theory of optimum currency areas: a critique

Introduction

In Chapter 1, we analysed the reasons why countries might find it costly to join a monetary union. This analysis, which is known as the theory of optimum currency areas (OCA), has come under criticism.[1] This criticism has been formulated at different levels. First, one may question the view that the differences between countries are important enough to bother about. Second, use of national monetary policies, including the exchange rate instrument, may not be very effective in correcting for the differences between nations. Third, not only may monetary and exchange rate policies be ineffective, they may do more harm than good in the hands of politicians.

In this chapter, we analyse this criticism in greater detail.

2.1 How relevant are the differences between countries?

There is no doubt that countries are different. The question, however, is whether these differences are important enough to represent a stumbling block for monetary unification.

Is a demand shock concentrated in one country a likely event?

The classical analysis of Mundell started from the scenario in which a demand shift occurs away from the products of one country in favour of those of another country. Is such a shock likely to occur frequently between the European countries that form a monetary union? Two views have emerged to answer this question. We will call the first one the European Commission view, which was defended in the 1990 report 'One Market, One Money'. The second view is associated with Paul Krugman.

According to the European Commission, differential shocks in demand will occur less frequently in a monetary union. The reason is the following. Trade between the industrial European nations is to a large degree intra-industry trade. The trade is based on the existence of economies of scale and imperfect competition (product differentiation). It leads to a

[1] See EC Commission (1990) and Gros and Thygesen (1998).

structure of trade in which countries buy and sell to each other the same categories of products. Thus, France sells cars to and buys cars from Germany, and vice versa. This structure of trade leads to a situation where most demand shocks will affect these countries in a similar way. For example, when consumers reduce their demand for cars, they will buy fewer French and German cars. Thus, both countries' aggregate demand will be affected in similar ways.

The removal of barriers with the completion of the single market will reinforce these tendencies. As a result, most demand shocks will tend to have similar effects.[2] Instead of being asymmetric, these shocks will tend to be more symmetric.

The second and opposite view has been defended by Paul Krugman. According to Krugman (1991), one cannot discard Mundell's analysis, for there is another feature of the dynamics of trade with economies of scale that may make Mundell's analysis very relevant. Trade integration, which occurs as a result of economies of scale, also leads to regional concentrations of industrial activities.[3] The basic argument here is that when impediments to trade decline this has two opposing effects on the localization of industries. It makes it possible to produce closer to the final markets, but it also makes it possible to concentrate production so as to profit from economies of scale (both static and dynamic). This explains why trade integration in fact may lead to more concentration of regional activities rather than less.

The fact that trade may lead to regional concentration of industrial activities is illustrated rather dramatically by comparing the regional distribution of automobile production in the USA and in Europe (see Table 2.1). The most striking feature of this table is that the US production of automobiles is much more regionally concentrated than the EU's. (This feature is found in many other industrial sectors; see Krugman 1991.) There is also no doubt that the US market is more highly integrated than the EU market, i.e. there are fewer impediments to trade in the USA than in the EU. This evidence therefore suggests that when the EU moves forward in the direction of a truly integrated market, it may experience similar kinds of regional concentrations of economic activities to those observed in the USA today. It is therefore possible that the automobile industry, for example, will tend to be more concentrated in, say, Germany (although we are not sure it will be Germany; it could also be another country). Sector-specific shocks may then become country-specific shocks. Countries faced

Table 2.1 Regional distribution of auto production

USA	%	EU	%
Midwest	66.3	Germany	38.5
South	25.4	France	31.1
West	5.1	Italy	17.6
North-east	3.2	UK	12.9

Source: Krugman (1991).

[2] Peter Kenen (1969) also stressed the importance of the similarity of the trading structure for making a monetary union less costly.

[3] This is an old idea that was developed by Myrdal (1957) and Kaldor (1966). For a survey, see Balassa (1961). Krugman (1991) gives a more rigorous underpinning of these ideas.

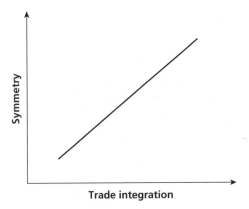

Figure 2.1 The European Commission view.

with these shocks may then prefer to use the exchange rate as an instrument of economic policy to correct for these disturbances.

The two views about the relation between economic integration and the occurrence of asymmetric shocks can be analysed more systematically using the graphical device represented in Fig. 2.1. Let us first represent the European Commission view. On the vertical axis we set out the degree of symmetry in the movements of output and employment between groups of countries (regions) that are candidates to form a monetary union.[4] On the horizontal axis we set out a measure of the degree of trade integration between these countries. This measure could be the mutual trade of these countries as a share of their GDP. The European Commission view can then be represented by an upward-sloping line. It says that as the degree of economic integration between countries increases, asymmetric shocks will occur less frequently (so that income and employment will tend to be more correlated between the countries involved). Symmetry increases.

We represent the second view, which we label the Krugman view, in Fig. 2.2. Instead of an upward-sloping line we have a negatively sloped line. Thus, when economic integration increases, the countries involved become more specialized so that they will be subjected to more rather than fewer asymmetric shocks.[5] Symmetry declines.

What is the right view of the world? A clear-cut answer will be difficult to formulate. Nevertheless it is reasonable to claim that a presumption exists in favour of the European Commission view. The reason can be formulated as follows. The fact that economic integration can lead to concentration and agglomeration effects cannot be disputed. At the same time, however, it is also true that as market integration between countries proceeds, national

[4] We could take as the measure of symmetry, the correlation coefficient between the growth rates of output of these countries. Thus when the correlation is 1, our measure of symmetry is 1. When the correlation is −1 our measure of symmetry would be 0, its minimum value.

[5] This view could be associated with Kenen (1969), who stressed that countries with a less diversified output structure are subject to more asymmetric shocks, making them less suitable to form a monetary union. The presumption is that small countries which are highly integrated with the rest of the world are also highly specialized. This leads to the paradox that small and very open countries should keep their own currencies and not join a monetary union (see Frankel and Rose, 1998, on this paradox and how it can be resolved).

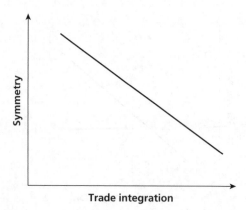

Figure 2.2 The Krugman view.

borders become less and less important as factors that decide the location of economic activities. As a result, it becomes more and more likely that concentration and agglomeration effects will be blind to the existence of borders. This creates the possibility that the clusters of economic activity will encompass borders. Put differently, it becomes more and more likely that the relevant regions in which some activity is centralized will cross one or more borders. For example, suppose that automobile manufacturing will not be centralized in Germany, but rather in the region encompassing south Germany and northern Italy. If this is the case, shocks in the automobile industry will affect Germany *and* Italy, so that the DM–lira rate cannot be used to absorb this shock.

Note that the argument we develop here is not that integration does not lead to concentration effects (it may do so) but rather that national borders will increasingly be less relevant in influencing the shape of these concentration effects. As a result, regions may still be very much affected by asymmetric shocks. The probability that these regions overlap existing borders, however, will increase as integration proceeds. We conclude that the economic forces of integration are likely to rob the exchange rates between national currencies of their capacity to deal with these shocks.

From the preceding arguments it should not be concluded that economists know for sure what the relationship is between economic integration and the occurrence of asymmetric shocks. All we can say is that there is a theoretical presumption in favour of the hypothesis that economic integration will make asymmetric shocks between nations less likely. The issue remains essentially an empirical one. There are two aspects to this empirical issue. The first one has to do with the question of whether monetary unions lead to increased economic integration. Rose (2000), Rose and van Wincoop (2001), and Glick and Rose (2002) have done important research clarifying this issue. They applied panel data analysis covering almost all countries in the world to analyse the effect of currency unions on the trade flows between the members of the union. They found that on average (and after correcting for many other variables that affect trade flows) the mere fact of belonging to the same monetary union doubles the size of trade flows.

These spectacular econometric results have led to a large literature. Part of that literature has criticized the Rose results on econometric grounds (see for example Persson 2001;

Nitsch 2001; and Baldwin 2006). Other studies have focused on the trade effects of the monetary integration in Europe (see Bun and Klaasen 2002; Micco et al. 2003; De Nardis and Vicarelli 2003; Flam and Nordstrom 2003; and Berger and Nitsch 2006). The conclusion from these studies is that the initially strong 'Rose effect' is probably biased upwards, and that the trade effect of monetary union in Europe is likely to be much smaller, i.e. in the order of magnitude of 5% to 20%. Put differently, monetary union in Europe could lead to an expansion of trade of 5% to 20%. But even this is uncertain, as was admitted recently by Glick and Rose (2015), we will return to some issues relating to the trade effects of a common currency in Chapter 3 when we discuss the benefits of the euro.

The second aspect of the empirical issue relates to the question of how this increased integration affects the asymmetry of shocks. Frankel and Rose (1998) have undertaken important empirical research relating to this issue. They analysed the degree to which economic activity between pairs of countries is correlated as a function of the intensity of their trade links. Their conclusion was that a closer trade linkage between two countries is strongly and consistently associated with more tightly correlated economic activity between the two countries. This is also confirmed in the studies of Rose (2000) and Rose and Engel (2001). Similar evidence is presented by Artis and Zhang (1995), who found that as the European countries became more integrated during the 1980s and 1990s, the business cycles of these countries became more correlated. In terms of Figs 2.1 and 2.2 this means that the relationship between symmetry and trade integration is positively sloped.

There is another piece of empirical evidence that enhances the view that economic integration may not lead to increased asymmetric shocks within a union. This has to do with the rising importance of services. Economies of scale do not seem to matter as much for services as for industrial activities. As a result, economic integration does not lead to a regional concentration of services in the way it does with industries. As services become increasingly important (today they account for 70% or more of GDP in many EU countries) the trend towards regional concentration of economic activities may stop even if economic integration moves forward. There is some evidence that this is already occurring in the USA. The OECD (1999a) came to the conclusion that the regional concentration of economic activities in the USA has started to decline after decades of increasing concentration. This result is also confirmed by Aiginger and Leitner (2002), who conclude that regional concentration is declining in both the US and the EU, suggesting that Europe may not be following the US in the direction of more regional concentration.

To summarize: the evidence seems to suggest, first, that monetary union intensifies trade integration (although the magnitude of this effect is still very uncertain), and, second, that integration in turn reduces asymmetric shocks. This is good news for countries that decide to form a monetary union. The very fact of starting a monetary union can create conditions that are favourable to the good functioning of the union. We come back to the dynamics of the process of monetary unification in Chapter 4.

Institutional differences in labour markets

The differences in the workings of the labour markets in different countries are well documented. These differences, however, have accumulated over the years, partly because European countries have experienced separate policy regimes. The issue is whether monetary

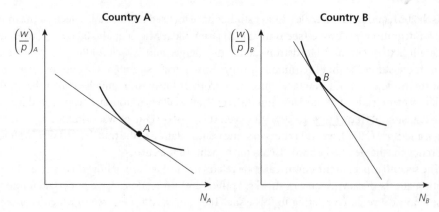

Figure 2.3 The Solow–McDonald model in two countries.

integration does not drastically change the behaviour of labour unions, so that the differences we observe today may disappear.[6]

An example may clarify this point. In Fig. 2.3, we present the labour markets of two countries that are candidates for a monetary union. The figure is based on the model of McDonald and Solow (1981).[7] On the vertical axis we have the real wage level and on the horizontal axis the level of employment (N). The convex curves are the indifference curves of the labour union. It is assumed that there is only one labour union in each country. The union maximizes its utility, which depends on both the real wage level and the employment of its members. The negatively sloped line is the economy-wide demand-for-labour curve. For the union, which maximizes its utility, the demand-for-labour curve is a constraint: thus, the union will select a point on it that maximizes its utility. This is represented in Fig. 2.3 by the points A and B.

The interesting feature of this model is that the employment line takes into account the reaction of the authorities to what the labour unions are doing. If we assume that the authorities give a higher weight to employment in their utility function than the labour unions do, we may have the following situation. When the labour unions set a wage that reduces the employment level below the level that the authorities find optimal, they will react by changing their policies. For example, they will engage in more expansionary monetary and fiscal policies to absorb the unemployed, they may create public jobs, etc. To the extent that labour unions take this reaction of the authorities into account, the constraint the unions face will change. More specifically, the employment line becomes steeper because an increase in the real wage level reduces private employment and, thus, induces the authorities to intensify their job-creating policies. As a result, an increase in the real wage level has a less pronounced effect on the total level of employment.[8] Thus, the steepness of this employment line also reflects the willingness of the authorities to engage in expansionary employment policies when the wage rate increases.

[6] See Chapter 9; Calmfors (2001); Boeri et al. (2001); Blanchard and Giavazzi (2003); and Hancke (2014).

[7] For a discussion of this model, see Carlin and Soskice (1990) and Carlin and Soskice (2005).

[8] This employment line must in fact be interpreted as the reaction curve of the government. The union acts as a 'Stackelberg' leader and selects the optimal point on this reaction line.

In Fig. 2.3, we have drawn the employment line of country B as being steeper than that of country A, assuming that the authorities of country B are more willing to accommodate the unions' wage-setting behaviour by expansionary employment policies. Monetary union now changes the ability of national governments to follow such accommodating policies. Monetary policies are now centralized, so that the unions of the two countries face the same reactions from the monetary authorities. This makes the employment lines similar, so that the two unions tend to select a similar combination of wage rates and employment levels.

The differences, however, are unlikely to disappear completely. National governments have other employment policies at their disposal besides monetary policies. For example, they can create jobs in the government sector, financing these extra expenditures by issuing debt. A monetary union does not necessarily constrain this accommodating government behaviour. Thus, although the differences in the behaviour of the labour unions will be less pronounced, they will certainly not be eliminated completely.

Finally, it should also be stressed that the previous analysis assumes a completely centralized labour union in both countries. As pointed out earlier, labour unions are different across countries because of different degrees of centralization. It is not clear how monetary union will change these institutional differences.

We conclude that the institutional differences in the national labour markets will continue to exist for quite some time after the introduction of a common currency. This may lead to divergent wage and employment tendencies, and severe adjustment problems when the exchange rate instrument has disappeared. We elaborate on this in Box 6.1 (Chapter 6).

Different legal systems and financial markets

Financial markets continue to work differently across the EU, creating the risk that the same monetary shocks are transmitted very differently. This is mainly due to different legal systems in the member states. Not all the differences in the workings of financial markets, however, are due to different legal systems. Some of them have arisen over time because of the fact that countries followed different monetary policies. An example will clarify this point. Before EMU (European Monetary Union), some countries managed to keep inflation low (e.g. Germany). Other countries experienced relatively high inflation (e.g. Italy). These systematic differences in inflation have affected the workings of financial markets in these countries. In an environment of high inflation, investors are typically very reluctant to buy long-term bonds. The reason is simple. The price of long-term bonds is very sensitive to unexpected inflation. Small increases in the latter can lead to large declines in the price of long-term bonds. This is much less the case for short-term bonds. As a result, in high-inflation countries, the long-term bond market barely exists. Instead, most issues of bonds are made in the short-term market. Thus, prior to EMU, a large part of the Italian government debt was short-term. This was not the case in low-inflation countries, like Germany. Because the inflation risk was low, investors were willing to invest in long-term bonds, and governments tended to supply these long-term bonds. We show some evidence in Table 2.2 for the year 1998, just preceding the start of EMU.

All this caused asymmetries in the way EU governments reacted to the same interest rate changes before EMU. When the interest rate increased, the Italian government budget was immediately affected. Because of the short maturity of the Italian debt, an increase in the

Table 2.2 Maturity distribution of government bonds (% of total), 1998

	Short term (<1 year)	Medium and long term (>1 year)	Of which long term (>5 years)
Italy	49.4	50.6	24.8
Germany	18.5	81.5	—
Netherlands	6.7	93.3	63.0

Source: OECD (1999*b*).

interest rate forced the Italian government to quickly spend more on interest payments, so that the budget deficit increased significantly. In low-inflation countries such as Germany, the budgetary effects of an interest rate increase were much slower to materialize.

These differences, which were due to large differences in inflation, disappeared in the European Monetary Union. As a result, the maturity structures of the bonds issued by the Italian and German governments converged, and so did the budgetary implications of the same interest rate shock.[9] Thus, monetary union eliminated some of the institutional differences that existed between national financial systems.

This trend has been reversed since the start of the sovereign debt crisis in the Eurozone in 2010. As has been noted in Box 1.2 (Chapter 1), government bond yields have started to diverge spectacularly in the Eurozone, reflecting not differences in inflation (which remain small) but divergent perceptions about the default risks of the bonds issued by the member states. The result has been that countries facing high perceived default risks have been forced to shorten the maturity structure of their bond issues. We learn from this recent episode that the monetary union by itself does not eliminate possible divergences in the maturity structure of government bonds. During the sovereign debt crisis, spreads surged giving incentives to national governments to reduce the maturity of the bonds they were issuing.

Booms and busts and the nation-state

Earlier, we argued that economic integration tends to reduce the probability that individual nations (in contrast to regions) are hit by asymmetric shocks. These are the exogenous asymmetric shocks that have been at the centre of attention from optimal currency area theory. We noted in Chapter 1 that there are also other types of asymmetric shocks. These could be called endogenously generated asymmetric shocks. They arise because of the inherent dynamics of capitalist systems, characterized by periods of optimism and pessimism (animal spirits) leading to booms and busts in economic activity. As we argued earlier, when these are desynchronized, major problems can arise in a monetary union. The question here is whether economic integration produces a synchronization of these business cycle movements.

The first thing to observe is that there does not seem to have been such a convergence in the Eurozone. We have already noted the wide divergence of the growth rates of GDP since the start of the Eurozone crisis in 2010. A similar strong divergence existed prior to the

---

[9] See Arnold and de Vries (1999) and Angeloni and Ehrmann (2003), who have shown that the maturities of government bonds have converged in the European Monetary Union.

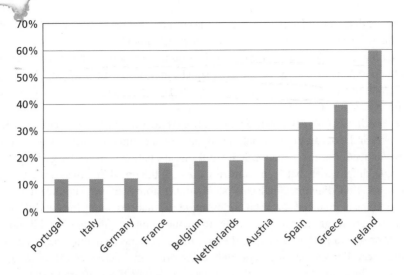

Figure 2.4 Cumulative growth of GDP (1999–2007).
Source: European Commission, AMECO databank.

crisis, as illustrated in Fig. 2.4, which shows the cumulative growth rates of GDP before the financial crisis in the Eurozone. We observe that, indeed, the differences in national growth rates in the Eurozone were very substantial. Some countries experienced booming economic conditions during 1999–2007 (Spain, Greece, Ireland); others experienced very slow growth (Portugal, Italy, Germany). Prior to the financial crisis of 2007, in countries such as Spain and Ireland there was strong optimism about the future, creating self-fulfilling expectations that intensified the boom. By contrast, such countries as Germany and Italy experienced low growth for many years, creating pessimism about the future of these countries. It seemed that the 'animal spirits' emerged at the national level, and not at the Eurozone level, creating wide divergences in booms and busts in the Eurozone.

Why did we observe these divergences? And why did the existence of a common currency not discipline these *national* animal spirits into *Eurozone-level* animal spirits? The answer has again to do with the incomplete nature of the monetary union as embodied in the Eurozone.

In the European Monetary Union, monetary policies are centralized, and therefore cease to be a source of asymmetric shocks. The member countries of the monetary union, however, continue to exercise considerable sovereignty in several economic areas. The most important one is the budgetary field. In the monetary union, most of the spending and taxing powers continue to be vested in the hands of national authorities. Today, in most EU countries, spending and taxation by the national authorities amount to close to 50% of GDP. The spending and taxing powers of the European authorities represent about 1% of GDP. This situation has not changed since the start of monetary union in 1999. By changing taxes and spending, the authorities of an individual country can create large asymmetric shocks. By their very nature, these shocks are well contained within national borders. For example, when the authorities of a country increase taxes on wage income, this only affects labour in that country and will influence spending and wage levels in that country. As a result, the aggregate demand and supply curves of the country involved will shift, creating disturbances that will lead to divergent price and wage developments.

The fact that countries maintain most of their budgetary powers in the monetary union creates the possibility that large asymmetric shocks may occur in the union. This raises the issue of how budgetary policies should be conducted in a monetary union. We will return to this issue in Chapter 10.

There are other aspects of the existence of nation-states that can be a source of asymmetric disturbances and that can induce a national dynamics of booms and busts. As was argued in the previous sections, many economic institutions are national. Wage bargaining systems, for example, differ widely between countries, creating the possibility of asymmetric disturbances. In addition, differences in legal systems and customs generate significant differences in the workings of financial markets. For example, regulations about the conditions under which mortgages are granted by banks differ from one country to another. In addition, differences in tax regulations that determine the amount borrowers can deduct from their income can lead to very different developments of housing prices in different countries. Many more examples can be given. The effect of these differences can be that countries experience very different economic conditions. These can trigger booming conditions in one country, while another country experiences a downturn in economic activity. There can be little doubt that part of the differences in economic growth that we showed in Fig. 2.4 is due to very different national economic policies and institutions. Thus the continued existence of nation-states with their own policies and institutions also created national 'animal spirits', i.e. waves of optimism and pessimism that were not synchronized and that contributed to the divergence.

These differences in the trends of economic activity can lead to another important phenomenon, i.e. the emergence of large divergences in the competitive positions of members of a monetary union. This is exactly what happened in the Eurozone. We show the evidence in Fig. 2.5, which presents the trends in the relative unit labour costs in the Eurozone

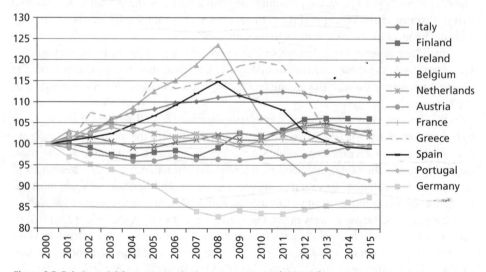

Figure 2.5 Relative unit labour costs in the Eurozone countries (2000–15).

Note: Performance relative to the rest of the EU—double export weights (PLCDQ).

Source: European Commission, AMECO databank.

during 2000–15. The relative unit labour cost is defined as the unit labour cost of one country (say Germany) relative to the average unit labour costs in the other member countries of the Eurozone. When the relative unit labour cost declines, as in the case of Germany, one can say that the unit labour costs of Germany declined relative to those of the other member countries. As a result, Germany improved its competitive position during the period 2000–8. Conversely Ireland, Italy, Greece, and Spain, among others, saw their unit labour costs increase relative to those of the other member countries. As a result, they lost competitiveness during 2000–8. After the emergence of the financial crises in 2008 we observe reverse movements in a number of countries that had lost competitiveness. We come back to this.

Note that the unit labour costs are defined as labour costs corrected for labour productivity.[10] It follows that unit labour costs can increase for two reasons. They increase when wages increase or when labour productivity declines. Thus, it appears that countries such as Italy, Spain, Portugal, and Ireland have lost significant competitiveness since 2000 because wages in these countries increased faster than labour productivity. This has led to serious adjustment problems. These countries have had to start a process of reductions of their wage levels relative to the other countries of the Eurozone (if they cannot raise productivity). This process is slow and painful.

In the past, when these countries were not in a monetary union, they would have been able to devalue their currencies, thereby making it possible to restore their competitiveness in just one stroke. We will come back to some of the issues these countries face during this painful process of adjustment.

From the discussion in this section and the previous ones we can conclude the following. While economic integration is likely to produce economic structures that can lead to more convergence, the continued existence of the nation-states in monetary unions can set in motion a macroeconomic dynamics that leads to strong divergences. Thus, despite the fact that at the microeconomic level trade integration may lead to fewer asymmetric shocks, the absence of a political union may set in motion a macroeconomic dynamics leading to large asymmetric shocks. Because the monetary union is incomplete, the dynamics of booms and busts continues to have mainly a national character, creating difficult adjustment problems for the member states. There is therefore a need to embed a monetary union in a stronger political union. We come back to this issue in Chapter 6.

2.2 How effective are national monetary policies?

The cost of relinquishing one's national currency lies in the fact that a country can no longer use national monetary policies and in particular the exchange rate to correct for differential developments in demand, or in costs and prices. But how effective are these national instruments of monetary policy?

---

[10] The unit labour cost is defined as: $ULC = W/(Q/L)$ where W is the wage rate, Q is the value of output, and L is the amount of labour used in production. Q/L is the average labour productivity. Note that the formula can also be rewritten as follows: $ULC = WL/Q$. This expression makes clear what unit labour cost means: it is the wage cost embedded in one euro (dollar) of output.

This is a crucial question. If the answer is that these instruments are ineffective, one may conclude that countries, even if they develop important differences between themselves, would not have to meet extra costs when joining a monetary union. The instrument they lose does not really allow them to correct for these differences.

In order to analyse this question of the effectiveness of national monetary policies, we return to the asymmetric disturbances analysed in Chapter 1.

National monetary policies to correct for permanent asymmetric demand shocks

Let us take the case of France developed in Section 1.1 of Chapter 1. We assumed that a shift occurred away from French products in favour of German products. In order to cope with this problem France can use expansionary monetary policies, which will lead to a depreciation of the currency, or alternatively, if it has a pegged exchange rate with Germany, it can devalue its currency. We concentrate on the latter case here.

As mentioned in Chapter 1, it is important to ask the question whether the demand shock has a permanent or temporary character. We first analyse the case of a permanent demand shock, and then turn to temporary shocks.

It is important to realize that in the case of a permanent demand shock, the price and costs (including wage costs) of French goods will have to decline relative to those of Germany if France is to return to its initial output level. Put differently, whatever the monetary regime that is used, the price of French goods will have to decline relative to that of German goods in order to stimulate demand for French goods and thereby to restore the initial output level. Can a depreciation of the French franc (FF) achieve this result in a permanent way? We present the situation in Fig. 2.6. As a result of the depreciation, aggregate demand in France shifts back upwards and corrects for the initial unfavourable demand shift. The new equilibrium point is F, which is the initial equilibrium point prior to the negative demand shock. Thus the price level of French goods (in French francs) has been restored. Since the French franc has depreciated against the German mark, the German mark price of French goods is

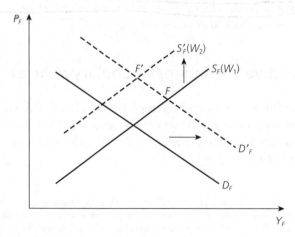

Figure 2.6 Cost and price effects of a currency depreciation.

now lower, while the French franc price of German goods is now higher. Thus it appears that the devaluation of the FF is the trick to reduce the price of French goods relative to German goods. Things seem to be going the right way.

However, it is unlikely that this new equilibrium point can be sustained. The reason is that the depreciation raises the French franc price of imported German goods. This raises the cost of production in France directly. It also reduces the real wage of French workers and will put upward pressure on the nominal wage level in France, as workers are likely to want compensation for the loss of purchasing power. All this means that the aggregate supply curve will shift upwards. Thus, the French price level increases and output declines. This price increase feeds back again into the wage-formation process and leads to further upward movements of the aggregate supply curve. The final equilibrium will be located at a point such as F'. The initially favourable effects of the FF depreciation on French output tend to disappear over time. In addition, the initially favourable effects of the FF depreciation on the relative price of French goods tend to dissipate. When moving from F to F' the relative price of French goods increases again. It is not possible to say here whether the initially favourable effects on output and relative prices will disappear completely. This depends on the openness of the economy, on the degree to which wage-earners will adjust their wage claims to correct for the loss of purchasing power. The latter also depends on institutional features of labour and product market (see Hancke (2013)). There is a lot of empirical evidence, however, that for most of the European countries this withering away of the initially favourable effects of a depreciation will be strong, although not always complete.[11]

The previous conclusion can also be phrased as follows. Nominal exchange rate changes have temporary effects on relative prices. Over time the nominal depreciations lead to domestic cost and price increases, which tend to restore the initial relative prices. In other words, nominal depreciations lead to temporary *real* depreciations. In the long run, nominal exchange rate changes leave the real exchange rate of a country largely unaffected.

Does this conclusion about the limited long-term ineffectiveness of exchange rate changes imply that countries do not lose anything by relinquishing this instrument? Not necessarily. We have to compare the adjustment process obtained here with the adjustment process in a monetary union described in Chapter 1. In order to do so, we set out both adjustment processes in Fig. 2.7. The left-hand panel of Fig. 2.7 shows what the adjustment looks like in a monetary union after the permanent negative demand shock in France. In order for the initial output level to be restored, nominal wages have to decline. This leads to a downward shift in the supply curve. Note that when the initial output (Y_1) is restored, real wages in France also decline. This may not be obvious from Fig. 2.7 because we see that both French nominal wages and the price of French products decline. We should keep in mind, however, that the price of imported German goods has not declined. Thus real wages in France decline. This is part of the process of relative price changes.

Let us now contrast this with the adjustment process when France keeps its national money and adjusts to the negative demand shocks by allowing its currency to depreciate. As we have seen, this shifts the demand curve back upwards. In order to restore the initial output level (Y_1) permanently, the upward pressure on the nominal wage rate (and thus on

[11] See EC Commission (1990), Chapter 6. See also Harberger (2008).

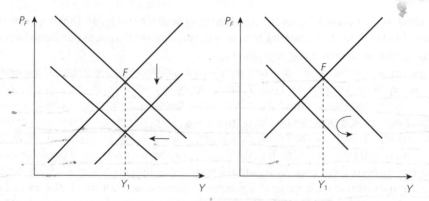

Figure 2.7 Currency depreciation and deflationary policies compared.

the supply curve) must be resisted. This can only be achieved if French workers are willing to accept the decline in their real wage that is implicit in settling at point F.

Thus, the condition needed to restore the initial output level is the same in the two monetary regimes: French workers must accept a decline in their real wages. This is difficult to achieve in both regimes. The question that then arises is the following. In which monetary regime can this condition be satisfied in the easiest way? The answer is that in a perfect world in which there is no money illusion, it does not make any difference. If French workers resist a decline in their real wages, they will resist it both in a monetary union and outside the monetary union. In both regimes, the relative price change will be difficult to achieve, and so also will the return to the initial output level. However, in a less perfect world in which workers have money illusion, these workers may resist real wage declines brought about by a drop in their nominal wage more forcefully than the same real wage decline brought about by price increases (while leaving the nominal wage constant). Thus, in such a world it can be said that it will be more difficult, and more costly in terms of lost output, to adjust to a demand shock in a monetary union than outside the monetary union.

This conclusion is strengthened when considering the budgetary implications of the two adjustment mechanisms. When, in a monetary union, a country has to reduce wages and prices, the ensuing decline in output also leads to an increasing budget deficit and a surge in the ratio of government debt to GDP. As we stressed in Chapter 1, members of a monetary union have no control over the money in which they have issued their debt. This makes them vulnerable to self-fulfilling speculative attacks that can lead to a liquidity crisis, which in turn can degenerate into a solvency crisis. Thus, during the period of adjustment these countries may face a sovereign debt crisis, which leads to a further downward movement in economic activity. This downward movement risks being intense and prolonged.

The contrast with a country that is not in a monetary union, and therefore has full control over the money in which it issues its debt, is important here. Such a country will be able to devalue, thereby avoiding the deflationary process and the ensuing increase in budget deficit and debt-to-GDP ratio.

There were several devaluations in the European Union prior to the start of the monetary union that were successful in restoring domestic and trade account equilibrium at a cost that was most probably lower than if it had not used the exchange rate instrument. The French devaluations of 1982–3 (coming after a period of major policy errors) stand out as success stories (see Sachs and Wyplosz 1986). Similarly, the Belgian and Danish devaluations of 1982 were quite successful in re-establishing external equilibrium without significant costs in terms of unemployment (see De Grauwe and Vanhaverbeke 1990).

National monetary policies to stabilize business cycle shocks *endogenous and temporary.*

In the preceding sections, we discussed the adjustment process to permanent (asymmetric) demand shocks. These were also exogenous in nature. Many demand shocks, however, are related to boom and bust dynamics. These are endogenous and temporary. These business cycle shocks can be asymmetric in that the business cycles of the different countries participating in the monetary union are not well synchronized.

The issue that arises here is one of macroeconomic stabilization. Let us return to Fig. 1.1. We now interpret this figure as representing completely asynchronous business cycle shocks, i.e. when there is a recession in France there is a boom in Germany. In the next period, it will then be the other way round, with a boom in France and a recession in Germany. If these two countries form a monetary union they have a problem. The common central bank is paralysed (see Box 1.1, Chapter 1): if it lowers the interest rate to alleviate the French problem, it will increase inflationary pressures in Germany; if it raises the interest rate to counter the inflationary pressures in Germany, it will intensify the recession in France. In addition, since the shocks are temporary, wage flexibility and mobility of labour cannot be invoked to solve this problem. For example, it would not be very sensible to try to induce French workers to leave France during the recession only to lure them back during the next French boom. In fact, in a monetary union there is simply no solution to this problem: the common central bank cannot stabilize output at the country level; it can only do this at the union level.

However, when France and Germany keep their own money they have the tools to stabilize output at the national level. Thus, when France is hit by a recession the French central bank can stimulate aggregate demand by reducing the interest rate and allowing the French franc to depreciate. Similarly, when Germany experiences a boom, its central bank can raise the interest rate and allow the currency to appreciate to dampen the boom. In a monetary union, these countries lose their ability to change the interest rate. What is worse is that in a monetary union, governments that have no control over the currency in which they issue their debt face distrust from financial markets during a recession. We analysed this problem in Chapter 1. This distrust then leads to increases in the interest rates on government bonds and adds to the forces of recession. In addition, as governments can be hit by sudden liquidity crises they can be forced to apply austerity, i.e. to reduce spending and increase taxes in the midst of a recession. Thus, in a monetary union, countries that face a recession can be forced to switch off the automatic stabilizers in government budgets.

We conclude that in a monetary union there is little scope for stabilization policies at the national level. Monetary policies cannot be used to stabilize nationally driven business cycles. In addition, these business cycle movements are likely to be exacerbated as government budgets lose their automatic stabilizing capacities. We come back to this issue in Chapter 5 and analyse some further implications.

?.

Productivity and inflation in a monetary union: the Balassa–Samuelson effect

Up to now we have assumed that national inflation rates are equalized in a monetary union. This is not necessarily true. We often observe that in existing monetary unions there are regional differences in inflation rates. Although these differences are relatively small, they can be significant. We show some evidence for the Eurozone. In Fig. 2.8, we present the average rates of inflation of the different members of the Eurozone during 1999–2011. It can be seen that these differences are certainly not zero: at one extreme Germany and Ireland had an average yearly rate of inflation of less than 1.5% while Italy, Greece, and Spain experienced a yearly inflation rate of between 2.5 and 3% during 1999–2011.

How can one interpret these phenomena? Balassa and Samuelson have provided a possible explanation.[12] The explanation is based on a distinction between traded and non-traded goods. We will assume that the price of non-traded goods (which are mostly services) consists of wage costs only. Let us now define inflation in Germany and Italy (two extreme observations during 1999–2011) in the following way:

$$\dot{p}_G = \alpha \dot{p}_{TG} + (1-\alpha)\dot{w}_G \qquad (2.1)$$

$$\dot{p}_I = \alpha \dot{p}_{TI} + (1-\alpha)\dot{w}_I \qquad (2.2)$$

where $\dot{p}_G$ and $\dot{p}_I$ are the rates of change in the *consumption* price indices in Germany and Italy. These are the ones shown in Fig. 2.8. They are a weighted average of the rates of price increases of tradables ($\dot{p}_{TG}$ and $\dot{p}_{TI}$), and non-tradables ($\dot{w}_G$ and $\dot{w}_I$) whereby the weights are given by α and $1-\alpha$, respectively. (We assume these weights to be the same in both countries.)

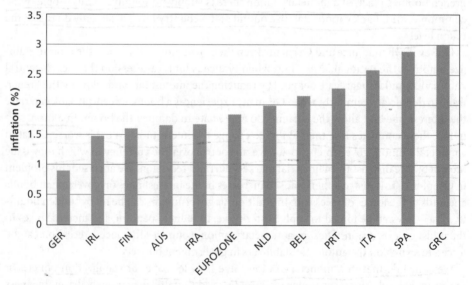

Figure 2.8 Average yearly inflation in Eurozone countries, 1999–2011.

Source: European Commission, *European Economy*.

[12] The basic insights come from Balassa (1964).

When Germany and Italy are in a monetary union, competition makes sure that price changes of tradable goods are equalized. Thus $\dot{p}_{TG} = \dot{p}_{TI}$. Such equalization, however, does not occur in the non-tradable goods sector, because no international competition occurs there. We can now subtract (2.2) from (2.1) and use $\dot{p}_{TG} = \dot{p}_{TI}$.

$$\dot{p}_G - \dot{p}_I = (1 - \alpha)(\dot{w}_G - \dot{w}_I) \tag{2.3}$$

In a well-functioning monetary union, differentials in wage increases must reflect differentials in productivity growth. This is necessary to make sure that countries maintain their competitiveness (see our discussion in the previous section, where we also showed that in the Eurozone this condition has not always been satisfied). We can write this condition as follows:

$$\dot{w}_G - \dot{q}_G = \dot{w}_I - \dot{q}_I \tag{2.4}$$

where $\dot{q}_G$ and $\dot{q}_I$ are the rates of productivity growth in the traded goods sectors of Germany and Italy.[13] Put differently, this is also a condition saying that unit labour costs must increase at the same rate in the two countries. Equation (2.4) can also be rewritten as:

$$\dot{w}_G - \dot{w}_I = \dot{q}_G - \dot{q}_I \tag{2.5}$$

We use this insight and substitute equation (2.5) into (2.3).

$$\dot{p}_G - \dot{p}_I = (1 - \alpha)(\dot{q}_G - \dot{q}_I) \tag{2.6}$$

From equation (2.6) we conclude the following. If there are differentials in productivity growth between countries in a monetary union, then the inflation rates (measured by the consumption price index) must also differ. This effect of productivity growth differentials on inflation is called the Balassa–Samuelson effect (see Balassa 1964). Thus, if productivity grows faster in Italy than in Germany, then Italian inflation will have to exceed German inflation in a monetary union. This higher inflation in Italy is then an equilibrium phenomenon. It reflects the higher productivity growth in that country.

It is important to understand that these inflation differentials should not be a source of worry. On the contrary, they are the result of an equilibrating mechanism. It is because productivity grows faster in Italy than in Germany that wages (and thus prices of non-tradables) must increase faster in Italy than in Germany so as to keep the competitive position of both countries' traded goods sectors unchanged.[14] Note, however, that in order to derive this conclusion we assumed that wage increases always reflect productivity growth.

The previous analysis should not be interpreted to mean that all observed differences in inflation rates in a monetary union are the result of this equilibrating mechanism. In fact we have documented in the previous section (Fig. 2.5) that in some countries (Spain, Ireland, Greece, and Italy) wages increased significantly faster than productivity. As a result, the higher inflation that resulted in these countries was not part of the equilibrating mechanism described in the Balassa–Samuelson model, and led to significant deteriorations of the competitive positions of these countries.

---

[13] Note that we assume implicitly that there is no productivity growth in the non-traded goods sectors.

[14] Canzoneri, Cumby, and Diba (1996) provide an interesting empirical analysis of these productivity-induced inflation differentials in Europe.

2.3 National monetary policies, time consistency, and credibility

The idea that when the government follows particular policies it plays a game with the private sector has dominated macroeconomic theory since the publication of the groundbreaking articles of Kydland and Prescott (1977) and Barro and Gordon (1983).[15] This literature stresses that economic agents follow optimal strategies in response to the strategies of the authorities, and that these private sector responses have profound influences on the effectiveness of government policies. In particular, the reputation governments acquire in pursuing announced policies has a great impact on how these policies are going to affect the economy.

This literature also has important implications for our discussion of the costs of a monetary union. It leads to a fundamental criticism of the view that national monetary policies (including the exchange rate) are policy tools that governments have at their disposal to be used in a discretionary way, in particular to stabilize the economy in the face of temporary shocks. In order to understand this criticism it will be useful to present first the Barro–Gordon model for a closed economy, and then to apply it to an open economy, and to the choice countries have of whether or not to join a monetary union.

The Barro–Gordon model: a geometric interpretation

Let us start from the standard Phillips curve, which takes into account the role of inflationary expectations. We specify this Phillips curve as follows

$$U = U_N + \alpha(\dot{p}^e - \dot{p}) \tag{2.7}$$

where U is the unemployment rate, U_N is the natural unemployment rate, $\dot{p}$ is the observed rate of inflation, and $\dot{p}^e$ is the expected rate of inflation.

Equation (2.7) expresses the idea that only unexpected inflation affects the unemployment rate. Thus, when the inflation rate $\dot{p}$ is higher than the expected rate of inflation, $\dot{p}^e$, the unemployment rate declines below its natural level.

We will also use the rational expectations assumption. This implies that economic agents use all relevant information to forecast the rate of inflation, and that they cannot be systematically wrong in making these forecasts. Thus, *on average* $\dot{p} = \dot{p}^e$ so that *on average* $U = U_N$. We represent the Phillips curve in Fig. 2.9. The vertical line represents the 'long-term' vertical Phillips curve. It is the collection of all points for which $\dot{p} = \dot{p}^e$. This vertical line defines the natural rate of unemployment U_N, which is also called the NAIRU (the non-accelerating-inflation rate of unemployment).

The second step in the analysis consists of introducing the preferences of the monetary authorities. The latter are assumed to care about both inflation and unemployment.

We represent these preferences in Fig. 2.10 in the form of a map of indifference curves of the authorities. We have drawn the indifference curves concave, expressing the idea that as

---

[15] The Barro–Gordon model has been applied to open economies by Mélitz (1988) and by Cohen and Wyplosz (1989), among others.

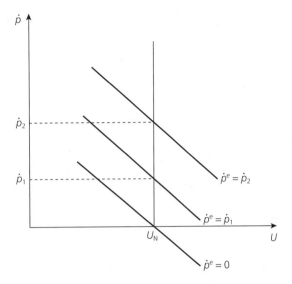

Figure 2.9 The Phillips curve and natural unemployment.

the inflation rate declines, the authorities become less willing to let unemployment increase in order to reduce the inflation rate. Put differently, as the inflation rate declines the authorities tend to attach more weight to unemployment. Note also that the indifference curves closer to the origin represent a lower loss of welfare, and are thus preferred to those farther away from the origin.

The slope of these indifference curves expresses the relative importance the authorities attach to combating inflation or unemployment. In general, authorities who care a good deal about unemployment ('wet' governments) have steep indifference curves: i.e. in order to reduce the rate of unemployment by one percentage point, they are willing to accept a lot of additional inflation.

On the other hand, 'hard-nosed' monetary authorities are willing to let the unemployment rate increase a lot in order to reduce the inflation rate by one percentage point. They

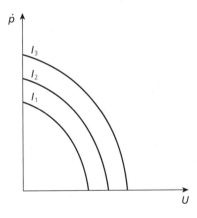

Figure 2.10 The preferences of the authorities.

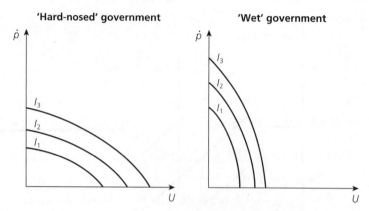

Figure 2.11 The preferences of the authorities: a 'hard-nosed' and a 'wet' government.

have flat indifference curves. At the extreme, authorities that care only about inflation have horizontal indifference curves. We represent two of these cases in Fig. 2.11.

We can now bring together the preferences of the authorities and the Phillips curves to determine the equilibrium of the model. We do this in Fig. 2.12.

In order to find out where the equilibrium will be located, assume for a moment that the authorities announce that they will follow a monetary policy rule of keeping the inflation rate equal to zero. Suppose also that the economic agents believe this announcement. They therefore set their expectations for inflation equal to zero. If the authorities implement this rule we move to point A.

It is now clear that the authorities can do better than point A. They could cheat and increase the rate of inflation unexpectedly. Thus, suppose that after having announced a zero inflation rule, the authorities increase the inflation rate unexpectedly. This would bring

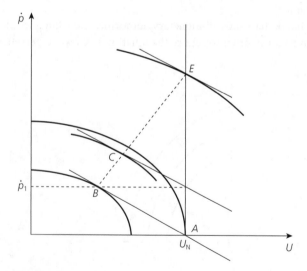

Figure 2.12 The equilibrium inflation rate.

the economy to point *B*, which is located on a lower indifference curve. One can say that the authorities have an incentive to renege on their promise to maintain a zero inflation rate.

Will the authorities succumb to this temptation to engineer a surprise inflation? Not necessarily. The authorities also know that economic agents are likely to react by increasing their expectations of inflation. Thus during the next period, the Phillips curve is likely to shift upwards if the authorities decide to increase the rate of inflation unexpectedly. The authorities should therefore evaluate the short-term gain from cheating against the future losses that result from the fact that the Phillips curve shifts upwards.

But suppose now that the authorities consist of short-sighted politicians who give a low weight to future losses, and that they decide to cheat. We then move to point *B*. This, however, will trigger a shift of the Phillips curve upwards. Given these new expectations, it will be optimal for the authorities to move to point *C*. This will go on until we reach point *E*. This point has the following characteristics. First, it is on the vertical Phillips curve, so that agents' expectations are realized. They therefore no longer have incentives to change their expectations further. Second, at *E* the authorities no longer have any incentive to surprise economic agents with more inflation. A movement upwards along the Phillips curve going through *E* would lead to an indifference curve located higher and therefore to a loss of welfare.

Point *E* can also be interpreted as the equilibrium that will be achieved in a rational expectations world when the authorities follow a *discretionary* policy, i.e. when they set the rate of inflation optimally each period given the prevailing expectations.

It is clear that this equilibrium is not very attractive. It is, however, the only equilibrium that can be sustained, given that the authorities are sufficiently short-sighted, and that the private sector knows this. The zero inflation rule (or any other constant inflation rule below the level achieved at *E*) has no credibility in a world of rational economic agents. The reason is that these economic agents realize that the authorities have an incentive to cheat. They will therefore adjust their expectations up to the point where the authorities have no incentive to cheat any more. This is achieved at point *E*. A zero inflation rule, although desirable, will not come about automatically.[16]

It should be stressed that this model is a static one. If the policy game is repeated many times, the authorities will have an incentive to acquire a reputation for low inflation. Such a reputation will make it possible to reach a lower inflation equilibrium. One way the static assumption can be rationalized is by considering that in many countries political institutions favour short-term objectives for politicians. For example, the next election is never far away, leading to uncertainty as to whether the present rulers will still be in place next period. Thus, what is implicitly assumed in this model is that the political decision process is inefficient, leading politicians to give strong weight to the short-term gains of inflationary policies. The politicians as individuals are certainly as rational as private agents; the political decision process, however, may force them to give undue weight to the very short-term results of their policies. This analysis has led to the view that the authorities that decide about monetary policies (the central bank) should be made independent from politicians. This view has been very influential, so much so that in many countries the central bank has been made politically independent.

---

[16] In the jargon of the economic literature it is said that the policy rule of zero inflation is 'time inconsistent', i.e. the authorities face the problem each period that a better short-term outcome is possible. The zero inflation rule is incentive incompatible.

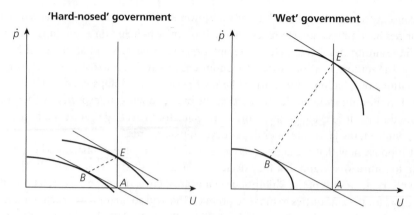

Figure 2.13 Equilibrium with 'hard-nosed' and 'wet' governments.

It can now easily be shown that the location of the discretionary equilibrium, and there-fore also the equilibrium level of inflation, depends on the preferences of the authorities. We show this in Fig. 2.13, where the cases of the 'wet' (steep indifference curves) and the 'hard-nosed' (flat indifference curves) governments are contrasted. Assuming that the Phil-lips curves have the same slopes, Fig. 2.13 shows that in a country with a 'wet' government, the equilibrium inflation will be higher than in a country with a 'hard-nosed' government.

Note also that the only way a zero rate of inflation rule can be credible is when the authori-ties show no concern whatsoever for unemployment. In that case the indifference curves are horizontal. The authorities will choose the lowest possible horizontal indifference curve in each period. The inflation equilibrium will then be achieved at point A.

The Barro–Gordon model in open economies

In the previous sections, we showed how authorities that are known to care about inflation and unemployment will not credibly be able to announce a zero inflation rate. They are therefore stuck in a suboptimal equilibrium with an inflation rate that is too high.

This analysis can be extended to open economies. Let us now assume that there are two countries that do not yet form a monetary union. We call the first country Germany, and assume its government is 'hard-nosed'. The second country is called Italy, where the govern-ment is 'wet'. We use the purchasing-power parity condition, which says that if inflation in Italy exceeds inflation in Germany, the Italian lira will have to depreciate against the German mark to compensate for this inflation differential, i.e.

$$\dot{e} = \dot{p}_I - \dot{p}_G \tag{2.8}$$

We show the inflation outcome in Fig. 2.14. Italy has a higher equilibrium rate of inflation than Germany. Its currency will therefore have to depreciate continuously. The problem of Italy is that it could achieve a much lower inflation equilibrium than point E if its govern-ment were able to convince its citizens that, once at point F, it would not try to reach point G.

This Barro–Gordon model for open economies allows us to add important insights into the discussion of the costs of a monetary union.

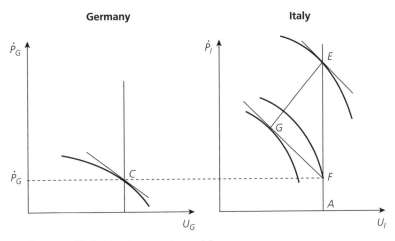

Figure 2.14 Inflation equilibrium in a two-country model.

Credibility and the cost of a monetary union

Can Italy solve its problem by announcing that it will join a monetary union with Germany? In order to answer this question, suppose first that Italy announces that it will fix its exchange rate with the German mark. Given the purchasing-power parity, this fixes the Italian inflation rate at the German level. In Fig. 2.14, we show this by the horizontal line from C. Italy appears now to be able to enjoy a lower inflation rate. The potential welfare gains are large, because in the new equilibrium the economy is on a lower indifference curve.

The question, however, is whether this rule can be credible. We observe that once at the new equilibrium point F, the Italian authorities have an incentive to engineer a surprise devaluation of the lira. This surprise devaluation leads to a surprise increase in inflation and allows the economy to move towards point G. Over time, however, economic agents will adjust their expectations, so that the equilibrium inflation rate will end up being the same as before the exchange rate was fixed. Thus, merely fixing the exchange rate does not solve the problem, because the fixed exchange rate rule is no more credible than a fixed inflation rate rule.[17]

There are, however, other arrangements that can potentially solve the high-inflation problem in Italy. Imagine that Italy decided to abolish its currency and to adopt the currency of Germany. If that arrangement could be made credible, i.e. if Italian citizens were convinced that once this decision was taken and the mark became the national money, the Italian authorities would never rescind this decision, then Italy could achieve the same inflation equilibrium as Germany. In Fig. 2.14, the horizontal line connecting the German inflation equilibrium with Italy defines a credible equilibrium for Italy. The point F is now the new Italian inflation equilibrium. Since Italy has no independent monetary policy any more, its monetary authorities (with 'wet' preferences) have ceased to exist and therefore cannot

---

[17] We will come back to this issue when we discuss the workings of *fixed exchange rate systems*. Some economists have argued that fixing the exchange rate can be a rule that inherently has more credibility than announcing a constant inflation rate rule.

devalue the lira. In the words of Giavazzi and Pagano (1989), Italy has borrowed credibility from Germany, because its government has its monetary hands firmly tied.[18]

This is certainly a very strong result. It leads to the conclusion that there is a large potential gain for Italy in joining a monetary union with Germany. In addition, there is no welfare loss for Germany. Thus, a monetary union only leads to gains. This analysis was very influential prior to the start of the Eurozone. It was especially so in high-inflation countries, which perceived the entry into the Eurozone as a free lunch allowing them to introduce macro economic stability at zero cost.

There are two considerations, however, that tend to soften this conclusion. First, it should be clear from the previous analysis that only a full monetary union establishes the required credibility for Italy. That is, Italy must be willing to eliminate its national currency, very much as East Germany did on 1 July 1990 when it adopted the West German mark. Anything less than full monetary union will face a credibility problem.[19] As was pointed out, when Italy fixes its exchange rate relative to the mark and keeps its own currency, the credibility of this fixed exchange rate arrangement will be in doubt.

Second, and more importantly for our present purpose, we have assumed that the central bank of the monetary union is the German central bank. In this arrangement, Italy profits from the reputation of the German central bank for achieving lower inflation. Suppose, however, that the new central bank is a new institution, where both the German and the Italian authorities are represented equally. Would that new central bank have the same reputation as the old German central bank? This is far from clear. If the union central bank is perceived to be less 'hard-nosed' than the German central bank prior to setting up the union, then the new inflation equilibrium of the union will be higher than the one that prevailed in Germany before the union. Italy may still gain from such an arrangement. Germany, however, would lose, and would not be very enthusiastic to form such a union. We return to these issues in Chapter 8, where we discuss problems of devising institutions that enhance the low-inflation reputation of the European Central Bank.

The Barro–Gordon model for open economies also allows us to understand why some countries decide to 'dollarize' their economies. 'Dollarization' is a monetary regime in which a country decides to unilaterally take over the dollar for domestic payments. Ecuador, El Salvador, and Panama are countries that have switched to a dollarized economy. Invariably these have been countries experiencing high inflation and facing great difficulties in bringing inflation down because of a lack of credibility of their domestic monetary authorities. Dollarization is then an instrument to solve the credibility problem by abolishing the national money and by taking over the dollar, which is backed by the credibility of the US Federal Reserve System. There are also countries in Central and Eastern Europe (Kosovo and Montenegro) that have decided to unilaterally take over the euro as their national currency for pretty much the same reasons as small Latin American countries decided to take over the dollar.

We conclude from the preceding analysis that problems of credibility are important in evaluating the costs of a monetary union. First, the option to allow for a depreciation of the

---

[18] See also Giavazzi and Giovannini (1989).

[19] Some countries (e.g. Argentina, Hong Kong) have experimented with currency boards. These are more constraining monetary regimes than fixed exchange rates, but fall short of a full monetary union. As a result, these countries have occasionally been subjected to intensive speculative attacks (see Box 5.2, Chapter 5). The Argentinian currency board arrangement did not survive the speculative attack of 2001.

currency is a two-edged sword for the national authorities. The knowledge that it may be used in the future greatly complicates macroeconomic policies. Second, the time-consistency literature also teaches us some important lessons concerning the costs of a monetary union: currency depreciations cannot be used to correct every disturbance that occurs in an economy. A depreciation is not, as it is in the analysis of Mundell, a flexible instrument that can be used frequently. When used once, it affects its use in the future, because it engenders strong expectational effects. It is a dangerous instrument that can hurt those who use it. Each time the policy-makers use this instrument, they will have to evaluate the advantages obtained today against the cost, i.e. that it will be more difficult to use this instrument effectively in the future.

This has led some economists to conclude that the exchange rate instrument should not be used at all, and that countries would even gain from irrevocably relinquishing its use. This conclusion goes too far. There were many cases, observed in Europe during the 1980s and 1990s, in which currency devaluations were used very successfully (see Section 2.2). The ingredients of this success have typically been that the devaluation was coupled with other drastic policy changes (sometimes with a change of government, e.g. Belgium and Denmark in 1982). As a result, the devaluation was perceived as an extraordinary change in policies that could not easily be repeated in the future. Under those conditions the negative reputation effects could be kept under control. Some countries, in particular Denmark in 1982, even seem to have improved their reputation quickly after the devaluation. Relinquishing the possibility of using this instrument for the indefinite future does imply a cost for a nation.

This conclusion is enhanced when taking into account the fact that when countries relinquish their national currencies the government debt will have to be issued in a currency that is not under the control of the government. As was argued earlier, this makes these governments more vulnerable to being involved in a debt crisis. Thus, it appears that there is a trade-off here. High-inflation countries can improve their inflation reputation by entering a monetary union. However, at the same time if their reputation in the budgetary field is not strong, their entry into the union makes them more vulnerable to a sovereign debt crisis. The entry into a monetary union does not create a free lunch.

2.4 Mundell once more

Robert Mundell's contribution to the theory of optimal currency areas is substantial. This is also the main reason why he received the Nobel Prize in 1999. On that occasion he was hailed as one of the fathers of the European Monetary Union. The latter may seem rather surprising, since his groundbreaking article, which laid the foundation for the subsequent analysis of the costs and benefits of a monetary union, was very sceptical about the chances of a successful monetary unification in Europe. There is another contribution by Mundell, however, written in 1973, which is much more optimistic about the benefits of a monetary union.

Mundell's reassessment is based on two arguments. First, he argued that a monetary union is a more efficient way to organize an insurance system to cope with asymmetric shocks than a system of national moneys with exchange rate uncertainty. In order to understand this, consider again the asymmetric shock hitting France and Germany. Suppose, though, that the asymmetric shock is temporary, e.g. the result of a desynchronization of the business cycles, or due to seasonal factors. When the two countries form a monetary union, there are automatic flows of capital that will soften the blow for French residents. French consumers who know that the shortfall of income is temporary and who wish to maintain their consumption levels will find it relatively easy to borrow from German consumers, who experience a temporary increase in income, at least if the capital markets are sufficiently integrated. It is likely that this will be the case in a monetary union. In the absence of a monetary union, such a mechanism will be more difficult, because the existence of separate moneys, and an exchange rate that can vary, will make the German consumers reluctant to lend to French consumers because of the risk involved. Thus, in the absence of a monetary union, temporary asymmetric shocks cannot easily be insured against.

A second reason why Mundell came to reassess his pessimism about monetary union has to do with the following. In an uncertain world, exchange rate movements are likely to be a source of asymmetric shocks instead of being a mechanism that allows countries to better adjust for asymmetric shocks. There is a lot of evidence indicating that exchange rate movements are often disconnected from underlying fundamentals such as inflation differentials or output growth. Exchange rates are often driven by psychological factors, herding behaviour, leading to great volatility that in turn feeds back into national economies. Based on these arguments, the 'new' Mundell came to view monetary union as a way to reduce asymmetric shocks and to improve the insurance against asymmetric shocks.

There is certainly an important grain of truth in this analysis. One should keep in mind, though, that one can easily exaggerate this optimism. First, Mundell's conclusion concerning insurance against asymmetric shocks holds when shocks are temporary. When these shocks are permanent, it is unlikely that the German consumers will be willing to extend credit to the French consumers indefinitely. Adjustment has to be undertaken by changing prices and wages. We are back in the 1961-vintage Mundell analysis. Second, even if the shocks are temporary, once financial markets start distrusting one or more member countries of a monetary union, the stabilizing insurance properties of financial markets disappear. The country experiencing a negative shock cannot count on financial flows from other countries; on the contrary, as we showed in Chapter 1, in a regime of distrust, investors are likely to sell the government bonds of the country hit by a negative shock, leading to an increase in the domestic interest rate and an outflow of liquidity. Financial markets cease to be a stabilizing force, and fail to facilitate insurance mechanisms against asymmetric shocks. Third, although exchange rate volatility can be an independent source of asymmetric shocks, it is still true that large shocks can occur that can more easily be dealt with when the exchange rate can be allowed to adjust.

2.5 The cost of monetary union and the openness of countries

In this chapter we have developed several ideas that bear on the question of how the openness of a country affects the cost of the monetary union. Here we concentrate on two of these, which, as will be seen, have opposite effects. First, there is the relation between the degree of openness (the degree to which a country is integrated with the rest of the world) and the

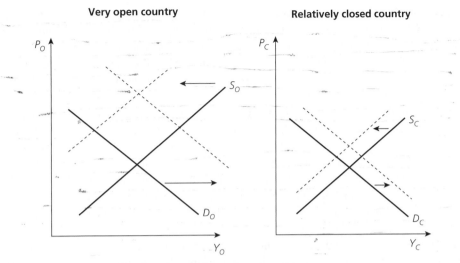

Figure 2.15 Effectiveness of currency depreciation as a function of openness.

occurrence of asymmetric shocks. We have presented two views: the European Commission view, which claims that more integration leads to more symmetry in shocks, and the Krugman view, which sees this relation between integration and symmetry as a negative one. According to the first view, we can conclude that more openness reduces the cost of a monetary union, as it reduces the probability that asymmetric shocks occur. According to the second view, however, this conclusion is reversed: the costs of a monetary union increase with the degree of openness of countries.

The second idea that matters in our analysis of how openness affects the cost of monetary union has to do with the effectiveness of the exchange rate in dealing with asymmetric shocks. Let us return to Fig. 2.6, where we analysed the effects of a currency depreciation. We now consider two countries, one relatively open, the other relatively closed. We represent these two countries in Fig. 2.15. Both the demand and the supply effects of a depreciation differ between the two countries. As far as the demand-side effects are concerned, the same depreciation has a stronger effect in the relatively open economy than in the relatively closed one. To understand this, consider two extreme cases. Suppose the relatively open economy exports 99% of its GDP, whereas the relatively closed one only exports 1% of its GDP. The same depreciation, say 10%, is bound to raise aggregate demand more in the former country than in the latter. In Fig. 2.15, we show this difference by the fact that the demand curve shifts further outward in the relatively open country than in the relatively closed country.

The two countries also differ with respect to the supply-side effects of the depreciation. One can expect that in the relatively open economy, the upward shift of the supply curve following the depreciation is more pronounced than in the relatively closed economy. This has to do with the fact that the more open economy imports more (as a percentage of total consumption) so that the CPI increases more, leading to a stronger wage–price spiral than in the relatively closed economy.

We now arrive at the following conclusion. The combined demand and supply effects of a depreciation in the two countries are such that we cannot say a priori in which country the depreciation is most effective in stimulating output. What we can conclude, however, is that the depreciation will be felt more strongly on the aggregate price level in the more open economy than in the relatively closed economy. This means that the systematic use of the exchange rate instrument will lead to more price variability in the more open economy than in the relatively closed one. We can generalize this point in the following way. The systematic use of monetary policy to stabilize output and employment is likely to lead to greater price variability in the more open economy than in the relatively closed economy. The reason is that these monetary policies will lead to exchange rate movements, i.e. an expansionary (or contractionary) monetary policy will lead to a depreciation (or appreciation) of the currency. These exchange rate movements will have more pronounced effects on domestic prices in the relatively open economy. To the extent that price variability involves costs, the systematic use of national monetary policies in the more open economy will be more costly. This point was first recognized by McKinnon (1963) in his important contribution to the theory of optimum currency areas.

From this discussion of the effectiveness of a currency depreciation in open and (relatively) closed economies, one can conclude that for the same effect on output, the depreciation is likely to be more costly in the open economy because of the higher price variability involved. Thus, the loss of the capacity to use national monetary policies is likely to be less costly for the relatively open economy than for the relatively closed one.

Combining the analysis of the effectiveness of a depreciation with the analysis of the relationship between openness and asymmetric shocks, one can derive the conclusion that the cost of a monetary union most likely declines with the degree of openness of a country. We show this in Fig. 2.16, which is borrowed from Krugman (1990). On the vertical axis, the cost of a monetary union is set out (i.e. the cost of relinquishing the exchange rate instrument). This cost is expressed as a percentage of GDP. On the horizontal axis, the openness of the country relative to the countries with which it wants to form a monetary union is set out. This openness is represented by the trade share in the GDP of the country considered here. We see that as the openness increases, the cost of joining a monetary union declines.

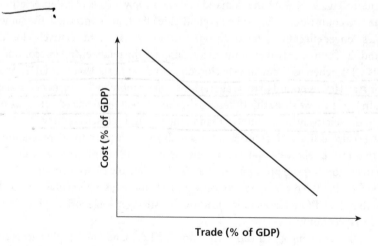

Figure 2.16 The cost of a monetary union and the openness of a country.

This conclusion, however, does not hold in general. We cannot exclude the possibility that the relationship is positively sloped. This situation may occur when the probability of asymmetric shocks increases significantly with the degree of openness of a country (the Krugman scenario). The presumption, however, is that this case is unlikely to happen. First, it is more likely that with trade integration, asymmetric shocks become less likely (see our analysis of the European Commission view). Second, even if trade integration leads to more asymmetric shocks, the cost of using the exchange rate instrument is likely to offset the former effect in more highly integrated economies. We will therefore maintain our presumption that the cost of the monetary union declines with openness.

2.6 Conclusion

The criticism of the traditional theory of optimal currency areas, as developed by Mundell and McKinnon, has enabled us to add important nuances to this theory. In particular, it has changed our view about the costs of a monetary union. The traditional theory of optimal currency areas tends to be rather pessimistic about the possibility of countries joining a monetary union at low cost. The criticism we have discussed in this chapter is less pessimistic about this, i.e. the costs of forming a monetary union appear to be less forbidding.[20] The main reasons why we come to this conclusion are twofold.

First, the ability of exchange rate changes to absorb asymmetric shocks is weaker than the traditional (Keynesian-inspired) OCA theory has led us to believe. Exchange rate changes usually have no permanent effects on output and employment.

Second, countries that maintain independent monetary and exchange rate policies often find out that the movements of exchange rates become a source of macroeconomic disturbances, instead of being instruments of macroeconomic stabilization. Paradoxically, the volatility of exchange rates may be a significant source of asymmetric shocks for countries maintaining their own currencies.

Contrary to the old view, exchange rate changes are not instruments that policy-makers can use flexibly and without cost.

Does this mean that the insights of traditional OCA theory have become irrelevant? The answer is no. Despite our criticism, the hard core of the OCA analysis still stands. This can be put as follows.

There are important differences between countries that are not going to disappear in a monetary union. Many, if not most, of these differences have a political and institutional origin. The nation-states that now make up the monetary union in Europe have maintained many of their national peculiarities. Labour markets continue to have special national institutional features. Legal systems are not identical, creating differences in the functioning of financial markets, of housing markets, and possibly of other markets. The governments of the member states of the monetary union use different tax systems and follow different spending policies. EMU by itself erases some of these differences, but certainly not all. The remaining ones lead to divergent movements in national output and prices, creating the need for difficult national adjustments. The absence of national monetary and

---

[20] See Tavlas (1993) for some further thoughts.

exchange rate policies to assist in this adjustment process is then felt as a cost of the monetary union.[21]

In addition, and most importantly, it appears that in a monetary union national governments not only lose their capacity to stabilize the business cycle by the use of monetary policies. They are also likely to lose the automatic stabilizers in the government budgets when, during a recession, financial markets panic about the capacity of these governments to continue to service their debts. This can lead to self-fulfilling liquidity crises forcing countries into severe austerity in the midst of a recession. We return to this important feature of monetary unions that lack a fiscal union in Chapter 5.

Thus when the EU countries joined EMU on 1 January 1999 they took a risk. The nature of this risk has become visible since the start of the sovereign debt crisis in the Eurozone. All this should serve as a warning for those countries that contemplate joining EMU, or for countries in the rest of the world moving into monetary unions of their own.

The risk of high adjustment costs in the face of asymmetric disturbances can be reduced by implementing two strategies. One consists of making markets more flexible, so that asymmetric shocks can be adjusted better. The other consists of speeding up the process of political unification. This will reduce national idiosyncrasies and thus the occurrence of asymmetric disturbances that have a political or institutional origin.

---

[21] Note that this and the previous sentence were not added since the eruption of the crisis in the Eurozone. These sentences were also to be found in the previous editions of this book. They were formulated in the future tense.

3 The benefits of a common currency

Introduction

Whereas the costs of a common currency have much to do with the *macroeconomic* management of the economy, the benefits are mostly situated at the *microeconomic* level. Eliminating national currencies and moving to a common currency can be expected to lead to gains in economic efficiency. These gains in efficiency have two different origins. One is the elimination of transaction costs associated with the exchanging of national moneys. The other is the elimination of risk coming from the uncertain future movements of the exchange rates. In this chapter we analyse these two sources of benefits of a monetary union. In addition, we will evaluate the benefits of creating a common currency, such as the euro, that has the potential of becoming an international currency.

3.1 Direct gains from the elimination of transaction costs

Eliminating the costs of changing one currency into another is certainly the most visible (and most easily quantifiable) gain from a monetary union. We all experience these costs whenever we exchange currency. These costs disappear when countries move to a common currency.

How large are the gains from the elimination of transaction costs? The EC Commission has estimated these gains, and arrives at a number between 13 billion and 20 billion euros per year.[1] This represents a quarter to a half of 1% of Community GDP. This may seem peanuts. It is, however, a gain that has to be added to the other gains from a monetary union.

It should be noted here that these gains that accrue to the general public have a counterpart somewhere. They are mostly to be found in the banking sector. Surveys in different countries indicate that about 5% of bank revenues are the commissions paid to banks in exchanging national currencies. This source of revenue for banks disappears with a monetary union.

The preceding should not give the impression that the gain for the public is offset by the loss for the banks. The transaction costs involved in exchanging money are a *deadweight* loss. They are like a tax paid by the consumer in exchange for which they get nothing. Banks, however, have a problem of transition: they have to look for other profitable activities. When this has been done, society has gained. The banks' employees, previously engaged in exchanging money, become free to perform more useful tasks for society.

---

[1] See EC Commission (1990).

An important point should be mentioned here. As long as payments systems are not fully integrated, bank transfers between member countries of EMU remain more expensive than bank transfers within the same country. The reason is that although the national payments systems are now linked up by the so-called TARGET system, these national systems are still in place. As a result, cross-border bank transfers follow a different, and more expensive, route from bank transfers within the same country (see Box 3.1).

In order to prevent banks in the Eurozone from applying charges to cross-border payments that are higher than those applied to national payments, a regulation was adopted to force banks to apply the same charges on Eurozone cross-border card payments, ATM withdrawals, and credit transfers of up to €50,000 as those for similar national payments. This regulation led Eurozone banks to create the European Payments Council, which in turn led to the creation of the Single Euro Payment Area (SEPA), which aims to simplify and codify payment standards across the Eurozone.

BOX 3.1 The TARGET payment system

In order for the Eurozone to function efficiently, the payment system must be integrated, so that cross-border payments can be handled as smoothly as payments within the same country. Key in this payment system are the transfers banks make to each other. These transfers are centralized at the central bank. This is also the reason why the central bank is called the 'bank of the banks'. Prior to the start of the Eurozone each country has its own payment system centralized by the national bank. There was therefore a need to integrate these payments systems in the Eurozone. This integration was achieved by the TARGET system. The main features of this system are the following:

- It is a real-time system. This means that the payments banks make to each other reach their destination 'instantaneously', i.e. with a delay of a few seconds or minutes.

- It is a gross settlement system. This means that the gross amount of each payment goes through TARGET. This requires the paying banks to provide collateral for each payment. This contrasts with a net settlement system, which is used in most national payments systems. In the latter, banks can accumulate net debtor or creditor positions during the day without having to provide collateral. These positions are settled at the end of the day.

- The fact that TARGET is a gross settlement system makes it an expensive one compared to net settlement systems. As a result, cheaper private payments systems have emerged based on net settlement.

- The reason why TARGET was selected is that it eliminates the risks that a bank default will have a domino effect on other banks involved in the payments chain.

- Since the sovereign debt crisis in 2010, major imbalances have occurred in the TARGET system, i.e. southern Eurozone countries that had accumulated large current account deficits were suddenly confronted with large liquidity outflows. The opposite occurred in the northern Eurozone countries that became the recipients of these liquidity flows. As a result, the southern Eurozone countries accumulated large liabilities in the TARGET system matched by claims of the northern European countries, mainly Germany. (See Sinn and Wollmershäuser, 2012, who have claimed that this will create large risks for the German taxpayer. See De Grauwe and Ji 2012 and Whelan 2012 for a criticism.) Since 2012 these imbalances in the TARGET system declined significantly as a result of reverse liquidity flows, i.e. liquidity inflows in southern Eurozone countries and outflows from northern Eurozone countries. Why this happened will be discussed in Chapter 6.

The European Commission issued a directive (the Payments Service Directive) that has given a legal basis to SEPA, which set in motion a process leading to a fully integrated payment system in the Eurozone. The first step was taken in January 2008 with the launch of the SEPA Credit Transfer. This allows banks that are active in the payment system to make transfers directly to all other participating banks. The final step was taken in November 2009. Since then customers of the banks have been able to make transfers across countries in the same way as they do within countries.[2] Thus, the transactions cost gains are fully realized in the Eurozone.

3.2 Indirect gains from the elimination of transaction costs: price transparency

The elimination of transaction costs also has an indirect (and less easily quantifiable) gain. The introduction of the euro should lead to more price transparency: i.e. consumers who now can see prices in the same currency unit are better able to make price comparisons, and to shop around. This in turn should increase competition. In the end this should benefit all consumers, who will face the same lower prices. The issue we want to analyse here is whether this effect is strong enough to lead to visible results in the way prices are set in the Eurozone.

There is much evidence that price discrimination is still practised widely in Europe. In Fig. 3.1, we illustrate this phenomenon for a wide range of brand-name products in the year

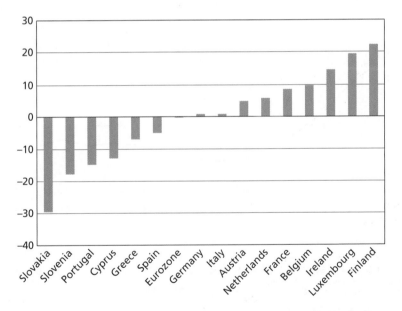

Figure 3.1 Price differentials for consumer goods (in percent) relative to Eurozone average (2011).
Source: Eurostat.

[2] For more detail, see European Central Bank (2008*a*).

2011. It shows the average price of a basket of goods and services in the Eurozone countries. The average price is expressed as an index relative to the Eurozone average. We observe that in Finland this basket of goods and services was 22% more expensive than in the Eurozone while in Slovakia this basket was 30% cheaper than the Eurozone average. Thus there was a price differential of 50% between the cheapest and most expensive country in the Eurozone.[3] These price differentials between countries are typically much larger than within countries. A similar phenomenon was observed by Charles Engel and Richard Rogers (Engel and Rogers 1995). They studied the price differentials of the same pairs of goods in different North American cities (in the USA and Canada). They found that crossing a border (in this case the US–Canadian border) is equivalent to travelling 2,500 miles within the same country. In other words, price differentials between Detroit and Windsor (which is just across the border) are of the same order of magnitude as the price differentials between New York and Los Angeles. Borders are quite powerful in segmenting markets and in introducing large differentials in prices. Thus, in Europe and North America the existence of borders continues to generate strong impediments to trade despite the fact that import tariffs and other explicit trade barriers have been abolished.

It is also useful to study the evolution of price convergence over time to see whether trends appear. We show the results of a study by Wolszczak-Derlacz (2006) in Fig. 3.2. It presents the price differentials (measured by the mean standard deviation) of 173 identical products across the Eurozone from 1990 to 2005. The remarkable observation is that price convergence occurred

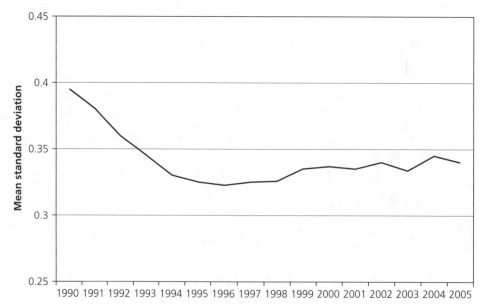

Figure 3.2 Evolution of price dispersion in the Eurozone, 1990–2005.

Source: Wolszczak-Derlacz (2006).

[3] Haskel and Wolf (2001) show that there are similar price differentials for exactly the same products sold by the furniture store IKEA across Europe. Price differentials in the automobile market are notorious. Baye et al. (2006) have shown that listed internet prices for a sample of items have not converged after the introduction of the euro.

prior to 1999 (mostly in the early 1990s).[4] Since the start of the Eurozone, price convergence has stopped.[5] This phenomenon has also been observed by the European Commission (see European Commission 2004). More recent empirical papers confirm that this lack of price convergence in the Eurozone is a continuing feature, i.e. there is no evidence that since 2005 price convergence has increased (see Parsley and Wei 2008 and Clementi et al. 2010). A recent study of the car markets in the Eurozone also confirms that the euro has had no effect in reducing the considerable price dispersion for the same cars within the Eurozone (Dvir and Strasser 2013).

Why does the introduction of the euro appear to be a weak force in bringing about price convergence? Many of the products in the sample of Wolszczak-Derlacz are supermarket products. The price differentials for supermarket products are the result of transaction costs. With or without the euro it remains very costly for individual consumers living in, say, Paris to make a trip to Berlin so as to profit from a price advantage for some (not all) groceries. Such arbitrage remains prohibitive in the Eurozone. But why then do we observe almost no price differentials for supermarket products within the same countries? The answer is that the retail business is still very much segmented nationally. In most countries, a few supermarket chains dominate the whole market. They conduct national commercial and advertising campaigns, setting prices for the whole national market. Part of the reason is that most of these supermarket chains are still very much national companies. The other part has to do with different regulations, customs, languages, and cultures. It is doubtful that the euro will overcome all this very soon.

Other products in the sample are electronic products (e.g. cameras, mobile phones, etc.). The price differentials for these products are due not so much to transaction costs. After all, it may pay to make a trip from Brussels to London to buy a portable PC. However, this is a sector of highly differentiated products, making precise price comparisons for consumers very difficult. This is also the reason why the price differentials for these products remain high also within countries with the same currency. Thus, although the euro may make price comparisons a little easier, it is doubtful that it will contribute much to eliminating the observed price differentials.

One may conclude that if the euro contributes to price convergence it will be not so much because it makes direct price comparisons for consumers easier. It will be because it may contribute to further economic integration in other ways. It is possible that the introduction of the euro stimulates financial integration (see Chapter 11 where we evaluate the extent to which the euro has stimulated financial integration). This in turn may set in motion a dynamics of integration in other areas. Financial market integration is likely to push for further legislative harmonization. Thus, the existence of the euro may become an important trigger for further integration in many other areas (political, legislative, regulations). If that occurs, a dynamic can be set in motion which is more important than the direct price comparison. It will take time, however, before it shows its effects.

3.3 Welfare gains from less uncertainty

Uncertainty about future exchange rate changes introduces uncertainty about future revenues of firms. It is generally accepted that this leads to a loss of welfare in a world populated

---

[4] This is also found by Engel and Rogers (2004).

[5] The slight increase in dispersion observed after 1999 is too small to be statistically significant.

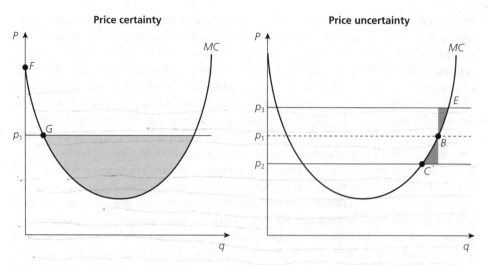

Figure 3.3 Profits of the firm under price certainty and uncertainty.

by risk-averse individuals. These will, generally speaking, prefer a future return that is more certain than one that is less so, at least if the expected value of these returns is the same. Put differently, they will only want to take the more risky return if they are promised that on average it will be higher than the less risky. Eliminating the exchange rate risk reduces a source of uncertainty and should therefore increase welfare.

There is one important feature of the theory of the firm that may invalidate that conclusion. Take a profit-maximizing firm that is a price-taker in the output market. Let us also assume that the firm exports its whole output. We represent its marginal cost curve and the price of its output in Fig. 3.3. The price the firm obtains is given by the price in the export market times the exchange rate. Suppose there are two regimes. In the first regime (presented in the left panel) the exchange rate is fixed. As a result, the price obtained by the firms is constant and perfectly predictable (assuming that the foreign currency price is constant). In the second regime (right panel) the exchange rate fluctuates randomly producing random price fluctuations. We assume here that the price fluctuates symmetrically between p_2 and p_3.

In the first regime of certainty, the profit of the firm in each period is given by the shaded area minus the area FGp_1. In the second, uncertain regime the profit will fluctuate depending on whether the price p_2 or p_3 prevails. We can now see that the profit will be larger on average in the uncertain regime than in the certain regime. When the price is low the profit is lower than in the certainty case by the area p_1BCp_2. When the price is high, the profit is higher than in the certainty case by the area p_3EBp_1. It can now easily be seen that p_3EBp_1 is larger than p_1BCp_2. The difference is given by the two shaded triangles.

This result may be interpreted as follows. When the price is high, the firm increases output so as to profit from the higher revenue per unit of output. Thus, it gains a higher profit for each unit of output it would have produced anyway, and *in addition* it expands its output. The latter effect is measured by the upper shaded triangle. When the price is low, however, the firm will do the opposite: it will reduce output. In so doing it limits the reduction in its total profit. This effect is represented by the lower shaded triangle.

If one wants to make welfare comparisons between a regime of price certainty and one of price uncertainty, the positive effect of price uncertainty on average profits should be compared to the greater uncertainty about these profits. The higher average profit increases the utility of the firm, whereas the greater uncertainty about these profits reduces the utility of the (risk-averse) firm. It is, therefore, unclear whether welfare declines when exchange rate uncertainty increases or, conversely, whether we can say with great confidence that the welfare of firms increases when national currencies are eliminated and a common currency is introduced.

Another way to put the preceding analysis is to recognize that changes in the exchange rate do not only represent a risk; they also create opportunities to make profits. When the exchange rate becomes more variable the probability of making large profits increases. In a certain sense, exporting can be seen as an *option*. When the exchange rate becomes very favourable the firm exercises its option to export. With an unfavourable exchange rate the firm does not exercise this option. It is well known from option theory that the value of the option increases when the variability of the underlying asset increases. Thus, the firm that has the option to export is better off when the exchange rate becomes more variable.

Many complications may be added to this theory. One may introduce the assumption of imperfect competition, or the assumption that firms face adjustment costs when they vary output.

These complications provide important insights into the effect of price uncertainty on average profits. In more complicated models, however, it is generally the case that price uncertainty *may* increase the average profits of the firm.

There is one aspect of uncertainty that is quite serious and that can undermine the relevance of the previous analysis. This is that exchange rate changes are not normally distributed. The nature of exchange rate movements is that there are periods of relative tranquillity followed by periods of great turbulence. During these turbulent periods, exchange rate changes can be very large and sustained in one direction, producing bubbles followed later by crashes. We show some examples involving the dollar versus the German mark and versus the euro in Fig. 3.4.

Such large movements in the exchange rate create 'tail risks', i.e. the risk of a very large change that occurs with low probability. When it occurs, the effect can be devastating. In the context of Fig. 3.3, the decline in the exchange rate can be so large that the price falls way below the marginal cost curve (and the average cost curve, which is not drawn here), forcing the firm to close its doors. The cost of bankruptcy and of reallocating the factors of production employed by these firms will typically be substantial, creating large costs of exchange rate movements.

Such large exchange rate movements are a recurrent problem with freely floating exchange rates. They create large adjustment costs and much economic misery. They also occurred massively within the European Union during the early 1990s, when some currencies (e.g. the Italian lira and the Spanish peseta) depreciated by 20 to 30% in a few weeks, creating large adjustment costs in countries like Germany and the Benelux.

These large exchange rate movements between the currencies of highly integrated countries were a major factor in convincing many leaders of these countries to move into a monetary union. There were two reasons for this. First, it was increasingly felt that it would be difficult if not impossible to manage exchange rates in an orderly fashion in a world of free capital mobility. We come back to this theme in Chapter 5, where we analyse why it is so difficult to manage exchange rates. Second, these exchange rate movements were increasingly seen as major sources of asymmetric disturbances, instead of being variables that could be used to adjust to asymmetric shocks.

German mark.

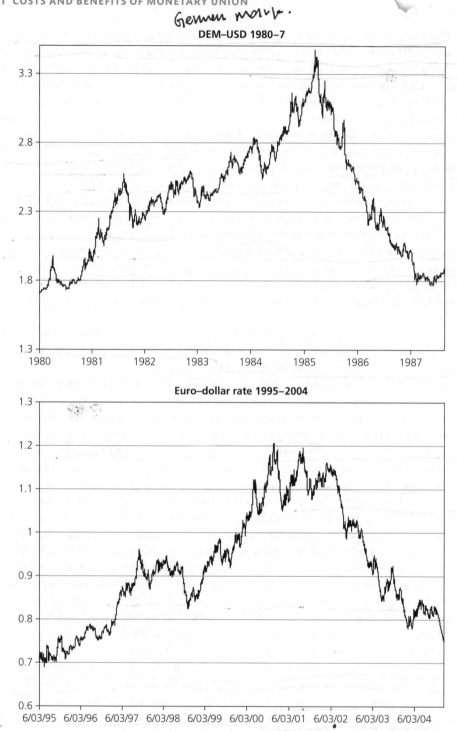

Figure 3.4 Bubbles and crashes in foreign exchange markets: two examples.

Note: The euro–dollar rate prior to 1999 is the DEM–dollar rate multiplied by the fixed DEM–euro conversion rate.

Source: De Grauwe and Grimaldi (2006).

3.4 Exchange rate uncertainty and economic growth

The argument that the elimination of the exchange risk will lead to an increase in economic growth can be made using the neoclassical growth model, and its extension to situations of dynamic economies of scale. This analysis featured prominently in the EC Commission report 'One Market, One Money' (1990), which in turn was very much influenced by Baldwin (1989). This analysis was very influential in selling the idea of a monetary union in Europe as a tool to boost economic growth.

The neoclassical growth model is represented in Fig. 3.5. The horizontal axis shows the capital stock per worker, and the vertical axis the output per worker. The line $f(k)$ is the production function, which has the usual concave shape, implying diminishing marginal productivities. The equilibrium in this model is obtained where the marginal productivity of capital is equal to the interest rate consumers use to discount future consumption. This is represented in Fig. 3.5 by the point A, where the line rr (whose slope is equal to the discount rate) is tangent to the production function $f(k)$. In this model, growth can only occur if the population grows or if there is an exogenous rate of technological change. (Note also that in this neoclassical model the savings ratio does not influence the equilibrium growth rate.)

We can now use this model as a starting point to evaluate the growth effects of a monetary union. Assume that the elimination of the exchange risk reduces the systemic risk. This will have the effect of lowering the real interest rate. The reason is that in a less risky environment, investors will require a lower-risk premium to make the same investment. In addition, when agents discount the future they will be willing to use a lower discount rate. We represent this effect in Fig. 3.6. The reduction of the risk-adjusted rate of discount makes the rr line flatter, twisting it to $r'r'$. As a result, the equilibrium moves from A to B. There will be an accumulation of capital and an increase in the growth rate while the economy moves from A to B. In the new equilibrium, output per worker and the capital stock each has at their disposal will have increased. Note, however, that the growth rate of output then returns to its initial level, which is determined by the exogenous rate of technological change and the rate of growth of the population. Thus, in

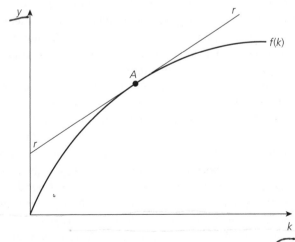

Figure 3.5 The neoclassical growth model.

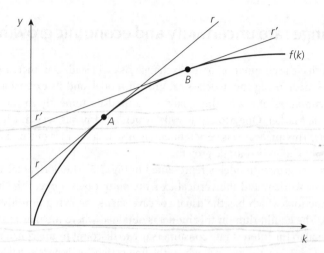

Figure 3.6 The effect of lower risk in the neoclassical growth model.

this neoclassical growth model, the reduction of the interest rate due to the monetary union *temporarily* increases the rate of growth of output. In the new equilibrium, the output *level* per worker will have increased. (Note also that the productivity of capital has declined.)

This model has been extended by introducing dynamic economies of scale (Romer 1986). Suppose the productivity of labour increases when the capital stock increases. This may arise because with a higher capital stock and output per worker there are learning effects and additional knowledge is accumulated. This additional knowledge then increases labour productivity in the next period. There may also be a public goods aspect to knowledge. Thus, once a new machine is in place the knowledge it embodies is freely available to the worker who uses it. All these effects produce increases in the productivity of labour over time when capital accumulates.

One of the interesting characteristics of these new growth models is that the growth path becomes endogenous, and is sensitive to the initial conditions. Thus, an economy that starts with a higher capital stock per worker can move on a permanently higher growth path.

A lowering of the interest rate can likewise put the economy on a permanently higher growth path. We represent this case in Fig. 3.7. As a result of the lower interest rate the economy accumulates more capital. Contrary to the static case of Fig. 3.6, however, this raises the productivity of the capital stock per worker. This is shown by the upward movement of the $f(k)$ line. The economy will be on a higher growth path.

How much of this promise has come through? Let's look at Fig. 3.8. We compare the growth of real GDP during 2000–14 of the euro area with the growth of real GDP in the US and in the EU-countries that are not members of the euro area (called EU-10). It is striking that GDP has increased at a significantly lower rate in the euro area than in the US and in EU-10. There may be many reasons why the growth rate was so low in the euro area, but if a monetary union was a growth-boosting machine, we would probably not have observed this. Note also the stagnation in the euro area since 2008 while the US and the EU-10 started a clear recovery. The impression we get is that there is very little evidence that the euro has boosted growth as was promised by the previous theoretical analysis.

Why is it that the theory predicting growth-boosting effects of monetary union does not seem to have been borne out? The main reason probably is that the reduced exchange rate

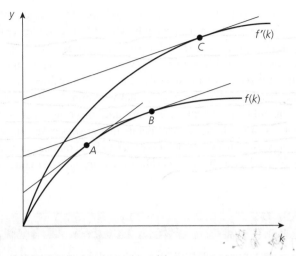

Figure 3.7 Endogenous growth in the 'new' growth model.

uncertainty within the union does not seem to have led to a significant decline in the real interest rate. There is very little evidence that the real interest rate in the Eurozone as a whole has come down.[6] Only in the 'catching up' countries such as Ireland, Spain, Portugal, and Greece did the real interest rate come down significantly. It is in these countries (with the exception of Portugal) that we observe an acceleration of economic growth as predicted by

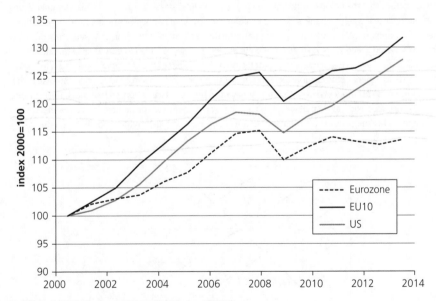

Figure 3.8 Real GDP in Eurozone, EU10, and US (prices of 2010).

Source: European Commission, AMECO.

[6] Note that since the financial crisis that erupted in 2007 the real interest rates have shown a tendency to decline. This phenomenon, however, has happened in most industrialized countries irrespective of whether they belong to the Eurozone or not (see Summers 2014 and Teulings and Baldwin 2014).

the theory. Much of this growth, however, turns out to have been temporary. In addition, the stagnation observed since 2008 is most probably related to the implementation of intense austerity programmes in a large number of Eurozone countries.

The weak link between exchange rate uncertainty, the real interest rate, and growth may also be due to the fact that the reduction in exchange rate uncertainty does not necessarily reduce the *systemic* risk. Less exchange rate uncertainty may be compensated by greater uncertainty elsewhere, e.g. output and employment uncertainty, and uncertainty about the sustainability of government debts. As a result, firms that operate in a greater monetary zone may not on average operate in a less risky environment. There is a whole theoretical literature, starting with William Poole (1970) that has analysed this problem. We present the main results in Box 3.2.

BOX 3.2 Fixing exchange rates and systemic risk

In a groundbreaking article, William Poole (1970) showed that fixing interest rates does not necessarily reduce the volatility of output compared to fixing the money stock. The argument Poole developed can easily be extended to the choice between joining a monetary union (irrevocably fixing the exchange rate) and staying outside the union (allowing for a flexible exchange rate).

We consider, first, random shocks occurring in the domestic goods market (business cycle shocks, for example). We present this by shifts in the *IS* curve. This now moves unpredictably between IS_U and IS_L.

Assume first that the country in question is a part of a monetary union. Thus, there is no longer any exchange rate to worry about. This implies that the domestic interest rate is equal to the union interest rate set by the union central bank. We represent the model graphically in Fig. 3.9.

Let us assume that the union central bank keeps the union interest rate unchanged. This is a rather strong assumption, since the central bank is likely to be influenced by what happens in the country analysed here, unless this country is small. Under those conditions the domestic interest rate is unchanged. Thus, output will fluctuate between y_L and y_U. Note that as the *IS* curve moves to, say, IS_U, the *LM* curve will automatically be displaced to the right, so that it intersects IS_U at the point *F*. This shift of the *LM* curve comes from the fact that the upward movement of the *IS* curve increases domestic income, which in turn leads to an increase in the domestic demand for money. This will attract money from the rest of the union, so that the domestic supply of money increases. Note again that we are assuming that the country involved here is small in relation to the union. If this is not the case, the domestic boom will put upward pressure on the union interest rate.

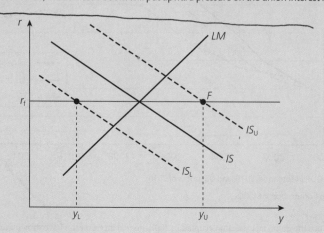

Figure 3.9 Shocks in the *IS* curve.

What happens if the country is not in the monetary union, and if it then allows its exchange rate to move freely? In this case the *LM* curve remains fixed. The same shocks in the *IS* curve now have no effect on the output level. The reason is the following. Suppose the *IS* curve shifts upwards (say, because of a domestic boom). This tends to increase the domestic interest rate. Since the exchange rate is flexible, there can be no increase in the money stock from net capital inflows. Instead, the increase in the domestic interest rate leads to an appreciation of the currency. This appreciation, in turn, tends to shift the *IS* curve back to the left. This will continue until the domestic interest rate returns to its initial level, which is only possible when the *IS* curve returns to its initial position.

We conclude from this case that being a member of the monetary union has led to more variability in the output market (and therefore also in the labour market) compared to being outside the union and letting the exchange rate vary. Joining the monetary union and thereby irrevocably fixing the exchange rate does not necessarily reduce systemic risk, because it leads to more uncertainty elsewhere in the system. Note that this is in essence the same conclusion as in the traditional theory of optimum currency areas in the presence of asymmetric shocks in the output market.[7]

This result, however, very much depends on the nature of the random shocks, which were assumed to come from the goods markets. Things are quite different if the random shocks originate from the money market.

Suppose that we have random disturbances in the demand for money (disturbances in velocity). We represent these by movements in the *LM* curve between the limits LM_L and LM_U in Fig. 3.10. Let us again consider the case where the country is in the monetary union. As before, this means that the domestic interest rate is fixed (assuming no shocks in the union interest rate). It can now immediately be established that there will be no change in output. The reason is the following. Suppose that the domestic demand for money has declined, leading to a rightward shift of the *LM* curve. This tends to reduce the interest rate. Such a reduction, however, is prevented by an immediate outflow of liquidity. The *LM* curve must return to its initial level. Thus, the domestic goods market is completely insulated from domestic money market disturbances when the country is in the union.

If the country is outside the union and allows the exchange rate to float, this will no longer be the case. Output will now fluctuate between the levels Y_L and Y_U. The intuition is that if the *LM* curve shifts to the right, the ensuing decline in the interest rate leads to a depreciation of the currency, whereas the domestic money supply remains unchanged. The decline in the interest rate and the depreciation tend to stimulate aggregate demand. This shifts the *IS* curve upwards until it intersects the LM_U line at point G. The goods market is not insulated from the money market disturbances.

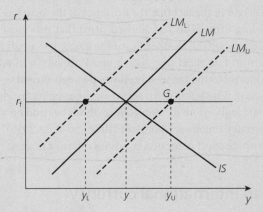

Figure 3.10 Shocks in the *LM* curve.

---

[7] The OECD provides some interesting evidence relating to this issue. It finds that output variability tends to be higher in member states of monetary unions. See OECD (1999*a*).

3.5 Monetary union and trade: the empirical evidence

Let us now concentrate on the trade effects of a monetary union. We identified two mechanisms through which a monetary union could increase trade among the members of a monetary union. The first one has to do with transaction costs: i.e. monetary union leads to fewer transaction costs and thus stimulates international trade. The second mechanism relates to exchange rate uncertainty. This could also be a factor that stimulates trade among the members of a monetary union.

What is the empirical evidence concerning the effects of a monetary union on trade? The first generation of econometric studies generally have found very little. These studies have typically been based on time series analysis, whereby bilateral trade flows were related to measures of exchange rate variability (and other control variables). Most of the time this relation was found to be weak and insignificant. Thus, it was concluded that eliminating exchange rate variability in the framework of a monetary union would have little effect on trade flows. (For a survey, see International Monetary Fund 1984.)

There is a second generation of econometric studies, pioneered by Andy Rose, which has come to very different conclusions. Using cross-section data, and controlling for a multitude of other variables that affect trade flows (e.g. income, distance, trade restrictions, language, and many more), Rose (2000) found that pairs of countries that are part of a monetary union have trade flows among themselves that, on average, are 200% higher than those among pairs of countries that are not part of a monetary union. We discussed these studies in Chapter 2 and we came to the conclusion that these trade effects of a monetary union are overestimated. In addition, in the absence of a good theory about how monetary union boosts trade, aggregate estimates of the correlation between monetary union and trade are unreliable (see Baldwin (2006)).

Several studies have attempted to overcome this criticism by looking at the sectoral and microeconomic evidence (Flam and Nordström 2006; Baldwin et al. 2008; Berger and Nitsch 2008; Nitsch and Pisu 2008). Estimates of the euro effect on trade within the Eurozone found in these studies vary between 5% and 20%. The mechanism through which the euro has boosted trade finds its origin in the fact that the existence of the euro has lowered fixed and variable costs of exporting firms. This has allowed firms that previously only catered for domestic markets to start exporting to other Eurozone countries. Small firms in particular seem to have profited from this effect (see Nitsch and Pisu 2008). In addition, firms that already exported have increased the range of products they sell abroad.

Finally in 2015 Glick and Rose published a surprising 'mea culpa' in which they admitted that using post-EMU data and various econometric methods 'we find no substantive reliable and robust effect of currency union on trade' (see Glick and Rose 2015). We conclude that the evidence about a positive effect of monetary unions on trade is weak.

3.6 Benefits of an international currency

When countries form a monetary union, the new currency that comes out of this union is likely to weigh more in international monetary relations than the sum of the individual currencies prior to the union. As a result, the new common currency is likely to find increasing use outside the union. This creates additional benefits of the monetary union. In this section, we analyse the nature of these benefits. In Chapter 11, we turn to the issue of whether and how quickly the euro can become an international currency like the dollar, and thereby reap the benefits that will be described here.

The advantages of having a currency that is used as a unit of account and a medium of exchange in the rest of the world are significant. We distinguish three sources of benefits.

First, when a currency is used internationally, the issuer of that currency obtains additional revenues. For example, in 1999 more than half of the dollars issued by the Federal Reserve were used outside the USA. This situation has the effect of more than doubling the size of the balance sheet of the Federal Reserve compared to a situation in which the dollar is only used domestically. It follows that the Federal Reserve's potential profits are also more than doubled. Since these profits go to the US government, US citizens enjoy the benefits of the worldwide use of the dollar in the form of lower taxes needed to finance a given level of government spending. If the euro becomes a world currency like the dollar, citizens of the Eurozone will enjoy similar benefits. In fact, there is some evidence that the euro is used in Central and Eastern Europe, creating revenues for the citizens of the Eurozone.

One should not exaggerate these benefits, however. The total profits of the US Federal Reserve amount to less than 0.5% of US GDP. Thus, the additional revenues from having an international currency remain relatively small.

A second source of benefit has to do with the fact that an international currency is also one that is held as international reserve by foreign central banks. Typically, these reserves are held not in the form of cash but as Treasury securities. Thus the Central Bank of China holds more than one trillion dollars in the form of US Treasury securities. Other Asian central banks also hold many hundreds of billions of dollars of US Treasury securities. These foreign holdings have been an important source of easy finance for US budget deficits during the last decade. The peculiarity of this finance is that the foreign holders bear the exchange risk. It is in this connection that the French President, de Gaulle, talked about the 'exorbitant privilege' of the US (see Eichengreen 2012).

The euro is increasingly held as a reserve currency by foreign central banks. According to the ECB, in 2010 the euro represented about 27% of all central banks' international reserves (against about 60% for the dollar). Thus it appears that euro area treasuries are also finding new sources of financing for their government budget deficits.

There is also a danger in such a trend. Easier finance can lead governments to make excessive use of this finance. During the decade prior to the financial crisis this was certainly the case with the US government, which did not hesitate to run large budget deficits thanks to the easy access to credit granted by Asian central banks. This in turn helped to finance an unsustainable consumption boom, which came to a crashing end in 2008.

A third benefit is probably larger, but also more difficult to quantify. When a currency becomes an international one, this will boost activity for domestic financial markets. Foreign residents will want to invest in assets and issue debt in that currency. As a result, domestic banks will attract business, and so will the bond and equity markets. This in turn creates know-how and jobs. Thus, if the euro becomes an international currency like the dollar, this is likely to create new opportunities for financial institutions in the Eurozone.

Here also a word of caution is necessary. Some countries such as the UK have been able to attract financial activities from the rest of the world without the support of a local currency that is a true international currency. The City of London is now a major centre of international finance, despite the fact that the pound sterling no longer plays a major role in the world. Thus, having an international currency is not a necessary condition for generating financial services that the rest of the world is willing to pay for. Nor is it a sufficient condition, for that matter. We come back to this issue in Chapter 11, when we discuss the conditions under which the euro could become a world currency.

3.7 Benefits of a monetary union and the openness of countries

As discussed in Chapter 1 on the costs of a monetary union, we can also derive a relationship between the *benefits* of a monetary union and the openness of a country. The welfare gains of a monetary union that we have identified in this chapter are likely to increase with the degree of openness of an economy. For example, the elimination of transaction costs will weigh more heavily in countries where firms and consumers buy and sell a large proportion of goods and services in foreign countries. Similarly, the consumers and the firms in these countries are more subject to decision errors because they face large foreign markets with different currencies. Eliminating these risks will lead to a larger welfare gain (per capita) in small and open economies than in large and relatively closed countries.

We can represent graphically this relationship between the benefits of a monetary union and the openness of the countries that are candidates for a union. This is done in Fig. 3.11. On the horizontal axis we show the openness of the country relative to its potential partners in the monetary union (measured by the share of their bilateral trade in the GDP of the country considered). On the vertical axis we represent the benefits (as a percentage of GDP). With increasing openness towards the other partners in the union, the gains from a monetary union (per unit of output) increase.

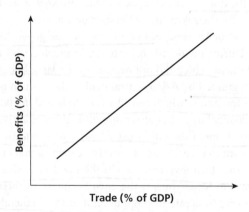

Figure 3.11 Benefits of a monetary union and openness of the country.

3.8 Conclusion

A common currency has important benefits. In this chapter several of these benefits were identified. First, a common currency in Europe decreases transaction costs. This produces not only direct but also indirect benefits in that it stimulates economic integration in Europe. Second, by reducing price uncertainty, a common currency improves the allocative efficiency of the price mechanism. This improves welfare, although it is difficult to quantify this effect. Third, the major welfare improvement resulting from eliminating exchange rates within the union is that it eliminates the extreme movements in the exchange rates. These extreme exchange rate changes that have occurred regularly within the European Union in the past lead to major macroeconomic disturbances. They themselves become sources of asymmetric shocks, instead of being instruments to adjust to asymmetric shocks. We should, however, also keep in mind that the existence of a common currency can create new risks. These arise when countries find it difficult to adjust to disturbances. A monetary union also creates specific risks for national governments. By entering into a monetary union they lose the capacity to guarantee that the outstanding stock of government bonds will always be repaid. This can unsettle the financial markets, creating new risks that did not exist outside the monetary union. As a result, the decline in exchange risk may not necessarily reduce systemic risk in EMU.

Fourth, the greater price transparency provided by the use of a common currency is likely to increase competition somewhat, benefiting consumers. However, we also concluded that it is not so much the greater price transparency that is the source of benefits. It is the fact that the existence of the euro can trigger integration in other areas (financial, institutional, political) that will lead to more competition and welfare gains. Fifth, if the new common currency graduates to become a truly global currency, additional benefits can be reaped in the form of government revenues and an expansion of the financial industry in the union.

4   Costs and benefits compared

Introduction

In the previous chapters, the costs and benefits of a monetary union were identified. In this chapter, we conclude this discussion by comparing the benefits with the costs in a synthetic way. This will allow us to evaluate the wisdom of the EU countries when they decided to launch EMU, and the risks they took. In addition it will make it possible to draw some conclusions about the economic desirability of joining EMU for the new EU member states that are waiting to enter and for those that today still hesitate to do so. We will also apply this cost–benefit analysis to other parts of the world: Latin America, East Asia, and West Africa.

4.1   Costs and benefits compared

It is useful to combine the figures (derived in the previous chapters) relating benefits and costs to the openness of a country. This is done in Fig. 4.1. The intersection point of the benefit and the cost lines determines the critical level of openness that makes it worthwhile for a country to join a monetary union with its trading partners. To the left of that point, the country is better off keeping its national currency. To the right it is better off when it relinquishes its national currency and replaces it with that of its trading partners.

Fig. 4.1 allows us to draw some qualitative conclusions concerning the importance of costs and benefits. The shape and the position of the cost schedule depend to a large extent on one's view about the effectiveness of national monetary policies, including exchange rate policies, in correcting for the effects of different demand and cost developments between the countries involved.

At one extreme, there is a view, which will be called 'monetarist', claiming that national monetary policies are ineffective as instruments to correct for asymmetric shocks, be they permanent or temporary. And even if they are effective, according to this view, the use of these policies typically makes countries worse off. In this 'monetarist' view the cost curve is very close to the origin.[1] We represent this case in Fig. 4.2(*a*). The critical point that makes it worthwhile to form a union is close to the origin. Thus, in this view, many countries in the world would gain by relinquishing their national currencies and joining a monetary union.

---

[1]   This is the view taken by the drafters of the influential EC Commission report (1990).

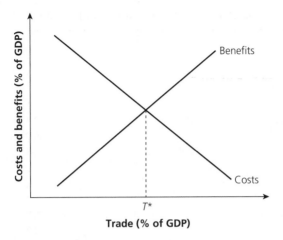

Figure 4.1 Costs and benefits of a monetary union.

At the other extreme, there is the 'Keynesian' view that the world is full of rigidities (wages and prices are rigid; labour is immobile), so that national monetary policies and the exchange rate are powerful instruments in absorbing asymmetric shocks. This view is well represented by the original Mundell model discussed in Chapter 1. In this view, the cost curve is far away from the origin, as shown in Fig. 4.2(*b*), so that relatively few countries should find it in their interest to join a monetary union. It also follows from this view that many large countries that now have one currency would be better off (economically) splitting the country into different monetary zones.

It is undeniable that since the early 1980s the 'monetarist' view has gained adherents, and has changed the view many economists have about the desirability of a monetary union. The popularity of monetarism helps to explain why EMU became a reality in the 1990s. The sovereign debt crisis that erupted in 2010 and the difficulties experienced in many Eurozone

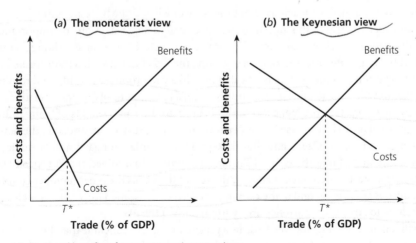

Figure 4.2 Costs and benefits of a monetary union: two views.

Table 4.1 Intra-EU exports of EU countries (% of GDP) in 2012

Slovakia	71.7
Hungary	67.2
Czech Republic	65.8
Belgium/Luxembourg	62.5
Netherlands	61.4
Slovenia	52.7
Estonia	49.5
Lithuania	42.6
Ireland	34.0
Latvia	31.8
Austria	30.4
Poland	28.5
Germany	24.9
Denmark	22.0
Portugal	19.5
Sweden	19.1
Malta	17.3
Finland	16.0
Italy	13.7
Spain	13.5
France	12.4
United Kingdom	10.8
Greece	6.0
Cyprus	5.1

Source: European Commission, *European Economy,* Statistical Appendix.

countries since then is likely to have reduced this popularity. It is not to be excluded that this may lead to a reappraisal of the desirability of a monetary union also by the present members of the Eurozone.

What does this analysis teach us about the issue of whether EMU is an optimal currency area? In order to answer this question, we first present some data on the importance of intra-EU trade for each EU country. The data are in Table 4.1, the most striking feature of which is the large differences in openness among the EU countries. This leads immediately to the conclusion that the cost–benefit calculus is likely to produce very different results for the different EU countries. For some countries with a large degree of openness relative to the other EU partners, the cost–benefit calculus is likely to show net benefits of being in EMU. This is most likely to be the case in the Benelux countries, Austria, Ireland, and the new EU member countries, the Czech and Slovak Republics, Estonia, Hungary, and Slovenia. It is very striking to find that the Central European countries that joined the European Union in 2004 are at least as well integrated with the rest of the EU as the older member countries. For countries at the other end of the ranking, the UK, Cyprus, and Greece, it is less clear that they belong to an optimal currency area with the rest of the EU.

It will remain difficult, however, to draw a precise line and to conclude that those above the line are part of an optimal currency area and those below do not form an optimal currency

area with the other EU member states. The reason is twofold. First, there are other important parameters that have to be drawn into the analysis, e.g. the degree of flexibility and the
degree of asymmetry of shocks. We will return to this issue in the next sections. Second, the
degree of 'completeness' of a monetary union matters for its costs and benefits. We take up
this issue in Section 4.4.

Additionally, some countries with a low trade share may nevertheless find it advantageous
to be in a monetary union. Our analysis of the credibility issues makes it clear that tradition-
ally high-inflation countries, such as Greece or Italy, might have decided that it was in their
interest to be in EMU despite the fact that their share of trade with the members of the union
is relatively low. In terms of the analysis of Fig. 4.2, this implies that the Greek and Italian
authorities did not consider the loss of their national monetary policy instruments costly,
so that the minimum trade share that makes the union advantageous is very low. Put differently, if one is sufficiently 'monetarist', one could argue that for countries with low degrees of
openness, the benefits could still outweigh the costs, and being in a monetary union could
also make sense for them from an economic point of view.

4.2 Monetary union, price and wage rigidities, and labour mobility

The cost–benefit calculus of a monetary union is also very much influenced by the degree
of wage and price rigidities. As will be remembered from our discussion in Chapters 1 and
2, when countries face permanent asymmetric shocks, requiring changes in relative prices,
losing the exchange rate can be a handicap in that it makes the adjustment to these shocks
more difficult. As a result, countries in which the degree of wage and price rigidities is low
experience lower costs when they move towards a monetary union. We show this in Fig. 4.3.

A decline in wage and price rigidities has the effect of shifting the cost line in Fig. 4.3
downwards. As a result, the critical point at which it becomes advantageous for a country to

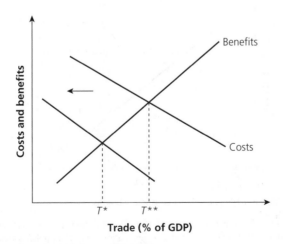

Figure 4.3 Costs and benefits with decreasing rigidities.

relinquish its national currency is lowered. More countries become candidates for a monetary union.

In a similar way, an increase in the degree of mobility of labour shifts the cost curve to the left and makes a monetary union more attractive. It should be noted, however, that not all forms of integration have these effects. As stressed in Chapter 2, economic integration can also lead to more regional concentration of industrial activities. This feature of the integration process changes the cost–benefit calculus, in that it shifts the cost curve to the right and makes a monetary union less attractive.

4.3 Asymmetric shocks and labour market flexibility

It is not only the degree of labour market flexibility (wage flexibility and labour mobility) that matters for determining whether a monetary union will be attractive to countries. Also important are the size and the frequency of asymmetric shocks to which they are subjected. This means that countries that experience very different demand and supply shocks (because their industrial structures differ greatly) will find it more costly to form a monetary union. In the framework of Fig. 4.3 this means that the cost line shifts to the right.

We are now in a position to analyse the relation between labour market flexibility and asymmetric shocks in a monetary union. This is done graphically in the following way (see Fig. 4.4). On the vertical axis we set out the degree of symmetry between regions (countries) that are candidates to form a monetary union. By symmetry is meant here the degree to which growth rates of output and employment are correlated. Thus, as we move up vertically, symmetry increases, or put differently the extent to which asymmetric shocks occur declines.[2] On the horizontal axis we have the degree of flexibility of the labour markets in these regions (countries). The flexibility here relates to wage flexibility and inter-regional (international) mobility of labour.

The central insight of the theory of optimum currency areas (OCAs) is that countries or regions that experience a lot of asymmetry in output and employment growth need much

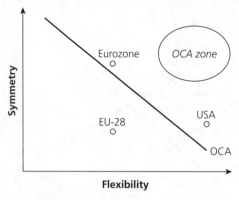

Figure 4.4 Symmetry and labour market flexibility in monetary unions.

[2] These asymmetric shocks are those that occur independently from the monetary regime, which were described in Chapter 1. Asymmetric shocks that are the result of divergent national monetary policies are not included. In a monetary union these would disappear.

flexibility in their labour markets if they want to benefit from monetary union, and if they wish to avoid major adjustment problems. Put differently, the lower the degree of symmetry, the greater is the need for flexibility in the labour markets to make a smoothly functioning monetary union possible. This relationship between symmetry and flexibility is represented by the downward-sloping line *OCA*. It shows the minimum combinations of symmetry and flexibility that countries must have in order for a monetary union to provide more benefits than costs. Countries or regions located below the *OCA* line do not have enough flexibility given the level of symmetry they face. They are likely to experience large adjustment costs as a result of asymmetric shocks. They do not form an optimum currency area. They are, therefore, well advised to maintain some degree of exchange rate flexibility. Of course, these countries are still free to form a monetary union. The theory, however, predicts that they will suffer economically from this decision. Conversely, countries to the right of the *OCA* zone have a lot of flexibility given the level of symmetry they face. In other words, they will be able to adjust to asymmetric shocks without incurring large adjustment costs. The benefits of a monetary union exceed the costs for these countries. They form an optimal currency area. We call the zone to the right of the *OCA* line the *OCA* zone.

Where should the European Union be located in Fig. 4.4? Since 2013, the European Union has consisted of 28 member countries. Ten new member countries were added to the union in May 2004, two more in 2007, and one in 2013. Most of the empirical studies have looked at this question from the point of view of the EU consisting of 15 member countries (EU-15). There is a broad consensus among economists, who have tried to implement the theory empirically, that the *EU-15 is not an optimum currency area.* (See Eichengreen 1990; Neumann and von Hagen 1991; Bayoumi and Eichengreen 1993, 1997; De Grauwe and Heens 1993; De Grauwe and Vanhaverbeke 1990; Beine et al. 2003.)[3] Some studies were undertaken analysing the optimality of a monetary union involving the European Union of 25 member countries (EU-25) that existed prior to the entry of Bulgaria and Romania in 2007 and Croatia in 2013 (see Korhonen and Fidrmuc 2001). These studies came to the same conclusion that the EU-25 was probably not an optimal currency area. Thus, according to these empirical studies, the EU-25 was located below the *OCA* line. As a result, from an economic point of view, a monetary union involving all EU member countries is a bad idea. The economic costs of a monetary union are likely to be larger than the benefits for a significant number of countries. (In Box 4.1, we present a case study illustrating the methodology used in many empirical studies.)

BOX 4.1 Empirical studies of the optimal size of monetary unions: methodological issues

Most of the empirical studies of the optimal size of monetary unions have concentrated on measuring the size and the nature of asymmetric shocks. The major problem encountered when doing this is that some of the asymmetric shocks may not be exogenous, i.e. these shocks may arise precisely because countries are not in a monetary union. For example, when a country has its own national money and central bank, it is likely to follow policies that are not identical to the monetary policies followed

(Continued...)

---

[3] A dissenting view is presented in EC Commission (1990). See also Gros and Thygesen (1998).

elsewhere. As a result, the movements of output and prices will be different from those observed in other countries. We will observe asymmetric shocks. These asymmetric shocks, however, are likely to disappear once this country joins a monetary union because national monetary policy will no longer be a source of asymmetric shocks.

In order to deal with this problem, Blanchard and Quah (1989) developed a statistical methodology, and Bayoumi and Eichengreen (1993) implemented it in the context of optimal currency areas. It consists of extracting from the price and output data the underlying demand and supply shocks. This is done by first estimating Vector Autoregressions (VAR). In a second step, demand and supply shocks are identified by assuming that demand shocks have only temporary effects while supply shocks have permanent effects on prices and output. Thus, the demand shocks are really temporary shocks while the supply shocks are permanent shocks (and could therefore also originate from the demand side). This extraction of demand and supply shocks is done for all the prospective members of the monetary union, and the correlation of these demand and supply shocks with the average of the union is then computed. The idea behind this exercise is that once in a monetary union, the asymmetric supply shocks (permanent shocks) that have a structural nature are likely to continue to exist, while the asymmetric demand shocks (temporary shocks) are more likely to disappear, if not completely then at least to a large degree.

We show the result of such an exercise performed by Korhonen and Fidrmuc (2001) in Fig. 4.5.[4] Each point represents the correlation coefficient of demand shocks with average demand shocks (vertical axis) and supply shocks with average supply shocks (horizontal axis) in the euro area. The results are quite instructive. First, we find relatively high correlations of the large countries (France, Germany, and Italy) with the euro area. This is not surprising because these large countries make up a significant part of the euro area. Second, although some Central European countries (Hungary and Estonia) are well correlated

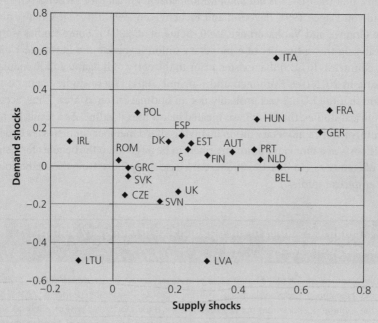

Figure 4.5 Correlation of demand and supply shocks within the Eurozone.

Source: Korhonen and Fidrmuc (2001).

---

[4] A similar analysis was performed by Frenkel et al. (2002).

with the euro area both for the demand and supply shocks, this is much less the case with others. A large number of them have negative correlations of their demand shocks (Lithuania, Latvia, Czech Republic, Slovenia, and Slovakia). Such negative correlations undoubtedly are partly the result of the fact that some of these countries pursued independent monetary policies when they were not in the Eurozone. Once in a monetary union, this source of asymmetry may disappear for those central European countries that joined the Eurozone (Lithuania, Latvia, Slovenia, and Slovakia). A more troublesome feature is that the correlation of the supply shocks of the Central European countries with the euro area is rather low. This source of asymmetry is unlikely to disappear in a monetary union.

Finally, the position of the UK is noteworthy. This country's correlation of demand shocks is also negative, reflecting to a certain degree the fact that it pursues its own national monetary policies quite independently from what happens in the euro area. At the same time, the correlation of the supply shocks with the euro area is rather low.

These exercises are interesting but incomplete. In order to obtain an estimate of the optimal size of the currency areas, the other dimensions of the problem should be investigated. In particular, the degree of flexibility of the labour markets does matter, and the microeconomic benefits of the monetary union should be added to the analysis.[5] All this makes it very difficult to obtain reliable estimates of the optimal size of currency unions.

Whereas there is a strong consensus among economists that the EU-28 should not form a monetary union, there is an equally strong conviction that *there is a subset of EU countries that form an optimum currency area*. The minimum set of countries for which a monetary union is optimal is generally believed to include Germany, the Benelux countries, Austria, and France. This conclusion is buttressed by the same empirical studies as those quoted earlier.

Some researchers, however, have tended to enlarge the group of EU countries that would benefit from monetary union; see the studies of Artis and Zhang (1995, 1997). Fidrmuc (2004), Mélitz (2004), and Boeri and Garibaldi (2006) arrive at similar conclusions.

Other empirical studies have cast doubts on the core–periphery view of monetary integration in the EU. Erkel-Rousse and Mélitz (1995) and Canzoneri, Valles, and Vinals (1996) find that in most EU countries monetary policies are powerless to affect real variables such as output and employment. Thus, even if EU countries are confronted with asymmetric shocks, their national monetary policy instruments cannot be used to deal with them effectively. As a result, the loss of these instruments for most of the EU countries is not very costly.[6]

Finally, another series of empirical studies has found that a large part of the asymmetric shocks in the EU countries occurs at the sectoral level and not so much at the national level. Put differently, many of the changes in output and employment in a country are the result of different developments between sectors (e.g. due to demand shifts or differential technological changes). These shocks cannot be dealt with by exchange rate changes (see Bini-Smaghi and Vori 1993; Bayoumi et al. 1995; and Gros 1996).

From this brief overview of empirical studies, it will be clear that it remains very uncertain how large the optimal currency area is in Europe. These empirical studies, however,

[5] Schadler (2004) has an analysis of the degree of flexibility of the labour markets in Central European countries and comes to the conclusion that labour market flexibility may be higher in these countries compared to the Eurozone countries.

[6] For a study of Portugal confirming this, see Costa (1996).

do not seem to undermine our conclusion that the EU-28 as a whole most probably does not constitute an optimum currency area. There is no consensus, however, about the size of the subset of countries that will profit from monetary union. Where should we place the present Eurozone consisting of 19 EU member countries in Fig. 4.4?[7] We have placed this group of countries (Eurozone) above the *OCA* line, but many economists may object to this and would put the Eurozone below the *OCA* line.[8] The recent Eurozone crisis lends some credence to the view that the present Eurozone is not an optimal currency area.

Because of the many difficulties in quantifying the costs of a monetary union, it will remain difficult, however, to obtain clear-cut results in this area. This situation generates ample scope for subjective judgement.

In Fig. 4.4, we have also located the USA above the *OCA* line. We are, of course, not really sure that the USA forms an optimum currency area. We are, however, much less uncertain about the relative positions of the EU and the USA. Note that we have placed the USA at about the same vertical level as the EU-28, expressing the fact that the degree of symmetry between regions in the USA is not much different from the symmetry observed between countries in the EU (see Krugman 1993 on this). The major difference between the USA and the EU seems to be the degree of flexibility of labour markets. Many empirical studies have documented this difference in the degree of flexibility of the labour markets in the USA and in Europe. For example, there is ample evidence that real wages in Europe respond less to unemployment than those in the USA.[9] Similarly, there is ample evidence that labour mobility is much higher within the USA than it is between member countries of the EU.

It should be stressed here that the analysis underlying Fig. 4.4 is based on the traditional theory of optimum currency areas. It does not deal with some of the problems we discussed in Chapter 2. For example, countries may find it difficult, for reasons of credibility, to follow low-inflation policies. The formation of a monetary union may reduce these problems. In addition, some of the asymmetric shocks one observes today in Europe may be the result of the absence of a monetary union. For example, the unsynchronized nature of the business cycle between the Eurozone and the UK may be due to the fact that the UK follows a monetary policy independent of the monetary policies on the continent. If the UK joins EMU these divergences are likely to become less important. As a result, one cannot really be sure that the EU-28 would not gain from a monetary union. Nevertheless, with the present state of our knowledge, it is not unreasonable to maintain our conclusion that the EU-28 may not be an optimum currency area.

The challenge for the EU-28 is to move into the *OCA* zone, i.e. to make a monetary union less costly. How can this be achieved? There are essentially two strategies. One is to reduce the degree of asymmetry of shocks (increase symmetry), and the other is to increase the degree of flexibility.

---

[7] Austria, Belgium, Cyprus, Estonia, Finland, France, Germany, Greece, Ireland, Italy, Latvia, Luxembourg, Malta, the Netherlands, Portugal, Slovakia, Slovenia, Spain, and (since 1 January 2015) Lithuania bringing the number of member countries to 19. When the Eurozone started in 1999 with 10 member countries, the present author decided to put the Eurozone above the *OCA* line. Today, with 19 members, he is very much tempted to bring the Eurozone below the *OCA* line.

[8] Many well-known American economists, e.g. Milton Friedman and Martin Feldstein, put the Eurozone below the *OCA* line.

[9] See Grubb et al. (1983) and Bruno and Sachs (1985).

The difficulty with the first strategy is that the degree of asymmetry of shocks is to a large extent dependent on factors over which policy-makers have little influence. For example, the degree of industrial specialization matters in determining how important asymmetric shocks are. There is very little policy-makers can do, however, to change regional specialization patterns.

There is one area, however, where policy-makers can do something to reduce the degree of asymmetry. This is in the field of political unification. We argued earlier that an important source of asymmetric shocks is the continued existence of nation-states with their independent spending and taxing policies, and with their own peculiarities as far as economic institutions are concerned. In order to reduce asymmetric shocks, more economic policy coordination and institutional streamlining will be necessary. (A special problem arises here: how should labour unions be organized in a monetary union? We take up this issue in Box 4.2.)

BOX 4.2 Labour unions and monetary union

During our discussion of the costs and benefits of a monetary union, we have stressed, on several occasions, the role of labour unions in determining the costs of a monetary union. Let us bring these insights together.

We established two rather opposite requirements for the optimal organization of labour unions in a monetary union. First, we stressed that in the presence of permanent *asymmetric* shocks, wages should be flexible, i.e. they should have different rates of change between countries (and regions). An example we gave is a differential in productivity growth between countries. In that case nominal wage growth should be different and should reflect the differences in productivity growth between these countries (see Chapter 2). This implies that centralized wage bargaining would be harmful. By imposing the same nominal growth rates of wages it would lead to great losses of competitiveness for the country (region) with a low growth in labour productivity. This problem also exists in individual countries. An example is Germany, where labour unions imposed centralized wage bargaining on the former East Germany after unification of the country. As a result, many East German firms failed to survive the shock of unification and employment was negatively affected. A similar problem exists in Italy: centralized wage bargaining has hurt the south of the country, where productivity is growing more slowly than in the north. The effect of this is that unemployment is four to five times higher in the south of Italy than in the north.

A second insight we obtained is that in the presence of the same, *symmetric* shock, different wage bargaining systems may lead to a different wage–price spiral and therefore to divergent developments in competitiveness between countries (see Chapter 2). This seems to suggest that when symmetric shocks prevail, the wage bargaining systems should be made more uniform across countries. Does this mean that a centralized wage bargaining system at the level of the union becomes desirable? Most probably not. The reasons are the following. First, we have noted that although in a unified Europe asymmetric shocks *between countries* may become less prevalent, specialization would still lead to large regional divergences. These regional asymmetries may even increase in a more unified Europe. The characteristic feature of this specialization is that it is likely to cross borders. In such an environment, a centralized wage bargaining system would be harmful for many of the European regions. Second, we have also stressed that technological changes tend to lead to uneven changes in output and employment between sectors. There is even a body of empirical evidence indicating that many of the asymmetric shocks occur within the same sectors (see Davis et al. 1996). Again, a centralized wage bargaining system would be very detrimental to output and employment in sectors that experience less favourable developments and for firms that lag behind others in the same sector.

To conclude, the future organization of labour unions in a monetary union will have to respect the inevitable requirements of flexibility in a world where shocks occur mostly at the sectoral and microeconomic level.

The other strategy for moving the whole of the EU into the *OCA* zone consists of increasing the degree of flexibility of labour markets (real wages and/or labour mobility). This strategy implies a reform of labour market institutions. Although such reforms are difficult to implement, they are necessary if one wants to have a monetary union involving the whole of the European Union.

We return to the issue of how to move into the *OCA* area in Section 4.5, where we will introduce another dimension of political union, i.e. budgetary union.

4.4 The degree of completeness of a monetary union

We argued in Chapter 1 that the degree of completeness of monetary unions matters for the cost of these unions. In an incomplete monetary union, i.e. one in which there is no budgetary union, there will be great fragility of the government bond markets. In addition, in such unions asymmetric shocks are likely to be intensified by disruptions in the government bond markets that impose high interest rates in countries experiencing negative shocks, forcing them to impose austerity measures in the midst of recessions. In monetary unions that are embedded in a budgetary union, these problems disappear and the cost of a monetary union is likely to be lower. We present these two types of monetary union in Fig. 4.6.

The left-hand graph in Fig. 4.6 presents the case of an incomplete monetary union. In this union, adjustment costs after asymmetric shocks are higher. Thus, we have drawn the cost curve further away from the origin. The right-hand graph presents the case of a full monetary union where, because of the budgetary integration, the cost curve is closer to the origin.

The previous analysis leads to the prediction that we are more likely to observe monetary unions that are budgetary unions at the same time. A budgetary union is an essential

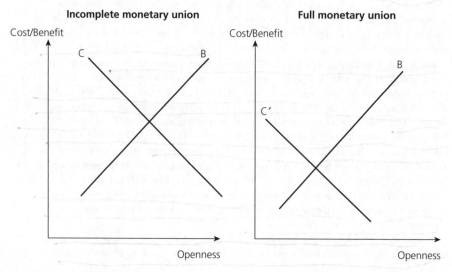

Figure 4.6 Costs and benefits and degree of completeness of monetary union.

component of a political union. Thus, a combination of monetary and political union is more likely to have fewer costs and therefore to function better than monetary unions that are not embedded in a political union. Indeed, the overwhelming evidence is that monetary unions are almost always embedded in a political union. The Eurozone is a big exception to this rule. We will come back to the problems that such an incomplete union leads to.

4.5 The trade-off between budgetary union and flexibility

The previous analysis allows us to derive a new *OCA* line that shows the trade-off between flexibility and budgetary union (Fig. 4.7). The idea of a trade-off between flexibility and budgetary union comes from André Sapir of the University of Brussels (see Sapir 2015). That's why we call it the OCA_S line. It allows us to obtain interesting insights about how countries can come closer to an optimal monetary arrangement.

The way this trade-off is constructed is as follows. On the vertical axis we set out the degree of budgetary union. The higher the degree of budgetary union the more we move upwards along the vertical line. On the horizontal axis we set out the same measure of flexibility we used in previous figures. The *OCA* line now measures the minimum combinations of budgetary union and flexibility needed to make a monetary union economically attractive (higher benefits than costs). It is negatively sloped for the following reason. When budgetary union increases, insurance against asymmetric shocks increases making the monetary union less costly. As a result, there is less need for flexibility. We move upward along the negatively sloped *OCA* line.

This is an important insight. Flexibility may sound great for many economists and central bankers. It is, however, costly for most people that are forced to be flexible. Flexibility means that these people may have to accept a wage cut or may be forced to emigrate. We learn from Fig. 4.7 that a movement towards budgetary union makes monetary union more acceptable to large segments of the population.

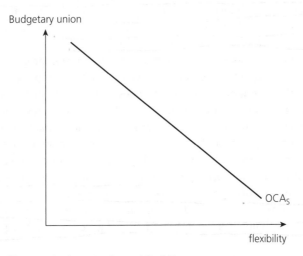

Figure 4.7 Trade-off between budgetary union and flexibility

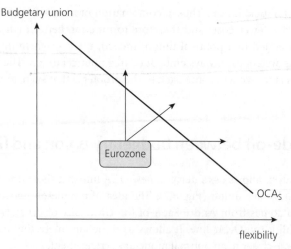

Figure 4.8 How to move the Eurozone towards the *OCA* area?

We can use the insights of Fig. 4.7 to analyse the importance of the nature of the asymmetric shocks. We have made the distinction between exogenous and endogenous asymmetric shocks. The former are permanent shocks like an increase in oil prices; the latter are the result of unsynchronized business cycle movements and are temporary. We have argued that when a permanent (exogenous) shock occurs flexibility is the only option to adjust to this shock. In contrast, when business cycle movements are desynchronized it is not optimal to use flexibility. In that case fiscal transfers are the appropriate response. This is provided by a budgetary union.

Let us now put the Eurozone of 19 members below the *OCA* line, suggesting that the present Eurozone is not an optimal currency area (Fig. 4.8).[10] When exogenous asymmetric shocks prevail, the Eurozone will have to move along the horizontal arrow to become optimal. In other words, more flexibility is needed. However, if the endogenous asymmetric shocks prevail, the Eurozone must move along the vertical arrow to become optimal. In this case flexibility does not help. Instead a common insurance mechanism (provided by a budgetary union) becomes necessary to deal with these shocks.

In practice, both types of asymmetric shocks occur. As a result, progress must be made on two fronts, i.e. more flexibility and more budgetary union. This is presented by the arrow moving in the North-Eastern direction. The steepness of this arrow depends on the relative prevalence of endogenous versus exogenous shocks. If the endogenous shocks prevail over the exogenous shocks, the arrow is steep and progress should be made mainly by budgetary integration. If, on the other hand, exogenous shocks occur more often, the arrow is flat, indicating that it is mainly through more flexibility that one can move into the *OCA* zone.

Fig. 4.8 leads to another interesting insight. Flexibility in labour markets is something national governments can do. There is no need for further integration to increase flexibility. Budgetary union, however, is of a different nature. It requires political integration. In other words, while flexibility is in the realm of national governments, budgetary union is a

[10] See the discussion of the previous section.

European affair (Sapir 2015). Thus when shocks are exogenous it has to be dealt with at the national level while when shocks are endogenous the response should be at the level of the Eurozone.

4.6 Costs and benefits in the long run

In the previous sections, we discussed the costs and benefits of a monetary union. Our analysis was mostly static. It will be useful to add some dynamics to this analysis so as to obtain a better insight into the question of how these costs and benefits of monetary union may evolve over time.

In order to analyse this question, we will use some of the tools introduced in Chapter 2, where we discussed the relationship between the degree of economic integration and the occurrence of asymmetric shocks. This relationship predicts whether the progress towards economic integration leads to economic convergence. We will now add the cost–benefit analysis.

In Fig. 4.9, we represent the model. On the vertical axis we set out, as before, the degree of symmetry between groups of countries. On the horizontal axis we have the degree of trade integration between the same groups of countries. The upward-sloping line (TT) says that as trade integration increases, the degree of symmetry between the countries involved increases, i.e. countries become more alike and face fewer asymmetric shocks. (We called this the European Commission view in Chapter 2. We will return to the Krugman view later.) The downward-sloping line (called OCA) represents the minimal combinations of symmetry and trade integration that make monetary union a break-even operation (costs = benefits). It is derived in a similar way to the other OCA line we have used in this chapter. Both integration and symmetry are qualities of countries that increase the benefits (reduce the costs) of a monetary union. Thus if, for example, symmetry increases (reducing the costs of a union) these countries can afford to have less integration (which increases benefits). All points on the OCA line are then combinations of symmetry and integration for which the monetary union has a zero net gain. It follows that all the points to the right of the OCA line are points for which the benefits of monetary union exceed the costs. We call it the OCA zone.

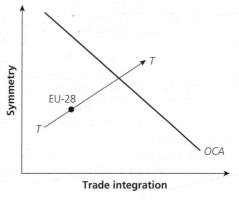

Figure 4.9 The European Commission view of monetary integration.

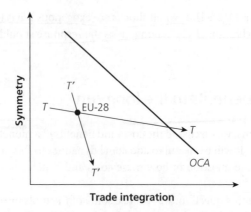

Figure 4.10 The Krugman view of monetary integration.

In Fig. 4.9, we have put the EU-28 on the upward-sloping TT line to the left of the OCA line, reflecting the conclusion that we arrived at in Section 4.3, i.e. that today (in 2016) the EU-28 is probably not an optimum currency area. As trade integration within the EU proceeds, however, this point will move upwards along the TT line. This will inevitably bring us into the OCA zone, at least if we can assume that the dynamics of integration will continue to work within the EU. Thus, in this view, monetary unification will over time be perceived to be beneficial for all countries in the EU. In this sense monetary union among all EU countries is inevitable.

This is the optimistic view about the long-term prospects for monetary integration in Europe. There is, however, also a pessimistic view, which one can derive from the Krugman analysis. It will be remembered that in the Krugman analysis, economic integration leads to less symmetry between countries. This is represented in Fig. 4.10 by the downward-sloping TT and $T'T'$ lines.

We now have to consider two possibilities for the long-term prospects of monetary union. One is represented by the TT line, the slope of which is flatter than the slope of the OCA line. In this case, although today the EU-28 may not be an optimum currency area, it will move into the OCA zone over time. In this case more integration leads to more specialization and thus more asymmetric shocks (less symmetry). However, the benefits of a monetary union also increase steeply with the degree of integration. As a result, despite the decline in symmetry, more integration will lead us into the OCA zone.

The second case is represented by the steep $T'T'$ line. Here integration brings us increasingly farther away from the OCA zone. This is so because the net gains of a monetary union do not increase strongly enough with the degree of integration. As a result, the costs of declining symmetry overwhelm all the other benefits a monetary union may have. In the long run the prospects for a monetary union of the EU-28 are poor. It should be noted that this case leads to an anomaly. It implies that a lowering of trade integration can bring us into the OCA zone. Thus, if the EU countries were to go back and disband, monetary union would become attractive. An odd result.

From the discussion of the Krugman model, we conclude that even if integration leads to more asymmetric shocks, this may still lead to increasing net gains of a monetary union for the EU-28.

A last but important point about the long-run dynamics of monetary integration is the following. The decision by an individual country to join the monetary union may speed up the integration process. In Chapter 2, we documented this by referring to empirical studies indicating how the existence of different national currencies helps to segment national markets. A decision by an individual country to join EMU, even if it does not satisfy the *OCA* criteria, would have a self-fulfilling character, at least if Fig. 4.9 is the right view of the world. In this case, the process of integration would be speeded up by the very decision to join the monetary union, so that this new country grouping moves faster into the *OCA* zone. In this sense, it can be said that there is an endogenous component in the criteria of an optimal currency area: i.e. when countries decide to form a monetary union, the criteria become more favourable. Put differently, the very decision to form a monetary union changes the cost–benefit outcome, and reduces the costs relative to the benefits. Conversely, by not forming a monetary union, an unfavourable cost–benefit balance remains unfavourable. The endogenous nature of the criteria for an optimal currency area has been analysed by Frankel and Rose (1998).[11]

Is there any evidence that the endogenous dynamics has been working within the Eurozone? Since the Eurozone has been in place since 1999, one may already see this dynamics at work. We consider the three *OCA* criteria here: economic integration, symmetry, and flexibility. We surveyed the literature on the effects of the euro on trade integration in Chapter 3, and we came to the conclusion that the existence of the euro may have added 5 to 20% to intra-Eurozone trade although more recent research casts doubt on this conclusion (Glick and Rose (2015)). This suggests that the integration criterion has not been moving much in bringing the member countries closer to (or deeper into) the *OCA* zone.

What about the asymmetry of shocks? We answer this question in Fig. 4.11. The figure presents the average bilateral correlation coefficients of the business cycle components of industrial production within the Eurozone during different periods.[12]

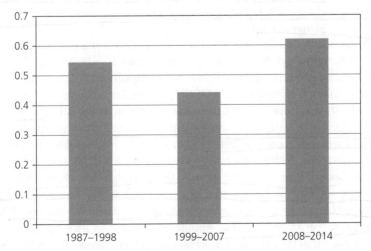

Figure 4.11 Mean Eurozone correlations of cyclical components of industrial production.

Source: OECD Dataset—production and sales.

[11] For a survey, see De Grauwe and Mongelli (2005).

[12] The procedure involves first extracting the business cycle component of the industrial production series using an HP-filter. These business cycle components are then correlated between pairs of countries. Then the average correlation coefficient is computed.

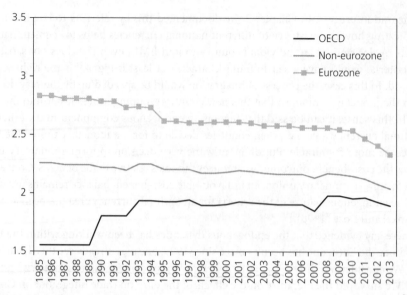

Figure 4.12 Employment protection legislation index (1985–2013)

Source: OECD

We observe the following. During the pre-crisis period (1999–2007), the mean correlation coefficient is marginally smaller than in the pre-Eurozone period (1987–98). During the post-crisis period (2008–14) the correlation increases. This may suggest that in the post-crisis period convergence of output has increased. It is likely, however, that this is mostly due to the strong decline in output that occurred in 2009 and that hit all countries together as a result of the 'Great Recession'. Thus, the strong increase in the correlation of output growth observed since 2008 may not last.

The third *OCA* criterion that was stressed in our previous analysis was flexibility. Here the evidence points to a significant increase in labour market flexibility (see Fig. 4.12). This shows the evolution of one indicator of labour market rigidities, i.e. the employment protection legislation index as compiled by the OECD. This measures the degree to which legislation makes it hard for firms to fire workers. We observe from Fig. 4.12 that the Eurozone has made progress in relaxing their employment protection legislation especially since the onset of the sovereign debt crisis of 2010. The Eurozone still remains above the average of the OECD countries as far as employment protection is concerned, but the gap has narrowed considerably. Countries that were hit most by the sovereign debt crisis (Ireland, Greece, Portugal, and Spain) went furthest in reducing employment protection. These countries have also attached tighter conditions to receiving unemployment benefit, and more flexibility in working hours has been introduced (see European Commission 2008, pp. 77–80).

On the whole, the evidence that there is an endogenous component in the *OCA* criteria receives only mixed support. The integration criterion does not show much evidence of moving in the right direction, while the flexibility criterion seems to be moving in the *OCA* direction. It is unclear, though, whether the symmetry criterion has been subject to an endogenous dynamics up to now (2015). In fact, it is likely that the sovereign debt crisis that erupted in 2010 has moved member countries of the Eurozone farther apart.

4.7 Should the UK join EMU?

The question of whether the UK should join EMU has been hotly debated in the past. In June 2003, Gordon Brown, at that time the UK Chancellor of the Exchequer, issued a massive study analysing the issue of the costs and benefits of monetary union for the UK.[13] The conclusion was rather pessimistic. The UK was not ready (at least in 2003) to join the Eurozone. At the same time, he promised that it was his intention to introduce structural reforms that would make it possible for the UK to join the Eurozone in the future.

The question of whether the UK should join EMU can only be answered by studying the costs and benefits of being part of EMU. Several of the cost and benefit items have been discussed in the previous sections.

There is some merit in bringing these together. This will allow us to gain better insights into this question.

Let us start with the cost side. We have identified several factors that affect the costs of a monetary union, i.e. openness, flexibility, and asymmetry of shocks.

- *Openness*. We have found that, with the exception of Greece and Cyprus, the UK has the lowest degree of openness towards the rest of the EU (see Table 4.1). It is even more striking to find that the UK is less open towards the EU than the Central European countries that joined the EU in 2004 (see also Table 4.1).

- *Asymmetry of shocks*. From Fig. 4.5 we have learned that the demand shocks in the UK are negatively correlated with the demand shocks in the EU. This is probably related to the fact that the UK has pursued an independent monetary policy. If that is the case, part of this asymmetry may disappear when the UK joins the union. This remains uncertain, however. We have also found that the supply shocks in the UK are only weakly correlated with those in the Eurozone. All this suggests that the divergence between economic movements in the UK and the Eurozone is relatively high, introducing potentially high costs of joining EMU. (A study by Beine et al. 2003 confirms this.)

- *Flexibility*. There is a general consensus among economists that the UK output and labour markets are more flexible than those of the Eurozone countries. The evidence is provided by the OECD. This organization has been producing indices of product market regulations and employment protection legislation. We show the evidence in Figs 4.13 and 4.14. Fig. 4.13 presents the OECD Index of Product Market Regulation. It can be seen that the UK has a lower level of product market regulation than any other Eurozone country. Similarly, Fig. 4.14 shows that the UK has the least stringent employment protection legislation. This evidence suggests that the UK product and labour markets are probably more flexible than those in the Eurozone.

---

[13] HM Treasury (2003). The costs and benefits for the UK were formulated as five economic tests. The first one dealt with economic convergence, the second one with flexibility, the third one with investment conditions offered in EMU, the fourth one with the competitive position of the UK's financial services industry, and the last one with the prospects for growth, stability, and employment in EMU. According to the Chancellor, the UK passed only the fourth test in 2003.

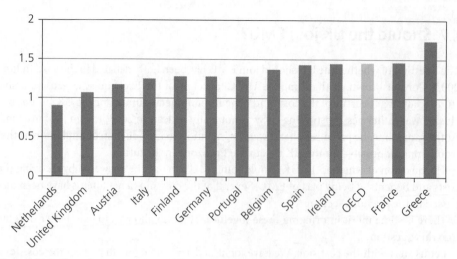

Figure 4.13 Indices of product market regulation in selected OECD countries (2008).
Source: OECD.

- *Debt issue*. The UK government issues debt in pounds sterling. As a result, it can guarantee that its debt will always be repaid. We have seen that this guarantee makes it less vulnerable to movements of distrust in financial markets. The power of that guarantee can be seen by looking at Figs 4.15 and 4.16. In Fig. 4.15, we show the debt-to-GDP ratios of the UK and Spain. The latter is a member country of the Eurozone, and therefore cannot give such a guarantee. We observe that since the start of the financial crisis up to 2014 the debt-to-GDP ratio in the UK has been higher than in Spain. Yet in Fig. 4.16 we see that since the start of the sovereign debt crisis in the

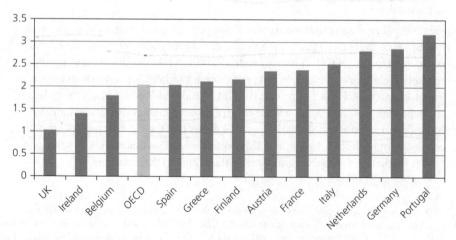

Figure 4.14 Indices of employment protection legislation in OECD countries (2013).
Source: OECD.

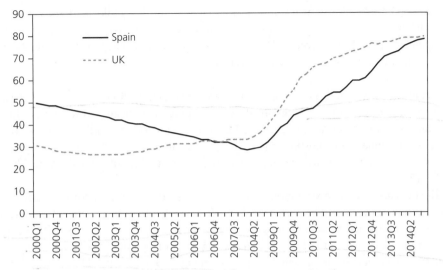

Figure 4.15 Gross government debt in Spain and the UK (as a percentage of GDP).

Source: Eurostat.

Eurozone in 2010, the financial markets have hit Spain, not the UK. Investors massively sold Spanish government bonds, thereby raising the interest rate on these bonds. As a result, from 2010 to 2014, the Spanish government paid more than 200 to 300 basis points extra on its debt than the UK government. It is likely that if the UK had been in the Eurozone, the unfavourable trend in its government debt ratio would have put it in the same position as Spain and would have forced it to pay significantly higher interest

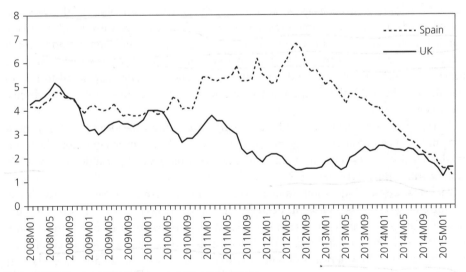

Figure 4.16 10-year government bond yields, UK and Spain.

Source: Eurostat.

rates on its debt. This in turn would have accelerated the debt build-up in the UK very much in the same way it did in Spain. We will come back to this comparison between Spain and the UK in Chapter 6. We also have to explain what happened after 2012 when the interest rate difference started to narrow.

Concluding the cost side of the analysis, one can state that the UK faces less integration and more asymmetric shocks, making monetary union potentially costly. However, flexibility is significantly more favourable than in the Eurozone countries, so that the UK may experience fewer problems in adjusting to these (higher) asymmetric shocks. In addition, having its own currency has shielded the UK from the debt crisis that raged in the Eurozone during 2010–12.

The benefits of a monetary union for the UK will be similar to those for the other countries, although they could be a little smaller. We have seen that the benefits of a monetary union are a function of openness, i.e. relatively less open countries have smaller benefits from a monetary union than more open economies. In the case of the UK, however, this negative effect may be compensated by the special position of the City of London as a major financial centre. Entry into the Eurozone is likely to consolidate the strong position of London as a financial centre; it is even likely to enhance it. As a result, relatively large benefits will accrue to the UK.[14]

Thus the cost–benefit analysis leads to the view that the various cost and benefit items look very different for the UK. The weights one attaches to these different costs and benefits are likely to have an important influence one one's conclusion as to whether or not the UK would benefit from joining the European monetary union.

4.8 Is Latin America an optimal currency area?

Latin American countries have experienced much monetary instability in the post-war period. High inflation and large exchange rate variability have negatively affected economic growth and welfare. In order to create more macroeconomic stability, Latin American countries have experimented with many different exchange rate regimes. Some have pegged the exchange rate to the dollar; others have chosen a currency board to import stability. On the whole these experiments have not worked well. In Chapter 5, we discuss the reasons for this.

As a result of the unstable nature of the exchange rate regimes, the idea of forming a monetary union in Latin America has gained some popularity. An important question, therefore, is whether this makes sense from an economic point of view, or put differently, is Latin America an optimal currency area?

The literature on this question is still in its infancy in Latin America. Nevertheless a broad picture emerges. We first look at the degree of openness, in Fig. 4.17. We compare the openness of South American countries among themselves with the openness of Eurozone countries. The differences are striking. Latin American countries have very low levels of trade with the rest of Latin America. This is due to two factors. First, these countries are relatively

---

[14] See also the HM Treasury (2003) report on this issue.

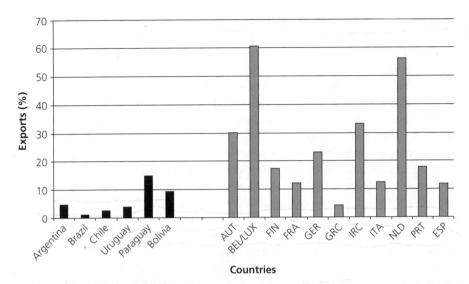

Figure 4.17 Intra-regional exports of goods and services, EU and Latin America, as a percentage of GDP (2010).

Notes: European data: exports of goods to EU-15 as percentage of GDP (2010). The exports of the Latin American countries are their exports to the whole of Latin America. (Export values for Bolivia are given in CIF whereas the numbers for all other countries correspond to FOB values.)

Source: European data: European Commission, *European Economy;* Latin American data: local central banks and local statistical offices.

closed towards the rest of the world in general. Second, the largest part of their trade is with regions outside Latin America (mostly the USA and Europe). Thus, our first criterion for forming an optimal currency area is quite unfavourable.

The other criteria are more difficult to evaluate because relatively little systematic research has been undertaken. On the degree of asymmetry of shocks there is evidence provided by Morandé and Schmidt-Hebbel (2000), Calderon et al. (2002), and Larrain et al. (2003) indicating that the degree of synchronization of output movements is low in Latin America, and that asymmetric shocks are relatively large.

Very little empirical research has been undertaken to measure the degree of flexibility of labour markets in Latin America, but it appears that the existence of segmented labour markets reduces the scope for adjustment to asymmetric shocks (see Hochreiter et al. 2002). On the whole, Latin America appears to be far from being an optimal currency area.

As we argued earlier, one of the main driving forces for the popularity of a monetary union is to be found in the fact that it allows high-inflation countries to import price stability. In order for this effect to work, however, the monetary union must provide for the right institutions guaranteeing price stability. This was the case in Europe, in that a significant number of countries joining EMU had experience with monetary stability. As a result, the monetary union that was created in Europe could profit from this experience with monetary stability, and could set up strong institutions guaranteeing price stability. Countries such as Italy, which had less experience with monetary stability, could benefit from joining a club whose members had much practical experience. This feature is certainly not present in Latin America today (2016). Almost all Latin American countries have gone through varying degrees of monetary instability and inflation in the recent past. Almost all the governments and central banks of these countries suffer from a bad record on inflation. It is, therefore, unlikely that the institutions that would have to be created in a Latin American monetary union would be strong enough to guarantee price stability.

The lack of credibility that the institutions in a Latin American monetary union would have is the major reason why such a union is unlikely to be created soon. There is a general perception in Latin America that such a union would not solve the continent's endemic problem of monetary instability.

This conclusion is confirmed by Larrain et al. (2003). These authors conclude that most Latin American countries would not profit from a Latin American monetary union, because such a union is unlikely to produce monetary stability. Conversely, according to the same authors, many Latin American countries would benefit from dollarization. This is a regime in which Latin American countries take over the dollar as their means of payment. In doing so, they also import the monetary stability provided by the US Federal Reserve. The same argument is developed very strongly by Hind (2006).

Dollarization, however, also implies that all monetary sovereignty is transferred to the USA. This creates strong political resistance. For this reason, it is unlikely that the larger Latin American countries will want to dollarize their economies, even if such a regime promises them a great deal of monetary stability. Dollarization can be attractive to smaller Latin American countries. Some of these (Ecuador, Panama, El Salvador) have already shown their preference to go for a monetary union with the USA in the form of dollarization.

4.9 The next monetary union in Asia?

The Asian financial crisis of 1997–8 generated considerable turbulence. Many Asian countries found out that in a world of free capital mobility they were unable to fix their exchange rates. Speculative attacks in the exchange markets forced them to devalue or to let their exchange rate float. This led to large macroeconomic disturbances and to distortions in trade flows. Initiatives were taken to prevent this from happening in the future. The most important one is the 'Chiang Mai Initiative' (CMI). The finance ministers of ASEAN, China, Japan, and South Korea announced the initiative in May 2000. It expanded a network of bilateral short-term credit arrangements among ASEAN countries, China, Japan, and South Korea. The CMI also initiated an economic review and policy dialogue process, which aims to eliminate macroeconomic and financial disequilibria that may lead to crises (see Xu Ning 2004).

There is a widespread view, however, that these new financial arrangements will not suffice to shield the Asian currencies from future speculative attacks. As a result, the idea of permanently locking the exchange rates of these currencies by moving into a monetary union has gained credence.[15] The question that arises then is whether Asia is ready for a monetary union. Or to put it differently, is Asia an optimal currency area? We will concentrate on East Asia here because this is the part of Asia that is most developed and where the financial crises of 1997–8 were felt most acutely.

---

[15] Genberg (2006) describes a strategy that could be used to move towards monetary union in East Asia.

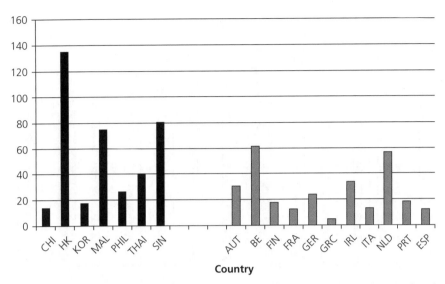

Figure 4.18 Intra-regional exports of goods and services, East Asia and EU, as a percentage of GDP (2010).

We start by analysing the evidence about the degree of trade integration and compare it with trade integration in the Eurozone. In Fig. 4.18, we present similar data to those in Fig. 4.17. We show the exports of East Asian countries to the rest of East Asia as a percentage of their GDP and compare these with the exports of Eurozone countries to the rest of the union (also as a percentage of GDP). The contrast with Latin America is striking. East Asian countries have strong degrees of integration with the rest of East Asia, very much as EU countries have with the rest of the EU. Note also that some countries in East Asia have extremely high integration ratios, in particular Hong Kong, which has a ratio exceeding 100%. This is due to the fact that exports are production data (which include imports) while GDP is value added data (excluding imports). Hong Kong's exports are to a large extent transit trade with little value added. As a result, the ratio exceeds 100%.

The second *OCA* criterion we want to analyse is the degree of asymmetry of shocks. This has been analysed in detail during the last few years. The consensus today is that East Asian countries do not experience more asymmetry in their shocks than the present Eurozone countries (see Bayoumi and Eichengreen 1993; Yin-Wong Cheung and Jude Yuen 2003; Xinpeng Xu 2004; Shin and Sohn 2007; and Sato and Zhang 2007). The study by Xinpeng Xu computes the percentage of the variation in demand and supply shocks that can be attributed to common shocks.[16] Thus, this percentage can be interpreted as expressing the degree of symmetry in the shocks. We show the results in Figs 4.19 and 4.20. Fig. 4.19 shows these percentages for the Asian countries, while Fig. 4.20 shows these percentages for the Eurozone countries. It is very striking to observe that the degree of symmetry in the demand and

---

[16] These percentages are computed by first extracting the demand and supply shocks using the Blanchard–Quah procedure (see Box 4.1). Then these demand and supply shocks are subjected to a factor analysis, which allows the extraction of a common component in the movements of these shocks.

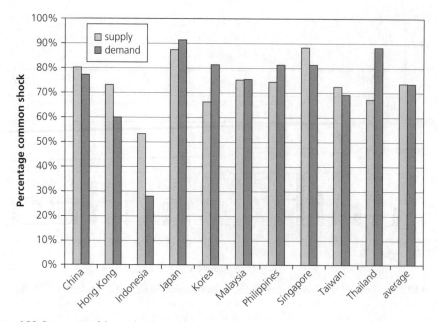

Figure 4.19 Percentage of demand and supply changes explained by common shock in East Asia.

Source: Xinpeng Xu (2004).

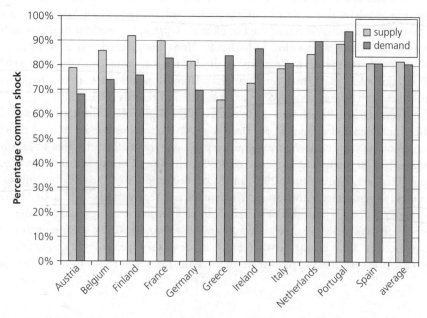

Figure 4.20 Percentage of demand and supply changes explained by common shock in the Eurozone.

Source: Xinpeng Xu (2004).

supply shocks of Asian and Eurozone countries is very similar.[17] The degree of symmetry of shocks in the Asian countries appears to be only marginally lower than in the Eurozone countries (see the averages in the figures).

We conclude that according to two of the *OCA* criteria, East Asia seems to be close to an optimal currency area (assuming that the Eurozone is a good benchmark). In addition, since the flexibility of the labour markets in these countries is at least as high, if not more so, than in Europe, it appears that East Asia comes close to forming an optimal currency area. So, why has monetary union not yet come about in Asia? The answer seems to be political. There is a widespread feeling in East Asia that the political obstacles to forming a monetary union are too large. These obstacles are themselves the result of historical developments that make it difficult for these countries to unite. In addition, there are large cultural differences that act as equally important impediments to a successful integration. The contrast with the European Union is important. Monetary unification became possible in Europe because of a strong political desire to unite the continent. This desire originated from the Second World War and led to the building up of European institutions such as the European Commission, the European Court of Justice, and the European Parliament, all of which embody some transfer of national sovereignty. In such an environment it became relatively easy to create a new supranational institution, the European Central Bank. This institutional infrastructure is still absent in Asia, making it difficult to envisage monetary union, even of the incomplete type as in the Eurozone, in the short and medium term.

4.10 Monetary unions in Africa

Africa represents an interesting case because three monetary unions have existed on the continent for about a half century: the two francophone monetary unions in West and Central Africa, and the Southern African monetary union.[18]

Today, Africa has several monetary union initiatives, which aim to extend the existing monetary unions. One such initiative is the monetary union project of the Economic Community of West African States (ECOWAS).[19] ECOWAS is a regional group of 15 countries in West Africa. It consists of the members of the existing monetary union, the West African Economic and Monetary Union (WAEMU), which comprises former French colonies Benin, Burkina Faso, Côte d'Ivoire, Guinea, Guinea-Bissau,[20] Mali, Niger, Senegal, Sierra Leone, and Togo, and also newcomers Cape Verde, Ghana, Gambia, Liberia, and Nigeria.

In April 2000, ECOWAS adopted a strategy of a two-track approach to the implementation of a monetary union in the whole area. As a first step, the non-WAEMU members of ECOWAS agreed to form a second monetary union, the West African Monetary Zone (WAMZ),

---

[17] The outlier is Indonesia, whose demand and supply shocks do not seem to be well synchronized with the rest of Asia. This may be due to the political upheavals experienced in this country having an effect on economic conditions.

[18] I am grateful to Romain Houssa for providing me with information about Africa and for insightful discussions.

[19] Apart from the monetary union project in West Africa there are other regional monetary integration initiatives in Africa: the Southern African Development Community (SADC) is working to establish a currency union by 2016; the East African Community envisages forming a monetary union in the future; the African Union even envisages the establishment of a monetary union for the whole of Africa in 2018.

[20] Guinea-Bissau is a former Portuguese colony that joined WAEMU in 1997.

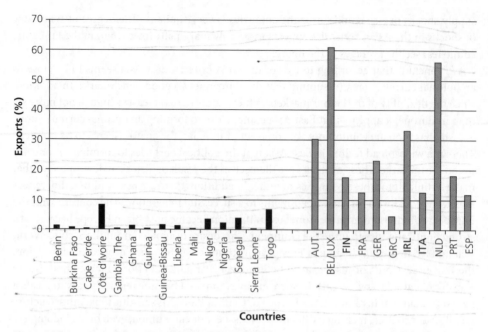

Figure 4.21 Intra-regional exports of goods and services in West Africa (2003) and the Eurozone (2010).

Source: For West Africa: Calculations based on data from IMF (DOTS) and World Bank for the year 2003. For EMU: European Commission, *European Economy.* The European data are for 2010.

made up of Gambia, Ghana, Guinea, Nigeria, and Sierra Leone.[21] Later on, WAEMU and WAMZ will merge to form a wider monetary union in ECOWAS.

We ask the same question here as we did in the previous section. Is this new monetary arrangement an optimal currency area? The first type of evidence we look at is the degree of trade integration among the West African countries, which we compare with the Eurozone. We show the result in Fig. 4.21.

The contrast between West Africa and the Eurozone is striking. The trade within West Africa makes up significantly less than 10% of most countries' GDP.[22] In the Eurozone, this intra-trade is for most countries significantly higher than 10%. Using the Eurozone as a benchmark this suggests that West Africa still has a long way to go to fully reap the benefits of a single currency. Note that the results we obtain for West Africa are very much comparable with the results for Latin America.

Some empirical studies have been undertaken to measure the degree of asymmetry of shocks in West Africa. Houssa (2008) uses a dynamic structural factor model to extract information on aggregate demand and aggregate supply shocks in each of the ECOWAS

[21] Liberia has declined to participate in the monetary union but it attends the WAMZ meetings as an observer. Cape Verde has fixed its currency to the euro with the support of Portugal.

[22] The reader should have in mind that these numbers may be biased because they concern only official trade. In developing countries a substantial part of trade goes through informal channels. See, for example, Lares (1998).

countries. The results show low or negative supply shock correlation across countries. However, demand shocks are more correlated among WAEMU countries, reflecting the existence of a common monetary union among them. All in all, it is not clear that the degree of asymmetry is larger in West Africa than it is in the Eurozone.

As far as flexibility is concerned, the literature review provided by Houssa (2008) suggests that labour mobility is intense. Asymmetric shocks seem to trigger relatively large movements of workers from one country to another. These movements are so large that they have led to major political disruptions in some countries (Côte d'Ivoire).

To conclude, when using the Eurozone as a benchmark, the evidence on whether West Africa forms an optimal currency area is mixed. On the one hand, the degree of integration among West African countries is low, yielding relatively few benefits of a monetary union. On the other hand, labour mobility is substantially stronger. At the same time, West African countries (the members of WAEMU) have already set into place a series of institutions, such as a common central bank (the members of WAEMU) and a monetary institute (the members of WAMZ), facilitating further steps towards a monetary union. This makes West Africa very different from Latin American countries and East Asia.

4.11 Conclusion

The arguments developed in this chapter have led to the following conclusions. First, it is unlikely that the EU as a whole constitutes an optimal currency area. Put differently, not all EU countries have the same interest in relinquishing their national currencies and in adhering to a European monetary union. The cost–benefit analysis of this chapter, therefore, also implies that a monetary unification in Europe better suits the economic interests of the different individual countries if it can proceed at different speeds, i.e. if some countries who today feel that it is not in their national interest to do so have the option to wait before joining the union.

Second, even the countries that are net gainers from a monetary union take a risk by joining the union. The risk is that when large shocks occur (like the one that occurred in some countries in the early 1980s or the more recent shocks resulting from the financial crisis), they will find it more difficult to adjust, having relinquished their national currencies. Thus, even for those countries that have joined a monetary union, it is not entirely academic to know whether they form an optimal currency area. As a result of the sovereign debt crisis, in some of these countries doubts are being voiced about whether it was a good idea to be in the Eurozone.

Third, the nature of the asymmetric shocks matters. If these are permanent, countries will have to focus mostly on making their labour and product markets more flexible. If, however, these shocks are temporary and result from unsynchronized business cycle movements, then efforts at increasing the degree of budgetary union become more important.

Finally, while most of the discussion on the optimality of currency unions is focused on Europe, this does not mean that the question of forming monetary unions is not topical in other parts of the world. In fact in Latin America, in Africa, and in Asia the issue of whether or not to form a monetary union is being debated. We conclude from our discussion that in Latin America the economic conditions for forming an optimal currency are as yet not fulfilled. This contrasts with East Asia where the conditions that could make a monetary union economically beneficial seem to be present. What seems to be lacking in East Asia is the political willingness to transfer sovereignty to an East Asian central bank. Finally, in West Africa the economic conditions for forming an optimal currency area are not as strong as in the Eurozone. The political conditions, however, seem to be favourable.

The discussion in this and the previous chapters has been based on an *economic* cost–benefit analysis. Countries may also decide to adopt a common currency for *political* reasons. A common currency may be the first step towards a political union that they wish to achieve. In the next chapters we pursue the analysis of the link between monetary and political union.

Part 2

Monetary union

The fragility of incomplete monetary unions

Introduction

In the previous chapters, we discussed the costs and benefits of monetary unions. We made a distinction between an incomplete and a full monetary union. The former is a monetary union where each member country maintains its own independent budgetary policy; the latter is characterized by budgetary unification. We argued that an incomplete monetary union is fragile, and may in the end be unsustainable. In this chapter we analyse the fragility of incomplete monetary unions more formally. This analysis is important because it can give us more insight into what has to be done about the fragility of incomplete monetary unions, and more specifically which steps have to be taken to reduce this fragility. The latter point will be taken up in Chapter 6.

Before analysing the fragility of the Eurozone type of incomplete monetary union that was studied in the previous chapters, it can be interesting to generalize the concept of incompleteness. In the real world, there exist many monetary arrangements between nations that are far removed from the Eurozone type of incomplete monetary union, and yet they also follow rules and constrain the national monetary policies of the participants. One such arrangement is a fixed exchange rate system. Some examples of fixed exchange rate systems in the post-war period are the Bretton Woods system and the European Monetary System (EMS). Many countries in the world peg their currency to another one, in particular to the dollar. In Europe, a number of countries peg their currencies to the euro (e.g. Denmark, Bulgaria). In doing so, they form an 'incomplete' monetary union with the country to which they peg. Clearly this is a monetary union that is much more incomplete than the Eurozone.

In this chapter, we analyse two types of incomplete monetary union. We start with the fixed exchange rate system, which is the less complete of the two. We then study the Eurozone type of incomplete monetary union, which is characterized by the existence of one common currency managed by one common central bank but also by the absence of a budgetary union. The comparison of the two types of incomplete monetary union will allow us to discover the similarities in the fragility and sustainability of these unions.

5.1 Fixed exchange rate regimes as incomplete monetary unions

In this section, we focus on fixed exchange rate regimes. One common feature of these regimes is that over time most of them tend to disintegrate after some crisis. The Bretton Woods system collapsed in 1973, as did the exchange rate mechanism (ERM) of the EMS in 1993. (Box 5.1 gives a description of how the EMS worked.) Similarly, many countries pegging their currency to another are hit, after some time, by a speculative crisis. These crises often end in the peg being abandoned. Examples are the South-East Asian currencies,

---

BOX 5.1 The European Monetary System: some institutional features

The European Monetary System was instituted in 1979. It was a reaction to the large exchange rate variability of community currencies during the 1970s, which was seen as endangering the integration process in Europe.[1] The EMS consisted of two elements: the Exchange Rate Mechanism (ERM) and the European Currency Unit (ECU).

Like the Bretton Woods system, the ERM was an 'adjustable peg' system. That is, countries participating in the ERM determined an official exchange rate (central rate) for all their currencies, and a band around these central rates within which the exchange rates could fluctuate freely. This band was set at 2.25% and -2.25% around the central rate for most member countries (Belgium, Denmark, France, Germany, Ireland, and the Netherlands). Italy was allowed to use a larger band of fluctuation (6% and -6%) until 1990 when it decided to use the narrower band. The three newcomers to the system, Spain (1989), the UK (1990), and Portugal (1992), used the wider band of fluctuation. The UK dropped out of the system in September 1992. In August 1993, the band of fluctuation was raised to 15% and -15%. On 1 January 1999, the EMS ceased to exist.

When the limits of the band (the margins) were reached, the central banks of the currencies involved were committed to intervene so as to maintain the exchange rate within the band. (This intervention was called 'marginal' intervention, i.e. intervention at the margins of the band.) The commitment to intervene at the margins, however, was not absolute. Countries could (after consultation with the other members of the system) decide to change the parity rates of their currency realignment.

These realignments were very frequent during the first half of the 1980s, when more than ten took place. They became much less frequent after the middle of the 1980s. During the years 1987–92 no realignment took place. In 1992–3, major crises erupted that led to several realignments. In August 1993, the nature of the ERM was changed drastically by the increase of the band of fluctuations to 15% and -15%.

The second feature of the EMS was the existence of the ECU. The ECU was defined as a basket of currencies of the countries that are members of the EMS. (This was a larger group of countries than the ERM members. It included all the EU countries except Austria, Finland, and Sweden.)

The value of the ECU in terms of currency i (the ECU rate of currency i) was defined as follows:

$$ECU_i = \sum_j a_j s_{ji} \tag{5.1}$$

where a_j is the amount of currency j in the basket, and S_{ji} is the price of currency j in units of currency i (the bilateral exchange rate).

On 1 January 1999, the ECU was transformed into the euro at the rate of 1 ECU = 1 euro. When the euro became a currency in its own right, the basket definition ceased to exist.

---

[1] For a fascinating account of the discussions that led to the establishment of the EMS, see Ludlow (1982). For a more detailed description of some institutional features of the system, see van Ypersele (1985).

which were hit by speculative attacks in 1997–8. Many of these countries abandoned their peg to the dollar. Similar crises involved Latin American currencies in the 1990s. In 2007–8, European countries pegging to the euro also got into trouble in the aftermath of the financial crisis. We will analyse the question of why pegged exchange rate regimes turn out to be so fragile.

The fragility of a fixed exchange rate system has to do with two features of a fixed exchange rate system (two features that we will also encounter in the Eurozone type of monetary union). First there is a credibility problem. When the authorities of a country announce that they will fix the exchange rate, they are making a promise: they pledge to keep the exchange rate fixed today and in the future. The problem with any promise, however, is that doubts may arise as to whether it will be kept. In other words, all promises lead to problems of credibility. Why would countries want to go back on a promise they made in the past? (Presumably, when they pledged to fix the exchange rate they must have considered that it was in their national interest to do so.) The answer is that circumstances may arise in which the fixed exchange rate arrangement ceases to be seen as serving the national interest of the country. In that case the country will have an incentive to renege on its promise. Economic agents will suspect this and will attack the currency. We then have a speculative crisis.

The second feature of a fixed exchange rate system that leads to great fragility arises from the fact that countries on a fixed exchange rate have a limited stock of international reserves (foreign exchange) with which to defend the fixed rate. As a result, the promise to convert domestic currency into foreign currency at a fixed exchange rate cannot be guaranteed because the central bank has an insufficient amount of foreign exchange. As investors know this, they will 'become nervous' when they see that the stock of international reserves gets depleted.

These two features interact with each other: the limited stock of international reserves reduces the credibility, and low credibility leads speculators to sell the domestic currency, forcing the central bank to sell foreign exchange, thereby depleting the stock of international reserves.

We now present a simple model that catches the essence of this fragility. Let us assume a country is on a fixed exchange rate. Everything looks fine, until a shock occurs that leads to a deterioration of its current account. This (asymmetric) shock could be due to a loss of competitiveness triggered by excessive domestic wage increases. As a result, the country finds it more difficult to export, and imports increase because foreign producers are more competitive. The current account deficit will have to be corrected over time. Note that when a country has a current account deficit it is spending more than it is producing. As a result, its foreign debt increases. This is unsustainable. The country will have to correct this deficit. It has two ways to do this. One is to keep the exchange rate fixed. In that case the authorities will have to follow a policy aimed at reducing aggregate spending. This can be achieved by raising taxes (so that households have less disposable income to spend from) and/or reducing government spending. This policy is likely to be costly for the government. First, taxation leads to resistance from the population, which may vote the government out of office. Second, a policy of expenditure reduction will have the effect of reducing output and increasing unemployment, especially if wages and prices are rigid (see Chapter 1). If this effect is strong enough, the country may experience a recession.

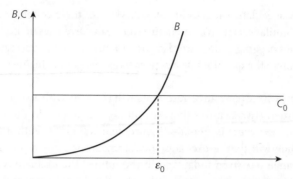

Figure 5.1 Benefits (*B*) and costs (*C*) of a devaluation.

A second way to correct for the external disequilibrium (the current account deficit) consists in devaluing the currency. As was argued in Chapter 1, this may be a less costly way to adjust to the current account deterioration. By devaluing, exports are made more competitive again. The government may now be tempted to devalue because it is perceived to be less costly.

We represent this analysis in Fig. 5.1. On the horizontal axis we set out the current account shock, i.e. the increase in the current account deficit (represented by ε). On the vertical axis we set out the benefits the government has from devaluing the currency. These benefits arise from the fact that by devaluing, the government avoids having to increase taxes and reduces the risk of a recession, which is costly in terms of output and employment.

In Fig. 5.1, we assume that the greater the current account shock, the higher is the benefit of a devaluation. This is so because when the current account deficit is high, the government will have to impose higher taxes and higher spending curbs if it does not devalue.

A devaluation not only has benefits for the government, it also has a cost. The cost is a loss of reputation for the government. Let us call this cost C_0, and let us assume it is fixed. We show the effect of this cost in Fig. 5.1. We now find that as long as $\varepsilon < \varepsilon_0$ the fixed exchange rate can be kept credible, i.e. the agents realize that the government will not devalue because the cost of losing reputation exceeds the benefits of devaluing. Thus, for small enough shocks in the current account, economic agents will expect that no devaluation will occur, which is borne out by the model. When $\varepsilon > \varepsilon_0$, however, the benefits of a devaluation exceed the cost, the authorities will be tempted to devalue the currency. As agents suspect this, they will massively sell the domestic currency, forcing the central bank to sell foreign exchange. Speculators know that this will lead to a depletion of the stock of international reserves. As a result, their speculative attack will be so large that the stock of international reserves will be depleted immediately, forcing the central bank to devalue the currency.

The analysis of Fig. 5.1 leads to an important insight. As time goes by, the probability that some shock will exceed ε_0 is positive.[2] As a result, sooner or later countries are hit by a shock that is large enough to make the fixed exchange rate non-credible. It will then collapse. Thus, fixed exchange rate commitments cannot stand the passage of time.

---

[2] The First World War was one such large shock, and it destroyed the gold standard. Similarly the EMS crisis of 1992–3 can be interpreted as the result of a large shock (the deep recession of 1992–3) that changed the cost–benefit calculus of maintaining the fixed exchange rate in major EMS countries.

The previous analysis is based on what has been called the 'first generation' models (Krugman 1979). These models stress that fixed exchange rates will inevitably collapse when the monetary authorities pursue domestic objectives, such as the stabilization of output and employment. Ultimately they will run out of reserves. Thus, the ultimate cause of a foreign exchange crisis always lies with the authorities that pursue inconsistent objectives (see, for example, Flood and Garber 1984). Speculators have the role of messengers who reveal this basic truth.

Things get more complicated, and more interesting, in the 'second generation' models (Obstfeld 1986). Consider the case of a country for which $\varepsilon < \varepsilon_0$ (see Fig. 5.1), i.e. the current account shock is small so that the cost of a devaluation exceeds the benefits. In this case no devaluation will occur, and this is actually borne out by the model. In other words, the fixed exchange rate is credible and can be sustained. Does this mean that no speculative crisis will occur? Not necessarily. To see this, we now introduce a new benefit curve, which shows the benefits of a devaluation if speculators expect a devaluation. Assume that for some reason (e.g. because they believe that there is a correlation between sunspots and devaluations) speculators expect the currency to be devalued. The authorities that want to maintain the fixed exchange rate will have to defend it against these speculators. Such a defence is, however, costly. The government will have to increase taxes even more and the central bank will have to raise the interest rate. All this is very costly and has an unfavourable effect on output and employment.

We show this in Fig. 5.2. We now draw two benefit curves. One is drawn under the assumption that speculators do not expect a devaluation. This was in fact the benefit curve used in Fig. 5.1. We call it the B_U-curve. The second benefit curve is drawn assuming that speculators expect a devaluation (the B_E-curve). The B_E-curve is located above the B_U-curve. The reason is the following. When a devaluation is expected (i.e. when there is a speculative attack) the central bank will have to raise the domestic interest rate to defend the fixed exchange rate regime. The increase in the interest rate has a negative effect on output and employment, and is thus costly. The need to raise the interest rate is absent when the devaluation is not expected, i.e. when there is no speculative attack. Thus, the maintenance of a fixed exchange rate will be more costly for the authorities when a devaluation is expected than when it is not expected. It follows that by devaluing, more benefits can be obtained when the devaluation was expected than when it was not.

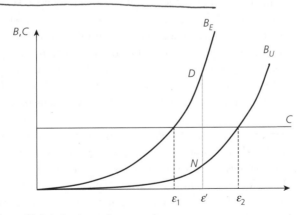

Figure 5.2 Multiple equilibria in foreign exchange markets.

We now consider three shocks: a small one, a large one, and an intermediate one. Let us first take a small shock: $\varepsilon < \varepsilon_1$. In this case, there will be no devaluation because the cost exceeds the benefits. Speculators know this. As a result, they will not expect a devaluation. Expectations are consistent with the outcome of the model. We have a no-devaluation equilibrium, and the fixed exchange rate is credible. Note that as it is credible, investors will be willing to invest in the domestic currency so that the current account deficit can easily be financed.

The large shock is the one when $\varepsilon > \varepsilon_2$. In this case, the devaluation is certain because the benefits exceed the cost. The fixed exchange rate is not credible. A devaluation is expected and this also happens in the model. The authorities will immediately lose their stock of international reserves, forcing them to devalue.

The really interesting case is the one when we have an intermediate shock, i.e. $\varepsilon_1 < \varepsilon' < \varepsilon_2$. We now obtain two possible equilibria, labelled N and D. Consider equilibrium N. At this point speculators do not expect a devaluation (there is no speculative attack). As a result, the cost of a devaluation exceeds the benefits. Thus, the authorities have no incentives to devalue, and they will not do so. Thus, point N is an equilibrium that is consistent with the expectations of the speculators, i.e. that there will be no devaluation. At point N the central bank will not have to raise the interest rate to defend the fixed exchange rate. Financing of the current account deficit will be forthcoming.

Things are very different at point D. At this point speculators expect a devaluation. Because of these expectations, the benefits of devaluation exceed the cost, leading the authorities to devalue the currency. Expectations again are model consistent. A devaluation is inevitable because the central bank will run out of international reserves.

Thus, when the shock is intermediate in size, there are two possible equilibria that depend solely on the state of expectations. When agents do not expect a devaluation the authorities have no incentive to devalue, so the exchange rate remains fixed. When, however, speculators expect a devaluation, the ensuing speculative attack creates an incentive for the authorities to devalue, and there will be a devaluation. Note also that expectations are self-fulfilling. It is sufficient to expect a devaluation for the devaluation to occur. This makes the fixed exchange rate arrangement very fragile.

It is important to realize that the existence of two equilibria ultimately depends on the fact that the central bank has a limited stock of international reserves. Suppose the central bank had an unlimited stock of international reserves. In that case, when a speculative attack occurs (speculators expect a devaluation) the central bank would always be able to counter the speculators by selling an unlimited amount of foreign exchange. The central bank would always beat the speculators. The latter would know this and would not start a speculative attack. In other words they would not expect devaluation. In terms of Fig. 5.2, the B_E-curve would coincide with the B_U-curve. There would be no scope for multiple equilibria.

This does not mean that devaluations would not occur when authorities have infinite international reserves. For shocks large enough, the authorities' cost–benefit calculus would lead them to conclude that devaluing the currency would be better than not doing so. As a result, they would devalue. The point is that when the authorities have no international reserve constraint, they cannot be forced to devalue by the speculators. If they devalue this is the result of a voluntary decision.

How can countries deal with the fragility of the fixed exchange rate? There are essentially two ways out. One is to move to a monetary regime in which these speculative attacks on the exchange rates are made impossible by abolishing exchange rates and exchange markets. This is achieved within a monetary union. The collapse of the EMS and the realization in Europe that it would be futile to manage a fixed exchange rate regime among EU countries on a permanent basis has influenced the readiness of EU policy-makers to move into a monetary union. But, as we will show in the next section, the fragility of an incomplete monetary union reappears in a new way.

The second way out of the fragility of the pegged exchange rate regime is to allow for more flexibility of the exchange rates. Thus, faced with the fragility of pegged exchange rate regimes, countries are tempted to move to one of two extremes: monetary union or more exchange rate flexibility. Empirical evidence seems to confirm this bipolar dynamics.

The bipolar view does not meet with universal approval. Many countries resist being forced to choose between the two extremes.[3] For quite a number of countries both of these extremes are uncomfortable. As a result, they have looked for a way out. This way out is made possible by re-imposing capital controls. Some countries, e.g. Malaysia, have in fact done this in the aftermath of the Asian financial crises. Other countries, such as China, have escaped the crises up to now by maintaining a heavy system of capital controls. It is doubtful, however, whether this is a long-term solution. The reason is that as economic integration proceeds, the necessity of opening up capital markets becomes more intense. Again, the case of China shows the importance of this effect. China embarked on a programme of liberalizing capital flows. Thus, sooner or later, countries with fixed exchange rates that integrate into the world economy are confronted with the increasing fragility of the fixed exchange rate.

Is there a way to reduce the fragility of the fixed exchange rate regime while maintaining the free movement of capital? The framework of Fig. 5.2 provides the answer. It consists of increasing the cost of devaluations. By shifting the C-curve upwards, countries can withstand larger shocks before they are hit by self-fulfilling speculative attacks.

Many countries that have chosen to maintain a fixed exchange rate have moved in the direction of increasing the cost of a devaluation. Some have achieved this by a currency board. Examples of currency boards are those of Hong Kong and Argentina from 1991 to 2002, which pegged their currencies to the dollar; and Bulgaria, Estonia (until 2011), and Lithuania (until 2015), which pegged their currencies to the euro. The essence of this type of regime is that the monetary authority is required to fully back the issue of domestic currency by holdings of the foreign currency (the dollar or the euro) to which the domestic currency is pegged. Thus when, say, the Hong Kong Monetary Authority wants to issue one Hong Kong dollar it has to acquire the equivalent amount of US dollars.[4] In addition, changing the peg is made very difficult by requiring legislative changes, and sometimes changes in the constitution. Recent history has shown, however, that currency board arrangements do not protect countries from speculative attacks. The most dramatic example was provided by Argentina, which abandoned its currency board in 2002 (see Box 5.2 for a discussion of some problems encountered in currency board systems).

---

[3] Calvo and Reinhart (2002) provide evidence that many countries, especially developing countries, have resisted such a move. See also McKinnon and Schnabl (2002).

[4] Since the HKD/USD is 7.8, the Hong Kong Monetary Authority must back the issue of 100 HKD by 12.8 USD.

BOX 5.2 What is a currency board?

A currency board is an institutional arrangement comprising the following elements:

1. The country fixes its exchange rate to an anchor currency (e.g. the dollar or the euro) and promises convertibility of its currency into the anchor currency at the fixed rate.

2. The country backs the issue of the domestic currency by holdings of the anchor currency. This backing is typically 100%. This 100% backing is done to provide credibility to the fixed exchange rate. The realization by market participants that the central bank has the reserves to convert the domestic money into the anchor currency should maintain their confidence in the arrangement.

3. There is a legal commitment to maintain the fixed exchange rate, which is inscribed in the law, and sometimes in the constitution.

The second element leads to a number of issues. First, a 100% backing of the issue of the domestic currency by the central bank will typically not be sufficient to back the domestic money stock. The reason is that the central bank only backs the issue of domestic currency (banknotes and coins), but not the demand deposits issued by commercial banks (which are typically much higher than the sum of banknotes and coins). The deposits can also be used by agents to convert into the anchor currency. Thus, in order for the fixed exchange rate to be fully credible, the whole money stock (currency plus demand deposits) should be backed by reserves of the anchor currency at the central bank. This implies that the reserves of the central bank should be higher than the currency in circulation (more than 100% backing).

A second issue relates to the role of the central bank as a lender of last resort. In a currency board regime the central bank cannot act as a lender of last resort. The reason is that lending of last resort typically means that the central bank injects liquidity into the banking system and that it does this by buying domestic assets from these banks. Thus, this kind of lending breaks the rule that every unit of domestic currency issued by the central bank should be backed by the anchor currency. The inability of the central bank to perform its duties of lender of last resort creates a risk in times of crises. This risk can be mitigated, or even resolved, by making sure that the domestic banks are branches of banks from the anchor currency countries. In this way these branches will profit from the lender of last resort capacity of their home country central bank.

A currency board system adds credibility to a fixed exchange rate. It is not a fool-proof system though. This is well illustrated by the experience of Argentina. In 1991, Argentina introduced a currency board and pegged the peso one-to-one to the dollar. At first it appeared that the introduction of a currency board would be a great success. Inflation dropped dramatically. Argentina was praised for having found the secret formula for success. In 2002, however, the Argentinean authorities had to abandon the peg in the face of a large speculative crisis, which made the maintenance of the fixed peg too costly. The reasons why this happened are diverse. First, Argentina experienced a deep recession, which was partly due to the fact that it pegged to the dollar, which appreciated a great deal during the second half of the 1990s. As a result the peso also appreciated against the other Latin American currencies, and Argentina lost its competitiveness vis-à-vis these countries. Second the Argentinian authorities were unable to keep the government budget under control. This led to an unsustainable debt explosion. These shocks created increasing doubts among the speculators that the authorities would be able (or willing) to maintain the fixed peg.

Successful currency boards are typically to be found in small countries (see Table 5.1). The reason is that a currency board implies that the central bank abstains from any desire to conduct a monetary policy geared toward achieving objectives other than the maintenance of the fixed exchange rate. In addition, it implies that the country has to accept the interest rate decisions decided by the anchor country. Thus, when the US Federal Reserve, say, increases its interest rate, the currency board country will have to accept this blindly by raising its domestic interest rate by the same amount. Thus, a currency board system (like any fixed exchange rate system) requires a de facto abdication of monetary sovereignty to a foreign country.

Table 5.1 Existing currency boards (2015)

Country	Years in operation	Pegged to
Antigua and Barbuda	42	dollar
Bulgaria	11	euro
Djibouti	58	dollar
Dominica	42	dollar
Grenada	42	dollar
Hong Kong	24	dollar
St Kitts and Nevis	42	dollar
St Lucia	42	dollar

In this connection, an interesting experiment was provided by the EU countries prior to the start of EMU. In the context of the Maastricht convergence criteria, countries had to maintain a fixed exchange rate (albeit with a large band). Failure to do so was punished by a ban on entry into EMU. As the political commitment to EMU was strong, the penalty for devaluation became very high during the transition period. The result was that the prospective EMU countries were spared foreign exchange crises during the transition. This happened while the rest of the world (Asia, Russia, Latin American countries) experienced major financial crises.

The previous analysis suggests that by increasing the cost of devaluations the credibility of fixed exchange rate regimes can be enhanced. We should have no illusions though. Time is generally against fixed exchange rate regimes. With the passage of time, some shock large enough to destroy the authorities' willingness to defend a fixed exchange rate commitment is bound to occur.

5.2 A monetary union without a budgetary union

In the previous section, we analysed the fragility of the fixed exchange rate regime, which as we have argued is a particular type of incomplete monetary union. In this section we analyse the Eurozone as another type of incomplete monetary union. The incompleteness arises because it is a monetary union without a budgetary union. It will be seen that this leads to a similar fragility as in the fixed exchange rate system.

In the Eurozone, there is one monetary authority (the ECB) and many independent national authorities that each control their own budget and issue their own debt. The characteristic feature of this set-up is that the national governments issue debt in the common currency. This is a currency that none of the national governments have direct control over.

In this section, a very simple model is developed that illustrates how in such a set-up multiple equilibria can arise, very much like in the model of the previous section. The starting point is that there is a cost and a benefit of defaulting on the debt, and that investors take this calculus of the government into account. Let us assume that a member country of the Eurozone is subject to a shock, which takes the form of a decline in government revenues.

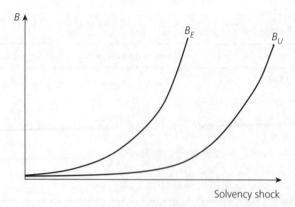

Figure 5.3 The benefits of default after a solvency shock.

austerity: difficult economic condition created by government measures to reduce public expenditure

The latter may be caused by a recession, or a loss of competitiveness. We'll call this a solvency shock. The greater this shock, the greater is the loss of solvency. Let us concentrate first on the benefit side. This is represented in Fig. 5.3. On the horizontal axis, the solvency shock is shown. On the vertical axis, the benefit of defaulting is represented. There are many ways and degrees of defaulting. To simplify, we assume this takes the form of a haircut of a fixed percentage. For example, the government can decide to repay only 50% of its debt (the haircut is then 50%). The benefit of defaulting in this way is that the government can reduce the interest burden on the outstanding debt. As a result, after the default it will have to apply less austerity, i.e. it will have to reduce spending and/or increase taxes by less than it would without the default. Since austerity is politically costly, the government profits from the default.

As in the previous section, there are two benefit curves. B_U is the benefit of a default that investors do not expect to happen, while B_E is the benefit of a default that investors expect to happen. Let us first concentrate on the B_U-curve. It is upward-sloping because when the solvency shock increases, the benefit of a default for the government goes up. The reason is that when the solvency shock is large, i.e. the decline in tax income is large, the cost of austerity is substantial. Default then becomes more attractive for the sovereign. We have drawn this curve to be non-linear, but this is not essential for the argument. There are three factors that affect the position and the steepness of the B_U-curve:

1. The initial debt level. The higher this level, the higher is the benefit of a default. Thus, with a higher initial debt level the B_U-curve will rotate upwards.

2. The efficiency of the tax system. In a country with an inefficient tax system, the government cannot easily increase taxation. Thus, in such a country the option of defaulting becomes more attractive. The B_U-curve rotates upwards.

3. The size of the external debt. When external debt takes a large proportion of total debt there will be less domestic political resistance against default, making the latter more attractive (the B_U-curve rotates upwards).

Let us now concentrate on the B_E-curve. This shows the benefit of a default when investors anticipate such a default. It is located above the B_U-curve for the following reason. When

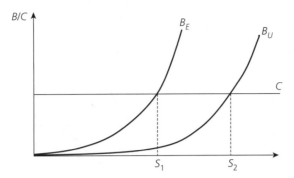

Figure 5.4 Cost and benefits of default after a solvency shock.

investors expect a default, they will sell government bonds. As a result, the interest rate on government bonds increases. This raises the government budget deficit, requiring a more intense austerity programme of spending cuts and tax hikes. Thus, default becomes more attractive. For every solvency shock, the benefits of default will now be higher than they were when the default was not anticipated.

Defaulting not only leads to benefits. There is also an important cost of default. The cost of a default arises from the fact that, when defaulting, the government suffers a loss of reputation. This loss of reputation will make it difficult for the government to borrow in the future. As in the case of the fixed exchange rate model, we will make the simplifying assumption that this is a fixed cost. We now obtain Fig. 5.4, where the fixed cost (C) is confronted with the benefit curves.

We now have the tools to analyse the equilibrium of the model. We will distinguish between three types of solvency shocks, a small one, an intermediate one, and a large one. Take a small solvency shock: this is a shock $S < S_1$ (this could be the shocks that Germany and the Netherlands experienced during the debt crisis). For this small shock the cost of a default is always larger than the benefits (both of an expected and an unexpected default). Thus, the government will not want to default. When expectations are rational, investors will not expect a default. As a result, a no-default equilibrium can be sustained. In this case investors will be willing to finance the shortfall in taxes by buying government bonds. There will be no liquidity shortage.

Let us now analyse a large solvency shock. This is one for which $S > S_2$ (this could be the shock experienced by Greece during the debt crisis). For large shocks such as this we observe that the cost of a default is always smaller than the benefits (both of an expected and an unexpected default). Thus, the government will want to default. In a rational expectations framework, investors will anticipate this. As a result, a default is inevitable. The government will not find the cash to finance its budget deficit.

We now turn to the intermediate case: $S_1 < S < S_2$ (this could be the shocks that Ireland, Portugal, and Spain experienced). For these intermediate shocks we obtain an indeterminacy, i.e. two equilibria are possible. Which one will prevail depends only on what is expected. To see this, suppose the solvency shock is S' (see Fig. 5.5). In this case there are two potential equilibria, D and N. Take point D. In this case investors expect a default (D is located on the B_E-line). This has the effect of making the benefit of a default larger than

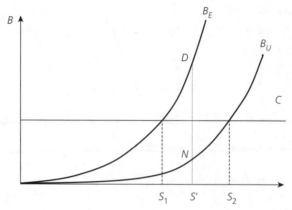

Figure 5.5 Good and bad equilibria.

the cost C. Thus, the government will default. D is an equilibrium that is consistent with expectations.

However, point N is an equally good candidate to be an equilibrium point. In the case of N, investors do not expect a default (N is on the B_U-line). As a result, the benefit of a default is lower than the cost. Thus, the government will not default. It follows that N is also an equilibrium point that is consistent with expectations.

Thus, we obtain two possible equilibria, a bad one (D) that leads to default, and a good one (N) that does not lead to default. Both are equally possible. The selection of one of these two points depends only on what investors expect. If they expect a default, there will be one; if they do not expect a default, there will be none. This remarkable result is due to the self-fulfilling nature of expectations.

Since there is a lot of uncertainty about the likelihood of default, and since investors have very little scientific foundation to calculate probabilities of default (until 2011 there had been none in Western Europe in the last 60 years), expectations are likely to be driven mainly by market sentiments of optimism and pessimism. Small changes in these market sentiments can lead to large movements from one type of equilibrium to another.

As in the case of the fixed exchange rate regime, it can be shown that the existence of two equilibria is the result of the liquidity constraint faced by the national governments in the incomplete monetary union. In order to see this, suppose that these governments did not face a liquidity constraint: i.e. like 'stand-alone' countries, they could be sure that the central bank (in this case the European Central Bank) would always provide the liquidity to pay out the bondholders at maturity. In that case, the government could always guarantee that the cash would be available. Bondholders would not expect a default, and thus would not try to force a default if the government did not want to default. The B_E-curve would coincide with the B_U-curve. There would be no scope for multiple equilibria. Put differently, a speculative selling of government bonds out of fear that the government may have insufficient cash would not be possible if the government could guarantee that the cash would always be available. Note that the government can still decide to default (if the solvency shock is large enough). But the country cannot be forced to do so by the whim of market expectations.

How can the fragility of the incomplete monetary union be reduced? There are three possibilities. First, by increasing the cost of a default the *C*-curve is raised, thereby shifting the area of self-fulfilling fears to the right. Some economists have argued that this can be done by creating the possibility of ejecting countries from the union in case of default.

A second possibility is to entrust the role of 'lender of last resort' to the European Central Bank, i.e. to allow the central bank to guarantee that it will always provide liquidity in the government bond markets. This amounts to making the ECB a central bank like the US Federal Reserve or the Bank of England, which provide the same guarantee to their own governments. We will return to this issue in Chapter 6.

A third possibility consists of consolidating national debt into one common debt. This is tantamount to a budgetary union. In doing so, the fundamental fragility of an incomplete monetary union is eliminated, essentially by completing the union. We return to this possibility in Chapter 6, where we discuss strategies for completing monetary unions.

As will be shown in the following chapters, the second and third possibilities are really part of one package that is necessary to make an incomplete monetary union like the Eurozone sustainable. As will be argued, the lender of last resort function of the ECB is needed to deal with crisis situations, while budgetary consolidation is necessary to make the Eurozone robust in the long run.

5.3 More bad news about bad equilibria: banking crises

In the previous sections, we discussed how countries in an incomplete monetary union can get stuck in a bad equilibrium that is characterized by the fact that it will be pushed into default in a self-fulfilling way. There is one feature of a bad equilibrium that is worth analysing further. This is that banks will also be affected, in two ways. First, when investors pull out from the domestic bond market, the prices of government bonds decline. Since the domestic banks are usually the main investors in the domestic sovereign bond market, this shows up as significant losses on their balance sheets. Second, domestic banks are caught up in a funding problem. As argued earlier, domestic liquidity dries up (the money stock declines), making it difficult for the domestic banks to roll-over their deposits except by paying prohibitive interest rates. Thus, the sovereign debt crisis spills over into a domestic banking crisis, even if the domestic banks were sound to start with. This feature has played an important role in the case of Greece and Portugal, where the sovereign debt crisis has led to a full-blown banking crisis. In the case of Ireland, there was a banking problem prior to the sovereign debt crisis (which in fact triggered the sovereign debt crisis). The latter, however, intensified the banking crisis.

The existence of a 'deadly embrace' between the sovereign and the local banking sector leads to the question of how this link can be broken. The answer is that a banking union can achieve this. A banking union makes it possible to spread the cost of a banking crisis that occurs in one country over the whole union, thereby insulating the local sovereign from the budgetary repercussions of this banking crisis (see Gros 2012) who compares Nevada and Ireland to shed light on this). The conditions to achieve such a banking union are not simple, though. We discuss these in Chapter 11.

5.4 More bad news about bad equilibria: automatic stabilizers

There is a second bad effect of being in a bad equilibrium. Once in a bad equilibrium, members of a monetary union find it very difficult to use automatic budget stabilizers. A recession leads to higher government budget deficits; this in turn leads to the distrust of markets in the capacity of governments to service their future debt, triggering a liquidity and solvency crisis. This then forces the government to institute austerity programmes in the midst of a recession.

Thus, member countries of a monetary union are downgraded to the status of emerging economies, which find it difficult if not impossible to use budgetary policies to stabilize the business cycle. This feature has been shown to produce pronounced booms and busts in emerging economies (see Eichengreen et al. 2005). In Box 5.3 we pursue this issue in the context of the Eurozone.

BOX 5.3 From liquidity crises to forced austerity in the Eurozone

In the this box, we provide evidence first that the strong increases in the government bond spreads in the Eurozone from 2010 were not only due to deteriorating fundamentals (such as government budget deficits and debt levels) but were driven mainly by market sentiments (i.e. by panic and fear). Second, we show that the ensuing spreads forced countries into severe austerity measures that in turn led to increasing government debt to GDP ratios.[5]

How much of the increase in the spreads observed since 2010 was due to deteriorating fundamentals, and how much to market sentiments? Fig. 5.6 shows some preliminary evidence. On the vertical axis

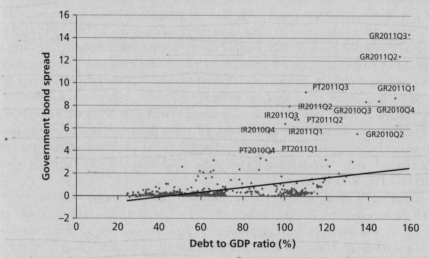

Figure 5.6 Government bond spreads and debt–GDP ratios (2000–11).
Source: De Grauwe and Ji (2013a).

---

[5] The discussion in this box is based on De Grauwe and Ji (2013a) and De Grauwe and Ji (2013b).

we set out the government bond spreads in the Eurozone. These are defined as the difference between the government bond rate in one particular country and the German government bond rates (10-year government bonds). On the horizontal axis we set out the government debt-to-GDP ratio, which is the most important fundamental variable affecting government bond spreads. Each point is a particular observation of one of the countries in a particular quarter (sample period 2000Q1–2011Q3). We also draw a straight line obtained from a simple regression of the spread as a function of the debt-to-GDP ratio.

We observe first that there is a positive relation (represented by the positively sloped regression line) between the spread and the debt-to-GDP ratio, i.e. higher spreads are associated with higher debt-to-GDP ratios.

A second observation to be made from Fig. 5.6 is that the deviations from the fundamental line (the regression line) appear to occur in bursts that are time dependent. We have labelled all observations that are more than three standard deviations from the mean, which are grouped in a triangle. It is striking to find that all these observations concern three countries (Greece, Portugal, and Ireland) and that these observations are highly time dependent, i.e. the deviations start at one particular moment of time and then continue to increase in the next consecutive periods. Thus, the dramatic increases in the spreads that we observe in these countries from 2010 on do not appear to be much related to the increase in the debt-to-GDP ratios during the same period. This is as predicted by the theory of the fragility of an incomplete monetary union.

In Fig. 5.6 only one fundamental variable, the debt-to-GDP ratio, is included in the analysis. In De Grauwe and Ji (2013a) an econometric analysis is performed using many other fundamental variables such as government budget deficits, the current account, foreign debt, and competitiveness. An econometric model linking the spreads to these fundamental variables is estimated. The question is then asked how much of the surge in the spreads observed during 2010–11[6] is explained by these fundamentals and how much by market sentiments. The latter is approximated by a time variable that is independent from the fundamentals. The result of this exercise is shown in Fig. 5.7. This shows the decomposition of the surge in the spreads. We find that, with the exception of Greece, the largest part of

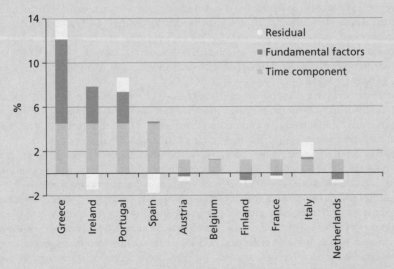

Figure 5.7 Decomposition of change in spreads: Eurozone (2008Q1–2011Q3).

Source: De Grauwe and Ji (2013a).

(Continued...)

[6] Since 2012 these spreads have declined again. We will return to this feature and we will argue that this occurred because of the announcement of the ECB becoming a lender of last resort in 2012.

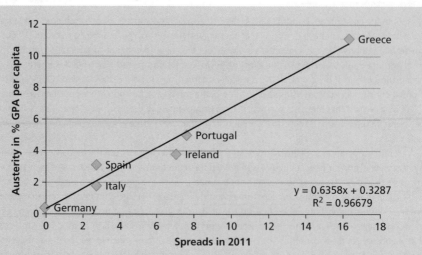

Figure 5.8 Austerity measures and spreads in 2011.

Source: De Grauwe and Ji (2013*b*).

the increase in the spreads observed during 2010–11 is the result of changing market sentiments that were unrelated to the changes in the fundamentals. In the case of Greece, we find that the largest part of the surge in spreads was due to deteriorating fundamentals. But note that in this case market sentiments also played a significant role, suggesting that market sentiments led to an excessive surge in these spreads.

How did the surge in the spreads that, as we showed, were mostly related to market sentiments affect the real economy? This is the question of how these spreads, and the ensuing liquidity problems, forced the governments of these countries into austerity.

We present some evidence in Fig. 5.8. This shows the average interest rate spreads[7] in 2011 on the horizontal axis and the intensity of austerity measures introduced during 2011 as measured by the *Financial Times*[8] (as a percent of per capita GDP) on the vertical axis. This measure of austerity is constructed in the tradition of the 'narrative approach' as pioneered by Romer and Romer (2010). It aims at producing exogenous measures of fiscal policy stance. By exogenous we mean here that they are not influenced by changes in GDP.

It is striking to find a very strong positive correlation between the spreads and the austerity measures in 2011 (the $R^2 = 0.97$). Note the two extremes. Greece was confronted with extremely high spreads in 2011 and applied the most severe austerity measures, amounting to more than 10% of GDP per capita. Germany, which did not face any pressure from spreads, did not apply any austerity.

Thus, financial markets exerted different degrees of pressure on countries. By raising the spreads they forced some countries to engage in severe austerity programmes. Other countries did not experience increases in spreads and as a result did not feel much urge to apply the austerity medicine.

We can now give the following interpretation of how the spreads exerted their influence on policy-makers and led them to apply severe austerity measures. As the spreads increased due to market panic, these increases also gripped policy-makers. Panic in the financial markets led to panic in the world of policy-makers in Europe. As a result of this panic, rapid and intense austerity measures were imposed on countries experiencing these increases in spreads. The imposition of dramatic austerity measures was also forced by the fact that countries with high spreads were pushed into a liquidity crisis by the same market

---

[7] These are defined as the difference between each country's 10-year government bond rate and the German 10-year government bond rate.

[8] *Financial Times*, http://www.ft.com/cms/s/0/feb598a8-f8e8–11e0-a5f7–00144feab49a.html#axzz2JSOwncy

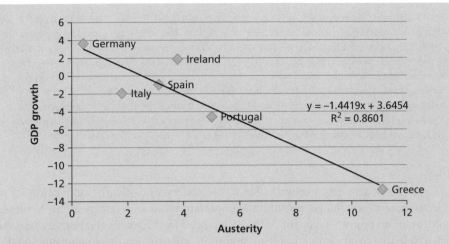

Figure 5.9 Austerity (2011) and GDP growth (2011–12).

Source: De Grauwe and Ji (2013b).

forces that produced the high spreads (De Grauwe 2011). This forced these countries to beg 'hat in hand' for funding from the creditor countries.

How well did this panic-induced austerity work? We provide some answers in Figs 5.9 and 5.10. Fig. 5.9 shows the relation between the austerity measures[9] introduced in 2011 and the growth of GDP over 2011–12. We find a strong negative correlation. Countries that imposed the strongest austerity measures also experienced the strongest declines in their GDP. This result is in line with the IMF's analysis (International Monetary Fund 2012).

Some will say that this is the price that has to be paid for restoring budgetary orthodoxy. But is this so? Fig. 5.10 may lead us to doubt this. It shows the austerity measures and the subsequent change in the

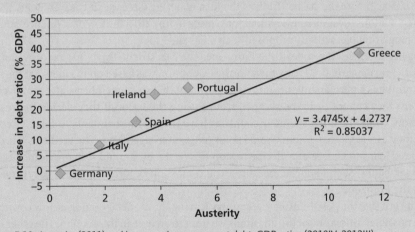

Figure 5.10 Austerity (2011) and increases in government debt–GDP ratios (2010IV–2012III).

Note: The Greek government debt ratio excludes the debt restructuring of end 2011, which amounted to about 30% of GDP.

Source: De Grauwe and Ji (2013b).

(Continued...)

[9] Note that the way the austerity measures are computed ensures that they are not influenced by the changes in GDP during 2011. Also, we show the austerity measures in 2011 and the growth rate during 2011–12.

debt-to-GDP ratios.[10] It is striking to find a strong positive correlation. The more intense the austerity, the larger is the subsequent increase in the debt-to-GDP ratios. This is not really surprising; as we learned from Fig. 5.9, those countries that applied the strongest austerity also saw their GDP (the denominator in the debt ratio) decline most forcefully. Thus, it can be concluded that the sharp austerity measures that were imposed by market and policy-makers' panic not only produced deep recessions in the countries that were exposed to the medicine, but also that this medicine did not work well. In fact it led to even higher debt-to-GDP ratios, and undermined the capacity of these countries to continue to service the debt. As a result of these policies of austerity many of these countries find themselves with a legacy of very high debt to GDP ratios that they will have to bring down in the future (See De Grauwe 2015).

This feature of a monetary union makes it potentially very costly. The automatic stabilizers in the government budget constitute an important social achievement in the developed world, as for many people they soften the pain created by the booms and busts in capitalist societies. If a monetary union has the implication of destroying these automatic stabilizers, it is unclear whether the social and political basis for such a union can be maintained. It is therefore important to design a governance structure that maintains these automatic stabilizers.

5.5 Grexit: can it happen and why? Is it desirable?

Greece was the country that triggered the Eurozone sovereign debt crisis in 2010. The severity of the Greek fiscal problems and the great difficulties this country experienced in adjusting to the crisis led economists and politicians to formulate an idea that would have been unthinkable before the crisis. This was the idea of letting Greece exit the Eurozone. During the negotiations towards a new bailout for Greece in July 2015 the German finance minister, Wolfgang Schäuble, actually proposed such a Grexit.

Legally countries cannot exit the Eurozone. The Maastricht Treaty has no provisions for an exit. The silence of the Treaty towards the exit option was based on the idea that the monetary union is a permanent one. It is clear, however, that since member-states are sovereign nations, they cannot easily be stopped from exiting the union if they decide to do so. In addition, while the other member countries have no legal instruments to force Greece to exit, they can force that country to do so in other, non-legal ways. The creditors who have provided loans to Greece may decide to stop this or the ECB could stop providing liquidity to Greek banks. Such financial measures would most likely force the Greek government to leave the Eurozone.

Why is it that the possibility of one country leaving the monetary union is now considered to be possible? This is one of the questions we want to analyse in this section. The other question will be how desirable it is for Greece to exit the Eurozone? We will conclude with a last question: How likely is a Grexit?

---

[10] In Greece, there was a debt restructuring at the end of 2011, which reduced the Greek government's debt by about 30% of GDP. We do not take this into account in the Greek numbers as we want to measure the total effect of austerity on government debt ratios.

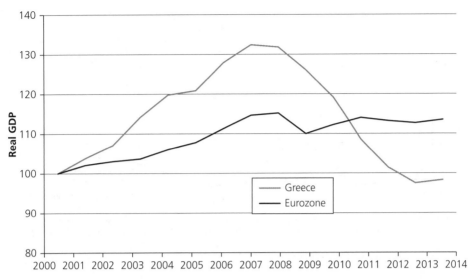

Figure 5.11 Real GDP Greece and Eurozone (2000=100)

Source: Eurostat.

How could this happen?

In order to shed light on this question it is useful to start with a discussion of macroeconomic developments in Greece since the start of the Eurozone. We do this in Figs 5.11 to 5.15. Fig. 5.11 compares the evolution of real GDP in Greece with the rest of the Eurozone. The

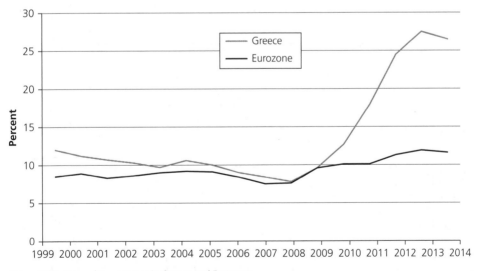

Figure 5.12 Unemployment rate in Greece and Eurozone

Source: Eurostat.

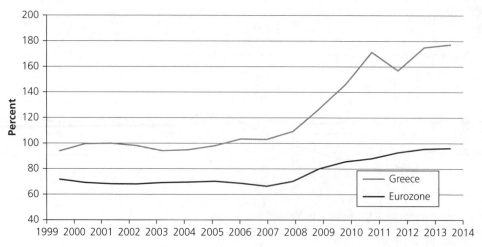

Figure 5.13 Government debt in Greece and Eurozone (%GDP)

Source: Eurostat.

striking feature of Fig. 5.11 is the fact that Greece experienced a much stronger growth in real GDP than the Eurozone as a whole during the period 2000–8. (The boom in Greece was comparable with the booms observed in Spain and Ireland). From Fig. 5.12 it appears that during these boom years, unemployment declined from about 12% to approximately 8%. So far so good.

The trouble with this boom is found in Figs 5.13, 5.14, and 5.15. In Fig. 5.13 we find that despite exceptionally high growth rates of GDP, the Greek government did not manage

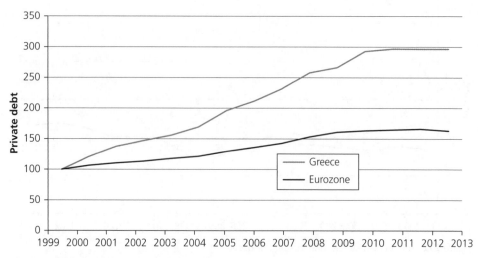

Figure 5.14 Private debt in Greece and Eurozone (1999=100)

Source: Eurostat.

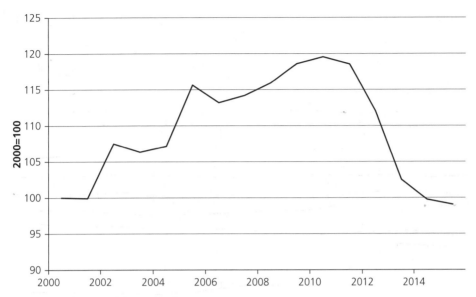

Figure 5.15 Relative unit labour costs Greece

Source: Eurostat.

to reduce its debt level. From 2003 to 2007, when the boom was at its peak, the Greek government accumulated budget deficits that led to an increase in the government debt from 94% to 103% of GDP. This illustrates the intense pro-cyclical nature of the fiscal policies of the Greek government during the boom years. Normally, during an economic boom, budget deficits tend to decline automatically. Not only did the Greek government switch out these automatic stabilizers, it added to government spending, thereby intensifying the boom.

Figure 5.14 tells us something important about the Greek boom. We observe that Greek private debt started to increase very rapidly from 2000 onwards, and tripled in 2010, while in the Eurozone it increased by a little more than 50%. (Note that other Eurozone countries, such as Spain and Ireland, also experienced very high increases of private debt. These countries would also get into trouble.)

Finally Fig. 5.15 illustrates how the boom led to a strong increase in relative unit labour costs. (We have defined this variable in Chapter 2.) From 2000 to 2010 Greek unit labour costs increased 20% faster than in the rest of the Eurozone. As a result, Greece experienced a strong deterioration of its competitiveness. This hampered its exports and stimulated imports leading to large current account deficits.

Putting all this together we obtain the following picture. Prior to the crisis Greece experienced a strong boom in economic activity. This was made possible by the fact that the private sector borrowed massive amounts of money. The money came mainly from banks in Northern Europe that were happy to lend to Greek banks that in turn lent the money to Greek consumers and Greek firms. Thus the boom was really based on a massive inflow of cheap money lent out to Greek consumers and firms. The problem with this is that these consumers and firms found themselves saddled by debt levels that would turn out to be unsustainable once the crash came. The same boom led to very large wage increases, which reduced the competitiveness of the Greek economy.

And the crash came in 2008, forcing the private sector to deleverage (i.e. to reduce) its debt levels. This, however, implied that consumers and firms had to reduce their spending massively. In addition, in order to restore competitiveness, wages were cut dramatically (Fig. 5.15), reducing spending even further. As a result, GDP collapsed, unemployment shot up to more than 25% of active population, and government debt exploded, mainly as a result of the imploding GDP, which reduced government revenues dramatically (see Figs 5.11 to 5.13). No other Eurozone member country faced such intense adjustments.

The intensity of the economic and fiscal crisis in Greece that we just described led to the phenomena we discussed in this chapter and in Chapter 1 (Sections 1.2 to 1.4). Holders of Greek government bonds massively sold these bonds, leading to record high interest rates in Greece, pushing the Greek government into illiquidity and forcing it to institute intense austerity. Put differently, Greece was forced to switch off the automatic budget stabilizers, intensifying the decline in GDP and the increase in unemployment. Greece was pushed into a bad equilibrium.

The Greek drama illustrates two points concerning the costs of a monetary union. First the adjustment costs after a large asymmetric shock can be very high in a monetary union. These adjustment costs are made more severe in a monetary union because the country cannot devalue the currency. In the case of Greece, devaluation would certainly have helped to reduce these costs, but being in the Eurozone Greece could not do so and was forced to engineer an 'internal devaluation'. When these adjustment costs take the intensity they have had in Greece the temptation to exit becomes strong.

Second, the fact that the government cannot issue debt in its own currency makes it prone to being pushed into illiquidity and insolvency. Such a dynamic makes the government helpless and forces it to look for help from creditors. The latter, however, impose their rule, which leads to a loss of sovereignty of the country.

From the previous discussion it appears that there is an important interaction between economics and politics. The adjustment mechanism in a monetary union can be extremely painful, leading millions of people into unemployment and poverty for prolonged periods. Such severe suffering can lead to political upheaval, leading politicians to power who promise a better life outside the monetary union. This, in a way, leads to the ultimate fragility of the Eurozone: large asymmetric shocks lead to such high adjustment costs that they trigger political instability, which ultimately can lead sovereign nations to decide they will be better off outside the monetary union.

The Greek drama illustrates something important about the governance of the Eurozone. In the absence of a full-fledged political union, a hegemonic form of political decision making has been put into place in the Eurozone. This is a decision mode where one or more creditor nations dictate policy to other countries. This has also happened in Portugal and Ireland. It is not clear that such a hegemonic decision mode is sustainable in the long run.

Should Greece exit the Eurozone?

This is the question of the desirability of Grexit; it leads to two sub-questions:

Will Greece be better off after Grexit?

Will the rest of the Eurozone be better off?

Will Greece be better off outside the Eurozone?

Economists have been debating this issue, but no consensus has emerged. There are important negative implications of a Grexit. The most important one is that a Grexit is likely to lead the Greek government to default on its debt, which in turn will lead to a banking crisis (because the Greek banks are major holders of Greek government bonds). All this will intensify the severity of the economic downturn. There are also positive effects of a Grexit. The likely devaluation of the new currency can boost the economy and speed up the recovery. However, if not carefully controlled, such devaluation can lead to an inflationary spiral. Thus there are benefits and costs of an exit for Greece. It is unclear how costs and benefits will evolve in the situation of a Grexit. Ultimately, if Greece were to exit, this will most likely be based on a political dynamic that we described in the previous section.

Does a temporary Grexit, as the German minister of finance, Wolfgang Schäuble, proposed recently, make sense?

The answer is most likely negative. A temporary Grexit it is like a temporary divorce. It leads to a dilemma. If Greece does well outside the Eurozone then it is unlikely to be willing to return to a club where it suffered so much. If, however, Greece does not do well (e.g. it is forced into large devaluations and increasing uncontrolled inflation), the other Eurozone countries will not want to let Greece in again. So a temporary Grexit makes little sense. It only serves to reduce the guilt feelings of those countries that have pushed out a member state from the monetary union.

Will the rest of the Eurozone be better off?

There are two views about this question. Let us discuss these.

According to the first view, a Grexit would transform a permanent union into a temporary one. Each time important asymmetric shocks occur, investors would ask the question of whether the adjustment costs of the country concerned may not become too high, leading to political pressures for an exit. 'Who is next' is the question investors would ask with each large economic disturbance. This by itself would introduce an unstable dynamic in the Eurozone as the expectations of an exit could become self-fulfilling.

In this connection, the idea of a redenomination risk is important. This is the risk that after an exit, firms in the exiting country may have to absorb large losses because they have more liabilities than assets vis-à-vis the other Eurozone countries. Prior to the exit such unmatched assets and liabilities vis-à-vis other Eurozone countries do not matter as assets and liabilities are expressed in the same currency, the euro. However, after an exit this is no longer the case because the assets and liabilities are suddenly expressed in a foreign currency.

If a Grexit occurs, firms in the Eurozone may be tempted to match their assets and liabilities they have in each of the other member countries of the Eurozone. This would in fact imply that financial integration in the Eurozone declines.

All this will make the future of the Eurozone (without Greece) more unstable and will lead to a general retrenchment of firms into their own countries. The Eurozone without Greece will become less of an optimal currency area. We represent this view in Fig. 5.16. It is similar to Fig. 4.4 of Chapter 4 and shows the trade-off between flexibility and symmetry in the monetary union. The effect of Grexit is to push the remaining members of the

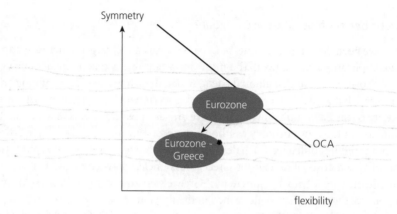

Figure 5.16 Grexit makes Eurozone less optimal

Eurozone farther away from the *OCA* line (i.e. it makes the Eurozone without Greece less of an optimal currency area and thus more likely to experience future problems).

The second view is optimistic about the effect of Grexit on the remaining Eurozone. According to this view, the Eurozone without Greece will face less asymmetric shocks because an outlier country has been ejected. This makes the remaining countries less asymmetric (more symmetric) and as a result increases the stability of the Eurozone.

We represent this view in Fig. 5.17. The effect of Grexit is to make the Eurozone more symmetric. As a result, the Eurozone (without Greece) is pushed upwards. This upward push may even put this new Eurozone safely into the *OCA* zone. The Eurozone will become more sustainable.

To conclude: Will there be a Grexit? At the time of writing, Greece was still in the Eurozone. It remains very difficult to predict whether or not Greece will leave the Eurozone. As will be clear from the discussion of this section, so many factors, both economic and political, influence such a decision. The reader will forgive the author of this book for not making a prediction. Such a prediction is just too difficult to make.

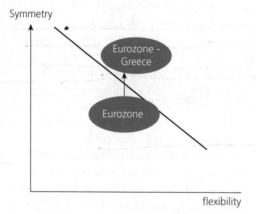

Figure 5.17 Grexit makes Eurozone (minus Greece) an *OCA*

5.6 Conclusion

In this chapter, we have analysed the inherent fragility of incomplete monetary unions. We focused on two incomplete monetary unions, i.e. a fixed exchange rate regime and a Euro-zone-type incomplete monetary union. We found that both types of union are characterized by a similar fragility. In both cases, a lack of confidence can in a self-fulfilling way drive the country to a devaluation (in the first case) or to a default (in the second case). Such fragility is problematic because it leads to questions of the sustainability of incomplete monetary unions. In the case of the Eurozone it has led to a situation in which several countries have been forced into severe austerity that pushed these countries into a bad equilibrium.

We also briefly discussed ways to reduce the fragility of these incomplete monetary unions so as to make them more sustainable. In Chapter 6 we discuss in more detail strategies aimed at making the Eurozone more sustainable.

6 How to complete a monetary union

Introduction

Many of the problems of a monetary union arise from the fact that it is incomplete. The Eurozone, in particular, is an incomplete construction. In the previous chapters, we argued that this incompleteness is at the core of its fragility. In this chapter, we analyse the question of how such a union can be completed so that it becomes sustainable in the long run. It will become clear from this chapter that all the proposals aimed at completing the Eurozone involve some transfer of sovereignty from national to supranational institutions. Thus, completing a monetary union really means moving towards more political union.

A monetary union should be embedded in a political union. Almost everybody will now agree with this.[1] Not so long ago, however, many observers, especially among the world of officials (see European Commission 2008; Issing 2008), disagreed and maintained that the Eurozone was all right and that no significant moves towards a political union were necessary. They have been proved spectacularly wrong. It is surprising to find out that 'practical men' have been living in a fictional world for so long.

While correct, the statement 'a monetary union should be embedded in a political union' is not really very helpful. Of course, if the Eurozone were to be embedded in a United States of Europe, its fragility would disappear. It is clear, however, that at this moment of history a 'deep variable' necessary to achieve full political union is lacking in Europe. This deep variable is a strong national sense of common purpose and an intense feeling of belonging to the same nation.[2] As long as this deep variable is missing it will be difficult to reach the nirvana of full political union. But that does not mean that one cannot make progress. A policy of small steps that creates a governance structure that helps to make the monetary union more sustainable is possible.

In this chapter, we first describe what these small steps look like and how they move us towards a more complete monetary union. Put differently, we give practical content to the idea that a monetary union should be embedded in a political union. We then show how these steps towards more political union can reduce the fragility of an incomplete monetary union.

The problem we identified in the previous chapters can also be reformulated as follows. Financial markets can drive the countries of a monetary union into a bad equilibrium that

---

[1] As always, there is dissent. For a recent one see Sandbu (2015).
[2] See Baldwin and Wyplosz (2006) on this issue.

is the result of a self-fulfilling mechanism. This can be interpreted as a 'coordination failure', i.e. the market fails to coordinate actions that lead to the best possible outcome. Instead, it coordinates financial agents' behaviour in a way that leads to a bad equilibrium. This market failure can in principle be solved by collective action aimed at steering countries towards a good equilibrium.

Collective action can be taken at two levels. One is at the level of the central banks, the other is at the level of the governments. We will argue that both levels of action are necessary, the first one as a way to deal with crisis situations and the second one as a way to structurally strengthen the union.

6.1 The role of the central bank: lender of last resort

Liquidity crises are avoided in stand-alone countries that issue debt in their own currencies mainly because the central bank can be forced to provide all the necessary liquidity to the sovereign. This creates an implicit guarantee to the bondholders that they will be paid out when the bond matures. This outcome can also be achieved in a monetary union if the common central bank is willing to provide the necessary liquidity in the different sovereigns' bond markets. This creates an implicit guarantee for the bondholders that they will always be paid out at maturity, as is the case in the bond market of stand-alone countries. By eliminating the threat of a liquidity crisis it can also prevent the market from pushing the member countries towards a bad equilibrium. Thus, in a monetary union there is a role for the central bank as a lender of last resort in the domestic bond markets. By guaranteeing that liquidity will always be available it reduces the fragility of an incomplete monetary union.

Note that the reason why central banks have a lender of last resort function in the government bond markets is the same reason why they have this responsibility in the banking sector. Banks borrow short and lend long. This creates great fragility in the banking sector. When deposit holders run to the bank together to convert their deposits into cash, the banks that hold relatively illiquid assets cannot produce the cash to pay out the deposit holders. As a result, the banking sector is very sensitive to movements of distrust that can create a self-fulfilling liquidity crisis. As banks try to find cash they sell assets, thereby lowering the price of their assets. This can lead to a solvency crisis. This well-known feature has led central banks to be lenders of last resort for the banks. The nice feature of this lender of last resort function is that when deposit holders are confident that the central bank will exert this function they will rarely run to their banks, so that the central bank rarely has to step in to provide cash to the banks.

Governments' assets and liabilities in a monetary union have a similar structure to those of the banks. Governments' liabilities are liquid, while most of their assets are illiquid (e.g. infrastructure, claims on taxpayers). Thus, when bondholders massively sell bonds, these governments may not be able to generate enough cash to pay out bondholders at maturity.

That the Eurozone needed a lender of last resort in the government bond markets was finally recognized by the ECB in September 2012, when it stepped in and committed itself to buying unlimited amounts of government bonds in times of crisis. Although the ECB prefers to call these operations 'Outright Monetary Transactions' (OMT), these are true lender of last resort operations. Unfortunately, the ECB attached a number of conditions to the

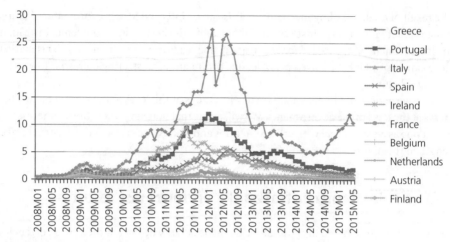

Figure 6.1 Spreads of 10-year government bond rates in the Eurozone, 2008–15.
Source: ECB.

application of its OMT facility, in particular that countries should apply for it and commit themselves to further austerity programmes. Nevertheless, the fact that the ECB provided a facility in which it committed itself to unlimited purchases of the bonds of troubled governments dramatically reduced the financial fragility of the system. It also took away the existential fear that existed in the Eurozone and that was destabilizing the system. Prior to the ECB's decision, investors feared that the Eurozone might collapse. The new stand taken by the ECB reduced this existential fear that had been destroying the Eurozone.

Fig. 6.1 shows that the government bond market has been pacified since 2012. We observe a dramatic decline in government bond spreads during 2012–13. During that period there was no significant improvement in fundamentals such as debt-to-GDP ratio, or external debt of the problem countries (see De Grauwe and Ji 2013*b*). The announcement alone that the ECB was committed to unlimited interventions in government bond markets was sufficient to bring down these spreads, especially the spreads of those countries that were highest before the announcement. Note that with the eruption of the second Greek crisis in 2015 after the election of the new Greek government, the spreads of the Greek government bonds started to surge again. This has to do with the stalemate between the creditor nations and Greece on the conditions to be applied on the liquidity support for Greece and on the perception that the ECB will not be willing to provide liquidity support to the Greek government. In contrast with 2010, the Greek crisis did not spill over into other bond markets, where the spreads continued to be low.

The ECB made the right decision to become a lender of last resort, not only for banks but also for sovereigns, thereby re-establishing the stabilizing force needed to protect the system from the boom and bust dynamics. This view was forcefully argued by a number of economists before the ECB decided to act (see De Grauwe 2011, Wyplosz 2012, Wolf 2012).

The view that the central bank has a role as lender of last resort in government bond markets remains controversial. It is severely criticized. The German Constitutional Court ruled in early 2014 that the OMT programme is illegal because its use leads the ECB to step outside its mandate. This, according to the German Constitutional Court, violates the German Constitution. The Court referred the case to the European Court of Justice (ECJ) and asked the latter to introduce restrictions on the use of OMT. The ECJ, however, rejected this request in June 2015 and ruled that OMT does not violate the Treaty and thus is in accordance with the European Law. This seems to settle the issue but a future clash between the German Constitutional Court and the ECJ is not to be excluded.

Three points of criticism have been formulated against the view that the ECB should be a lender of last resort in the government bond markets. They play an important role in the legal discussions between the German Constitutional Court and the ECJ.

Risk of inflation

A first argument against an active role for the central bank of a monetary union as a lender of last resort in the sovereign bond market is that this would lead to inflation. This criticism was very strong when the ECB started buying government bonds of member states in 2010. It was said that the ECB increased the money stock, thereby leading to a risk of inflation. Does an increase in the money stock not always lead to more inflation, as Milton Friedman taught us? Two points should be made here.

First, a distinction should be introduced between the money base and the money stock. When the central bank buys government bonds (or other assets) it increases the money base (currency in circulation and banks' deposits at the central bank). This does not mean that the money stock increases. In fact, during periods of financial crisis both monetary aggregates tend to become disconnected. An example of this is shown in Fig. 6.2. One observes that prior to the banking crisis of October 2008 both aggregates were very much connected in the Eurozone. From October 2008 on, however, the disconnect became quite spectacular.

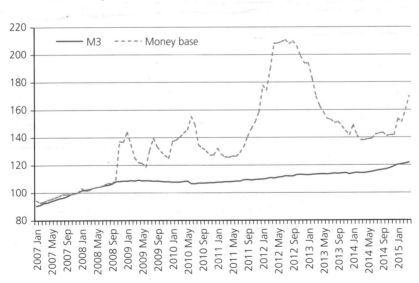

Figure 6.2 Money base and money stock (M3) in the Eurozone (2007–15); 2007 December = 100.

Source: ECB, Statistical Data Warehouse.

Over the period 2008 (October) to 2015 (April), the money base increased by more than 70% while the money stock increased by a mere 20%.

This suggests that the money multiplier (the ratio of the money stock to the money base) has dropped dramatically. This dramatic decline in the money multiplier has everything to do with the liquidity trap (Krugman 2010). Banks, which accumulate reserves as a result of liquidity injections by the ECB, hoard these reserves. Their degree of risk aversion is such that they do not use their cash reserves to expand bank credit. As a result, the money stock (M3) does not increase much, despite the massive increase in the money base. A similar phenomenon has been observed in the US and the UK.

Another way to understand this phenomenon is to note that when a financial crisis erupts, agents want to hold cash for safety reasons. If the central bank decides not to supply the cash, it turns the financial crisis into an economic recession and possibly a depression, as agents scramble for cash. When instead the central bank exerts its function of lender of last resort and supplies more money base, it stops this deflationary process. That does not allow us to conclude that the central bank is likely to create inflation.

All this was very well understood by Milton Friedman, the father of monetarism, who cannot be suspected of favouring inflationary policies. In his classic book, co-authored with Anna Schwartz, *A Monetary History of the United States*, he argued that the Great Depression was so intense because the Federal Reserve failed to perform its role of lender of last resort, and did not increase the US money base sufficiently (see Friedman and Schwartz 1963). Friedman and Schwartz argued forcefully that the money base should have increased much more and that the way to achieve this was by buying government securities. Much to the chagrin of Friedman and Schwartz, the Federal Reserve failed to do so. Those who today fear the inflationary risks of lender of last resort operations would do well to read Friedman and Schwartz (1963).

There is a risk of inflation in the future when the economy starts booming again. At that moment, the extra liquidity held by banks could be used to expand credit. The central bank, however, can then withdraw the liquidity by selling government bonds or by increasing minimum reserve requirements of banks.

Fiscal consequences

A second criticism is that lender of last resort operations in the government bond markets can have fiscal consequences: if governments fail to service their debts, the central bank will make losses and these will have to be borne by taxpayers. Thus, by intervening in the government bond markets, the central bank is committing future taxpayers. The central bank should avoid operations that mix monetary and fiscal policies (see Goodfriend 2011).

All this sounds reasonable. Yet it fails to recognize that all open market operations (including foreign exchange market operations) carry the risk of losses and thus have fiscal implications. When a central bank buys private paper in the context of its open market operation, there is a risk involved, because the issuer of the paper can default. This will then lead to losses for the central bank.[3] These losses are in no way different from the losses the central bank can incur when buying government bonds. Thus the argument really implies that a

---

[3] The same is true with foreign exchange market operations, which can lead to large losses as has been shown by the recent Swiss experience.

central bank should abstain from any open market operation. It should stop being a central bank. The truth is that a central bank should perform (risky) open market operations. The fact that these are potentially loss-making should not deter the central bank. Losses can be necessary, even desirable, to guarantee financial stability. In addition, a central bank can make losses without going bankrupt. The reason is that it has the power to print the money that will be accepted to cover its losses. No other institution can do this. Put differently, a central bank is not constrained by solvency requirements the way a private company is. In fact a central bank does not need equity to function properly (see De Grauwe and Ji 2013c).

There is another dimension to the problem that follows from the fragility of the government bond markets in a monetary union. It was argued in Chapter 5 that financial markets can in a self-fulfilling way drive countries into a bad equilibrium, where default becomes inevitable. The use of the lender of last resort can prevent countries from being pushed into such a bad equilibrium. If the intervention by the central banks is successful, there will be no losses and no fiscal consequences.

Moral hazard

As with all insurance mechanisms there is a risk of moral hazard. By providing a lender of last resort insurance in the government bond markets, the common central bank gives an incentive to governments to issue too much debt. This is indeed a serious risk. But this risk of moral hazard is no different from the risk of moral hazard in the banking system. It would be a mistake if the central bank were to abandon its role of lender of last resort in the banking sector because there is a risk of moral hazard. In the same way it is wrong for the central bank to abandon its role of lender of last resort in the government bond market because there is a risk of moral hazard.

The way to deal with moral hazard is to impose rules that will constrain governments in issuing debt, very much the way moral hazard in the banking sector is tackled by imposing limits on risk-taking by banks. In general, it is better to separate liquidity provision from moral hazard concerns. Liquidity provision should be performed by a central bank and the governance of moral hazard by another institution, the supervisor. This has been the approach taken towards the banking sector: the central bank assumes the responsibility of lender of last resort, thereby guaranteeing unlimited liquidity provision in times of crisis, irrespective of what this does to moral hazard; the supervisory authority takes over the responsibility of regulating and supervising the banks.

This should also be the design of the governance within a monetary union, in particular in the Eurozone. The common central bank assumes the responsibility of lender of last resort in the sovereign bond markets. A different and independent authority takes over the responsibility of regulating and supervising the creation of debt by national governments. In fact the European Commission is that authority. It has been vested with the power to control and to implement budgetary discipline in the European Union under the so-called Stability and Growth Pact (SGP). Since the eruption of the sovereign debt crisis, the European Commission's authority in policing budgetary discipline under the SGP has been enhanced significantly. This will be described in greater detail in Chapter 10. This disciplining and sanctioning mechanism should relieve the ECB of its fear of moral hazard. These mechanisms, of course, imply a willingness of the member states to subject their budgetary policies to outside control. It will be argued later that this implies some transfer of sovereignty in the budgetary field. This is necessary in order for the common central bank to be assured that some national governments in the monetary union will not create too much debt by exploiting the implicit guarantee that the common central bank provides.

6.2 Consolidating government budget and debts

The second building block in the completion of the monetary union is budgetary. We have seen that the existence of national government budgets and debts is at the core of the fragility of a monetary union. Collective action at the union level is necessary to solve this problem. The key is that parts of the national budgets and debt should be consolidated into one central component. There are two reasons why this is necessary. First, such a consolidation creates a common fiscal authority that can issue debt in a currency under the control of that authority. In so doing, it protects the member states from being forced into default by financial markets. It also protects the monetary union from the centrifugal forces that financial markets can exert on the union. Second, by consolidating (centralizing) national government budgets into one central budget, a mechanism of automatic transfers can be organized. As was stressed in Chapter 1, such a mechanism works as an insurance mechanism transferring resources to the country hit by a negative economic shock.

This solution to the systemic problem of the Eurozone requires a far-reaching degree of political union, i.e. member countries should be willing to transfer sovereignty over taxation and spending to European institutions. Economists have stressed that such a political union will be necessary to sustain the monetary union in the long run (see EC Commission 1977 and De Grauwe 1992). It is clear, however, that there is little willingness in Europe today to significantly increase the degree of political union. This unwillingness to go in the direction of more political union will continue to make the Eurozone a fragile construction.

This does not mean, however, that one should despair. One can move forward by taking small steps. Such a strategy of small steps not only allows us to solve the most immediate problems. It also signals the seriousness of European policy-makers in moving forward in the direction of more political union.

A strategy of small steps

(a) The joint issue of common bonds

A potential step towards political union and thus towards strengthening the Eurozone consists of the joint issue of Eurobonds. A joint issue of Eurobonds is an important mechanism for internalizing the externalities in the Eurozone that were identified above.

By jointly issuing Eurobonds, the participating countries become jointly liable for the debt they have issued together. This is a very visible and constraining commitment that will convince the markets that member countries are serious about the future of the euro (see Verhofstadt 2009; Juncker and Tremonti 2010). In addition, by pooling the issue of government bonds, the member countries protect themselves against the destabilizing liquidity crises that arise from their inability to control the currency in which their debt is issued. A common bond issue does not suffer from this problem.

The proposal to issue common Eurobonds has met stiff resistance in a number of countries (see Issing 2008). This resistance is understandable. A common Eurobond creates a number of serious problems that have to be addressed. We will discuss these in Chapter 10. Here we want to stress one of these problems: the moral hazard risk. The common Eurobond issue contains an implicit insurance for the participating countries. Since countries are collectively responsible for the joint debt issue, an incentive is created for countries to rely on this implicit insurance and to issue too much debt. This prospect creates a lot of resistance in other countries that behave responsibly. It is unlikely that these countries will be willing to step into a common Eurobond issue unless this moral hazard risk is resolved (Chapter 10).

(b) A banking union

A banking union is necessary to cut the 'deadly embrace' between sovereign and banks that we have stressed earlier. A common bank resolution mechanism allows the cost of resolving banking crises to be spread over the whole union. This is a key ingredient of the banking union that exists in the United States. It has allowed states such as Nevada, which experienced a similar real estate boom and bust as that in Ireland, to escape from the deadly embrace. Many Nevada banks that, like their Irish counterparts, were heavily involved in the real estate boom faced bankruptcy when the crash occurred. The resolution of the crisis was carried out by the US federal government, so that the Nevada state government was shielded from the budgetary fallout of this resolution. Daniel Gros (2012) has estimated that this centralization of the cost of resolving the Nevada banking crisis amounted to a transfer from the federal government of more than 10% of Nevada's GDP. No such central mechanism existed in the case of Ireland. As a result, the Irish government had to bear the whole burden of the costs of bank resolution. This pulled the Irish government into a default crisis, forcing extreme austerity and depression with increases in unemployment. The same happened in Spain.

A prerequisite to setting up a common resolution mechanism for banking crises is that the supervision of banks should also be centralized. One cannot have common resolution without a common supervisory system. In fact, the Eurozone countries decided in 2012 to set up such a common supervisory framework. It became operational in November 2014 and it is managed by the European Central Bank. (We describe this new supervisory framework in Chapter 8.)

The discussion above makes clear that a workable banking union also implies some form of fiscal union. In times of crisis there must exist one or more European institutions with sufficient resources that can be mobilized immediately to intervene and to recapitalize banks. Such an institution, the Resolution Fund, was created in the context of the banking union. It will have approximately €55 billion available to be used in times of crises and to recapitalize banks. One can doubt, however, whether this institution has sufficient resources to act in times of crisis. Certainly it can deal with individual cases, but probably not with systemic banking crises involving large parts of the Eurozone banking system.

6.3 Coordination of budgetary and economic policies

A second important step in the process towards political union is to set some constraints on the national budgetary and economic policies of the member states of the Eurozone. The fact that while monetary policy is fully centralized the other instruments of economic policies have remained firmly in the hands of the national governments is a serious design failure of the Eurozone. We discussed this design failure in Chapter 2 and we have argued that it is responsible for divergent movements in wages and prices within the Eurozone (see also Box 6.1 below). Some of these divergences have become unsustainable and have to be corrected. It is usually very painful to make these corrections.

Ideally, countries should hand their sovereignty over the use of national instruments of economic policies to European institutions. However, the willingness to take such a drastic step towards political union is weak. Here also small steps should be taken.

Some progress has been achieved in setting up new rules of economic governance in the Eurozone. A so-called 'six pack' of measures strengthening control of budgetary policies and coordinating macroeconomic policies have been adopted and are being put into place. These measures include a tightening of the mutual control on each member's budgetary situation, as mentioned earlier (Stability and Growth Pact), including a stronger sanctioning procedure; the 'European Semester', which requires national governments to present their annual budgets to the European Commission prior to their approval in national parliaments; and the monitoring of a number of macroeconomic variables (current account balances, competitiveness measures, house prices, and bank credit) aimed at detecting and redressing national macroeconomic imbalances. Failure to take action to eliminate these imbalances could trigger a sanctioning mechanism very much in the spirit of the sanctioning mechanism of the Stability and Growth Pact. We will discuss these features in greater detail in Chapter 10.

The different steps towards completing the monetary union are complementary. They should be taken together. The role of the ECB as a lender of last resort can only be fulfilled if at the same time steps are taken to reinforce the coordination of budgetary policies and to strengthen the mutual control on national governments' deficits and debts. This is necessary because as we have stressed earlier, giving lender of last resort support in government bond markets creates a risk of moral hazard. This could lead to a dynamics tending towards the creation of excessive deficits and debts.

Such a tightening of mutual control of government debts and deficits is also necessary to make a joint issue of Eurobonds feasible. The moral hazard risk implicit in such a joint issue can be reduced by mutual control. In Chapter 10, we return to this problem and we discuss additional features for making joint issues immune to moral hazard risk.

6.4 The theory of optimal currency areas and political union

In the previous sections, we discussed the steps that should be taken to complete the monetary union. Put differently, we studied how one could move towards the kind of political union that the monetary union needs to be embedded in. In this and the following sections we go back to the theory of optimal currency areas and we show how such steps towards a political union have the effect of making the monetary union an optimal currency area.

There is a fundamental difference between the monetary union of the US and that of Europe. The US federal government has a monopoly of the use of coercive power within the union, and will surely prevent any state from seceding from the monetary union. The

Figure 6.3 Symmetry and flexibility as *OCA* criteria.

contrast with the member states of the Eurozone is a very strong one. There is no suprana-tional institution in the EU that can prevent a member state of the Eurozone from seceding. Thus, for the Eurozone to survive, the member states must continue to perceive their membership of the zone to be in their national interest. If that is no longer the case, the temptation to secede will exist and at some point this temptation may lead to secession.[4]

The theory of optimal currency areas determines the conditions that countries should satisfy to make a monetary union attractive, that is, to ensure that the benefits of the monetary union exceed its costs. We used this theory to analyse whether countries should join a monetary union. It can also be used to study the conditions in which existing members of a monetary union will want to leave the union.

We perform this analysis using the same framework as the one used in Fig 4.4. Fig. 6.3 presents the minimal combinations of *symmetry* and *flexibility* that are needed to form an optimal currency area as the downward-sloping *OCA* line. Points on the *OCA* line define combinations of symmetry and flexibility for which the costs and the benefits of a monetary union just balance. We discussed earlier why this is a negatively sloped line. To the right of the *OCA* line, the degree of flexibility is sufficiently large given the degree of symmetry to ensure that the benefits of the union exceed the costs. To the left of the *OCA* line there is insufficient flexibility for any given level of symmetry.

Fig. 6.4 presents the minimal combinations of *symmetry* and *integration* that are needed to form an optimal currency area. The *OCA* line represents the combinations of symmetry and integration among groups of countries for which the costs and benefits of a monetary union just balance. Points to the right of the *OCA* line represent groupings of countries for which the benefits of a monetary union exceed its costs.

We have put the present Eurozone to the left of the *OCA* zone, reflecting the idea that the Eurozone as it is today is incomplete, and as such is a grouping of countries for which some of the members may have more costs than benefits from being in the union. This makes the Eurozone unsustainable in the long run.

---

[4] See the discussion of a potential 'Grexit' in Chapter 5.

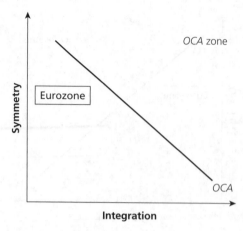

Figure 6.4 Symmetry and integration as *OCA* criteria.

6.5 How does political integration affect the optimality of a monetary union?

As argued earlier, political integration affects the optimality of a monetary union in several ways. First, political union makes it possible to centralize a significant part of national budgets at the level of the union. This in turn makes it possible to organize systems of automatic fiscal transfers that provide some insurance against asymmetric shocks. Thus when one member country is hit by a negative economic shock, the centralized union budget will automatically transfer income from the member states that experience good economic conditions to the member state experiencing a negative shock. We have argued in Chapter 4 (Section 4.5) that this insurance mechanism is particularly important when shocks are temporary and occur as a result of movements in the business cycle. When such an insurance mechanism exists, member states will perceive adherence to the union to be less costly. Second, by consolidating part of the national government debts into a jointly issued union debt, the fragility of the union is reduced, allowing the union to better withstand the movements of distrust afflicting national governments that cannot issue their own money.

Third, a political union reduces the risk of asymmetric shocks that have a political origin. We give some examples that are relevant for the Eurozone. Today, spending and taxation in the Eurozone remain in the hands of national governments and parliaments. As a result, unilateral decisions to lower (or increase) taxes create an asymmetric shock. Similarly, social security and wage policies are decided at the national level. Again, this creates the scope for asymmetric shocks in the Eurozone, as in the case of France when that country decided on its own to lower the working week to 35 hours. We show the implications of this in Box 6.1. From the preceding, it follows that political unification reduces the scope for such asymmetric shocks.

The way one can represent the effect of political unification is twofold (see Fig. 6.5). First, the existence of a centralized budget makes it possible to alleviate the plight of countries hit by a negative shock and reduces the scope for liquidity crises hitting individual member

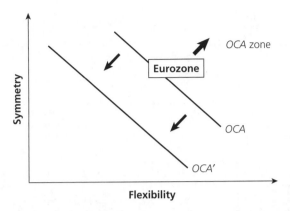

Figure 6.5 Political integration and the optimality of the Eurozone.

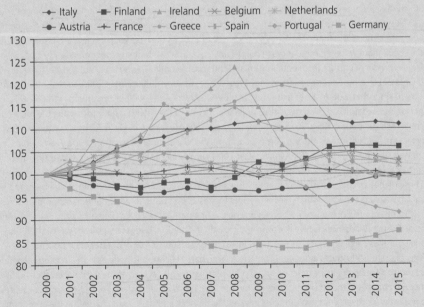

BOX 6.1 Divergences in competitive positions in the Eurozone

The European monetary union started in 1999. One of the surprises of the functioning of that monetary union (called the Eurozone) has been the extent to which the competitive positions of the member countries have diverged. We show the real effective exchange rates in the Eurozone (based on unit labour costs) since 2000 in Fig. 6.6. These indices were discussed in Chapter 2 and measure the evolution of the wage costs of one country relative to the other Eurozone countries after correction for different productivity growth rates (see Fig. 2.5). They can be interpreted as measuring trends in competitiveness of the countries. A declining index means that in the country considered, unit wage costs have decreased relative to the other Eurozone countries, and vice versa. We observe from Fig. 6.6 that prior to the emergence of the Eurozone crisis (from

Figure 6.6 Relative unit labour costs in the Eurozone (2000–15); 2000 = 100.

Note: Performance relative to the rest of the former EU-15: double export weights (PLCDQ).

Source: European Commission, Ameco.

(Continued...)

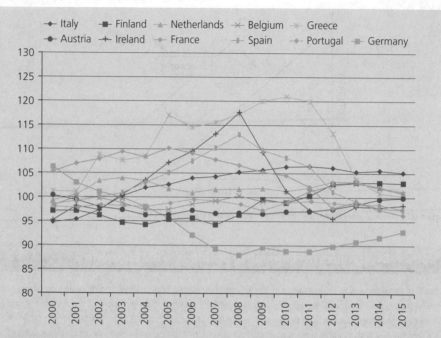

Figure 6.7 Relative unit labour costs in the Eurozone (1999–2015); 1991–2013 = 100.

Note: Performance relative to the rest of the former EU-15: double export weights (PLCDQ).

Source: European Commission, Ameco.

2000 to 2008-9) some countries (Ireland, Greece, Spain, and Italy) lost a significant amount of competitiveness. The only country that gained a significant amount of competitiveness during that time was Germany.

One may criticize this figure because of the choice of 2000 as the base year. Indeed, this choice assumes that in 2000 there were no imbalances in competitive positions, so that any movement away from the 2000 level was a departure from equilibrium and thus problematic. This is surely not the case (see Alcidi and Gros 2010). A number of countries may have been far from equilibrium in 2000, so that movements observed since that date could conceivably be movements towards equilibrium. In order to take this criticism into account, we present relative unit labour costs of the member countries using the long-term average over the period 1991–2013 as the base. The results are shown in Fig. 6.7. The divergence is less spectacular, but still very significant. Fig. 6.8 confirms this: the standard deviation of the yearly indices increased significantly during 2000–2008. After 2008 we observe convergence again, suggesting that countries have adjusted their competitive positions.

These divergent movements in competitiveness within the Eurozone are the result of divergent movements in wage agreements, which are themselves the result of divergent movements in economic conditions. Some countries experienced booms during the first part of the 2000s (Ireland, Spain, Greece); others such as Germany experienced weak economic growth. In addition, budgetary policies were different. Some countries such as Greece and Portugal failed to follow sufficiently tight budgetary policies.

This case study illustrates a deeper problem. A large part of economic policies is still in national hands. Spending and taxation, wage policies, social policies: they are all decided at the national level. In addition, structural changes in the labour markets follow the lines of national borders. This state of affairs creates the potential for divergent developments in wages and prices and significant changes in the competitive position of member countries of the monetary union. It also leads to difficult adjustment problems. These can no longer be facilitated by exchange rate adjustments.

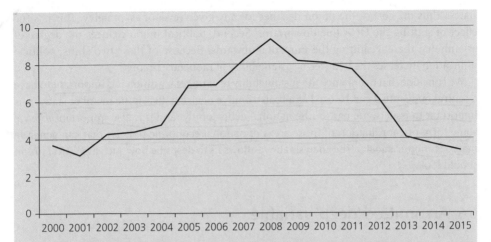

Figure 6.8 Standard deviation in relative unit labour costs in the Eurozone (in percent).

Note: Computed using data from Fig. 6.7.

The countries that lost competitiveness during the boom years from 1999 to 2008 (Greece, Portugal, Spain, Ireland) could improve it only by lowering their wages and prices relative to the other Eurozone countries. This is sometimes called an 'internal devaluation' (in contrast with a devaluation proper, which can no longer be used). Some, including Portugal, Spain, Ireland, and Greece, have made such an improvement, and in fact have been quite successful in engineering such an internal devaluation. Note also from Fig. 6.8 that the standard deviation started to decline after 2008, reflecting the convergence of unit labour costs made possible by these internal devaluations.

These internal devaluations, however, can only be achieved by deflationary macroeconomic policies (mainly budgetary policies). Inevitably, this first leads to a recession and thus (through the operation of the automatic stabilizers) to increases in budget deficits. Most of the analyses in current textbooks merely note that this is a slow and painful process. The analysis of the previous sections, however, allows us to go a little further and to link it with the debt dynamics described earlier. As countries experience increasing budget deficits while they attempt to improve their competitiveness, financial markets are likely to get nervous. Distrust may install itself. If strong enough, this may lead to a liquidity crisis as described before. This then inevitably triggers a solvency crisis.

Thus, the period during which countries try to improve their competitiveness is painful *and* turbulent: painful, because of the recession and the ensuing increase in unemployment; turbulent, because during the adjustment period the country can be hit by sovereign debt and banking crises. This is what has happened in Greece, Ireland, and Portugal. When this happens, the deflationary spiral is bound to be intensified: in such a case the domestic long-term interest rate increases dramatically, forcing the authorities to apply even more budgetary austerity, which in turn leads to an even more intense recession. The banks that are trapped in a funding crisis reduce their credit to the economy. The country finds itself stuck in a bad equilibrium, characterized by austerity programmes that lead to ever increasing government debt-GDP ratios because of the downward pressure on GDP (see Chapter 5). The path towards recovery for members of a monetary union is likely to be crisis-prone.

This also leads to political problems in a democracy. The resistance against the pain inflicted by the austerity programmes destabilizes governments in power and strengthens the position of extreme political parties from the right or the left. The spectre of political instability and upheaval emerges. This has certainly been the case most spectacularly in Greece where an extreme left government came to power in January 2015. But also in other countries (e.g. Spain and Portugal), the deep recessions and large increases in unemployment led to an upheaval in the political landscape.

states. Thus the cost of the union declines for any given level of asymmetry. This has the effect of shifting the *OCA* line downward.[5] Second, political union reduces the degree of asymmetry, thereby shifting the Eurozone upwards. Because of these two shifts, political unification increases the long-term sustainability of monetary unions.[6]

We conclude that to enhance the sustainability of a monetary union it is important to have a central budget that can be used as a redistributive device between the member states; it is important to issue some part of the national debts jointly; and it is also important to have some form of coordination of those areas of national economic policies that can generate macroeconomic shocks. The analysis above allows us to describe how such a political union should look.

6.6 An omitted 'deep' variable

The monetary union between West and East Germany that came about in 1990 after a transition period of barely six months stands in great contrast to the European monetary union. The German monetary union was part of a larger political union. Thus, on 1 July 1990 the monetary union was established together with a unification of all important macroeconomic instruments (budgetary policies, transfer system, wage bargaining, social security, regulatory environment). There can be no doubt that such a comprehensive political union came about as a result of a strong national sense of common purpose and an intense feeling of belonging to the same nation.[7] In a way, it can be said that this sense of common purpose was the deep variable that made the monetary and political union possible in Germany. Put differently, monetary and political union were endogenous variables that were driven by a common force. The existence of this deep variable made it inconceivable that Germany would have started with a monetary union without having a centralized budget capable of making large transfers between regions, or without a unified social security system.

This deep variable is weakly developed at the European level. It is this weakness of the deep variable that makes progress towards political union so difficult in Europe. The weakness of the deep variable also explains why Europe started with monetary union. The latter can be considered to be the easy part on the road to political union. But at the same time it puts the whole process at risk. Without a sense of common purpose it is very doubtful that further progress will be made towards political union. And as we have argued, without these steps towards political union the monetary union will remain a fragile construction.

From this perspective, the enlargement of the Eurozone that occurred with the entry of Slovenia (1 January 2007), Slovakia (1 January 2009), Estonia (1 January 2011), Latvia (1 January 2014), and Lithuania (1 January 2015) creates a risk. There can be little doubt that the enlargement will weaken the sense of common purpose. The deep variable that

---

[5] It is important that these transfers be reversible so that they maintain their insurance character. If these transfers attain a permanent one-way character they are likely to become unpopular in the donor country, leading to a perception of a high cost from the monetary union. This calls for the use of transfers only to alleviate the effects of temporary asymmetric shocks (business cycle movements) or, in the case of permanent asymmetric shocks, making such transfers temporary, allowing receiving countries to spread the adjustment cost over a longer time.

[6] A similar analysis can be done using the symmetry–integration space of Fig. 6.3.

[7] See Baldwin and Wyplosz (2006) on this issue.

drives the dynamics towards political union may therefore become even weaker than it already is.

6.7 Conclusion

The long-term success of the Eurozone depends on the continuing process of political unification. Such a political unification is needed to reduce the scope for the emergence of asymmetric shocks, to reduce the structural fragility of the union in which governments issue debt in a currency over which they have no control, and to embed the Eurozone in a wider system of strong political ties that are needed to take care of the inevitable divergent economic movements within the Eurozone.

Put differently, a political unification is needed because the Eurozone has dramatically weakened the power and legitimacy of nation-states without creating a nation at the European level. In the long run this is not sustainable.

The transition to a monetary union

Introduction

In December 1991, the heads of state of the EU signed a historic treaty in the Dutch city of Maastricht. The Maastricht Treaty went well beyond purely monetary affairs. Nevertheless it is best known for the blueprint it provided for progress towards monetary unification in Europe.

The Maastricht Treaty strategy for moving towards monetary union in Europe was based on two principles.[1] First, the transition towards monetary union was seen as a gradual one, extending over a period of many years. Second, entry into the union was made conditional on satisfying convergence criteria. In this chapter, we analyse this Maastricht strategy. It remains relevant since those EU countries wishing to join EMU in the future will have to abide by it.

It is important to be aware that the Maastricht strategy was not the only one available. In fact, throughout history, monetary unification has quite often been organized in a very different way. Take as an example the German monetary unification, which happened on 1 July 1990. The characteristic features of the German monetary union were its speed and the absence of any convergence requirement. The decision to go ahead with monetary union was taken at the end of 1989, and six months later German monetary union was a reality. As will be seen in the next section, it took the EU more than ten years to do the same. In addition, East Germany was allowed into the West German monetary area without any conditions attached. Surely, had Maastricht-type convergence requirements been imposed on East Germany, German monetary union would not have occurred. All this shows that a monetary union *can* be established quickly and without prior conditions. It does not show, of course, that this was the desirable way to organize a monetary union in Europe.

7.1 The Maastricht Treaty

The approach set out in the Treaty was based on principles of gradualism and convergence. Let us analyse the details of this approach.

---

[1] In this, the Treaty was very much influenced by the Delors Committee Report, which was issued in 1989. See Committee on the Study of Economic and Monetary Union (1989).

As mentioned earlier, the Maastricht Treaty was signed in 1991. Twelve years later, monetary union in the EU was a fact. This period of 12 years was one of gradual transition. The main characteristic of this transition process was the requirement that candidate countries had to go through a process of convergence of their economies. This convergence process was described in detail in the Treaty. The Treaty stipulated that the transition to the final stage of monetary union was conditional on a number of 'convergence criteria'. A country can join the union only if:

1. its inflation rate is not more than 1.5% higher than the average of the three lowest inflation rates among the EU member states;

2. its long-term interest rate is not more than 2% higher than the average observed in these three low-inflation countries;

3. it has joined the exchange rate mechanism of the EMS and has not experienced a devaluation during the two years preceding the entrance into the union;

4. its government budget deficit is not higher than 3% of its GDP (if it is, it should be declining continuously and substantially and come close to the 3% norm, or alternatively, the deviation from the reference value of 3% 'should be exceptional and temporary and remain close to the reference value', Art. 104c(a));

5. its government debt should not exceed 60% of GDP (if it does, it should 'diminish sufficiently and approach the reference value (60%) at a satisfactory pace', Art. 104c(b)).

It was decided in May 1998 that 11 EU countries (Austria, Belgium, Finland, France, Germany, Ireland, Italy, Luxembourg, the Netherlands, Portugal, and Spain) satisfied these convergence criteria. Greece did not satisfy these criteria at that time, but did so very soon afterwards so that it was ready to introduce the euro on 1 January 2002 with the other 11 countries.[2] Monetary union in Europe was a fact. Three countries (Denmark, Sweden, and the UK) decided to stay out of the Eurozone despite the fact that they satisfied the convergence criteria. The UK obtained the right to opt out and Denmark the right to subject its entry to a national referendum. Sweden decided not to join and used a loophole in the Treaty, i.e. it refused to enter the exchange rate mechanism of the EMS before the start of the third stage, thereby deliberately failing to satisfy one of the entry conditions. On 1 January 2007, Slovenia became the 13th member of the Eurozone. Cyprus and Malta followed on 1 January 2008, Slovakia became the 16th member country on 1 January 2009, Estonia the 17th member on 1 January 2011, Latvia the 18th member on 1 January 2014, and Lithuania the 19th member on 1 January 2015. The euro is now (in 2016) used by more than 320 million Europeans as their everyday currency.

One peculiarity about the start of EMU should be noted. Technically monetary union started on 1 January 1999. This was the moment when the European Central Bank took over control from the national central banks, and the euro came into existence. From 1 January 1999 until 31 December 2001, however, the euro did not exist in physical form; it only existed in the books

[2] It turned out afterwards that the budgetary numbers used to decide on the convergence of Greece had in fact been falsified by the Greek government. Greece would never have been allowed to join if the Maastricht convergence criteria had been based on the true numbers.

of the banks. The national currencies continued to circulate in each country, and the exchange rates between them were irrevocably fixed. On 1 January 2002 the euro was introduced in physical form (banknotes and coins) and the national currencies were taken out of circulation.

It should be noted that the national central banks have not disappeared since the start of EMU. They are part of what is called the Eurosystem. These national banks, however, no longer make independent decisions about monetary and exchange rate policies. They are there to implement the decisions taken by the ECB. In this respect the Eurosystem resembles the US Federal Reserve system. National central banks, however, maintain their decision-making powers in the important field of banking supervision.[3] (We will return to some issues relating to the operation of the Eurosystem in Chapters 8 and 9.)

7.2 Why convergence requirements?

We noted earlier that past transitions to monetary unions were usually organized in a different way from the Maastricht Treaty's approach, i.e. once the decision was taken to have a monetary union, this was done quickly without any Maastricht-type convergence requirements being imposed on the prospective members. What is more, the theory of optimum currency areas, which we discussed in previous chapters, is silent about Maastricht-type convergence criteria. Instead, the OCA theory stresses the need to have labour market flexibility and labour mobility as important requirements for a successful monetary union. In addition, it stresses the need to create a budgetary union as a way of strengthening the monetary union, without which it remains incomplete. According to this theory, if these conditions are satisfied, there is no need to wait more than ten years to achieve it. Conversely, if these OCA conditions are not satisfied, it is not a good idea to allow countries to enter the union, even though the Maastricht convergence criteria are met. Why then did the designers of the Treaty stress so much *macro*economic convergence (inflation, interest rates, budgetary policies) prior to the start of EMU, while the theory stresses *micro*economic and political conditions for a successful monetary union?

Inflation convergence

The answer has to do with the fear that the future monetary union would have an inflationary bias. In order to understand this concern it is useful to go back to the Barro–Gordon model that we developed in Chapter 2, and which we now represent in Fig. 7.1. We assume that there are two countries, called Germany and Italy. The two countries are assumed to be identical except for the preferences of the authorities. (We do not really need this assumption. We do this only to be able to put both countries in the same figure.) The German authorities give a high weight to reducing inflation, and the Italian authorities a low weight. This is shown by flat indifference curves for the German authorities and steep ones for the Italian authorities. The natural unemployment rate, u_N, is the same in the two countries, and

---

[3] In some countries the responsibility for banking supervision is vested not in the national central bank but in a separate agency. In these countries, the national bank has few remaining responsibilities. It should also be noted that the supervisory power of the national central banks has been constrained by the creation of a European Banking Authority. In addition, from November 2014 the ECB has become the single supervisor of the systemic banks in the Eurozone. We analyse the functions of this new authority and of the ECB in Chapters 8 and 9.

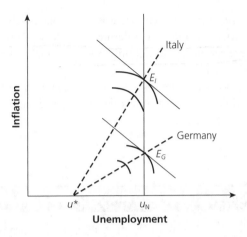

Figure 7.1 The inflation bias in a monetary union.

so is the target unemployment rate of the authorities, u^*. Inflation equilibrium is achieved at E_G in Germany and E_I in Italy. Thus, inflation is on average higher in Italy than in Germany without any gain in unemployment for Italy.

A monetary union between the two countries implies that a common central bank takes over. Two propositions can now easily be established. First, the low-inflation country (Germany) reduces its welfare by forming a monetary union with the high-inflation country. This is so because the union's central bank is likely to reflect the average preferences of the participating countries. As a result, the union inflation rate increases and will be located between E_G and E_I. (There are of course other sources of gains in a monetary union, e.g. lower transaction costs, lower risk, etc., which we discussed in Chapter 3, and which are outside the model of Fig. 7.1. These efficiency gains must then be compared with the welfare losses resulting from higher inflation.)

The second proposition follows from the first: since the low-inflation country, Germany, loses when it joins the union with Italy, it will not want to do so unless it can impose conditions. It follows from the analysis of Fig. 7.1 that one condition must be that the union's central bank should have the same preferences as the German central bank. This can be achieved in two ways. One is that the European Central Bank should be a close copy of the Bundesbank. What this means will be analysed in Chapter 8.

This condition, however, may not be sufficient from the point of view of Germany, because the European Central Bank is composed of representatives of the participating countries. Even if the ECB is made a close copy of the Bundesbank, these representatives may still have different inflation preferences. The German representative may be put in a minority position, so that the equilibrium inflation rate in the union would exceed the German one. In order to avoid this outcome Germany wants to control entry into the union, so that only those countries with the same preferences join the union (see Morales and Padilla 1994).

The Maastricht inflation entry conditions can now be interpreted from this perspective. Before the union started, the candidate member countries were asked to provide evidence that they cared about a low inflation rate in the same way as Germany did. This they did, by bringing down their inflation rate to the German level. During this disinflationary process, a temporary increase in the unemployment rate was inevitable (a movement along the short-term Phillips curve). This self-imposed suffering was added evidence for Germany that countries like Italy were serious about fighting inflation. Once the proof was given, these countries could be let in safely.

As it turned out, inflation stayed low in these countries after the introduction of the euro, although there were widespread perceptions that the introduction of the euro led to an acceleration of inflation (see Box 7.1).

BOX 7.1 The introduction of the euro and perceived price increases

One major surprise about the introduction of the euro is its unpopularity in a number of Eurozone countries. In Italy, Germany, and Greece, the introduction of the euro is associated with large price increases.

The official response to this strong perception of the euro as an engine for large price increases has been first to deny it, and then later to acknowledge it but to argue that it is quantitatively unimportant. And yet the evidence we now have is that, indeed, in some countries the introduction of the euro has coincided with large price increases in certain product categories. In Table 7.1, we show the price increases of different food categories in Italy from November 2001 to November 2002. These calculations are based on a sample of 150 food items. It appears that food prices in Italy increased on average by 30% during the year following the introduction of the euro.

The purchase of food is a very repetitive behaviour occurring almost daily. In addition, there is a sense of basic needs involved. As a result, such price increases have created a strong perception in Italy, and also in other countries, that the introduction of the euro has led to a loss of purchasing power and a general impoverishment of consumers. The authorities reacted by stressing that because of their low weight in the consumption basket, these price increases barely affected the rate of inflation (which is correct). This reaction in no way reduced the perception of consumers of a strong general price increase after the introduction of the euro.

Table 7.1 Price increases of food products in Italy (from November 2001 to November 2002)

Breakfast (bread, snacks)	23.3%
Pasta, bread, rice	20.1%
Beverages	32.9%
Meat, eggs, and fresh fish	22.1%
Cold meats	27.5%
Canned food	30.9%
Fruit and vegetables	50.8%
Frozen food	23.6%
Average	29.2%

Source: Eurispes (2003).

Few economists expected such large price increases to occur in basic consumption items. Yet they did. How did this happen? One possible answer is the following: food products are sold in markets that are relatively competitive. At the same time, the price elasticity of the demand for food is low. In normal circumstances, it is very difficult for individual suppliers to exploit the low price elasticity and to raise the price without being punished by a loss of business. In order to raise the price of food and to exploit the low price elasticities, it should be raised by all suppliers at the same time. Collective action is necessary. But under normal circumstances, the cost of collective action is high. Once in a while, however, a window of opportunity arises that lowers the costs of collective action. The introduction of the euro was such a window of opportunity. In some countries, the possibility arose of rounding up the prices in euros at the same time. This could only be done at one moment, i.e. the introduction of the euro, which was an eminently collective decision. At the moment of the introduction of the euro it appeared as if the authorities were blowing a whistle that allowed the suppliers to coordinate their action and jointly raise their prices.

The preceding analysis is confirmed by a study by three Italian economists, Giancarlo Marini, Fabrizio Adriani, and Pasquale Scaramozzino (see Marini et al. 2004). They document large increases in restaurant prices within the Eurozone compared to non-Eurozone countries just after the changeover to the euro. It should be added, however, that some economists dispute that these changes in restaurant prices have been large enough to be accounted for by the introduction of the euro (see Gaiotti and Lippi 2004).

We have learned our lesson for the future. Similar experiences are likely to occur in the new member states when these join the Eurozone. It thus appears that the introduction of the euro in the new member states of the European Union may have to be accompanied by a system of temporary price controls. Such a system can prevent the large price increases brought about by a temporary lowering of the collective action costs of raising prices at the same moment. Such a system will also avoid the post-natal depressions that have occurred in several countries after the birth of the euro.

For the same reasons, the Central European countries wishing to enter the Eurozone have to go through the same disinflationary process. In doing so they prove to the existing members of EMU that they pursue the same objectives of inflationary stability.

Budgetary convergence

Can the budgetary convergence requirements (3% norm for the budget deficit and 60% norm for government debt) be rationalized in a way similar to the inflation convergence requirement? The answer is positive. Let us take again the case of Italy and Germany. Italy has a high debt-to-GDP ratio (more than 100% during the 1990s before its entry into the Eurozone). A high government debt creates incentives for the Italian government to engineer a surprise inflation. The reason is that some of the Italian government bonds are long term. The interest rate on these bonds was fixed in a previous period based on the then prevailing expectations of inflation. If the government now creates an unexpectedly higher inflation, the real value of these bonds will be eroded and the bondholders will obtain insufficient compensation because the interest rate on their bonds does not reflect this inflation upsurge. Bondholders lose. The Italian government gains. (Obviously, if the bondholders are rational, they will no longer be willing to invest in Italian bonds unless they obtain an extra risk premium on these bonds. Thus, the systematic use of surprise inflation by the Italian authorities may become quite costly in the long run. Rational governments, therefore, will not systematically produce surprise inflation. The problem here is that the political system may create a very short-term outlook for politicians, who will continue to be tempted to create inflation surprises.)

From the preceding analysis, it follows that a monetary union between low- and high-debt countries creates a problem for the low-debt country. In the union, the low-debt country will be confronted with a partner who will have a tendency to push for more inflation. This may happen even if these countries have the same preferences regarding inflation. As long as one country has a higher debt–GDP ratio it will have an incentive to create surprise inflation. As a result, the low-debt country stands to lose and will insist that the debt–GDP ratio of the highly indebted country be reduced prior to entry into the monetary union. In order to achieve this, the high-debt country must reduce its government budget deficit. Once this is achieved the incentives for that country to produce surprise inflation disappear, and it can safely be allowed into the union.[4] Note again that the argument for debt and deficit reduction prior to entry into EMU is made not because countries with high debt and deficits cannot form a monetary union, but because allowing these countries into the union increases the risk of more inflation in the future EMU.

Other arguments have been developed to justify deficit and debt reductions as conditions for entry into the union. One is that the authorities with a large debt face a higher default risk. If they are allowed into the union, this will increase the pressure for a bailout in the event of a default crisis. The fear that this may happen also explains the *no-bailout* clause that was incorporated into the Maastricht Treaty, i.e. the clause that says that neither national governments nor the European Central Bank can be forced to bail out other member countries.[5] In Chapter 10, where we discuss fiscal policies in monetary unions, we will return to this issue.

Whereas serious arguments can be found to justify the requirements that countries should reduce their government debts and deficits prior to entry, the numerical precision with which these requirements have been formulated is much more difficult to rationalize. This has led many economists to criticize the 3% and 60% norms as arbitrary, or worse, as some form of voodoo economics (see Buiter et al. 1993 and Wickens 1993 among others). But let us at least find some rational grounds for imposing the budgetary numbers of 3% and 60%.

The 3% and 60% budgetary norms seem to have been derived from the well-known formula determining the budget deficit needed to stabilize the government debt:[6]

$$d = gb$$

where b is the (steady state) level at which the government debt is to be stabilized (as a percentage of GDP), g is the growth rate of nominal GDP, and d is the government budget deficit (as a percentage of GDP).

The formula shows that in order to stabilize the government debt at 60% of GDP, the budget deficit must be brought to 3% of GDP if and only if the nominal growth rate of GDP is 5% ($0.03 = 0.05 \times 0.6$).

---

[4] It can be argued that if the Italian authorities reduce the maturity of their debt, the incentives to create surprise inflation are reduced. Thus, as a substitute for a debt reduction, one could ask the Italian authorities to reduce the maturity of their debt prior to entry into the EMU. The problem with this is that when the maturity of the debt reduces, it becomes more vulnerable to changes in the interest rate, which may lead to liquidity crises as the authorities find it difficult to roll over their debt.

[5] The no-bailout clause is often (mis)interpreted to imply that it is forbidden for one country to voluntarily bailout another country. The Maastricht Treaty does not forbid altruism if this is voluntary. The no-bailout clause should be interpreted as a no-liability clause, i.e. governments cannot be forced to take over the debt of other countries against their will.

[6] This is confirmed in Bini-Smaghi et al. (1993). The formula is derived as follows. The budget deficit (D) is financed by issuing new debt:

$$\dot{B} = D$$

(where B is the government debt and a dot above a variable signifies a rate of increase per unit of time). By definition one can write:

$$\dot{B} = \dot{b}Y + b\dot{Y}$$

The rule is quite arbitrary on two counts. First, it is unclear why the debt should be stabilized at 60%. Other numbers, e.g. 70% or 50%, would do as well. In that case, the deficit to be aimed at should also be different, i.e. 3.5% and 2.5%, respectively. The only reason why 60% seems to have been chosen at Maastricht was that at that time this was the average debt–GDP ratio in the EU. Second, the rule is conditional on the nominal growth rate of GDP. Some countries, e.g. the new member states from Central Europe, have high nominal growth rates allowing them to have higher budget deficits that stabilize the government debt at 60%. In contrast some countries experience lower nominal growth rates. This implies that if they want to stabilize their debt to GDP ratio at 60% of GDP they have to run lower budget deficits.

In the preceding paragraphs we have focused on the inflation and budgetary convergence requirements. Let us briefly discuss the rationale of the other convergence rules, i.e. the no-devaluation rule and the interest rate convergence requirement.

Exchange rate convergence (no-devaluation requirement)

The main motivation for requiring countries not to have devalued during the two years prior to their entry into the EMU is straightforward. The requirement prevents countries from manipulating their exchange rates so as to force entry at a more favourable exchange rate (a depreciated one, which would increase their competitive position). The stringency of this requirement, however, has been reduced considerably since the Maastricht Treaty was signed. This has to do with the peculiar way the no-devaluation condition is formulated in the Treaty. According to the Treaty, countries should maintain their exchange rates within the 'normal' band of fluctuation (without changing that band) during the two years preceding their entry into the EMU. At the moment of the signing of the Treaty, the normal band was $2 \times 2.25\%$. Since August 1993, the 'normal' band within the EMS has been $2 \times 15\%$, a considerably larger band of fluctuation.

The exchange rate arrangements for the potential newcomers (the new member countries of the EU: Denmark, Sweden, and the UK) are similar but not identical. They will be discussed in Section 7.4.

Interest rate convergence

We come finally to the interest rate convergence requirement. The justification for this rule is that excessively large differences in interest rates prior to entry could lead to large capital gains

---

[6] *continued* (where $b = B/Y$ and Y is GDP). Combining the two expressions yields:

$$D = \dot{b}Y + b\dot{Y} \quad \text{or} \quad \frac{D}{Y} = \dot{b} + b\frac{\dot{Y}}{Y}$$

which is rewritten as follows:

$$\dot{b} = d - gb$$

$$\left(\text{where } d = \frac{D}{Y}, g = \frac{\dot{Y}}{Y} \right)$$

In the steady state, $\dot{b} = 0$ which implies that $d = gb$.

and losses at the moment of entry into EMU. Suppose, for example, that the UK decides to join EMU and that at the moment of entry its long-term bond rate is 5% while the long-term bond rate in euros is 4%. At the moment of entry the euro–sterling rate will be fixed irrevocably. As a result, it will be quite attractive for bondholders to arbitrage, i.e. to sell low-yield euro denominated bonds and to buy high-yield sterling denominated bonds. Since the exchange rate is irrevocably fixed there is no exchange risk involved in such an arbitrage. As a result, it will continue until the return on euro and sterling bonds is equalized. This will lead to a drop in the price of euro bonds and an increase in the price of sterling bonds, until the yields are equal. Thus, economic agents (mainly financial institutions in the Eurozone) holding euro bonds will make capital losses, and economic agents holding sterling bonds (mainly UK financial institutions) will make capital gains. These could create disturbances in national capital markets. In order to limit these disturbances the interest differentials have to be reduced prior to entry into EMU.

The peculiarity of this rule is its self-fulfilling nature. The rule says that the long-term government bond rate of a prospective member should not exceed the interest rate level (+ 2%) in the Eurozone.[7] Now consider the UK again. Suppose it is expected to join in, say, 2017 (a very unlikely event). It can easily be seen that the long-term bond rate will start converging prior to entry. As a result, the capital gains and losses (which are inevitable) will be borne long before the entry into the union. At the start of the union, these capital gains and losses will be very small. The upshot of all this is that the interest rate convergence criterion is redundant. As soon as countries are expected to satisfy the other criteria, market forces make sure that interest rates quickly converge. This also happened prior to the start of EMU. Once countries were expected to join EMU, long-term interest rates converged automatically. For countries like Spain, Ireland, Greece, Portugal, and Italy, where interest rates had previously been very high, this led to strong declines in the long-term interest rates prior to the start of EMU. This also contributed to strong economic booms in some of these countries at the beginning of EMU.

7.3 Technical problems during the transition: how to fix the conversion rates

The transition to EMU created a number of technical problems. These problems were mastered quite skilfully, but it remains important to analyse them because they will re-emerge when other countries decide to join EMU.

On 1 January 1999, the exchange rates of the national currencies within the euro were fixed irrevocably. This took place remarkably smoothly. How was this done? The problem faced prior to the conversion date was the following. The Treaty, together with a decision taken at the Madrid Council of 1995, implied that on 1 January 1999 one ECU would be converted into one euro. At the same time, the conversion rates of the national currencies into the euro had to be equal to the market rates of these currencies against the ECU at the close of the market on 31 December 1998. The latter condition was introduced to make sure that the start of EMU would not be accompanied by jumps in the exchange value of the currencies, thereby creating large capital gains and losses.

---

[7] Note that prior to the start of EMU the requirement was that the interest rate of the prospective members had to be at most 2% above the interest rate of the three EMS countries with the lowest rates of inflation.

Table 7.2 Conversion rates of EMU currencies into the euro

Belgian franc	40.3399
Spanish peseta	166.386
Irish punt	0.787564
Luxembourg franc	40.3399
Austrian schilling	13.7603
Finnish markka	5.94573
German mark	1.95583
French franc	6.55957
Italian lira	1936.27
Dutch guilder	2.20371
Portuguese escudo	200.482

These conditions created the potential for self-fulfilling speculative movements of exchange rates prior to 31 December 1998. The reason can be explained as follows. (In Box 7.2 we go into this problem in a more technical way.) Since the authorities had announced that the market rates of the last day prior to EMU would be used as the conversion rates to be fixed forever on the next day, any movement on the last day would be self-validating. Thus, if on that last day some Soros of this world were to drive up the value of, say, the German mark relative to the French franc, this higher DM/FF exchange rate would then be irrevocably fixed the next day. In other words, there was nothing to anchor the beliefs of the market, so that the exchange rates could drift in any direction as one approached the conversion date.

Such a result had to be avoided, for it could lead to permanently fixing wrong values for the exchange rates, creating a situation in which some currencies would be undervalued and others overvalued almost permanently. A number of academic researchers solved this problem by proposing that the authorities announce long enough in advance the fixed values at which the currencies would be converted into each other at the start of EMU.[8] If these announcements were credible, then the market would smoothly drive the market rates towards the fixed conversion rates announced.

This is exactly what happened. The authorities announced the fixed bilateral conversion rates in May 1998. They are shown in Table 7.2. They chose the central rates of these currencies in the EMS. The authorities made this announcement credible by also announcing that the central banks of the EMU candidate countries would closely cooperate in setting monetary policies. They also made it clear that they would be willing to intervene to an unlimited degree to make sure that the market rates were driven towards the fixed conversion rates announced. In fact, very little intervention was necessary. Market participants were very confident that the announced rates would also be the conversion rates. As a result, speculation became stabilizing. As we moved closer and closer to the date of conversion, the market rates converged more and more closely with the fixed conversion rates. In addition, the variability of these market exchange rates declined progressively as we moved closer to 31 December 1998. (In Box 7.2 we show why this had to happen.) All this happened while the world was being hit by major financial crises during the second half of 1998 (in South-East Asia and Russia).

[8] Begg et al. (1997) and De Grauwe and Spaventa (1997) made such a proposal.

BOX 7.2 How to fix conversion rates

In order to analyse the nature of the problem, we use a simple model of the determination of the exchange rate. Let us assume that the exchange rate to be fixed at the start of EMU is the DM/FF rate. We can write that exchange rate as follows:

$$S_t = Z_t + bE_t\Delta S_{t+1} \tag{7.1}$$

where S_t is the DM/FF rate at time t, $E_t\Delta S_{t+1}$ is the expectation held at t about the change in the exchange rate at $t+1$, and Z_t is a vector of fundamental variables at time t affecting the exchange rate at time t. These fundamentals can be the money stock, prices, the current account, etc. Equation (7.1) can be rewritten as:

$$S_t = (1-\beta)Z_t + \beta E_t S_{t+1} \tag{7.2}$$

where $\beta = \dfrac{b}{1+b}$ and $(1-\beta) = \dfrac{1}{1+b}$.

This equation says that the current exchange rate is a weighted average of current fundamentals and the expected future level of the exchange rate.

One can now solve this equation assuming rational expectations as follows. Rational expectations imply that agents use all available information to forecast the future exchange rate. This means that when forecasting the future exchange rate, they will use the same model as in (7.2), i.e.:

$$E_t S_{t+1} = (1-\beta)E_t Z_{t+1} + \beta E_t S_{t+2} \tag{7.3}$$

Substituting (7.3) into (7.2) yields:

$$S_t = (1-\beta)Z_t + \beta[(1-\beta)E_t Z_{t+1} + \beta E_t S_{t+2}] \tag{7.4}$$

When forecasting S_{t+2}, rational agents will proceed in exactly the same way, i.e. using (7.2). Continuing this process of forecasting future exchange rates yields:

$$S_t = (1-\beta)[Z_t + \beta E_t Z_{t+1} + \dots \beta^{T-t-1}E_t Z_{T-1}] + \beta^{T-t}E_t S_T \tag{7.5}$$

where T is the time of the start of EMU (the conversion date). Thus, the exchange rate at time t is a weighted average of the fundamental variables that agents forecast up till the start of EMU (at time T) and their forecast of the conversion rate that will be applied. As time moves forward, more and more terms in the brackets drop out and so do the weights attached to the fundamentals. Note also that β can be considered as a discount factor, so that as we move closer and closer to T, β converges to 1. Thus, in the limit as we have moved arbitrarily close to T we obtain

$$S_t = E_t S_T$$

which becomes $S_t = S_T$ when $t = T$.

This result illustrates the indeterminacy of the exchange rate when the authorities announced that the conversion rate at time T would be equal to the market rate obtained just prior to the date of conversion. In that case, any expectation that the market had about the conversion rate would be self-validating. In other words, there are infinitely many exchange rates that satisfy this condition.

In order to anchor the market's expectations it was necessary to announce in advance what the conversion rate would be. This is what the authorities did in May 1998. Let us call the announced DM/FF rate S^* (a fixed number). The DM/FF exchange rate then becomes:

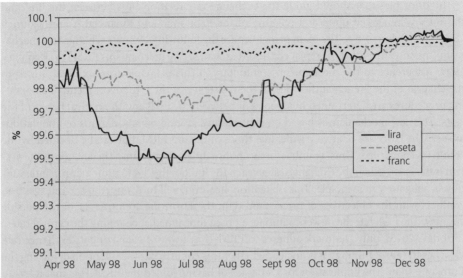

Figure 7.2 Market exchange rates of DM in 1998 relative to conversion rates.

Note: For more detail, see De Grauwe et al. (1999).

Source: Datastream.

$$S_t = (1-\beta)[Z_t + \beta E_t Z_{t+1} + \beta^2 E_t Z_{t+2} + ... \beta^{T-t-1} E_t Z_{T-1}] + \beta^{T-t} S^* \tag{7.6}$$

As we move closer to T, the exchange rate must smoothly converge towards the fixed number S^*.

Note also that the variance of S_t can be written as the sum of the variances and covariances of the present and future fundamentals. As we move closer to T, more and more fundamentals between the brackets drop out and so do their variances and covariances. In addition, the weight of the final conversion rate increases. Since the final conversion rate is a fixed number, its variance is zero. Thus, as we move closer to T the variance of S_t also converges to zero. All this, of course, assumes that the announced conversion rate S^* is fully credible.

The prediction of this simple model came out beautifully. We illustrate this graphically in Fig. 7.2. This shows a number of exchange rates against the DM. We observe the smooth convergence towards the announced conversion rate (normalized at 100). We also observe that as we moved towards the date of conversion, the variability declined.

Note that the model we have used here is an application of a well-known exchange rate model introduced by Mussa (1979). In normal exchange markets that are not assumed to disappear at some final date (as we have assumed here), the last term in equation (7.5) disappears, i.e. as $T \rightarrow \infty$, $\beta^{T-t} E_t S_T \rightarrow 0$ since $|\beta| < 1$ (assuming that S_T does not go to infinity).

7.4 How to organize relations between the 'ins' and the 'outs'

Today (2016) EMU consists of 19 out of 28 EU member countries. This situation leads to the issue of how exchange rate relations should be organized between these two groups of countries. The main issue that arises here is the exchange rate regime that should be set up between the euro and the currencies of the 'outs'.

The principles that should guide the exchange rate relationships between the 'ins' and the 'outs' were agreed upon at a meeting of the Economic and Financial Affairs Council (ECOFIN) in June 1996. The main principles are the following. A new exchange rate mechanism (the so-called ERM-II) replaced the old exchange rate mechanism (ERM) on 1 January 1999. Adherence to the mechanism is voluntary.[9] (This principle was accepted, much to the chagrin of the French authorities, at the insistence of the UK government.) Its operating procedures are determined in agreement between the ECB and the central banks of the 'outs'. The new mechanism is based on central rates around which margins of fluctuations are set. The latter are relatively wide, like those of the old ERM, but can be decided by the countries concerned. Thus, countries may choose different margins. The anchor of the system is the euro. When the exchange rates reach the limit of the fluctuation margin, intervention is obligatory in principle. This obligation, however, will be dropped if the intervention conflicts with the objectives of price stability in the Eurozone countries or in the outside country. The ECB has the power to initiate a procedure aimed at changing the central rates.

Today (2015), only Denmark adheres to ERM-II as a way of stabilizing its exchange rate vis-à-vis the euro, although it is unclear whether this country has the intention of joining the Eurozone soon. The implication for Denmark of having joined the ERM-II is that it has to follow the decisions of the ECB to raise or lower the interest rate very closely, without having a say in the decisions made by the ECB.

The UK, the most prominent outsider, has made it clear that it does not want to be constrained by an ERM type of arrangement, even when the band of fluctuation is relatively wide. There is thus very little choice but to have a floating sterling–euro exchange rate until the UK decides to join the Eurozone, if it does. This may create problems if in the future this exchange rate fluctuates a great deal and creates large movements in the competitive position of the UK economy relative to the Eurozone economy. The only conceivable constraint that could exist for the UK, while it stays outside the Eurozone, is given by Article 109 m of the Treaty. This says that member states that do not participate in EMU should 'treat their exchange rate policies as a matter of common interest and it is accordingly agreed that exchange rates should be monitored and assessed at the Community level with a view, in particular, to avoiding any distortion in the single market'. Up to now this has remained a dead letter.

Another EU country that has not adhered to the ERM-II is Sweden. As will be remembered, Sweden decided to stay out of the Eurozone by not joining the ERM prior to 1999. Entering this exchange rate arrangement would legally bind Sweden also to enter the Eurozone (provided the other convergence criteria are satisfied). Thus Sweden is using a loophole in the Treaty to avoid having to enter the Eurozone, despite the fact that it is committed to do so. Other EU member countries that today are not in the Eurozone are likely to use the same loophole if they do not wish to enter the Eurozone despite their commitment to become part of the monetary union.

Finally, there is the issue of the intervention commitment of the ECB. The principles agreed upon today stipulate that the ECB should stand ready for unlimited intervention when, say, the Danish kroner drops below the lower limit of the band, unless this intervention would

---

[9] Note, however, that as mentioned earlier, countries that want to enter the Eurozone have to be a member of the ERM-II for two years prior to entry.

jeopardize price stability in the Eurozone. This may seem to seriously reduce the intervention commitment of the ECB. However, it is very unlikely that ECB interventions could destabilize price levels in the Eurozone. The countries that are now in ERM-II or that may join in the future are small relative to the whole of the euro area, so that the intervention activities of the ECB will have a small quantitative impact in the euro money market. In addition, the ECB is likely to sterilize these interventions so that they will not affect the Eurozone money markets. It is therefore reasonable to conclude that if the ECB is committed to intervene, it can do so without jeopardizing price stability in the Eurozone.

To conclude, it should be stressed that the ERM-II arrangement makes sense only in the framework of a temporary regime that facilitates the quick convergence and acceptance of the 'outs' into the Eurozone. If the prospects for quick entry by the 'outs' are weak, then an ERM-II arrangement may be undesirable. It may then face similar problems to those the EMS experienced in 1992–3 with speculative crises and a collapse of the arrangement.

7.5 Conclusion

The Maastricht strategy followed by the EU countries was successful in bringing about EMU in Europe. Few observers had expected this success in the early 1990s. The transition towards EMU was based on two principles, gradualism and convergence. The latter requires prospective members to satisfy convergence requirements. These will continue to be important for the Central European countries, the UK, Denmark, and Sweden when and if these countries decide to join the Eurozone.

The technical problems associated with the start of EMU were solved remarkably well. In particular, the decision to announce fixed conversion rates in May 1998 stabilized the exchange markets in Europe. This stability was maintained despite the world financial upheavals in the second half of 1998.

The theory of optimum currency areas, which we discussed in previous chapters, is silent about Maastricht-type convergence criteria. Instead, the OCA theory stresses the need to have labour market flexibility and labour mobility as important requirements for a successful monetary union. In addition, it stresses the need to create a budgetary union as a way to strengthen the monetary union, without which it remains incomplete. According to the OCA theory, if these conditions are not satisfied, it is not a good idea to allow countries to enter the union, even though the Maastricht convergence criteria are met. We argued that the Maastricht convergence criteria were invented to solve a political problem, i.e. the reluctance of Germany to enter into a monetary union with countries that had a history of high inflation and high government debts and deficits.

It is unclear to what extent the emergence of the sovereign debt crisis in the euro area has affected the desire of the new member states of Central Europe to join the euro area. Much will depend on how this debt crisis is resolved. Smaller countries such as Estonia, Latvia, Slovakia, and Lithuania decided to join (respectively in 2009, 2011, 2014, and 2015). It is as yet unclear how the other Central European countries will decide.

8 The European Central Bank

Introduction

The centrepiece of the European Monetary Union is the European Central Bank (ECB). This is the institution that took over the monetary decision-making powers from the national central banks when the Eurozone was created in 1999. In this chapter, we analyse the nature of that institution. We look at how it was designed and the characteristic features of this design. We also develop some criticism of the way the ECB was designed. These design failures have now become apparent with the eruption of the financial crisis.

8.1 The design of the ECB: the Maastricht Treaty

In the post-war period, two models of central banking evolved. One may be called the *Anglo-French model*, and the other the *German model*. These two models differed from each other on two counts. One was concerned with the objectives a central bank should pursue, and the other related to the institutional design of the central bank.

- *The objectives of the central bank.* In the Anglo-French model, the central bank pursues several objectives, e.g. price stability, stabilization of the business cycle, maintenance of high employment, and financial stability. In this model, price stability is only one of the objectives and does not receive any privileged treatment. This is very different in the German model, where price stability is considered to be the primary objective of the central bank. And, although the central bank can pursue other objectives, this is always conditional on the requirement that their pursuit does not endanger price stability.

- *The institutional design of the central bank.* The Anglo-French model is characterized by the political dependence of the central bank, i.e. monetary policy decisions are subject to the government's (the minister of finance's) approval. Thus, in this model, the decision to raise or to lower the interest rate is taken by the minister of finance. Things are very different in the German model, where the guiding principle is political independence. Decisions about the interest rate are taken by the central bank without interference from political authorities. This principle is enshrined in the statutes of the central bank and jealously guarded by the central bank authorities.[1]

---

[1] In the German model, there is some ambiguity about who is responsible for the exchange rate policy: the central bank or the government. We return to this issue at a later stage.

When the European countries negotiated the Maastricht Treaty, a choice between these two models had to be made. It may now be said that the Anglo-French model was discarded as a guide to the design of the European Central Bank, and that the German model prevailed. This is made clear by analysing the statutes of the ECB, which are enshrined in the Maastricht Treaty.

On the objectives of the ECB, the Treaty is very clear. According to Article 105, the primary objective of the ECB is the maintenance of price stability. The same Article adds:

> Without prejudice to the objective of price stability, the ECB shall support the general economic policies in the Community with a view to contributing to the achievement of the objectives of the Community as laid down in Article 2 *(Article 105(1))*.

Article 2 of the Treaty defines these objectives, which include 'a high level of employment'. Thus, the Treaty recognizes the need for the ECB to pursue other objectives. However, these objectives are seen as secondary, i.e. they should not interfere with the primary objective of price stability.

In a similar vein, the Treaty is very clear on political independence. This principle is formulated in very strong language in Article 107:

> When exercising the powers and carrying out the tasks and duties conferred upon them by this Treaty … neither the ECB nor a national central bank, nor any member of their decision-making bodies shall seek or take instructions from Community institutions or bodies, from any Government of a Member State or from any other body.

In addition, the Treaty recognizes that political independence is a necessary condition for ensuring price stability. In the absence of political independence, the central bank can be forced to print money to finance government budget deficits. This is the surest way to inflation. In order to exclude this, the following sentence was included in the Treaty:

> Overdraft facilities or any other type of credit facility with the European Central Bank or with the national central banks of the Member States … with Community institutions or bodies, central governments, regional or local authorities, public authorities … shall be prohibited, as shall the purchase directly from them by the ECB or national central banks of debt instruments *(Article 104(1))*.

One may conclude that the Bundesbank was the role model for the ECB. In fact, the language used by the drafters of the statutes of the ECB is tougher on inflation and political independence than the statutes of the Bundesbank. The political independence of the ECB is certainly greater than that of the Bundesbank. The reason is that a simple majority in the German parliament can change the statutes of the Bundesbank. Changes in the statutes of the ECB are much more difficult. They can be made only by a revision of the Maastricht Treaty, requiring unanimity among all EU member states, including those that are not members of EMU. (This feature has in fact led some to criticize the ECB for a lack of democratic accountability. We will come back to this issue.)

8.2 Why has the German model prevailed?

The success of the German model of central banking is an intriguing phenomenon. After all, when the EU countries negotiated the Maastricht Treaty, the Anglo-French model of central banking prevailed in almost all the EU member states. Why, then, was this model rejected in favour of the German one? Two reasons may be identified. One has to do with an intellectual development, i.e. the 'monetarist counter-revolution'; the other has to do with the strategic position of Germany in the process towards EMU.

During the 1950s and 1960s, Keynesianism triumphed. High economic growth and low unemployment were seen as objectives for which monetary and fiscal authorities were responsible. Expansionary monetary and fiscal policies were seen as instruments to reach these objectives. The 1970s were a watershed. Backed by increasing evidence that these policies had produced an inflationary bias, monetarism erupted as a counter-revolution. In the monetarist view, which is very well synthesized by the Barro–Gordon model, monetary authorities cannot systematically lower the unemployment rate below its natural level. They can only lower unemployment temporarily. If they seek to set the unemployment rate below the natural one, they will do this at a price, i.e. they will create a systematic inflation bias. The only way to lower unemployment permanently is by lowering the natural unemployment rate. This can only be achieved by 'structural policies', i.e. by introducing more flexibility in the labour market and by lowering labour taxes. Conversely, the central bank must occupy itself only with what it can control, namely the price level.[2]

This monetarist view also led to a new view about the nature of the relations between the central bank and the government. Since the pressures to follow expansionary monetary policies aimed at stimulating the economy typically come from politicians pursuing short-term electoral gains, the central bank should be protected from these political pressures by being independent.

These theoretical prescriptions were given a strong empirical backing by a series of econometric studies that appeared during the 1980s and early 1990s (see Box 8.1 for a brief overview). These demonstrate that countries in which central banks were politically independent had managed their economies better. These countries had maintained lower inflation on average without experiencing costs in terms of higher unemployment or lower economic growth. We discuss some of the issues relating to these empirical models in Box 8.1. We also show in Box 8.1 that there are some problems with the interpretation of the results. The main one is that political independence and inflation are jointly determined by deeper social and political factors. Therefore, it is not obvious that imposing independence in the statutes of the central banks will automatically lead to lower inflation. In order for political independence to lead to the desired price stability, it must be backed by a social and political consensus favouring price stability. Despite this criticism, there is a general consensus that political independence, although not sufficient to guarantee price stability, is necessary to achieve and to maintain it.

It is no exaggeration to state that, since the 1980s, the monetarist paradigm has become the prevailing one, especially among central bankers. In annual reports and countless speeches by central bank officials, the monetarist analysis and prescriptions have become the dominant intellectual framework. Central bankers throughout the world, and especially in Europe, have become the greatest champions of monetarism.

It is no surprise, therefore, that when the central bankers drafted the Delors report (which provided the intellectual framework for the Treaty) they were willing to take the Bundesbank

---

[2] This view was first formulated by Friedman (1968) in his celebrated presidential address to the American Economic Association.

BOX 8.1 The case for independence: the empirical evidence

The idea that political independence will lead to less inflation has been subjected to much empirical analysis. There have been studies by Bade and Parkin (1978), Demopoulos et al. (1987), Grilli et al. (1991), Cukierman (1992), Alesina and Summers (1993), and Eijffinger and Schaling (1995) showing that central banks that are politically independent tend to produce less inflation than central banks that have to take orders from the government. In Fig. 8.1, we show an example of such an empirical test. On the vertical axis the average yearly rate of inflation of industrial countries (1972–91) is represented. On the horizontal axis, an index of political independence of the central banks as computed by Cukierman (1992) is represented. We observe that there is a negative relationship, i.e. countries where the central banks have a great deal of political independence enjoy a lower rate of inflation, on average.[3]

Of course, many problems arise in testing this hypothesis. One concerns the measurement of political independence. It must be said that much careful analysis has been carried out using alternative measures of political independence. On the whole, the empirical results remain robust for these alternative measures.

An important aspect of these empirical studies is that they also reveal that on average and in the long run political independence does not lead to more unemployment or to a lower growth rate of the economy. All this seems to suggest that political independence is a desirable institutional feature of the ECB.

An important question that arises here is whether the explicit recognition, in the Statutes of the ECB, of political independence is sufficient to guarantee price stability. One may express doubts about

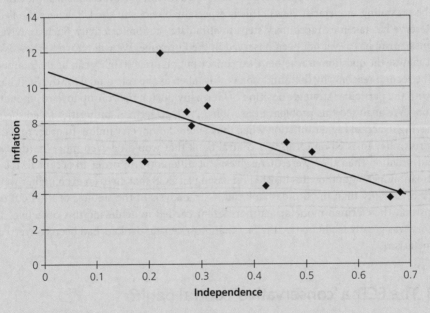

Figure 8.1 Average annual inflation and political independence (1972–91).

Source: de Haan and Eijffinger (1994).

(Continued...)

[3] A regression exercise involving 21 industrial countries confirms this conclusion (t-statistics in parentheses):
inflation = 11.2 − 9.4 independence
           (8.7)(−2.9)
$R^2 = 0.88$.

this. In this connection, Posen (1994) has conducted very interesting research about the link between political independence and inflation. His main conclusion is that both are the result of deeper social and economic interests. Some countries have strong pressure groups against inflation (e.g. financial institutions). In these countries we observe that the central bank tends to be politically independent and that inflation is low. In other countries, the major pressure groups are less opposed to inflation. In these countries, central banks will be less independent and inflation will be higher. This research teaches us that central banks' behaviour is very much influenced by underlying social and economic forces, so that a mere change of the statutes of the central bank will not by itself change behaviour.[4]

One should not, however, go too far in a neo-Marxian interpretation of the issue. In this interpretation economic forces drive institutions. A more balanced view recognizes that institutions (and incentives) can also change behaviour. Thus, the incorporation in the statutes of the central banks of political independence as a means to guarantee price stability can help in influencing behaviour and in changing society's view about the role of monetary policy. In addition, there is scope for the strengthening of these institutions so that the risk of inflation is reduced.

as their model. By stressing price stability as the primary objective and political independence as the instrument to achieve it, the Bundesbank appeared to be the living embodiment of the new monetarist paradigm.

The financial crisis that erupted in 2007 has seen a revival of Keynesianism at the expense of the prevailing monetarist views. This is especially obvious in the US, where the Federal Reserve has taken extraordinary steps to stimulate economic activity. Such a revival of Keynesianism has as yet not been observed in the Eurozone. We will return to these issues and analyse the question of whether the primacy put on price stability can be maintained.

The second reason why the Bundesbank was taken as the role model for the ECB has to do with the particular strategic position of Germany during the run-up towards monetary union. (We analysed this problem in Section 7.2.) The German authorities faced the risk of having to accept higher inflation when they entered monetary union. In order to reduce this risk, they insisted on creating a central bank that would be even more 'hard-nosed' about inflation than they were themselves. Put differently, in order to accept EMU, the German monetary authorities insisted on having an ECB that gives an even higher weight to price stability than the Bundesbank did. Our analysis of the statutes of the ECB confirms that the German monetary authorities succeeded in achieving this objective. This victory was greatly facilitated by the fact that most central bankers had been converted to monetarism.

8.3 The ECB: a 'conservative' central bank?

The monetarist counter-revolution and the German strategic position have led to the creation of a European Central Bank with a strong mandate for price stability and a weak responsibility for stabilizing output and employment fluctuations. In this sense one may say that the ECB is a 'conservative' central banker, i.e. an institution that attaches greater weight to price stability and less weight to output and employment stabilization than the rest of society.

---

[4] See Hayo (1998) for an interesting analysis.

Is there evidence that the ECB has acted as a conservative central bank? It is of course very difficult to answer this question. One way to try to do this is to compare the ECB's policy actions to those of the US Federal Reserve. We do this in Fig. 8.2, which shows the short-term interest rates that these two central banks control. (In Box 8.2, we compare the different use made of non-traditional monetary policy tools by the ECB and the Fed during the recent financial crisis.) It is striking to find that the Federal Reserve seems to have used the interest rate much more actively than the ECB. In 2001, it reacted very strongly to the economic slowdown, cutting its interest rate from a peak of 6.5% at the end of 2000 to less than 2% at the end of 2001. (Many observers have been arguing that the Federal Reserve kept the interest rate too low for too long, thereby fuelling the bubble in the housing markets that started around that time.) From 2004 it started to tighten monetary policy again and raised the interest rate above 5% until the eruption of the financial crisis in August 2007, when it lowered the interest rate in a spectacular fashion.

The contrast with the ECB is striking. The ECB appears to have been much more cautious in changing its policy rate. We clearly see that during the recession of 2001–3 it lowered its interest rate much less aggressively than the Federal Reserve, and during the boom of 2006–7 raised it less. Again, when recession struck in 2008, it reacted more slowly and less intensely than the Fed. Thus the ECB lowered the short-term interest rate to (practically) zero five years after the Fed had done so.

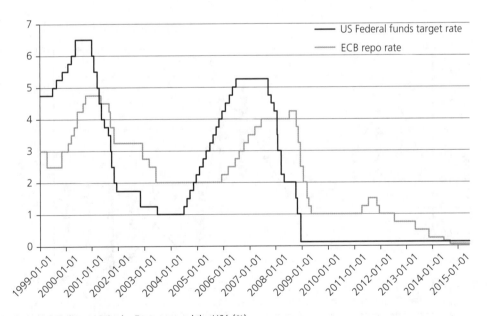

Figure 8.2 Policy rates in the Eurozone and the USA (%).

Note: From June 2000 to October 2008, the ECB repo rate is the minimum bid rate used in variable-rate tenders; before and after this period, this policy rate is the fixed rate used in fixed-rate tenders. On December 16, 2008, the Federal Open Market Committee established a target range for the federal funds rate of 0 to 1/4 percent; 0.13 is the average level.

Sources: Board of Governors of the Federal Reserve System and European Central Bank.

The difference in activism between the Federal Reserve and the ECB can also be gauged from the fact that the standard deviation of the US policy rate was 2.2% during 1999–2015 (compared to 1.4% for the ECB policy rate (while the mean of these interest rates was the same in both countries, i.e. 2.2%)).

This simple comparison of the interest rates, however, does not take into account that the underlying economic conditions were different in the USA and the Eurozone. In order to deal with this problem, we show the evolution of the short-term interest rates together with the output gaps in the Eurozone and in the USA in Figs 8.3 and 8.4. A comparison of these figures leads to the following conclusions. First, it appears that the ECB reacts to movements in the output gap, i.e. when the output gap is small the ECB tends to reduce the interest rate to boost the economy, and vice versa. Thus, it appears from the evidence that the ECB gives some weight to output stabilization. There is additional empirical evidence substantiating this conclusion (see Begg et al. 2002 and Sauer and Sturm 2007). There is one problem with this interpretation, though. This is that even if the ECB only cares about inflation and gives zero weight to output stabilization, it would still react to output gap movements because these have a good predictive power for future inflation. Thus, if the output gap increases (i.e. economic activity accelerates) it is likely to increase inflation in the future. A central bank that only cares about inflation will then react to the output gap. Whether this is the reason why the ECB has systematically reacted to output gap movements is difficult to detect. Probably, the ECB has been motivated both by the fact that the output gap is a good predictor of future inflation and by a genuine desire to stabilize output movements.

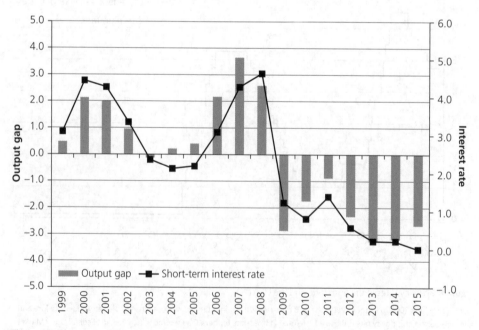

Figure 8.3 Short-term interest rate and output gap in the Eurozone (1999–2015).

Source: OECD, *Economic Outlook*, Statistical Annex Tables.

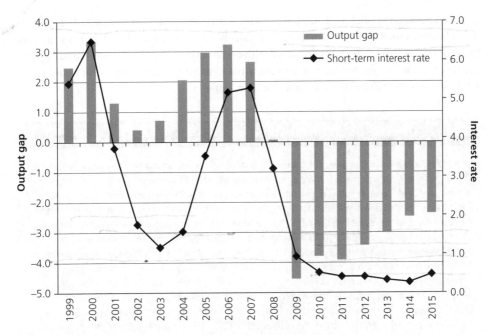

Figure 8.4 Short-term interest rate and output gap in the USA (1999–2015).

Source: OECD, Economic Outlook, Statistical Annex Tables.

A second conclusion one can draw from a comparison of Figs 8.3 and 8.4 is that the ECB reacts less intensely to movements in the output gap than the US Federal Reserve. It is true that the strong interest rate cut of the Federal Reserve in 2001 was motivated by the steep decline in the US output gap during the same year. Conversely, the ECB did not cut the interest rate by as much during the same period because the decline in the output gap was less pronounced. However, it can also be seen that by 2003–4 the decline of the Eurozone output gap was at least as strong as in the USA in the previous years, and yet the ECB did not react with a similarly strong cut in the interest rate. Put differently, in 2003–5 the output situation in the Eurozone was comparable to that in the USA in 2001–3, but the ECB was certainly not willing to stimulate it as much as the US Federal Reserve had done. Could this be explained by the fact that the inflation performance was significantly worse in the Eurozone than in the USA, thereby forcing the ECB to be more cautious with stimulating the economy of the Eurozone? The answer is no. Over the period 1999–2015 the average yearly inflation rate was 1.9 % in the Eurozone and 2.1% in the USA. Thus, it appears that the more cautious attitude of the ECB vis-à-vis output stabilization was not due to greater inflation risks in the Eurozone as compared to the USA. All this confirms that the ECB attaches less importance to output stabilization than the US Federal Reserve.

From the analysis above, one can conclude that the ECB appears to be more conservative than the US Federal Reserve in that it seems to attach greater importance to price stability, and it is more cautious in reacting to movements in the business cycle than the US Federal Reserve. From such a comparison one cannot conclude that the Federal Reserve followed better policies than the ECB. There is now a consensus among economists that the Federal

Reserve's monetary policies during 2001–4 were too expansionary for too long, thereby fuelling a boom in the US housing market. This can also be seen from Fig. 8.4, illustrating how the Federal Reserve may have overreacted to the economic downturn of 2000–1 and kept the interest rate too low for too long. It also contributed to a general consumption boom in the USA. These booms came to a spectacular end in 2007.

BOX 8.2:   QE in the US and in the Eurozone

One of the legacies of the financial crisis has been that inflation was pushed downwards in many countries. This was especially the case in the Eurozone as can be seen from Fig. 8.5 where inflation became negative at the end of 2014. There were similar pressures in the US. These deflationary pressures also pushed nominal interest rates towards zero as was illustrated in Fig. 8.2. As a result, central banks that wanted to stimulate the economy so as to prevent inflation falling further had to use 'unconventional' methods of monetary stimulus, called quantitative easing (QE). This consisted in buying government bonds. In doing so, the central bank was increasing liquidity (money base[5]) in the system. One implication of QE is that it increased the balance sheet of the central bank. (We explain in more detail how QE works in the next chapter.)

Again, the US Federal Reserve was much quicker and more aggressive in applying QE to limit the deflationary tendencies in the US economy than the ECB. This is shown quite dramatically in Fig. 8.6, which shows the balance sheets of the US Fed and the ECB. We observe that the Fed applied QE forcefully from the end of 2012 to stimulate the US economy. The ECB in fact allowed its balance sheet to decline during 2013–14 when inflation declined strongly. Only in early 2015 did it start its own QE programme, but it had waited to do so until inflation had become negative.

Figure 8.5 Inflation in the US and the Eurozone 2010–15.

Source: Eurostat.

[5] Money base is the money created by the central bank. It consists of currency in circulation and deposits held by commercial banks at the central bank.

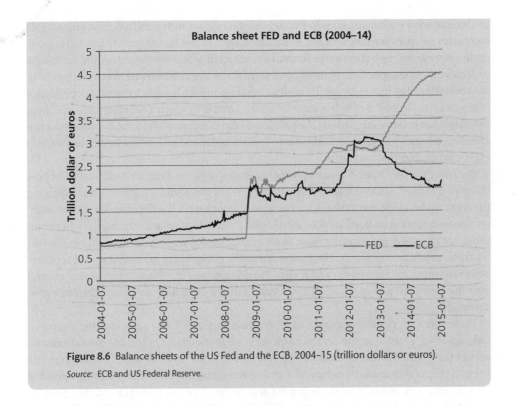

Figure 8.6 Balance sheets of the US Fed and the ECB, 2004–15 (trillion dollars or euros).
Source: ECB and US Federal Reserve.

8.4 Independence and accountability

The Maastricht Treaty gave a mandate to the ECB to maintain price stability but also to stabilize output and employment (provided the latter does not endanger price stability). In order to achieve these objectives, a wall was erected around the ECB to protect it from political interference. We argued earlier that there are good reasons for ensuring the political independence of the central bank. However, there are also problems. These have to do with the low level of accountability of the ECB.

The ECB has to fulfil its mandate. It can, however, like any other institution, make systematic mistakes. It can also be led to do things that go against its mandate. For example, we have shown in the previous section that the ECB could systematically fail to stabilize output and employment even though it could do so without endangering price stability. Errors in the other direction are also possible. The ECB could just fail to provide for price stability.

It is, therefore, important that a mechanism should exist to check whether the ECB is fulfilling its mandate, and, if it is not doing so, that sanctions are applied. This is simply the application of a general democratic principle. In a democracy, citizens delegate power to politicians. The politicians exercise this power until they face the electorate again. Thus, delegation of power to the politicians has two stages. The first one starts when the politicians are vested with power. During this stage they exercise this power independently of the electorate. The second stage is the accountability stage, when the electorate evaluates the record of the politicians and perhaps applies sanctions.

Much of what politicians do is to further delegate power to specialized institutions. This secondary delegation must have the same two stages. In the first stage, the politicians delegate power to the institution in the form of a contract in which the objectives and the means to achieve them are specified. In the second stage the politicians evaluate the performance of the institution. The first stage can be seen as the stage in which some form of independence is granted; the second one is the stage in which control is exerted (accountability). These two stages are inextricably linked. The politician who is accountable to the electorate cannot afford to delegate power to an institution (make it independent) unless he or she can also exert control over that institution.

The more the politician delegates power, the better organized the control must be of how this power is used. If there is little delegation, there is little need for control. Thus (applying these principles to the central bank), if the government makes the decisions about the interest rate then there is no need for the central bank to have explicit accountability. If, however, the government delegates much power to the central bank, there is a corresponding need for it to have much accountability. The reason is that the government maintains its full accountability to voters, and therefore cannot afford to delegate power without maintaining control over the use of this power. Thus, independence and accountability are part of the same process of delegation.

These ideas are given a graphical interpretation in Fig. 8.7. We represent the degree of independence granted to the central bank on the vertical axis. On the horizontal axis, we set out the degree of accountability of the central bank. The upward-sloping line represents the optimal combinations of independence and accountability from the politician's point of view. The more independence the politician grants, the more risk they take and therefore the more they want to hedge their risks by organizing a system of control over the performance of the central bank.

In Fig. 8.7, the empirical evidence about the degree of independence of three central banks, the Federal Reserve, the Bundesbank, and the ECB, is used. This evidence is based on Cukierman (1992) and an update by Bini-Smaghi and Gros (2000). Using several indicators of independence (e.g. who sets the targets? Who formulates the policy? What are the limitations on lending to governments? What is the length of the terms of office?), Bini-Smaghi

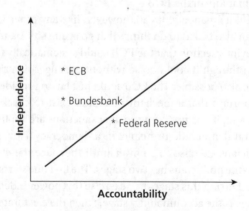

Figure 8.7 Optimal relation between independence and accountability.

and Gros conclude that the ECB is the most independent central bank, followed by the Bundesbank and the Federal Reserve.[6]

Can it also be concluded that the ECB has the strongest degree of accountability? This does not seem to be the case. On the contrary, the evidence suggests that the degree of accountability of the ECB is less well developed, at least compared to that of the Federal Reserve (see Buiter 1999, Eijffinger and de Haan 2000, and de Haan et al. 2005 on this issue).[7] Although the presidents of both central banks have to appear regularly before the parliament, the implications are very different. When the chairman of the Federal Reserve appears before Congress, he or she faces an institution that can change the statutes of the Federal Reserve by a simple majority. The chairman therefore cannot afford systematically to disregard the opinions of the Congressmen. When the president of the ECB appears before the European parliament, he or she faces an institution that has no power to change the statutes of the ECB. These can be changed only by changing the Treaty, which requires unanimity of all EU member states (including those that do not participate in EMU). As a result, the balance of power is very much tilted in favour of the ECB.

Thus, the ECB is an institution that was granted more independence than the other major central banks, while the degree of accountability it is subjected to appears to be weaker than in these central banks. This goes against the theory developed here, which stresses that accountability should be increased in line with the degree of independence.

There is an additional problem in the way power was delegated to the ECB. Delegation of power implies the writing of a contract in which the objectives to be pursued are defined, together with the method to be used to achieve them, and the sanctioning procedure if the objectives are not met. A crucial issue is the precision with which the objectives are described.[8] If objectives are left vague, it will be difficult to monitor the behaviour of the central bank. Accountability will be weak. The more precise the definition of the objectives is, the easier it is to monitor the central bank. How does the ECB compare here with other central banks?

As pointed out earlier, the Maastricht Treaty has singled out price stability as the primary objective of the ECB. At the same time, the Treaty mandates the ECB to support the general economic policies of the Community, provided this does not interfere with price stability. Two issues arise here. First, the concept of price stability has not been given a precise content in the Treaty. This has made it possible for the ECB to fill the void and to define this concept itself (see Section 9.2, which describes the Monetary Policy Strategy of the ECB). Thus, in a sense the ECB has filled out for itself the fine print of the contract it has with the politicians.

Second, the other objectives the ECB should pursue (provided price stability is guaranteed) have been left vague in the Treaty—so vague that it is unclear what these other objectives are. This state of affairs has made it possible for the ECB to develop its own interpretation of the

---

[6] See also Eijffinger and de Haan (2000), who come to the same conclusion.

[7] It is unclear how the Bundesbank compares with the ECB as far as accountability is concerned. There is no legal requirement for the Bundesbank president to appear before the German parliament. On the other hand, the statutes of the Bundesbank can be changed by a simple majority in parliament, thereby giving the members of parliament greater leverage in controlling the Bundesbank. In Fig. 8.6, we have taken the view that there is not much difference in the accountability of the ECB and the Bundesbank, but this can be criticized.

[8] There are other issues, e.g. how detailed the contract should be, and how to design the right incentives for the agent. We do not discuss these issues here. (See Walsh 1998.)

objectives it should pursue. This interpretation has been made public in the ECB's Monetary Policy Strategy (see Section 9.2). Given the vagueness of the Treaty about the other objectives besides price stability, the ECB has interpreted this to mean that it has to pursue only price stability. All reference to other objectives has been dropped. As a result, the ECB has restricted the domain of responsibilities about which it can be called to account.

The fact that for all practical purposes the ECB has set its own objectives is an undesirable situation that will lead to conflicts in the future. There is an increasing consensus that it is the task of elected officials to set the objectives, and not the central bank. Once the objectives have been defined, the central bank has to pursue these objectives in a way that it sees fit. This idea has been called 'instrument independence': the central bank is independent in the sense that it can choose how to achieve the objectives that society, through its representatives, has mandated.

The contrast with other central banks is significant. US legislation makes the Federal Reserve responsible for movements in employment and inflation. There is no way that it could decide on its own that the employment objective is none of its business. As a result, the area of responsibilities for which the Federal Reserve is accountable is broader than the ECB's.

To summarize, the accountability of the ECB is weak for two reasons. First, there is an absence of strong political institutions in Europe capable of exerting control over the performance of the ECB. Second, as a result of the Treaty's vagueness in defining the objectives of the ECB (apart from price stability), the ECB has effectively restricted its area of responsibility to inflation, so that it will be accountable only for its anti-inflation performance. In this connection it is significant that when Jean-Claude Trichet, the President of the ECB during 2003–11, departed from the ECB, he explicitly stated that 'there is only one needle on the radar screen in Frankfurt and that is inflation'. All other objectives, including financial stability, were shifted onto the shoulders of the 'politicians'.

This state of affairs creates a long-term problem for the political support of the ECB. Modern central banks have a wider responsibility than simply price stability. Their responsibility extends to macroeconomic stability in general, i.e. reducing business cycle fluctuations, avoiding deflation, and maintaining financial stability. It is difficult to see how European politicians will continue to support an institution to which great power has been delegated and over which they have so little control.

The ECB could do much to defuse these conflicts. First, in order to compensate for the lack of formal accountability, it could enhance informal accountability. This can be achieved by greater transparency. This would mean, for example, that the ECB would inform the public about its objectives and the way it wants to achieve them. It would also require openness in the decision-making process so that the public is aware of why the ECB is making certain decisions. Put differently, the ECB can compensate for the lack of formal accountability by volunteering information about its policies. Given its high degree of independence, the ECB should in fact do more voluntarily than other central banks. It must be recognized that the ECB has gone some way in this direction (see de Haan et al. 2005, Ehrmann and Fratzscher 2007, and Sturm and de Haan 2011 on this). It publishes a *Monthly Bulletin* in which it explains its policies in detail. In addition, after each monthly meeting of the Governing Council dealing with monetary policy, the ECB president explains to the press what has been decided and why.

Accountability can be improved indirectly by other means. Some economists (e.g. Svensson) have argued that inflation targeting promotes informal accountability. The reason is that by announcing a particular target for inflation the central bank is forced to explain to the public any subsequent failure to achieve the target.[9] Similarly, the ECB could announce its estimate of the natural unemployment rate. If the observed unemployment rate exceeds the natural unemployment rate, the ECB would be expected to do something about it. If it does not want to stimulate the economy, it would have to explain why it does not want to do this. All of these measures would promote informal accountability. It is interesting to note that the US Federal Reserve and the Bank of England announced in 2013 that they would keep the interest rate at its (historically) low level as long as the unemployment rate remained above the natural unemployment rates in their respective countries.

In this connection, the issue arises of whether or not the ECB should publish the minutes of the meetings of the Governing Council. Some central banks, e.g. the Federal Reserve, do this, and include the voting record of the members of the Board. The advantage of such publication is that it informs the public better about the process by which the central bank has made the decision. This tends to improve accountability. Until recently, the ECB refused to do this. It claimed that it is forbidden by the Treaty to do so. Indeed, Article 10.4 of the Statutes can be interpreted to mean that publication of the minutes and votes is prohibited.[10] In 2015, the ECB reconsidered its position and it decided that the minutes would be published, however, without referring to comments made during the meetings to particular members of the Governing Council (see next section where the role of the Governing Council is discussed).

8.5 The ECB: institutional framework

The continuing importance of nation-states in the EU made it necessary to construct monetary institutions for the Eurozone that are sufficiently decentralized and yet that maintain unity in the conduct of monetary policy. The result has been an institutional framework that is quite unique in the world. We first describe this institutional framework and then ask what its strengths and weaknesses are.

The institutions of the Eurozone: the Eurosystem

The institutions of the Eurozone were established in the Maastricht Treaty. Monetary policy is entrusted to the Eurosystem.[11] This consists of the European Central Bank (ECB) and the national central banks (NCBs) of the EU countries that have joined EMU. Today (in 2015) there are 19 such NCBs.[12]

---

[9] We shall return to inflation targeting when we analyse it more technically.

[10] For a dissenting interpretation, see Buiter (1999), who comes out very strongly in favour of publication of the minutes and votes.

[11] For a good description and discussion, see Gros and Tabellini (1998).

[12] On 1 January 2015 the Lithuanian Central Bank became the 19th NCB in the Eurosystem.

The governing bodies of the Eurosystem are the Executive Board and the Governing Council. The Executive Board consists of the President, the Vice-President, and the four Directors of the ECB. The Governing Council consists of the six members of the Executive Board and the governors of the 19 national central banks.

The Governing Council is the main decision-making body of the Eurosystem. It formulates monetary policies and takes decisions concerning interest rates, reserve requirements, and the provision of liquidity in the system. It meets every two weeks in Frankfurt.[13] During these meetings, the 25 members of the Governing Council deliberate and take the appropriate decisions. Each of the members has one vote. Thus, unlike the European Council of Ministers, the Governing Council of the Eurosystem has no qualified voting. The rationale for this is to be found in the Treaty. This mandates that the members of the Governing Council should be concerned with the interests of the Eurozone as a whole, and not with the interests of the country from which they originate. Qualified voting would have suggested that the members of the Governing Council represent national interests. Whether the national governors sitting in the Governing Council will set aside their national interests so as to promote the interests of the Eurozone exclusively remains to be seen.

The Executive Board implements the monetary policy decisions taken by the Governing Council. This includes giving instructions to the NCBs. In addition, the Executive Board sets the agenda for the meetings of the Governing Council. Thus, it has a strategic position and can have a large influence on the decision-making process in the Governing Council. We illustrate the organizational structure of the Eurozone's monetary institutions, as described above, in the form of a flow chart in Fig. 8.8.

This whole decision-making structure is called the Eurosystem. The ECB is only a part of this system and cannot take decisions on its own about monetary policies in the Eurozone. Nevertheless, we shall continue to use the label ECB as a synonym for the Eurosystem, mainly because this has become common practice. The reader should, however, bear in mind that the label ECB then refers to a broader concept than its legal definition.

Is the Eurosystem too decentralized?

The organizational structure we have just described combines unity of decision-making with decentralization in structure and in implementation of the decisions. This can also be seen from Fig. 8.8. This shows that the national central banks are fully involved in the decision-making process within the Governing Council. The decisions of the Governing Council are then implemented by the ECB. Following the instructions of the ECB, the NCBs carry out these decisions in their own national money markets.

The question arises here of whether this system is not too decentralized. Put differently, is not the influence of the NCBs in the Governing Council too great, so that national interests will tend to prevail at the expense of system-wide interests? We analyse this question here.

Some observers have argued that the system is indeed too decentralized.[14] The governors of the NCBs have a clear majority (19 out of 25 members) in the Governing Council. This

---

[13] The Governing Council sometimes meets in the national capitals of the Eurozone.
[14] See Begg et al. (1998) and Gros and Tabellini (1998).

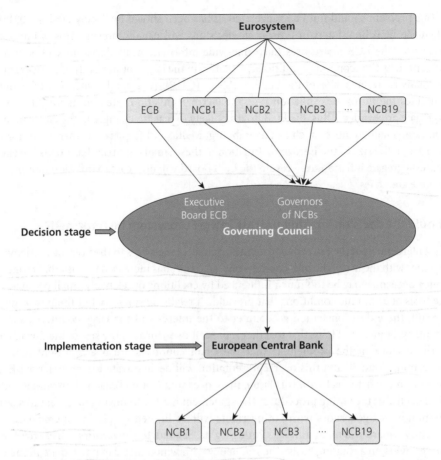

Figure 8.8 Organizational framework of the Eurosystem.

contrasts with other decentralized central banks. For example, the US Federal Reserve System's decision-making body is the Federal Open Market Committee (FOMC). It consists of 12 members, five of whom are presidents of regional banks. The other seven members, the Board members, are appointed by Congress and represent the interests of the system as a whole.[15] Thus, the regional banks' presidents, who could be said to represent regional interests, are always in a minority position. The US Federal Reserve System used to be more decentralized during the 1920s and 1930s than it is today. In *A Monetary History of the United States*, Milton Friedman and Anna Schwartz (1963) argued that in the early 1930s the Federal Reserve System failed to take decisive action to avert the banking crisis because the System was torn by opposing regional interests. There was no authority looking at the system-wide interests and strong enough to overcome divergent regional interests. This exacerbated the Depression, in their view.[16]

---

[15] Research by Meade and Sheets (2002) shows that the Board members are also influenced by the economic conditions prevailing in the region from which they come.

[16] Friedman and Schwartz (1963). See also Eichengreen (1992) on this issue.

This problem should not be exaggerated. It has been shown by Aksoy et al. (2002) that when the ECB Board acts in unison, its decisions will usually prevail. This is important because as the ECB Board uses Eurozone-wide information, its decisions will be heavily influenced by the economic conditions prevailing in the large countries. To give an example, Germany represents 30% of the Eurozone's size (GDP). As a result, when the ECB Board computes the Eurozone's inflation rate, the German inflation rate counts for 30% in the aggregate price index. Thus, the ECB Board is likely to react to changes in the German inflation rate. Small countries such as Luxembourg, Malta, and Cyprus together count for less than 1% of the size of the Eurozone. Inflation in these small countries has no visible effects on the aggregate inflation. As a result, the ECB Board will not react to inflation rate changes in these countries.

Should the decision-making process in the Eurosystem be reformed?

The enlargement of the Eurozone from the original 12 members to the present 19 members, together with the use of the one-country-one-vote rule, has increased the risk that monetary policy decisions may be too much influenced by coalitions of relatively small countries on the basis of economic conditions that prevail in a relatively small part of the Eurozone. As a result, these decisions could go counter to the interests of the large countries, such as Germany, France, and Italy, that together represent two-thirds of the size of the Eurozone.

The essence of the problem is that the small countries are overrepresented in the Governing Council, and this overrepresentation will be aggravated in an enlarged Eurosystem. In order to deal with this issue, the Governing Council reached an agreement in 2002 to change the voting procedure. The agreement has the following main features. First, the number of governors with voting rights will be limited to 15. The members of the Executive Board will maintain their voting rights. Second, the governors will exercise their voting rights on a rotating basis. The frequency with which they can participate in the voting will depend on the relative size of the country they come from. Thus, governors from large countries will exert their voting power more frequently than governors from small countries.

This proposal was formally adopted by the Heads of State by a unanimous decision in March 2003. This new system was supposed to be put into effect as soon as the number of national governors exceeded 15. This was achieved on 1 January 2009 when Slovakia became the 16th member country. However, the Governing Council decided to postpone the implementation of the rotating system until the number of member countries exceeds 18. This occurred on 1st January 2015 when Lithuania became the 19th member country.

The new rotating system works as follows. Euro area countries are divided into two groups according to the size of their economies and their financial sectors. The Governors from the five biggest countries (Germany, France, Italy, Spain, and the Netherlands) form the first group. They share four voting rights. All others (14) are in the second group and share 11 voting rights. The Governors take turns using the rights on a monthly rotation. Thus, in the first group Governors vote 80% of the time. In the second group Governors vote 78.6% of the time (11/14). Thus it turns out that today the difference between the voting rights of the two groups is very small. This will change when more members join the second group (the 11 voting rights are fixed).

Whatever the voting system, it can be argued that the Governing Council has become too large.[17] The risk exists that it will be very difficult to come to decisions quickly, especially when economic conditions in the Eurozone diverge or when major decisions have to be made. There is some evidence that this was the case when the ECB had to decide whether or not to buy government bonds in the secondary markets in 2011. Similarly the decision to start with the OMT programme (see the next section) came more than two years after the start of the sovereign debt crisis in early 2010.

It should also be pointed out that the new voting procedure implies that the principle of one-country-one-vote will be abandoned. Although this principle appeared quite attractive because it was based on the idea that the members of the Governing Council were representing the interests of the Eurosystem as a whole and not of their countries of origin, the enlargement of the Eurozone makes it difficult to maintain this.

8.6 The ECB as lender of last resort

In October 2008, the banks in the Eurozone were gripped by a full-scale liquidity crisis. The collapse of Lehman Brothers put a number of European banks that had bought insurance from Lehman Brothers in grave difficulties. They had to sell assets, thereby creating solvency problems for themselves and other banks. As a result, deposit holders (especially in the interbank markets) withdrew their money, precipitating a liquidity crisis. For a few days the banking system was close to collapse as the interbank market completely dried out.

The ECB stepped in with massive liquidity injections, using open market operations (see Chapter 9 for a description of how these function in practice). These liquidity injections succeeded in averting a collapse of the banking system. Thus, the ECB stood its first big test as a lender of last resort in times of crises. And it succeeded.

The contrast with the ECB's role of lender of last resort in the government bond markets of the Eurozone could not be greater. We argued in Chapter 6 that it is essential for the ECB to take on this role in the government bond markets in the Eurozone, because the latter are characterized by the same fragility as the banking sector. That is, governments issue liquid liabilities (government bonds) while most of their assets are illiquid. This feature makes them prone to self-fulfilling liquidity crises, unless the central bank stands ready to provide liquidity in the government bond market. In contrast with its readiness to provide massive support to banks, the ECB has been very hesitant to provide the necessary liquidity in government bond markets.

In September 2012, the ECB announced its readiness to act as lender of last resort in government bond markets, i.e. to buy unlimited amounts of government bonds in the secondary markets. It called this programme 'Outright Monetary Transactions' (OMT). As shown in Chapter 6, this announcement had an immediate effect in reducing the government bond rates in the countries most hit by the sovereign debt crisis (Greece, Ireland, Portugal, Spain).

---

[17] In a fascinating paper Anne Sibert analyses the optimal size of Central Bank Committees (Sibert 2006). She comes to the conclusion that committees should not be much larger than five to develop efficient decision procedures. The Governing Council is clearly too big.

The ECB, however, attached a number of conditions to the use of the OMT programme. These went much further than those formulated in the Bagehot doctrine, as discussed in Box 8.3. First, the ECB will restrict its bond purchases to bonds with a maturity of 3 years or fewer. There is no good economic argument to impose such a restriction. In fact, it may even increase the fragility of the sovereigns. These will now have an incentive to issue bonds with shorter maturities than they would have done otherwise, making them more vulnerable to liquidity crises. Second, countries in need of OMT support will have to subject their budgetary policies to an austerity programme supervised by the European Stability Mechanism (ESM). This is a European Fund created in the wake of the sovereign debt crisis and funded by national governments of the Eurozone. Only when an austerity programme dictated by the ESM has been accepted by the government calling for OMT support will the ECB provide this support. It looks like that the carrot provided by the ECB (OMT support) will be accompanied by a big stick.

Second, the ECB condition to the use of the OMT programme that the countries concerned apply to the European Stability Mechanism (ESM), may then

---

BOX 8.3 The Bagehot doctrine

Ideally, the lender of last resort function should only be used when banks (or governments) experience liquidity problems. It should not be used when they are insolvent. This is the doctrine formulated by Walter Bagehot (1873). The central bank should not bail out banks or governments that are insolvent.

This is certainly correct. The problem with this doctrine, however, is that it is often difficult to distinguish between liquidity and solvency crises. As argued earlier, when sovereign debt crises erupt they are very often a mix of liquidity and solvency problems. Liquidity crises raise the interest rate on the debt issued by governments and therefore quickly degenerate into solvency problems. Solvency problems often lead to liquidity crises that intensify the solvency problem. It is therefore easy to say that the central bank should only provide liquidity to governments or banks that are illiquid but solvent. It is often very difficult to implement this doctrine.

The doctrine also leads to a paradox. If it were easy to separate liquidity from solvency problems, the markets would find it easy to do so. Thus, if a government came under pressure, financial markets would be able to determine whether this government suffered from a liquidity or solvency problem. If they determined it was a liquidity problem, they would be willing to provide credit to the government. The central bank would not have to step in. If they determined it was a solvency problem, they would not want to provide credit and rightly so. The Bagehot doctrine would come to the same conclusion: the central bank should not bail out the insolvent government. The conclusion is that if solvency and liquidity crises can be separated, there is no need for a lender of last resort. Financial markets would take care of the problems.[18] Who wants to believe this these days?

There is one way in which the Bagehot doctrine could be used by the common central bank in a monetary union. Bagehot put forward the principle that in times of crisis, the central bank should provide unlimited liquidity at a penalty rate. This was seen by Bagehot as a way to take care of the moral hazard problem. The common central bank could apply this principle by committing itself to provide unlimited liquidity as soon as the government bond rate of country A exceeded the risk-free rate (say the German bond rate) by more than, say, 200 basis points (it could also be another number). The ECB, to a certain degree, could take care of moral hazard concerns in this way.

---

[18] This seems to have been the belief of Alan Greenspan. See Greenspan (2007).

subject these countries to additional austerity programmes. This creates the problem that countries are pushed further into a recession as a condition of obtaining relief from the ECB. This condition was influenced by the perception that the recipients of the liquidity support might reduce their efforts to balance the government budget (moral hazard).

These conditions create some governance issues. As argued earlier, the proper separation of responsibilities is for the ECB to act as a lender of last resort, and for the European Commission to control the moral hazard risk produced by these lender of last resort activities. The OMT programme, however, makes it clear that the ECB wants both to provide liquidity and to police moral hazard risk. This also appears from the fact that the ECB is actively involved in the 'Troika' (European Commission, ECB, IMF) that monitors countries' budgetary policies. This monitoring, however, is highly political. Thus the ECB gets involved in decisions about how much governments should spend, which spending cuts to apply, and what taxes to raise.

These are highly political decisions. A central bank that cherishes its political independence endangers this independence if it is involved in political decision-making processes in member countries.

This being said, the ECB's decision to provide unlimited liquidity support in government bond markets is a positive one. It probably constitutes the most important institutional change to make it possible to stabilize government bond markets in the Eurozone. It can even be argued that without this institutional change the Eurozone might have collapsed during 2012.

Despite this success, the OMT programme is still vehemently opposed in a number of countries. In Chapter 6 we analysed the criticisms that have been levelled against the idea that the ECB should be a lender of last resort in government bond markets, and found most of them wanting (except the moral hazard risk). Here we concentrate on some legal issues.

8.7 Did the ECB violate its statutes when it announced its government bond buying programme (OMT)?

It is often said that the ECB's decision to buy government bonds represents a violation of its statutes, which, it is claimed, forbid such operations. This was also the view of the German Constitutional Court (see Chapter 6). A careful reading of the Treaty, however, makes clear that this is not the case. Article 18 of the 'Protocol on the Statute of the European System of Central Banks and the European Central Bank' clearly states that 'the ECB and the national central banks may operate in financial markets by buying and selling … claims and marketable instruments'. Government bonds are marketable instruments, and nowhere is it said that the ECB is forbidden to buy and sell these bonds in financial markets. This is also the position of the ECJ which ruled in early 2015 that the OMT programme does not violate the ECB's statutes.

What is prohibited is spelled out in Article 21: the ECB is not allowed to provide 'overdrafts or any other type of credit facilities' to public entities, nor can the ECB directly purchase 'debt instruments' from these public entities.

The distinction between these two types of operations is important and is often confused. According to its statute, the ECB is allowed to buy government bonds in the secondary markets in the context of its open market operations. In doing so, the ECB does not provide credit to governments. What it does is to provide liquidity to the holders of these government bonds. These holders are typically financial institutions. In no way can this be interpreted as a monetary financing of government budget deficits.

By contrast, the prohibition on buying debt instruments directly from national governments is based on the fact that such an operation provides liquidity to these governments and thus implies a monetary financing of the government budget deficit.

8.8 The new financial regulatory and supervisory structure in the EU: towards a banking union

The banking crisis of 2008 has been the trigger for a fundamental overhaul of the way banks and financial markets are regulated and supervised in the Eurozone and in the EU. The fact that regulation and supervision that existed before the crisis was mainly national was seen as having contributed to the crisis and as impeding its effective resolution.[19] The need was felt to create a centralized framework of regulation and supervision. It should be noted that the new framework applies to all EU countries and thus is not restricted to the Eurozone.

We first discuss the new regulatory framework and the common supervisory framework.

A common regulatory framework

In Fig. 8.9, we show the new regulatory structure as it came into existence on 1 January 2011. First, a new European Systemic Risk Board, presided over by the President of the ECB, has been given the task of analysing sources of potential systemic risks that may affect the financial system and issuing early warnings of impending problems. The Board has no executive power but is assumed to carry enough weight for its warnings to have the effect of pushing the supervisory authorities into action. Second, three new supervisory authorities at the European level have been created. These ESAs consist of three independent authorities: the European Banking Authority (EBA) headquartered in London; the European Insurance and Occupational Pensions Authority (EIOPA) with headquarters in Frankfurt; and the European Securities and Markets Authority (ESMA) based in Paris.

The ESAs are supposed to draft new technical standards that should become EU law, and to issue recommendations that should be applied by the national supervisors. These recommendations, however, should not have budgetary implications for national governments. The ESAs have the power to investigate breaches of the EU law by national supervisors. If the national supervisors fail to comply, the ESAs can take decisions that will directly bind firms and market participants in the member states. They can temporarily ban certain financial activities, and in times of crisis they can take decisions that have binding force for the national supervisors. Finally, ESAs can collect information from the national regulators that they need in order to satisfactorily perform their duties.

---

[19] This criticism has been formulated by the IMF (1998). A good survey of the issues is in Lannoo (1998). See also Borio (2003); European Central Bank (2008b); and González-Páramo (2008). In 2009, the Larosière Committee proposed the creation of a European Systemic Risk Council, which would issue macro-prudential risk warnings leading to mandatory action by EU authorities. In addition, it proposed the setting up of a European System of Financial Supervision.

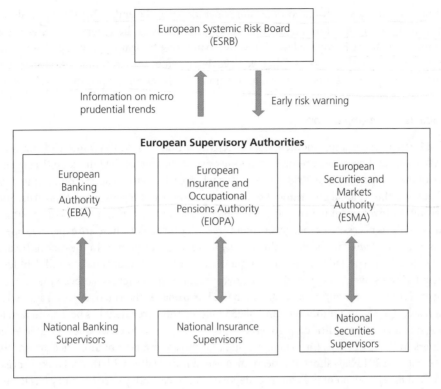

Figure 8.9 The new financial regulatory structure in the EU.

Source: Adapted from Lannoo (2011).

A common supervisory framework

In June 2012, it was decided to create a common supervisor for the Eurozone. As the creation of a new institution would have required a Treaty change and the prospect of lengthy procedures to have a new Treaty accepted, it was decided that the ECB would take over the responsibility of the common supervisor of banks in the Eurozone. In November 2014 the ECB became the common supervisor in the Eurozone.

Within the ECB there is a Board of Supervisors consisting of representatives of the 19 Eurozone member states and four ECB representatives. This Board has the authority to supervise the 'systemic' banks in the Eurozone. These are the banks with a balance sheet exceeding €30 billion or 20% of the national GDP (about 200 banks). This supervisory authority includes the auditing of balance sheets, the imposition of fines, the recapitalization of the banks, and even their closing down when necessary. As can be seen, these are very intrusive powers that have been given to the ECB.

The supervision of the 6,000 smaller banks remains vested with the national supervisors. However, the ECB Board of Supervisors is empowered to issue instructions to these smaller banks if the national supervisors fail to act.

This new supervisory framework became operational at the end of 2014. It certainly signifies an important step towards the transfer of sovereignty in the supervisory power from member states to the European level. The move to more centralization of financial regulation and supervision in the Eurozone that we have described in this section can be interpreted as a movement towards more political unification. This is certainly a positive development.

Towards a banking union

What is still missing at this moment is an effective common resolution framework, i.e. a system that makes it possible to resolve a banking crisis at the level of the Eurozone. The experience of the banking crisis of 2008 has been that when such a crisis erupts in one country, e.g. Ireland, it is the national government that is solely responsible for resolving this crisis. Such a resolution involves taking over insolvent banks and restructuring them by disposing of bad assets. This necessitates that governments recapitalize banks. These are expensive operations, the cost of which is borne exclusively by national governments. In the case of Ireland, the crisis led to a spectacular increase in the Irish government budget deficit and debt level, precipitating a solvency crisis of the Irish government. Some progress has been made in setting up a common resolution mechanism in the Eurozone. At the end of 2013, an agreement was reached to set up a resolution fund of €55 billion. This agreement has been criticized for being insufficient. In addition, its governance is so complex as to raise issues about its effectiveness in times of crisis. One can conclude that the common resolution mechanism that was created in 2013 falls short of a mechanism capable of dealing with future banking crises.

A final missing element is a common deposit insurance. Today every country has its own national deposit insurance mechanism. Since it is national it implies that the contributions to the insurance scheme are national. This means that if a new banking crisis were to erupt in a country, the losses of the depositors would be compensated by the national insurance system. In a large-scale crisis, however, the national insurance systems turn out to have insufficient resources; thus it would again be the national governments that would have to step in. In other words, the 'deadly embrace' between the banks and the sovereign would not be cut. That is why a common Eurozone deposit insurance mechanism is necessary at the Eurozone level. This would make it possible for the cost of compensating the deposit holders in one country to be spread over the Eurozone as a whole, pretty much as this is done in the US. This of course necessitates a willingness of member-countries to transfer resources to a member-country hit by banking crisis. Up to now the willingness to do so has been very thin.

We can conclude that we are still far removed from a full banking union. Such a banking union consists of three components: common supervision, common resolution, and common deposit insurance. The first component is a reality; the second one is partially realized; the third one is completely absent.

8.9 Conclusion

The Eurosystem is a remarkable construction, unique in history. In designing the Eurosystem, it was necessary to take into account existing national sensitivities and the desire of national banks to retain some power in the formulation and implementation of monetary policies. At the same time, a clear and unified decision-making process was needed to make the monetary union work. What has come out is a fine compromise that balances these opposing desires.

There are, however, a number of shortcomings in the design as discussed in this chapter. One is the lack of clear accountability. The strong degree of independence that the ECB has obtained (a positive feature) is not matched by an equally strong procedure to control the performance of the ECB. The only way to compensate for this shortcoming today is for the ECB to develop a climate of transparency so that its policy actions are well understood and a broad consensus can be developed.

The decision of the ECB in 2012 to be a lender of last resort in the government bond markets of the Eurozone (OMT) is certainly a major institutional change. It will still have to be tested. Up to now the ECB has not had to activate the OMT programme. This may become necessary in the future. The resolve of the ECB will then be tested.

The ECB has acquired major responsibilities in the common supervision of the systemic banks in the Eurozone. As a result, the ECB is now responsible for monetary policy in the Eurozone and for supervision. Its powers have been increased dramatically. This makes the need for accountability of that institution even more intense.

Finally, important steps have been undertaken to create a banking union in the Eurozone. This banking union is far from complete. Important steps will have to be taken to strengthen the common resolution mechanism and to create a common deposit insurance system.

Monetary policy in the Eurozone

Introduction

In Chapter 8, we discussed fundamental problems relating to the design of the ECB.[1] In this chapter we discuss more practical problems that have to do with the conduct of monetary policies in the Eurozone.

We first identify the major problem with which the ECB is confronted, i.e. how to conduct monetary policies in a union where asymmetric shocks occur. We then shift our focus towards the formulation of intermediate and ultimate targets of monetary policy. In this connection, we will discuss the ECB Monetary Policy Strategy. Finally, we discuss the instruments the ECB uses to achieve these targets.

9.1 Central banking and asymmetries of shocks

The Eurozone is regularly hit by asymmetric shocks. How does the existence of such asymmetries affect policy-making by the ECB? In Fig. 9.1, we analyse this issue by presenting the same two-country model used in Chapter 1 (Fig. 1.1). This allows us to analyse the effects of a 'pure' asymmetric shock. We show one country hit by a boom (France) produced by an increase in aggregate demand, and the other hit by a recession (Germany) produced by a decline in aggregate demand. We assume that the positive shock in one country is exactly offset by the negative shock in the other country. This assumption makes it a pure asymmetric shock. The ECB, which is responsible for maintaining price stability and for stabilizing the economy *in the Eurozone as a whole*, aggregates the numbers. As a result, when observing the economic conditions prevailing in the Eurozone, it will decide that, since prices and output have remained unchanged, no change in policies is called for. The result is a greater fluctuation in output (and thus employment) in the individual countries. In Germany, for example, output declines to Y_{G1}. If Germany could set its own interest rate it would probably lower it, thereby stimulating aggregate demand. Output would be higher than Y_{G1}. The opposite holds in France. There output increases to Y_{F1}. The inflationary pressure this creates in France would have led an independent Banque de France to

[1] As mentioned in the previous chapter, we shall use the label ECB in a broad sense, indicating the institutions that formulate and implement monetary policies in the Eurozone (the Eurosystem).

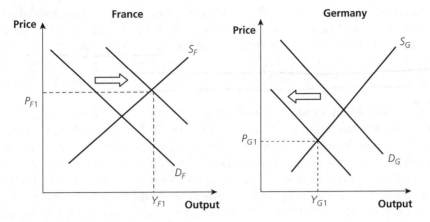

Figure 9.1 Asymmetric shock and monetary policy of the ECB.

increase the interest rate, thereby reducing aggregate demand. Output in France would be lower than Y_{F1}.

In this extreme case of a pure asymmetric shock, the ECB never stabilizes. The ECB is completely paralysed. It behaves as if the weight the ECB attaches to output stabilization is zero.

The symmetric case is shown in Fig. 9.2. We now assume that the shock is exactly the same in both countries, i.e. the aggregate demand curve shifts downwards in both France and Germany. The ECB observes a decline in prices and in output in the Eurozone as a whole. Given its desire to stabilize, it takes action and lowers the interest rate. This tends to shift the aggregate demand curves at least partially up again (not shown in the graph), thereby reducing the loss in output. Although from the German point of view, the shock is the same, the ECB is now capable of stimulating output in Germany.

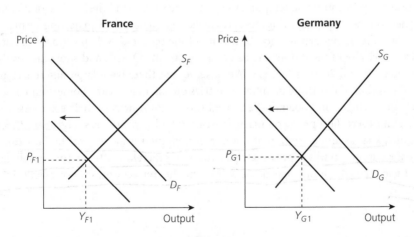

Figure 9.2 Symmetric shock and monetary policy of the ECB.

Thus, the effectiveness of the ECB in stabilizing output in individual countries depends on whether the shocks are symmetric or asymmetric. In practice, shocks are always some mixture of symmetric and asymmetric movements. We can derive the following important conclusion. To the extent that there is some asymmetric component in the shocks, the ECB generally stabilizes too little from the point of view of the individual member state.

Can this problem of insufficient stabilization be resolved? The answer is negative. The analysis we have carried out is just an extension of the analysis we conducted in Chapters 1 and 2 when we discussed the theory of optimum currency areas. There we found that if countries are subject to temporary asymmetric shocks, they will find it costly to be in a monetary union. The analysis of the current chapter gives practical content to this theory. Thus, if countries do form an optimum currency area (in the sense of not being subjected much to asymmetric shocks) then the ECB has a relatively easy time stabilizing shocks, and there are few conflicts between member states and the ECB. Conversely, if countries do not form an optimum currency area then the ECB has a hard time stabilizing output and employment.

Have these asymmetric shocks been important in the operation of the Eurosystem since 1999? We answer this question by first looking at the growth rates of output and the inflation rates in the 12 members of the Eurosystem from 2003 to 2014 (see Figs 9.3 and 9.4).[2] It is very striking to observe that there was a relatively wide range of experiences, especially in the growth rates of GDP. In most years, the differentials between the high- and low-growth countries exceeded 5%. The year 2003 is noteworthy. In 2003 some countries experienced strong booms, while others experienced recessions. Inflation differentials between the lowest and the highest inflation countries are also important, regularly exceeding 3%.

The evidence presented in Figs 9.3 and 9.4 is to a certain extent misleading. Part of the observed differences in output growth and inflation may be the result of permanent asymmetric shocks. As we argued in Chapter 2, monetary policy, whether at the national or the European level, can do very little about permanent shocks that require a change in relative prices. It can only help smooth the adjustment towards the long-term equilibrium.

In order to concentrate on temporary asymmetric shocks and the stabilization issue, we focus next on the output gap. This measures deviations of output from its long-term growth path. Thus, the output gap is a good measure of the business cycle position of a country. We use a measure of the output gap as computed by the OECD, and show the results for the years 2008 and 2010 in Fig. 9.5. We observe that there were large differences in the cyclical position of Eurozone member countries during these years. Some countries, such as Ireland, Portugal, and Spain, experienced severe slowdowns of their economies, while (mostly) northern European countries experienced a boom in 2008. The year 2008 is an interesting year as an illustration of the role of asymmetric shock. For the Eurozone as a whole the output gap was approximately 0. There was therefore little reason to stabilize the output gap. The conditions prevailing within the different countries, however, were very divergent.

---

[2] Malta, Cyprus, Slovenia, Slovakia, Estonia, Latvia, and Lithuania have not been included in this analysis.

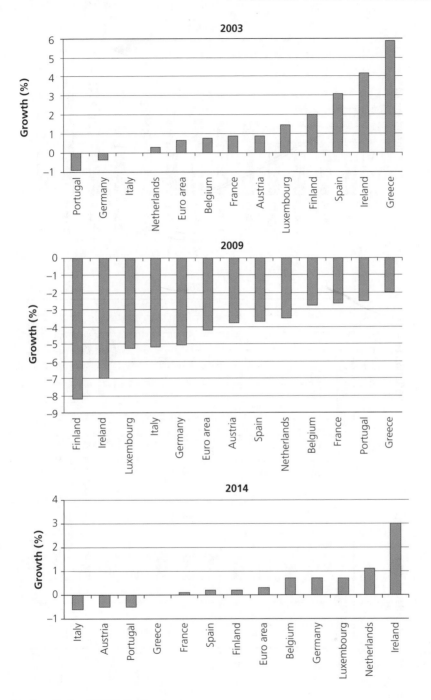

Figure 9.3 Growth of real GDP in the Eurozone.

Source: European Commission, *European Economy.*

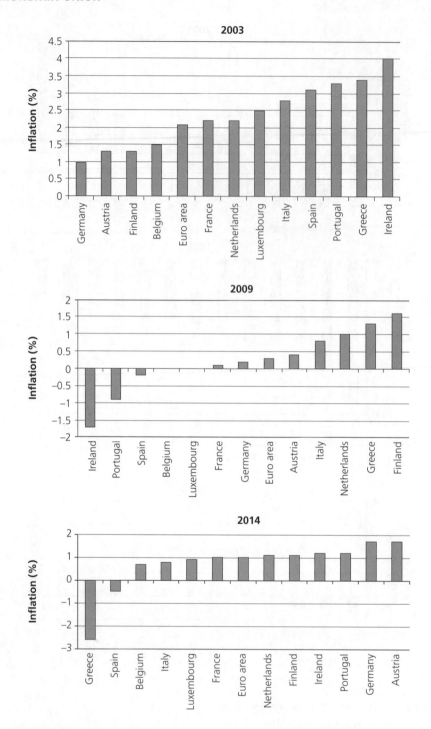

Figure 9.4 Inflation in the Eurozone 2014.

Source: European Commission, *European Economy.*

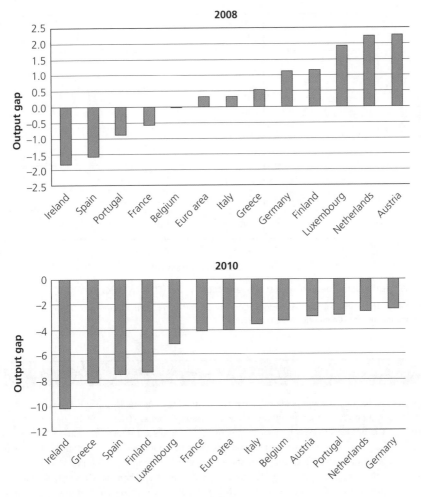

Figure 9.5 Output gaps in the Eurozone in 2008 and 2010.

Source: OECD, *Economic Outlook* 83 database.

Another way to look at the size of the asymmetries is to ask what the optimal interest rate would be for each country, given the rates of inflation and output gaps observed in these countries. In order to compute these desired interest rates we used the Taylor rule. This rule describes how the central bank sets the interest rate to counter changes in the rate of inflation and the output gap. In Box 9.1, we explain this in greater detail. We applied the analysis to the year 2010, but the same could be done for other years. We show the results in Fig. 9.6. We observe a wide range of desired interest rates. We have also added the relative size of each country (which is measured on the vertical axis) and the average interest rate that the ECB Board is computing using the same Taylor rule for the Eurosystem as a whole. This is represented by the dotted line. Given our discussion in Chapter 8, the ECB Board's wishes are likely to prevail. Note also that the wishes of the ECB Board and of the large countries are very close. We also discussed in Chapter 8 why this is so.

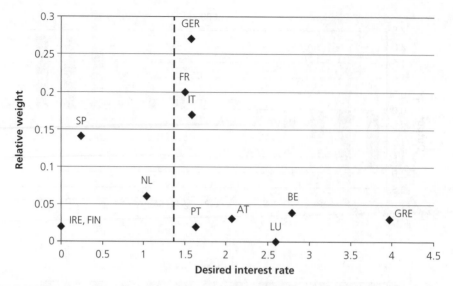

Figure 9.6 Distribution of desired interest rates and country sizes (EU-12) (Taylor rule, 2010).

Source: Inflation and relative country size: European Commission, *European Economy;* Output gap: OECD, *Economic Outlook;* for Luxembourg: European Commission, *European Economy.*

BOX 9.1 The Taylor rule

The Taylor rule has become a popular instrument in the analysis of monetary policies. It was first formulated by John Taylor as a description of how central banks behave (Taylor 1993). The central idea is that central banks react to deviations of the inflation rate from its target level. In addition, they react to changes in the output gap (the difference between observed output and capacity output) to the extent that they care about economic activity. More specifically, when inflation exceeds (or falls short of) the target, the central bank raises (or lowers) the short-term interest rate. When the output gap is positive (or negative) they raise (or reduce) the interest rate. More formally, each central bank computes its desired interest rate using the following rule:

$$r_t^* = p + \dot{p}* + a\left(\dot{p}_t - \dot{p}* \right) + bx_t$$

where r_t^* is the desired interest rate, p is the long-term real interest rate, $\dot{p}^*$ is the inflation target, and x_t is the output gap.

In order for this rule to lead to a stable inflation rate, the coefficient a should be larger than 1. The reason is that when the inflation rate exceeds the target, the nominal interest rate should increase by more than the increase in the inflation rate, so that the real interest rate goes up. This increase in the real interest rate is essential in bringing the inflation rate back to its target level. Taylor found that modern central banks tend to do this.

In the exercise reported in the main text, we assume that each governor uses the same Taylor rule (expressing identical preferences). The only difference between the governors is that their national inflation rates and output gaps differ. The ECB Board does the same exercise, using the Eurozone-wide averages of these two variables. We set $p = 2\%$, $\dot{p}^* = 2\%$, $a = 1.5$, and $b = 0.5$. The latter two coefficients have often been found to have such orders of magnitude (see Alesina et al. 2001). We applied the exercise to the year 2010 using OECD, *Economic Outlook*, as shown in Table 9.1.

Table 9.1 Desired interest rate using the Taylor rule (2010)

Countries	Desired interest rate	Relative size
Finland	0.00	0.02
Ireland	0.00	0.02
Spain	0.24	0.14
Netherlands	1.04	0.06
ECB Board	1.41	
France	1.50	0.20
Germany	1.57	0.27
Italy	1.59	0.17
Portugal	1.64	0.02
Austria	2.07	0.03
Luxembourg	2.60	0.00
Belgium	2.80	0.04
Greece	3.97	0.03

Source: Inflation: European Commission, *European Economy*; Output gap: OECD, *Economic Outlook*.

Fig. 9.6 illustrates that many countries are likely to be less than enthusiastic about the interest rate decisions of the ECB. Similar divergences are observed for other years (see De Grauwe 2009, where a similar exercise was performed for 2007).

The wide divergence in desired interest rates, which is the result of asymmetric developments in the member countries, also helps to explain the great caution the ECB exerts in manipulating its interest rate. As was shown in Chapter 8, the ECB did not react much to the slowdown in economic activity during 2003–5, nor in the Great Recession of 2008–9, at least when compared to the US. Similarly, we observed that during booms in economic activity the ECB was more reluctant to raise the interest rate than the US Fed. We interpreted this to imply that the ECB gave a relatively low weight to output stabilization, i.e. that it is a conservative central banker. There is an alternative interpretation that is possible: the large differences in desired interest rates due to asymmetric shocks paralyse the ECB and prevent it from taking action.

It should be pointed out that the discussion above may lead to a distorted view of the policy problem facing the ECB. As we saw in Chapter 2, countries that experience higher growth rates of productivity will naturally experience more inflation (in the CPI index) than countries with low rates of productivity growth. Thus, if the source of inflation differentials lies in productivity growth differentials, there is nothing to worry about. In fact, the higher inflation in the high-productivity-growth countries is an equilibrating mechanism. This is the Balassa–Samuelson effect discussed in Chapter 2. We observe from Fig. 9.4 that this effect may have played a role in 2003, but is much less likely to have been important in later years.

Another qualification should be made here. Systematic inflation differentials affect real interest rates and may affect asset markets (in particular the housing market). We explore this issue in Box 9.2.

BOX 9.2 Asymmetric shocks and housing prices

In Fig. 9.4, we illustrated the very different inflation experiences of the Eurozone countries. These large inflation differences within the Eurozone have important implications. Since the start of the Eurozone in 1999 the nominal interest rate as set by the ECB in the zone has applied to all members. As a result, the large inflation differentials imply that the real interest rates have been very different. In Eurozone countries with high inflation rates, real interest rates tended to be low, while in low-inflation countries real interest rates were significantly higher. To give some examples, Ireland experienced a yearly rate of inflation of 3.3% during 1999–2008 and the long-term nominal interest rate (government bond rate) was on average 4.8%. As a result, the real interest rate was 1.5%. In Germany, the rate of inflation was 1.3% while the government bond rate was on average 4.6%. As a result, the real interest rate amounted to 3.3%. We show the average real interest rates within Eurozone countries during 1997–2008 in Fig. 9.7. These differences in real interest rates were not without consequences for housing markets in the Eurozone countries. In general, low real interest rates stimulate the demand for houses (and real estate in general). This in turn will tend to raise house prices.

The reverse is likely to happen in countries with high real interest rates. There is strong evidence that this happened in the Eurozone countries from 1997 until the start of the financial crisis in 2008. We show the evidence in Figs 9.8 and 9.9. Fig. 9.8 shows house price increases during 1997–2008 in a number of Eurozone countries. These statistics are compiled by *The Economist*, and cover only seven (albeit the largest) of the Eurozone countries. We observe very large differences. In Ireland and Spain, house price increases were truly spectacular. They more than doubled in Spain, and more than tripled in Ireland. In contrast, in Germany, house prices barely moved during the same period. In Fig. 9.9, we plot house price increases on the vertical axis and the real interest rate on the horizontal axis. We observe that there seems to be a negative relationship between real interest rates and house price increases. Countries that enjoyed low real interest rates experienced very strong price increases in their housing markets.

All this leads to important policy issues. The low real interest rates in countries such as Ireland and Spain have fuelled a strong housing bubble. Such bubbles spill over into the credit markets. Local banks that see the collateral of their housing loans increase are tempted to increase credit, thereby fuelling

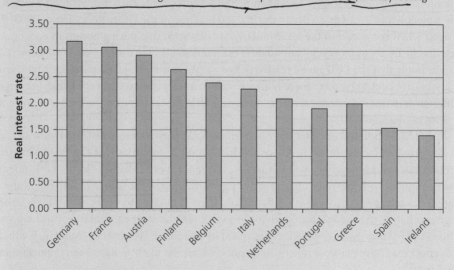

Figure 9.7 Average real interest rates in Eurozone countries (1997–2008).

Source: European Commission, *European Economy.*

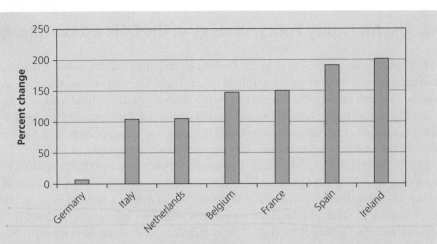

Figure 9.8 House price indices (% change over 1997–2008).

Source: The Economist, 6 December 2008, and Global Property Guide.

the bubble. Since nominal interest rates are fixed centrally by the ECB, such a credit expansion can be done at unchanged nominal interest rates. There is very little to check this bubble. The danger is that when the crash comes (which happened in 2008), the economy will go through a wrenching deflationary adjustment, when consumers find out that their borrowings exceed the (deflated) values of their houses.

In order to reduce these risks of booms and busts, bank supervisors can use macro-prudential stabilizers. This can be achieved by lowering the loan–value ratio (i.e. the ratio of the mortgage loan to the value of the house) during boom conditions, and to increase it again during downturns. Thus, when house prices increase, the size of the mortgage loan that banks are able to grant declines as a percentage of the value of the house, thereby automatically limiting the extension of credit during boom periods.

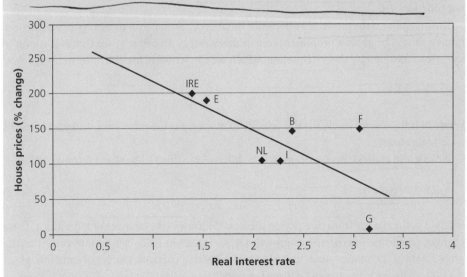

Figure 9.9 Real interest rate and house prices (% change over 1997–2008).

Source: The Economist, 6 December 2008; Global Property Guide; and European Commission, European Economy.

9.2 The Monetary Policy Strategy of the ECB: a description

The ECB has formulated the strategy it follows to set monetary policies in the Eurozone. This strategy starts out by defining the ultimate targets (inflation, output) and the intermediate targets. As is well known, the ultimate targets are often affected by central bank actions very indirectly and with long lags. Therefore, central banks select intermediate targets that are known to influence the ultimate targets, and that they can influence more directly. We first describe the ECB strategy. In the next section we critically evaluate it.

The first step in the formulation of the Monetary Policy Strategy (MPS) consists of giving a precise definition of price stability. The Governing Council of the ECB has adopted the following definition: 'price stability shall be defined as a year-on-year increase in the Harmonised Index of Consumer Prices (HICP) for the euro area of below 2%' (*ECB Monthly Bulletin* January 1999, p. 46).[3] As this definition does not have a lower bound, it led at some point to fears that the ECB would not be concerned with deflation (negative inflation rate). In 2003, the ECB clarified this definition of price stability by stating that it pursued an inflation objective below, but close to, 2%. Price stability according to this definition 'is to be maintained over the medium run'. This means, for example, that if inflation suddenly increases above the target range due to a large disturbance, the ECB will allow for a gradual adjustment back to the target range. The ECB, however, does not define what the 'medium run' is.

Having identified the target of monetary policies, the ECB then developed a strategy to achieve it. At the start of the Eurozone, the ECB proposed a 'two-pillar' approach. Later it changed that strategy when it realized that it did not work well. Let us first describe this two-pillar strategy as initially conceived by the ECB. This will then allow us to find out why it did not function well.

The first pillar is the monetary one. Since inflation is ultimately a monetary phenomenon, money should be given a prominent role in this strategy. In order to see this, it is useful to start from the quantity theory equation, which we can write (in log-linear form) as follows:

$$m + v = p + y \tag{9.1}$$

where m is the money stock, v is the velocity of money, p is the price level, and y is real GDP, all in logarithms.

We can also express this equation in first differences. This yields, after rearranging:

$$\Delta m = \Delta p + \Delta y - \Delta v \tag{9.2}$$

where Δ is the change from one year to the next. Since we take changes of logarithms, these changes should be interpreted as growth rates.[4] Equation (9.2) can be interpreted as the growth rate of the money stock that is consistent with a particular target of inflation, given the underlying growth rates of GDP and of velocity.

---

[3] The HICP is a price index for the euro area constructed from a harmonized definition of the national price indices.

[4] Note that this is only approximately true.

The first pillar of the ECB strategy can now be described as follows. The ECB makes a forecast of the future trend growth of real GDP (Δy). In its *Monthly Bulletin* of January 1999, this was estimated to be approximately 2%. Next the ECB forecasts the future velocity of money. In the same *Monthly Bulletin*, velocity was estimated to decline in a trendwise fashion by approximately 0.5% per year. Thus, $\Delta v = -0.5\%$. With these two numbers fixed, the ECB finds the growth rate of the money stock that is consistent with the inflation target, which is at most 2%. As a result, the money stock should not be increasing by more than 4.5% per year.[5] This is then the target for the money stock growth. The ECB selected M3 as the relevant money stock definition.

This is a similar procedure to that followed by the Bundesbank in the past. The ECB, however, stresses that the 4.5% money stock number should not be considered as a target, but rather as a 'reference value'. This means that if the actual increase in M3 exceeds 4.5%, the ECB may (or may not) take action to reduce the growth rate of M3 (by raising short-term interest rates, for example). Thus, the deviation between the actual money growth and the target value is interpreted flexibly by the ECB. Although the wording was somewhat different, this was also the attitude of the Bundesbank towards the use of the money growth target.

The second pillar in the Monetary Policy Strategy identifies a number of variables that provide important information to forecast future inflation. 'These variables include, *inter alia*, wages, the exchange rate, bond prices and the yield curve, various measures of real activity, fiscal policy indicators, price and cost indices and business and consumer surveys' (*ECB Monthly Bulletin* January 1999, p. 49). Thus if, for example, wages increase markedly in the Eurozone, the ECB may deem this to threaten future price stability and may therefore take appropriate action (in this case increase the short-term interest rate and/or reduce liquidity in the system). Similarly, a depreciation of the euro against the dollar would set in motion inflationary pressures that might lead the ECB to raise the interest rate. Note in this connection that the ECB would not try to influence the exchange rate directly. It would react to exchange rate changes only to the extent that these changes were forecasted to affect future inflation. The list of potential indicators in this second pillar is an open-ended one. Others may be added, and those on the list may or may not receive much attention.

In a nutshell, the Monetary Policy Strategy of the ECB sets an inflation target of 2% at most. In order to steer actual inflation towards that target, the ECB watches a number of variables that influence future inflation. The most prominent of these variables (the intermediate target) is the growth rate of M3. In the next section we evaluate this monetary policy strategy.

9.3 The Monetary Policy Strategy of the ECB: an evaluation

Academic economists and market analysts alike have criticized the Monetary Policy Strategy of the ECB. We present this criticism in this section and we focus on two problems with this strategy. One has to do with the objectives pursued by the ECB, the other with the instruments. From the outset, it should be said that the ECB has been receptive to some of this criticism and has been willing to adapt its Monetary Policy Strategy accordingly.

---

[5] This number could change in the future if the ECB deems that the trend growth of GDP and/or of velocity changes.

The selection of the target

The ECB recognizes only one target of monetary policy. This goes counter to the Maastricht Treaty, which mandates that the ECB should also pursue other targets, if these do not interfere with price stability. We criticized the ECB in Chapter 8 for this reinterpretation of the Treaty and for narrowing its responsibilities. If we are to accept this narrowing down of the ECB's responsibility then it must be admitted that the ECB has been quite successful in achieving the objective of price stability. This is shown in Fig. 9.10. During the whole period of its existence (1999–2015) the ECB has kept inflation on average equal to 1.87%. This is indeed below but close to 2%. However, from Fig. 9.10 it appears that, since the start of the financial crisis in October 2008, the success of the ECB in keeping the rate of inflation close to 2% has been less clear. We first observe large fluctuations of inflation with a pronounced decline in inflation during the Great Recession of 2008–09 and again since early 2012, when the rate of inflation declined substantially to reach negative territory at the end of 2014. Second, since the start of the financial crisis, the average inflation in the Eurozone had, at 1.41%, ceased to be close to 2%. Thus we conclude that the ECB experienced difficulties in stopping the deflationary dynamics that emerged in the wake of the sovereign debt crisis. This is probably the reason why in early 2015 the ECB decided to engage in a large bond-buying programme (QE) aimed at increasing the money base, which the ECB hopes will tend to push up the rate of inflation again.

It is useful to point out here that the exclusive targeting of inflation does not necessarily mean that other objectives cannot be realized at the same time. In particular, inflation targeting also leads to output stabilization when the source of the shock comes from the demand side (see Bofinger 1999 and Clarida et al. 1999 on this issue). This is illustrated in Fig. 9.11.

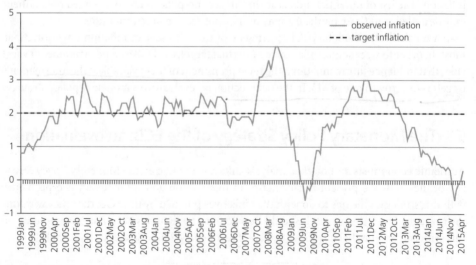

Figure 9.10 Inflation rate in the Eurozone (1999–2015).

Source: European Central Bank, *Monthly Bulletins.*

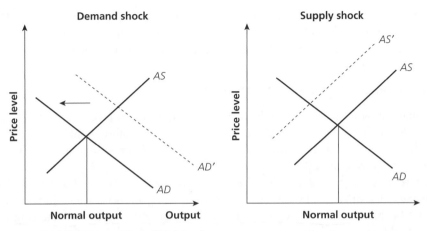

Figure 9.11 Shocks in aggregate demand and supply.

The left panel of Fig. 9.11 shows an economy experiencing a boom, which is the result of a high level of aggregate demand (represented by the dotted AD′ line). As a result, output exceeds full capacity level (the normal level). To prevent inflationary pressures, the ECB will follow restrictive monetary policies (shown by the arrow, which shifts the AD′ line back to its normal level). This has the effect of stabilizing both the price level and the output level. There is no trade-off between price and output stabilization when shocks in aggregate demand occur.[6]

In reinterpreting its mandate, the ECB has been influenced by the theory of flexible inflation targeting as developed by Svensson[6] (1995, 1998; see also Alesina et al. 2001 and Mishkin and Schmidt-Hebbel 2001). The central claim made by this theory is that inflation targeting makes it possible for the central bank not only to stabilize inflation, but also to do the best possible job of stabilizing output around potential output (its 'natural' level in long-run equilibrium). This is clear from Fig. 9.11. By stabilizing the price level, the central bank also stabilizes the output level. In this view there is no need to target output explicitly.

Things are more complicated when shocks originate in the supply side of the economy. We show this in the right panel of Fig. 9.11. The economy has experienced a negative supply shock, which lowers output but increases prices. When the ECB targets the price level, it will tend to reduce aggregate demand, thereby lowering the price level again at the expense of an even lower output level. In this case, there is a trade-off between inflation and output stabilization.[7] In its official pronouncements, the ECB has made it clear that when there is such a trade-off, it will pursue price stabilization.

It should be pointed out that the ECB has left the door open for some output stabilization even in this case of a supply shock. As mentioned earlier, the ECB defines price stability over the 'medium run'. Thus, if, after a supply shock, prices start to rise, the ECB may apply gradualism in its response. This means that it would not immediately react by applying restrictive monetary policies aimed at stopping the price increases. Instead, it would try to lower the inflationary pressures gradually. In doing so, it would avoid a sharp decline in output.

[6] Note that in this model the ECB stabilizes the price *level* rather than the inflation rate. One can develop the same analysis in terms of inflation rates, however. See Clarida et al. (1999).

[7] Note that we assume here that the supply shock is temporary. If the supply shock is permanent, the central bank will have to bring down the price level, and there is no trade-off between output and inflation stabilization.

It should be mentioned that proponents of inflation targeting (e.g. Svensson 1997, 1998) have stressed that the *gradual* transition to the inflation target after a shock is the right approach and allows a central bank to also pay attention to output stabilization.

Financial stability: an additional objective?

The financial crisis of 2007–8 and the ensuing government debt crisis that started in 2010 have called into question the mainstream view that price stability should be the primary objective of a central bank. Is financial stability not equally important, or more so, as an objective of the central bank?

Before the emergence of the crisis, the standard response to that question was, first, that by maintaining price stability the central bank was doing all that it could do to maintain financial stability. In other words, price stability was seen as a strategy that would minimize the risk of financial instability. Second, the main responsibility for maintaining financial stability is in the hands of the supervisors and regulators.

There can be no doubt that the responsibility of the supervisors and the regulators is a formidable one. But does this absolve the central bank from its responsibilities? To answer this question, we have to formulate another one. Is it conceivable that there is a trade-off between price stability and financial stability (much in the same way as there can be a trade-off between price stability and output stability when supply shocks occur)? If there is none, the central bank can indeed claim that by maintaining price stability it is doing all that it can to also maintain financial stability. If there is a possible trade-off between price stability and financial stability, then the central bank will have to make a choice. In that case, the issue arises of which of the two objectives should have precedence: price stability or financial stability.

Is there a trade-off between price stability and financial stability?

Much of central banking has to do with resolving trade-offs. The one that has occupied most of the attention both of practitioners and theorists is the trade-off between inflation and output that we discussed in the previous section.

Does there exist a similar trade-off between inflation and financial stability? At first sight, there does not seem to be a trade-off like the one between price stability and unemployment. There are no macroeconomic models that say that reducing inflation reduces financial stability, in the short run or in the long run. Thus, the choice faced by the central bank does not seem to be comparable to the choice between inflation and unemployment. Nevertheless, trade-offs between inflation and financial stability may appear in a different form. In order to analyse these different trade-offs it is useful to trace how bubbles work through demand and supply, and in so doing create trade-offs between inflation and financial stability.

Let us take the case of the IT-driven asset bubble of the late 1990s as our prototype bubble.[8] A new technology leads to great optimism about the future potential of that technology. This leads to large increases in stock prices. These increases reduce the cost of attracting capital, which in turn increases investment in these new technologies. The primary effect of such a shock is to increase productivity so that the aggregate supply curve shifts to the right. The same shock, however, also increases aggregate demand. New technologies create new

---

[8] See Kindleberger (2005) for an analysis of similar technology-driven bubbles in history.

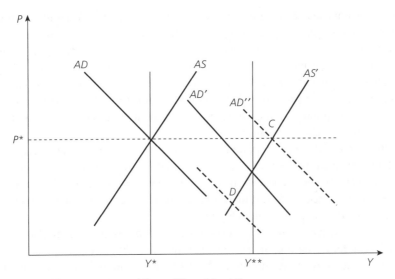

Figure 9.12 Trade-off between price stability and financial stability.

products and thus lead consumers to spend more. We will assume here that the supply effect is larger than the demand effect. We show this case in Fig. 9.12. The new technology shifts demand and supply to the right (from *AD* to *AD'* and *AS* to *AS'*). However, the supply effect is stronger than the demand effect. As a result, in the new equilibrium the aggregate price level has declined.

Much of the subsequent dynamics now depends on the policy regime. Suppose the central bank targets the price level at the level *P** (in practice it targets inflation, but the argument could be phrased in terms of inflation). We then immediately see that the central bank will respond by a policy of monetary stimulus (lower interest rate, higher money stock) so as to raise demand and the price level. We show this by a shift of the demand curve from *AD'* to *AD''*. The economy settles at point *C*. The result of this monetary accommodation is to keep the price at its pre-technological shock level. Thus, the central bank maintains price stability. The monetary stimulus, however, increases asset prices even further, creating a risk that this could degenerate into a bubble. Since bubbles inevitably lead to crashes and since financial institutions are usually involved in asset price inflation, financial stability is endangered.

Thus, there seems to be a trade-off here between price stability and financial stability in the presence of a technology shock. The trade-off arises because the technology shock has the effect of reducing the aggregate price level. The central bank, however, targets a price level corresponding to the pre-technology shock. As a result, it is forced to react to the shock by a monetary stimulus, creating an environment that makes a bubble more likely, while keeping the price level unchanged.

This analysis comes close to what Kindleberger (2005) has identified to be the main sources of the development of a bubble. There is first a technological revolution, and second a monetary accommodation. The two together provide the cocktail that in history most often leads to bubbles and later crashes.[9]

---

[9] It is also the dynamics underlying the IT bubble during the second half of the 1990s. The US monetary authorities identified this shock as a productivity shock that tended to lower prices and thus made a monetary expansion desirable. See Greenspan (2007).

The equilibrium reached at point C is unsustainable and therefore can only be temporary. Output is beyond full capacity. It is sustained at that level by an interest rate that is too low and by the high level of asset prices that create a positive wealth effect on aggregate demand.

Point C is unsustainable; a crash is inevitable. The crash leads to a decline in aggregate demand. It is likely to lead to an overreaction, as consumers and producers who have indebted themselves have to improve their balance sheets again. Thus, the demand curve shifts to the left. A new (temporary) equilibrium is reached at point D. The economy is in a recession, with output located below full capacity.

It should be noted that once at point D, the trade-off for the central bank disappears. The central bank, by targeting the price level, will stimulate aggregate demand, thereby allowing the price level and the output level to increase. Whether this monetary stimulus is effective is another matter, which we do not analyse here. Chances are that a monetary stimulus may have become ineffective (as a result of liquidity traps).

The analysis underlying Fig. 9.12 stresses the importance of technological shocks. These were important for explaining the IT bubble of the late 1990s that crashed in 2001. Not all bubbles are technology driven, however. The stock market bubble that started in 2003 and crashed in 2007–8 does not appear to have been driven by a technology shock. It is not fully clear how this bubble was triggered. It appears, though, that it was mainly caused by a combination of 'animal spirits', i.e. optimistic beliefs of investors, and excessive credit creation.

We analyse this case in Fig. 9.13 because we believe that this is the type of bubble most relevant to understanding the macroeconomic disequilibria in the Eurozone during 2003–7. We start from the initial equilibrium at point C. A bubble is now set in motion as a result of 'animal spirits'. This raises stock prices and lowers the cost of capital. The supply curve shifts down from AS to AS'. At the same time, the bubble in asset markets raises aggregate demand due to wealth effects and the increased availability of credit. The latter arises because the banks' balance sheets move upward with the bubble. The mechanism is that the higher price of assets increases the collateral value of these assets and thus the potential for bank credit.[10] The aggregate demand curve shifts to the right from AD to AD'. We assume that these two effects are of the same magnitude. They do not have to be. The important point is that both

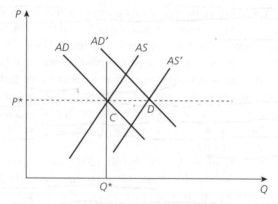

Figure 9.13 The trade-off between price stability and financial stability due to 'animal spirits'.

[10] Note that 'mark-to-market' rules reinforce this effect.

demand and supply shift. As a result, the central bank, which is targeting P at the level P^*, decides that there is nothing to worry about.

There is, however, a lot to worry about. The expansion of output is unsustainable because it is based on credit creation, which is linked to artificially high asset valuations. In addition, in this process of excessive credit creation, households and firms accumulate excessive debt that will have to be scaled down. This happens when the bubble bursts. At that moment both demand and supply shift to the left. They will typically undershoot, creating a recession. All this will lead to banking problems and a financial crisis.

From the preceding analysis we conclude that important trade-offs between price stability and financial stability arise when technological developments trigger booms in asset markets. When 'animal spirits' create a cycle of booms and busts, there may not be a trade-off but the central bank may fail to see the underlying boom–bust dynamics when it focuses exclusively on inflation. Thus, a central bank that uses a lexicographic ordering favouring price stability over other objectives is likely to fuel the boom inadvertently (in the case of a technology-driven bubble) or will decide to do nothing (in the case of an 'animal spirits bubble'), allowing a process of excessive credit creation. This is what happened during the period 2000–7. Major central banks (including the ECB) focused mainly on price stability, and were quite successful in keeping inflation low during that period. They failed, however, to see the bubbles in asset markets that were threatening financial stability and that they were fuelled inadvertently by allowing excessive credit creation to develop. These are situations in which central banks should have given equal weights to the inflation target and to financial stability.

We also conclude that the lexicographic ordering of the objectives of the ECB should be abandoned. Strict inflation targeting cannot be maintained because it can conflict with financial stability and also because it can blind the central bank into believing that everything is all right (see Borio and Lowe 2002 for a similar conclusion).[11]

Promoting financial stability to a level at par with price stability creates a number of issues, however. We discuss two issues here. The first one has to do with the definition and the monitoring of financial stability; the second one has to do with the instruments a central bank can use to reach the objective of financial stability (this issue will be discussed in Section 9.4).

How to define and monitor financial stability?

While the definition of price stability and thus its monitoring is relatively easy, this cannot be said of the objective of financial stability. Defining financial stability is more difficult than defining price stability because the former has different dimensions that do not lend themselves to being captured by one index in the way that price stability is described. As a result, the monitoring of financial stability is also inherently more difficult than the monitoring of price stability (through the use of the Consumer Price Index).

The literature offers few formal definitions of financial stability. For example, Ferguson (2002) defines financial stability through its contrary: financial instability. Financial instability is a situation in which 'a) some important set of financial asset prices seem to have diverged

---

[11] This is certainly not the mainstream view. The mainstream view is represented by Svensson (2003), who argues that the central bank should focus on its objective of price stability, with financial stability concerns only entering in an extreme scenario when a crisis is underway. This was also the Greenspan (2007) view and was very much influenced by Bernanke and Gertler (2001).

Figure 9.14 Growth rate of total bank loans (left) and stock price index (right) in the euro area.

Note: The index of stock prices is the Euro STOXX-50.

Source: European Central Bank.

sharply from fundamentals; and/or b) market functioning and credit availability, domestically and perhaps internationally, have been significantly distorted; with the result that c) aggregate spending deviates (or is likely to deviate) significantly from the economy's ability to produce'.

Borio and Lowe (2002) use a similar definition of financial instability. According to these authors, sustained rapid credit growth combined with large increases in asset prices increases the probability of an episode of financial instability (see also Borio 2003). This view of the simultaneous occurrence of bubble-like developments in asset markets and excessive credit growth as twin indicators of threats to financial stability is also to be found in Kindleberger (2005) and forms the basis of our theoretical analysis.

Thus, by focusing on two types of variables, i.e. asset prices and credit growth, the monetary authorities can obtain important information about ongoing developments that can threaten financial stability. We show an example of a recent episode. In Fig. 9.14, we present the Euro STOXX-50 Price Index and the yearly growth of bank credit in the euro area during 1999–2008. The stock market bubbles and crashes in the euro area appear to have coincided with strong accelerations and decelerations of bank credit in the euro area. Take the bubble and crash in the stock market that started in 2003. We observe that the yearly growth rates of total bank loans in the euro area increased from less than 4% per year in 2003 to double-digit growth rates during 2006–7 (which was the period during which stock prices reached their peaks). Thus, during the bubble in the euro stock markets from 2003 to 2007, during which stock prices almost doubled, bank credit in the Eurozone increased by 60% (from 95% of euro area GDP to 115%).

Thus, during the period 2003–7 statistical evidence was available to detect threats to financial stability.[12] The period 2003–7 showed the classic combination of asset bubbles fuelled

[12] There were also observers at the BIS (Bank for International Settlements) and in academia who, based on similar evidence, warned of imminent financial crises.

by excessive bank credit, which ultimately leads to a crash and a financial crisis. (See also Borio 2003 on this issue, with more empirical evidence of the importance of these twin variables in explaining subsequent financial crisis.) We conclude that it is possible for a central bank to monitor the risk of financial crisis by focusing on a limited number of indicators.

One issue that arises here is why central bankers in Europe (the ECB, the Bank of England) and the US (the Federal Reserve) put so little weight on these indicators. There were probably many factors that influenced the failure of central bankers to detect the threats to financial stability. There is one factor that we want to stress here. Central bankers were 'fed intellectually' by macroeconomic models developed in academia. These models were based on the assumption of perfectly informed and superbly rational agents who cannot make systematic errors, and who understand the great complexity of the world in which they live. In these 'dynamic stochastic general equilibrium' models (DSGE-models) that are now widely used in central banks, bubbles and crashes cannot occur. Prices always reflect underlying fundamentals. Financial crises cannot occur. There is no need to do anything about asset prices.

These models tell the policy-makers to focus on price stability and suggest that all the rest—growth and stability—will be given to them by the efficient working of the markets.[13] Such an intellectual framework can easily work as an intellectual device that prevents policy-makers from seeing emerging problems in the financial markets, because in the models these problems can simply not arise. And when they do arise they are just exogenous shocks that could not be seen in advance.

Since the eruption of the financial crises, these DSGE-models have been amended by introducing a banking sector. These models then make it possible for financial crises to occur (see Gertler et al. 2012, Boissay et al. 2013). It is surprising though that one had to wait until financial crises erupted for mainstream macroeconomists to accept that crises were theoretically possible.

Excessive reliance on the money stock?

The ECB has been very much influenced by the Bundesbank legacy,[14] which itself was much influenced by the monetarist analysis made popular by Milton Friedman, i.e. that inflation is always and everywhere a monetary phenomenon. This view led the ECB to give a prominent role to money in its monetary policy strategy (the so-called first pillar) until 2003 when it de-emphasized this first pillar without, however, eliminating the monetary analysis from its policy analysis.

[13] For a strong formulation of this view see Stark (2008) in a speech of 18 November 2008: 'The mandate of the ECB is to maintain price stability over the medium term. This mandate must be adhered to both in normal times and in times of crisis. The monetary policy stance appropriate to fulfill our mandate depends exclusively on our assessment of the balance of risks to price stability, and nothing else … There is no trade-off between price stability and financial stability.' For another sceptical note on the existence of a trade-off between financial stability and price stability, see Bini-Smaghi (2008).

[14] There is strong evidence that the Bundesbank was not very successful in its money stock targeting. Half of the time the actual money stock numbers fell outside the targeted range (see Clarida and Gertler 1996 and Bernanke and Mihov 1997). This has led these authors to conclude that the strong reputation of the Bundesbank had nothing to do with money targeting (which the Bundesbank failed to apply successfully). It had everything to do with its success at keeping inflation low.

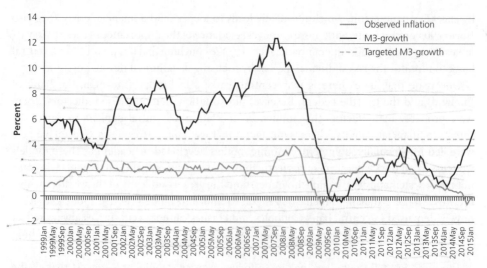

Figure 9.15 Inflation and money growth (M3) in the Eurozone.

Source: ECB, Monthly Bulletin.

How successful was this monetarist strategy? Sometimes a picture is worth a thousand words. We show the picture in Fig. 9.15. It is useful to split the whole period into two, the pre- and post-crisis periods. During the pre-crisis period (1999–2008), we observe that apart from a very brief period in 2000–1, M3 growth has permanently exceeded by far the reference value of 4.5%. The average yearly growth rate of M3 was 7.4% while inflation amounted to 2.2% a year (see Table 9.2). Thus it appears that the ECB's monetary strategy, which consisted in keeping inflation low by controlling the growth rate of the money stock, failed dismally. While inflation remained remarkably stable during this period, the growth rate of M3 by far exceeded the reference value of 4.5% that the ECB had said should not be surpassed to maintain inflation below 2%. It dramatically surpassed that value, and yet this did not affect inflation. The troubleshooter was velocity, which declined on average by more than 3% per year.

Things changed during the post-crisis period. During 2010–14 it appeared that there was again some correlation between money growth and inflation, but this was only temporary. During the second half of 2014 the two growth rates diverged significantly again. M3-growth increased above 4% while inflation continued to move downwards.

Table 9.2 Average yearly growth rates of M3, prices, output, and velocity (1999–2015)

	1999–2008	2009–15
Mean growth rate M3	7.4%	2.1%
Mean inflation rate	2.2%	1.4%
Mean growth rate output	2.0%	0.0%
Velocity growth	−3.2%	−1.4%

What do we learn from this? First, the ECB has managed to keep inflation low throughout 1999–2015 despite the fact that it completely failed in its announced strategy of controlling inflation via monetary control. Second, it tells us much about the signalling power of money growth in the Eurozone: that M3 growth has had almost no power to predict future inflation in the Eurozone since 1999. The only exception occurred during the 'Great Recession' of 2008–9 when the deflationary forces of this recession pulled down both M3 growth and the rate of inflation.

The question that arises next is why money growth has so little information value for future inflation. There is a great deal of evidence that in a low-inflation environment and in a world of frequent financial innovations, the money supply numbers are very unreliable as signals of future inflation. We analyse this issue further in Box 9.3.

BOX 9.3 The information content of money growth in low inflation countries: cross-section evidence

How much information do money growth numbers reveal about inflation? We analyse the question using cross-section evidence about the relation between inflation and money growth in Fig. 9.16. It shows a very tight relation between the 30-year average of inflation and money growth in a sample of more than 100 countries. Subjecting this kind of evidence to regression analysis invariably reveals that

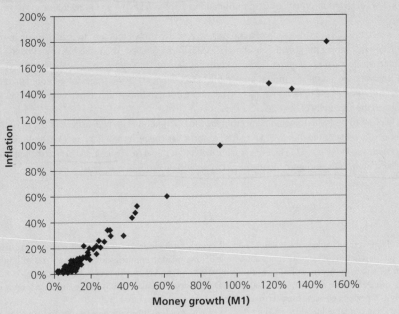

Figure 9.16 Inflation and money growth (1970–99) (average yearly changes; full sample).

Source: IMF, *International Financial Statistics*, CD-ROM, August 2001.

the hypothesis of strict proportionality between inflation and money growth cannot be rejected and that most, if not all, of the differentials in inflation between countries can be explained by differentials in money growth. This kind of cross-section evidence has invaded textbooks to show that the evidence in favour of the quantity theory is overwhelming (see for example Parkin et al. 2000). It was also used by Lucas (1996) in his Nobel Lecture.

When one looks at a subsample of countries with low inflation, things get fuzzier. We show this in Fig. 9.17, where we present a subsample of countries that experienced an average rate of inflation of 5% or less during 1970–99. We observe that there is very little relation between inflation and money growth in these 'low'-inflation countries.[15] Put differently, long-term sustained differences in money growth between countries are uninformative about the differences in their rates of inflation, and this finding is not altered when one corrects for differences in the growth of output.[16]

It is not difficult to understand this result. Money supply statistics are full of noise. In a low-inflation environment where inflation is only a few percent a year, the observed differences in the money supply growth numbers contain mostly noise, and say little about differences in monetary policies (the signal). Thus, paradoxically, it is the success of central banks in reducing inflation that makes money growth numbers unreliable as a signal of inflationary tendencies. In a low-inflation environment, where the central banks do not systematically increase the supply of money above the growth potential of the economy, the money stock is subjected to shocks that come mostly from the demand for money (velocity changes, financial innovations, and other shocks). They no longer reflect systematic policy changes (see Gerlach 2002 on this).[17]

All this confirms what many critics have been saying about the first pillar of the ECB monetary policy strategy, i.e. that the prominence given to money in guiding monetary policies is mistaken (see for example Svensson 1998; Gerlach 2002; and Woodford 2006). Given that it is the ambition of the ECB to keep the rate of inflation below 2%, success on the inflation front makes the yearly money growth numbers even less informative about the inflationary potential in the economy than appears from Fig. 9.17.

In fact, the ECB became aware of this problem. We have shown that the strategy of trying to control inflation by keeping the growth rate of money (M3) in check failed. The result has been that the ECB has had to ignore the money supply numbers most of the time. This has led to a credibility problem. The ECB announced a target for money growth but in fact did not take this target into account in its policy decisions most of the time. It thus gave signals about its intentions which it then failed to follow. This harmed the credibility of the ECB.

In order to deal with this credibility problem, the ECB amended its 'two-pillar' strategy in 2003. It decided to relegate the money stock to the second pillar, calling it monetary analysis, and to elevate the previous second pillar to the first one, calling it economic analysis. Thus, it decided to maintain its two-pillar strategy using monetary analysis as a cross-check of economic analysis.

---

[15] Many central bankers today would not call a yearly rate of inflation of 4% or 5% maintained during 30 years a low rate of inflation. If we restrict our subsample of low-inflation countries to those countries with inflation of less than 3% a year, the absence of a link between inflation and money growth is even more striking.

[16] See De Grauwe and Grimaldi (2001) and De Grauwe and Polan (2005) where a more elaborate econometric analysis is performed using long-term cross-section data.

[17] There is a large literature on the question of whether the European money demand equation is more predictable than national money demand equations (see Monticelli and Papi 1996). The evidence indicates that in the past the European money demand was more stable than the national money demand functions. It has been stressed by Arnold and de Vries (1997) that this is due to the fact that the uncorrelated error terms of the national money demand functions tend to offset each other in the aggregation process towards a European money demand function.

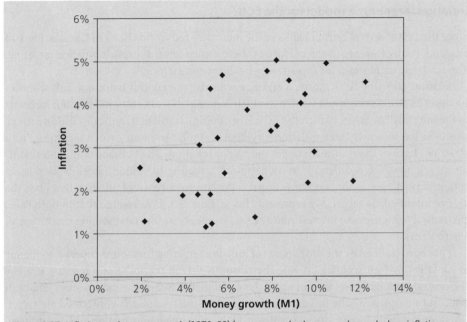

Figure 9.17 Inflation and money growth (1970–99) (average yearly changes; subsample: low-inflation countries).

Source: IMF, *International Financial Statistics*, CD-ROM, August 2001.

The rapid expansion of M3 during the pre-crisis period, especially after 2005, signalled something very different from future inflation. It was a signal of future financial upheavals. The rapid expansion of M3 was nothing but the counterpart of the massive expansion of the balance sheets of banks. As argued earlier, banks were allowed to increase their risky credit portfolios both nationally and internationally in an unprecedented way. As a result, their balance sheets became closely linked to the consecutive bubbles that were developing in asset markets (real estate markets, stock markets, commodities markets). Thus, the spectacular expansion of M3 (which reflects broadly the liabilities side of the banks) was a mirror image of the bubble-driven expansion of bank credit (the asset side), and should have been a warning signal of possible future financial instability. This expansion of the balance sheets of banks led not to inflation in consumption goods but to inflation in asset markets, until the bubble burst.

The single-minded focus of the ECB on inflation worked as a blind spot, preventing it from seeing that the danger did not come from CPI inflation but from asset inflation. (There was a similar blind spot about the danger of public debts and deficits, which were seen as the most important danger for the stability of the Eurozone. This led to an elaborate Stability and Growth Pact aimed at checking public debt. This pact, however, prevented policy-makers from seeing that the danger did not come from excessive government debt but from excessive private debt made possible by the unsustainable expansion of bank credit.)

Inflation targeting: a model for the ECB?

Since the 1990s, several central banks in the industrialized world (Bank of Canada, Bank of England, Bank of Sweden, Bank of Norway) have shifted towards explicit inflation targeting. The academic enthusiasm for this strategy has been quite strong.[18]

Inflation targeting here means a strategy whereby the central bank not only chooses inflation as its ultimate target (which the ECB is doing), but also uses its inflation forecasts as the intermediate target (which the ECB is not doing). It will then typically also announce this inflation forecast. Thus, inflation targeting is similar to money stock targeting. Both strategies have as their ultimate target the rate of inflation. Their choice of the intermediate target, however, is different. In money stock targeting the money stock is used as an intermediate target; in inflation targeting it is the current forecast of inflation that plays the role of intermediate target. We represent this in Table 9.3. (We assume that in both cases the central bank uses the interest rate as its instrument. See the next section on the use of instruments.)

It has been claimed by the proponents of inflation targeting that this is superior to money stock targeting (see Svensson 1998). The reason is that in the inflation-targeting strategy the central bank uses information on all the variables (including the money stock) that will affect future inflation. The inflation forecast is then the best possible intermediate target. This contrasts with money stock targeting, which omits much information and, in addition, uses irrelevant information also (because as we argued earlier, the money stock today can change for reasons that have nothing to do with inflation).

Although inflation targeting is clearly superior to money stock targeting, the issue arises of whether inflation targeting guarantees the best possible outcome for macroeconomic stability. We have discussed this issue earlier in this chapter. We argued that central banks can be quite successful in targeting inflation, but that this does not prevent bubbles in the asset markets from emerging. A much debated topic is whether the central bank should take movements in asset prices into account in setting its monetary policies (see Cecchetti et al. 2000; Bernanke and Gertler 2001; Bordo and Jeanne 2002; and Borio and Lowe 2002).

We argued earlier that besides targeting the inflation rate, the central bank must and can also monitor the evolution of bank credit and asset prices. This could be achieved by formulating a new 'two-pillar' strategy. In the first pillar, the central bank would target the rate of inflation as described in Table 9.3. This is the pillar that has to be used in normal times. In the second pillar, the central bank would keep track of bank credit and asset prices (stock prices and real estate prices). Bubbles usually develop when asset prices and bank credit increase together. We showed that this feature occurred quite strikingly in the Eurozone in Fig. 9.14. In this new two-pillar approach, the ECB would be responsible for limiting the movements

Table 9.3 Money and inflation targeting compared

	Instrument		Intermediate target		Ultimate target
Money stock targeting	interest rate	⇒	money stock	⇒	inflation
Inflation targeting	interest rate	⇒	inflation forecast	⇒	inflation

[18] For an evaluation, see Bernanke et al. (1999).

in bank credit. In order to do so, it would need sufficient instruments. We return to this issue in Section 9.4.

The practical implementation of the two pillars must be quite different. Inflation targeting can be implemented in a very precise way, i.e. by specifying a numerical target and by monitoring how close to this target inflation has stayed. No such precision is possible when monitoring bank credit and asset prices. More judgement is necessary.

9.4 The instruments of monetary policy in the Eurozone

In the previous sections, we discussed the choice of the intermediate and ultimate targets of the ECB. In this section, we analyse the instruments that the ECB uses to steer the economy towards these targets.

The ECB uses three types of instruments: open market operations, standing facilities (credit lines), and minimum reserve requirements.[19]

Open market operations

Open market operations are the most important instrument of the monetary policy of the ECB. They imply the buying and selling of marketable securities with the aim of increasing or reducing money market liquidity. Open market operations can be conducted in different ways. The ECB can engage in outright buying and selling of securities in the 'open market'. These are open market operations in the traditional sense. Prior to January 2015, the ECB rarely used this traditional instrument. Since then it has started a programme of 'Quantitative Easing' (QE), which is nothing else than the buying of government bonds in the open market (and possibly future sales of these bonds again). We discuss this QE-programme in the section 'QE: How does it work?'

The main technique that the ECB has been using up to 2015, however, is not these outright transactions but transactions using tenders. The ECB calls these its *main refinancing operations*. In this technique, the ECB provides liquidity to financial institutions in exchange for collateral. The latter also consists of marketable securities. We describe this technique in more detail because it also illustrates the role the interest rate plays as an instrument of monetary policy.

Main refinancing operations: how do these work?

The first crucial decision the Governing Council makes is to set the interest rate that will be applied to the main refinancing operations. We show the evolution of this interest rate (called the repo rate) during 1999–2015 in Fig. 9.18.

The ECB then announces a tender procedure. This can be a fixed-rate or a variable-rate tender. In the case of a fixed-rate tender, the interest rate chosen by the Governing Council is the fixed rate at which financial institutions can make their bids. Private financial institutions are invited to make a bid to obtain a certain amount of liquidity in exchange for delivering collateral (called eligible assets). These bids are collected by the NCBs and centralized by

[19] For detailed institutional information on the use of these instruments, see European Central Bank (2002).

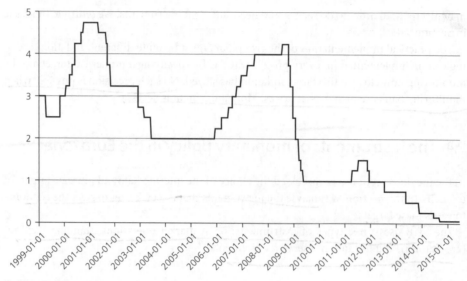

Figure 9.18 ECB policy rate (repo rate).

Note: Before June 2000, the refinancing rate was the fixed rate used in fixed-rate tenders; during 2000–8, it was the minimum bid rate used in variable-rate tenders; from 2008 it has again been the fixed rate used in fixed-rate tenders.

Source: ECB, *Monthly Bulletin.*

the ECB. The ECB decides the total amount to be allotted, and distributes this to the bidding parties pro rata to the size of the bids.

We illustrate this by a numerical example in Table 9.4. The 'Bid' column presents the amounts each bank is bidding. The total amount of the bids is 250 million euros. We assume that the amount the ECB decides to allot is 150 million euros. This is 60% of the total bids. The ECB then applies this 60% to all the individual bids to obtain the individual allotments (last column). In practice, this allotment ratio turns out to be very low. During 1999–2000, it was often less than 10%, mainly because banks overbid to obtain the desired amount of liquidity. It is for this reason that the ECB decided that, as from the operations to be settled on 28 June 2000, the main refinancing lending facility of the Eurosystem would be conducted as variable tender rates.

Table 9.4 Hypothetical example of bids and allotments in a fixed-rate tender (million euros)

	Bid	Allotment
Bank 1	30	18
Bank 2	40	24
Bank 3	50	30
Bank 4	60	36
Bank 5	70	42
Total	250	150

Source: European Monetary Institute (1997).

Table 9.5 Hypothetical example of a variable-rate tender (million euros)

Interest rate (%)	Bank 1	Bank 2	Bank 3	Total bids	Cumulative bids
3.07				0	0
3.06		5	5	10	10
3.05		5	5	10	20
3.04		5	5	10	30
3.03	5	.5	10	20	50
3.02	5	10	15	30	80
3.01	10	10	15	35	115
3.00	5	5	5	15	130
2.99	5		10	15	145
Total	30	45	70	145	

The variable-rate tender system, which was used between 2000 and 2008, implies that banks bid for the amounts of liquidity they want to buy at successive interest rates. The interest rate decided by the Governing Council (the repo rate) acts as a minimum bid rate, below which the ECB will not accept bids from the financial institutions. In Table 9.5, we provide an example of a variable-rate tender.

Let us assume that the minimum bid rate set by the Governing Council is 3%. We now distinguish three cases. Suppose first that the ECB decides to allot 80 million euros; then all bids of 3.02% and more are satisfied. In this case the minimum bid rate does not bind. Secondly, suppose that the ECB decides to allot 150 million. In this case the minimum bid rate is binding. All bids of 3% and more are accepted (130), but the allotted amount of liquidity (150) is not exhausted. Finally, assume that the ECB decides to allot 120 million euros. In this case there is unsatisfied bidding at the minimum bid rate of 3%, i.e. there is a total amount of bidding of 15 at the minimum rate while the remaining allotment of liquidity is only 5. In this case, all bids at 3.01% and more are accepted, and in addition, each bank is allotted one-third (5/15) of the amounts they bid at the minimum rate.

As indicated earlier, open market operations are the main tools by which the ECB affects monetary conditions. By increasing or reducing the interest rate on its main financing operations it affects market interest rates. In addition, by changing the size of the allotments it affects the amount of liquidity directly.

After the banking crisis of October 2008, the ECB returned to the use of fixed-rate tenders 'with full allotment'. This means that banks obtain all the desired liquidity at the predetermined rate. This was done in the context of the ECB's role as a lender of last resort. We discussed this role in Chapter 8 and in Section 9.5 of this chapter.

It is important to stress that the Eurosystem provides liquidity against collateral provided by the banks. Thus, in the example of Table 9.5, Bank 1, which has successfully bid for, say, 25 million euros, will have to provide collateral worth 25 million in exchange for the liquidity that the Eurosystem is transferring to the bank.

The Eurosystem accepts a broad range of assets as collateral although they have to be of a certain quality to be eligible. The Eurosystem applies two sets of eligibility criteria. The first one relates to marketable assets. Typically credit ratings will be used here as an eligibility criterion. The second relates to non-marketable assets (e.g. asset-backed securities that are not traded in markets). Here the Eurosystem applies its own risk assessment (see European Central Bank 2008b). The purpose of this is to minimize the risk for the Eurosystem when it acquires assets from the banks in exchange for liquidity. Since the banking crisis of October 2008, the ECB has relaxed the eligibility requirements of collateral presented by banks. If it had not done so, many banks would not have had a sufficient amount of collateral and would have been unable to face deposit withdrawals. This would have led to an even deeper banking crisis.

QE: How does it work?

As a result of the continuing decline in the rate of inflation that we documented in Fig. 9.10, the ECB decided to start a massive programme of quantitative easing (QE).[20] This is often presented as a non-conventional policy instrument. In fact it is not. Open market purchases (and sales) of government bonds are part of the traditional toolkit of modern central banks. The only novelty is the size of the announced purchase. The ECB announced that it would buy every month about €60 billion of member countries government bonds until September 2016. This is a cumulative total of €1,260 billion.

It took the ECB a long time to decide on this QE programme. The US Fed and the Bank of England started buying large amounts of government bonds at least five years earlier, mainly as a tool to stimulate their economies. The ECB was very reluctant to follow suit mainly as a result of internal opposition coming from some Northern Eurozone countries (Germany, Netherlands, Finland). The main fear of these countries was that QE could potentially lead to large fiscal transfers between member countries if one of the governments of the member countries were to default on its government bonds. Much of this fear is ill-founded, as is explained in De Grauwe and Ji (2015). But fears are what they are and become a reality one has to take into account. That is why the ECB structured QE in such a way that fiscal transfers will remain very limited. The way this is done is by having each national central bank buy a given amount of the government bonds of its own country. These amounts are determined by the equity shares in the Eurosystem of each member country. We show these equity shares in Table 9.6. The total amount of cumulative bond purchases is then allocated to each central bank using these equity shares. Each central bank then keeps 80% of these purchases on its own balance sheet. To give an example: the Bundesbank buys a cumulative amount of German government bonds equal to €341 billion. It keeps 80% of this (i.e. €273 billion) on its balance sheet (the rest is put on the balance sheet of the ECB). This implies that the German government will pay interest to the Bundesbank each year and at the end of the year the Bundesbank will transfer the interest back to the German government. Thus, there will be no transfer of German interest rates to other countries. The same holds true for the other national central banks. Only the fraction of 20% that is held by the Eurosystem can lead to transfers between countries because these interest payments are pooled together and are then redistributed to each national central bank using the same equity shares presented in Table 9.6.

[20] For more detail on this programme see ECB: https://www.ecb.europa.eu/press/pr/date/2015/html/pr150122_1.en.html

Table 9.6 Equity shares of member-countries in Eurosystem and QE bond purchases (cumulative)

	Equity shares	Bond purchase (billion €)
Nationale Bank van België	3.5	44
Deutsche Bundesbank	27.1	341
Central Bank of Ireland	1.6	20
Bank of Greece	2.8	
Banco de Espana	11.9	150
Banque de France	20.3	256
Bank d'Italia	17.9	226
De Nederlandsche Bank	5.7	72
Oesterreichische Nationalbank	2.8	35
Banco de Portugal	2.5	32
Suomen Pankki-Finlands Bank	1.8	23
Others	2.1	26
Total	100	1260

Note: as of 2015 Greece is not part of the QE programme
Source: ECB

Standing facilities

Standing facilities aim to provide and absorb overnight liquidity. Banks can use the *marginal lending facility* to obtain overnight liquidity from the NCBs. The Governing Council fixes the marginal lending rate. It is typically 1% above the interest rate used in the main financing facility. Banks can borrow from this facility without limit provided they present adequate collateral. The marginal lending rate acts as a ceiling for the overnight market interest rate.

Similarly, banks can use the *deposit facility* to make overnight deposits. The Governing Council fixes the interest rate on the deposit facility. It is typically 1% below the interest rate used in the main financing facility. This interest rate acts as a floor for the overnight market interest rate. In June 2014, the interest rate used in the main financing facility fell to 0.05% As a result, the deposit rate dropped below 0% and became −0.2%. Thus, since June 2014 banks that deposit funds overnight have to pay 0.2% to the ECB instead of receiving an interest rate on their deposits as was the case before. All this is part of a policy aimed at giving banks the incentives to increase their lending to households and firms.

These two facilities are administered by the NCBs in a decentralized manner. By changing the interest rate on these two facilities, the Governing Council affects the short end of the interest rate structure.

Minimum reserves

The third instrument of the ECB's monetary policy is the imposition of minimum reserves for banks. By manipulating reserve requirements, the ECB can affect money market conditions. For example, an increase in the reserve requirements increases the shortage of liquidity and tends to reduce the money stock.

The use of reserve requirements was very much promoted by the Bundesbank but was strongly resisted by commercial banks, which felt that this instrument would give them a competitive disadvantage with respect to foreign (e.g. British) banks that were not subject to reserve requirements. In order to alleviate this problem, it was decided that the ECB would pay interest on these minimum reserves.

The ECB does not use the minimum reserve requirements as an instrument of monetary policy. Rather, it uses them as an instrument to smooth short-term interest rates. This is achieved by computing the minimum reserve requirement as a monthly average of daily reserve ratios. This gives the banks incentives to smooth the effects of temporary liquidity fluctuations.

We argued earlier that the financial crisis calls for extending the objectives of the ECB to also include financial stability more explicitly. We formulated a new two-pillar strategy in which, apart from pursuing an inflation target, the ECB also monitors asset prices and bank credit. The minimum reserve requirements could be a useful instrument for the ECB to control bank credit (which as we have seen is strongly correlated with asset prices). Thus, the ECB could increase the minimum reserve requirements when bank credit is expanding too quickly. This was the case, for example, during the period 2003–7 when bank credit increased by close to 10% a year (see Fig. 9.14). If the ECB had increased the minimum reserve requirements, it is unlikely that bank credit would have ballooned as it did.

The ECB could also use other instruments to control bank credit. One such instrument is macro-prudential control. By that we mean the use of prudential rules to control the total amount of credit. An example is the loan-to-value ratios applied in mortgage lending. This is the ratio of the value of the mortgage loan to the value of the house used as collateral. By lowering this ratio, the central bank discourages mortgage lending and thus checks the expansion of bank credit.

Macro-prudential control is not part of the toolkit of the ECB (in contrast to reserve requirements). Its use by the ECB would require institutional changes. The new regulatory structure that was introduced in 2011–12 and that we discussed in Chapter 8 does not give this power to the ECB but it can, however, be used by national central banks.

9.5 The Eurosystem as lender of last resort during the financial crisis

In Chapter 8, we discussed the role of the ECB as a lender of last resort in the banking sector and in the government bond markets. The ECB has been an active lender of last resort in the banking sector since October 2008. The most spectacular intervention occurred during 2011–12 when the ECB provided more than €1 trillion of liquidity to the banking sector. At about the same time, it bought about €165 billion of government bonds in the context of its 'Securities Market Programme' (SMP). This was a programme of limited purchases of government bonds at a time of extreme pressure in the government bond markets for a number of southern Eurozone countries. It should not be confused with the OMT programme that we discussed in Chapter 8. The latter is a programme in which the ECB commits itself to buying an unlimited number of government bonds in times of crisis. The SMP programme was very different. The ECB announced that it would buy a limited amount of bonds during a limited period of time. This programme backfired: it gave a signal to the holders of government bonds to sell as quickly as possible (because the time it would be able to sell to the ECB was limited). As a result, the ECB had to buy a lot of these bonds. The OMT programme did not lead to this problem because the ECB's commitment was unlimited in size and time. As a result, up to now (2016), the ECB has not had to buy government bonds at all in the context of the OMT programme. The confidence that the ECB will be in the market if needed has been sufficient for bondholders to keep the government bonds of troubled countries, and even to buy them, so that interest rates declined dramatically (see Fig. 6.1 in Chapter 6).

One important implication of these various liquidity injections is that the balance sheet of the Eurosystem expanded massively. It will be remembered from our discussion of the open market operations that the central banks provide liquidity to the banks by accepting eligible assets as collateral. Thus, the Eurosystem acquired large claims on the banks in the Eurozone.

We show the evolution of the total assets held by the Eurosystem since 2007 in Fig. 9.19[21] and we observe that in October 2008 there was a large increase in the total amount of assets held by the Eurosystem. This increase amounted to about €500 billion. Fig. 9.19 also shows that the expansions of the balance sheets of the Bank of England and the Federal Reserve were even more spectacular. The Federal Reserve's balance sheet more than doubled while the Bank of England allowed its balance sheet to triple. Thus, the ECB appears to have been more cautious in using its role of lender of last resort. Note also that during 2012–13 the ECB started to reduce the size of its balance sheet. The opposite happened in the US, where the Federal Reserve decided to expand its balance sheet in the context of its 'quantitative easing' programme. As was discussed earlier, this was a programme aiming at injecting liquidity into the financial system so as to stimulate the US economy. The ECB was reluctant to do this and waited to January 2015 to start its own QE programme.

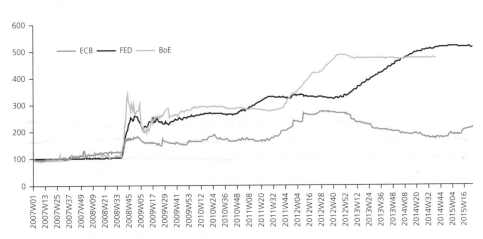

Figure 9.19 Balance sheet of Eurosystem, US Fed, and Bank of England; 2007 = 100.

Sources: European Central Bank, Federal Reserve, Bank of England.

[21] Note that this is a similar Figure to Fig. 8.6 except that in Fig. 8.6 we expressed the balance sheets in trillion dollars and trillion euros, and that we did not include the Bank of England. Here we present indices so as to better gauge the relative changes in these three central banks.

The expansion of the balance sheet of the Eurosystem creates a number of problems. We discussed these in Chapters 6 and 8. There we argued that the inflation risk and the fiscal implications of the lender of last resort's actions are limited. The only significant risk is moral hazard. The latter, however, cannot be invoked as a reason not to provide lending of last resort, as this creates an even bigger risk, i.e. the implosion of a fragile financial system. Moral hazard requires the use of other instruments, i.e. regulation and supervision.

Note also that the problems of the lender of last resort role of the ECB apply when the ECB exerts this role both in the banking sector and in government bond markets. In addition, there is a very strong connection between the two. The reluctance of the ECB to perform its role of lender of last resort in government bond markets during 2010–11 had the effect of forcing the ECB to provide liquidity support to Eurozone banks in 2011. This should not have come as a surprise. Banks are the largest holders of government bonds. When as a result of the sovereign debt crisis of 2010 bond prices in a number of Eurozone countries dropped, banks made large losses. As a result, a bank crisis erupted in a number of these countries (Greece, Portugal, Spain), forcing the ECB to provide large amounts of liquidity to banks in these countries.[22] It is surprising that while the ECB showed much resistance to providing liquidity in government bond markets at that time, it was happy to provide the necessary liquidity to banks.

The open market operations we have described up to now are operations that are not geared towards the support of one particular bank. They are designed to provide liquidity in the market in a non-discriminatory way. However, during a liquidity crisis NCBs may provide emergency liquidity assistance (ELA) to particular illiquid (but solvent) banks. The provision of ELA is undertaken at the discretion of the competent NCB, and only in exceptional circumstances. The potential losses on emergency liquidity assistance (for example, the loan provided by the National Bank of Belgium to Fortis and the one provided by the Bundesbank to Eurohypo) are, however, borne only by the NCB in question. But here also national governments have agreed to guarantee the collateral presented at the NCB, thereby shielding the NCBs and the Eurosystem from losses.

9.6 Conclusion

The European Central Bank has set itself the overriding objective of keeping inflation below, but close to, 2%. It can be concluded that it has achieved this objective during the first 15 years of its existence. However, since the start of the sovereign debt crisis it has experienced increasing difficulties in keeping inflation close to 2% as inflation continued to slide downwards. This led the ECB in January 2015 to finally start expanding the money base by buying large amounts of government bonds in the hope of pushing inflation up again.

Paradoxically, while the ECB had announced that it would achieve its inflation objective by closely watching the growth rate of the money stock, it can now also be concluded that the money stock has played no useful role in the ECB's strategy of controlling inflation. During the pre-crisis period (1999–2008), the growth rate of the money stock was systematically

---

[22] In December 2011 and February 2012, when a new banking crisis emerged, the ECB massively supported the banks. The effect was that the ECB's balance sheet increased by €1 trillion.

higher than the reference value that the ECB claimed to be the value that should not be exceeded to maintain price stability.

This massive expansion of M3 during 2000–08 did not announce inflation. What it reflected was a massive build-up of the balance sheets of the banks in the Eurozone. This expansion in turn reflected bubbles that were going on in various asset markets. It should have warned the ECB not of future inflation but of future financial crises.

The main responsibility for the financial crisis, however, does not lie at the door of the ECB. It is to be found in the failure of bank supervision and regulation, which were nationally organized while the banking sector became increasingly international. This failure of bank supervision occurred not only in the Eurozone but also in many other highly developed countries (e.g. the US and the UK).

Although the major responsibility for the financial crisis is to be found in a failure to supervise and to regulate banks that were expanding credit in an unsustainable way, it is also true that the ECB bears part of the responsibility. The reason is that its excessive focus on inflation prevented it from taking action aimed at checking the ballooning expansion of bank credit during the pre-crisis period. That is why we have proposed that the ECB should widen its objectives and include financial stability explicitly as an objective at par with price stability. We also discussed the instruments that could be used to achieve this dual mandate.

The banking crisis of October 2008 has severely tested the capacity of the Eurosystem to be a lender of last resort. It must be recognized that the Eurosystem withstood this test during 2008–9. It injected liquidity massively and in a timely way, thereby averting a full-scale banking crisis. However, when the government debt crisis erupted in 2010, the ECB stood on the sidelines until 2012. It initiated a government bond purchasing programme (SMP) but applied this with great hesitation, and announced that this would be temporary. The effect of this was that the programme lacked credibility, inducing investors to continue to sell government bonds and forcing the ECB to buy large amounts of these bonds.

In the 9th edition of this book we concluded this chapter as follows: 'The right approach would have been for the ECB to announce its full commitment to buying government bonds, making it clear that it would use its unlimited capacity to create liquidity to stabilize bond prices. Such a strategy would have created confidence in the market that bond prices would stop falling. As a result, investors would have stopped their large sales of government bonds and the ECB would not have been forced to buy as many bonds as it did.' The ECB came to the realization that this was indeed the right approach when it announced its OMT programme in September 2012.

Fiscal policies in monetary unions

Introduction

The traditional theory of optimum currency areas, which was discussed in Chapters 1 and 2, offers interesting insights into the conduct of national fiscal policies in a monetary union. In this chapter, we start out by developing these ideas. We then challenge this theory by introducing issues about the credibility and sustainability of fiscal policies.

The analysis of this chapter will allow us to answer questions such as:

- What is the role of fiscal policy in a monetary union?
- How independent can national fiscal policies be?
- Does a monetary union increase or reduce fiscal discipline? What rules, if any, should be used to restrict national fiscal policies? This will lead us into an analysis of the 'Stability and Growth Pact'.

10.1 Fiscal policies and the theory of optimum currency areas

In order to analyse what the theory of optimum currency areas has to say about the conduct of fiscal policies, it is useful to start from the example of an asymmetric demand shock as developed in Chapter 1. Suppose again that France experiences a recession while Germany is gripped by a boom in economic activity. We reproduce Fig. 1.1 from Chapter 1 here (as Fig. 10.1). What are the fiscal policy implications of this disturbance? We analysed some of the implications in Chapter 1. Here we go into some more detail.

Suppose first that France and Germany, being members of the same monetary union, have also centralized a substantial part of their national budgets to the central European authority. In particular, let us assume that the social security system is organized at the European level, and that income taxes are also levied by the European government.

It can now be seen that the centralized budget will work as a shock absorber. In France, output declines and unemployment tends to increase. This has a double effect on the European budget. The income taxes and social security contributions collected by the European government in France decline, whereas unemployment benefit payments by the European authorities increase. Exactly the opposite occurs in Germany. There, output increases and unemployment declines. As a result, tax revenues collected by the European government in

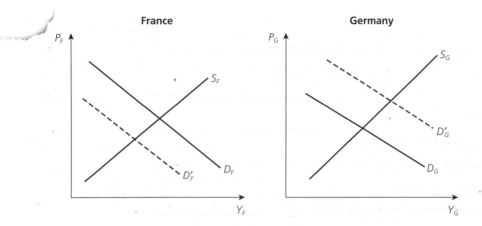

Figure 10.1 Asymmetric shock in France and Germany.

Germany increase, while European government spending in Germany declines. Thus, the centralized European budget automatically redistributes income from Germany to France, thereby softening the social consequences of the recession in France. It can be considered as an insurance system whereby those countries (and individuals) hit by a negative shock are compensated by automatic transfers raised in the countries experiencing a positive shock.

This is a very important feature of a centralized budget. This becomes particularly evident when one of the national governments experiences payment difficulties. Let us take an extreme case and suppose that one of the governments were to default. In that case, the centrally organized social security system would still function and continue to pay unemployment benefits and pensions, and the health service would still be operational in the country of the defaulting government. Thus the social security system would be insulated from the payment crisis of the government. Clearly this would not be the case in the absence of a budgetary union.

In addition, by centralizing national budgets into one, the fragility of the government bond markets in the monetary union that we identified in Chapter 1 is reduced considerably. In particular, in this example of a pure asymmetric shock, France obtains automatic funding through the centralized budget, without having to issue government bonds. In fact, to the extent that the deficit of France is matched by the surplus of Germany, no net bond issue needs to be done. If that is not the case, e.g. because the French deficit exceeds the German surplus, the centralization of the budget implies that the European government issues common bonds. Thus, we achieve the situation of 'stand-alone' countries that issue their debt in a currency over which they have full control.

Consider now what would happen if France and Germany form a monetary union without centralizing their government budgets. It can easily be demonstrated that the negative demand shock in France will lead to an increase in the French government budget deficit, because tax receipts decline while unemployment benefit payments by the French government increase. The French government will have to increase its borrowing. In Germany, we have the reverse. The German government budget experiences increasing surpluses (or declining deficits). If capital markets work efficiently, the need for the French government to borrow can easily be accommodated by the increasing supply of savings coming from Germany.

In this case of decentralized budgets, France increases its external debt, which will have to be serviced in the future. Thus, we no longer have a regional insurance system, since those who receive a transfer during hardship, the French, are supposed to pay back the Germans later. The French people will make this future repayment. As a result, this decentralized system is an insurance whereby future generations of French people pay for the hardship of today's French people. In addition, this decentralized system will reduce the degrees of freedom of future French fiscal policies. This contrasts with the case where the national budgets are centralized: in such a system, France will not have to face such external debt problems, as German residents automatically transfer income to France.

Note that, as was stressed in Chapter 1, the insurance system (whether centralized or decentralized) should only be used to deal with temporary shocks (e.g. shocks that arise as a result of desynchronized business cycles). We have also called these shocks endogenous as they are the result of booms and busts that are endemic in a market system. In this case, it is desirable to allow the insurance mechanisms to function properly. If the shocks are permanent, however, the insurance mechanism should only be applied in a temporary way so as to allow time for fundamental adjustments (e.g. wage adjustments) to be undertaken. In this case, it is important that there should be a sufficient degree of wage and price flexibility and/or labour mobility. In the absence of such flexibility the insurance mechanism may become unsustainable, as it implies permanent transfers from one country to the other (in the centralized system) or exploding government debt levels (in the decentralized system).

In the previous chapters, we have stressed that a monetary union with decentralized national budgets is incomplete and fragile and that such a system is unlikely to be sustainable in the long run (see Chapters 5 and 6). It is important to stress here that if a country is pushed into a bad equilibrium as analysed in Chapter 5, the insurance mechanism will not function well. The reason is that when countries are stuck in a bad equilibrium, investors distrust the debt issued by these countries. As a result, the negative shock is unlikely to be financed by the market. On the contrary, as the negative shock leads to a further lack of confidence, investors will require to be compensated by an even higher risk premium, making it difficult if not impossible for the countries experiencing a negative shock to finance the ensuing budget deficit. The insurance mechanism breaks down.

The theory of optimum currency areas leads to the following implications for fiscal policies in monetary unions (see Kenen 1969). First, it is desirable to centralize a significant part of the national budgets at the European level. A centralized budget allows countries (and regions) that are hit by negative shocks to enjoy automatic transfers, thereby reducing the social costs of a monetary union. In addition, by consolidating government debt issues, it reduces the fragility of a monetary union. This was also a major conclusion of the influential MacDougall Report, published in 1977. The drafters of that report argued that monetary union in Europe would have to be accompanied by a significant centralization of budgetary power in Europe (more precisely a centralization of the unemployment benefit systems). Failure to do so would impose great social strains and endanger monetary union. (In Box 10.1, we ask how much centralization of national budgets is desirable.)

Second, if such a centralization of the national government budgets in a monetary union is not possible (as appears to be the case in the context of European monetary union), then national fiscal policies should be used in a flexible way. That is, when countries are hit by negative shocks, they should be allowed to let the budget deficit increase through the built-in (or automatic) budgetary stabilizers (declining government revenues, increasing social outlays).

This requirement that fiscal policies respond flexibly to negative shocks also implies that substantial autonomy should be reserved for these national fiscal policies. In the logic of the traditional optimum currency area theory, countries lose an instrument of policy (the exchange rate) when they join the union. If there is no centralized budget that automatically redistributes income, countries have no instrument at their disposal to absorb the effects of these negative shocks.[1] The fiscal policy instrument is the only one left.

BOX 10.1 How much centralization of government budgets in a monetary union is desirable?

The theory of optimum currency areas stresses the desirability of a significant centralization of the national budgets to accommodate for asymmetric shocks in the different regions (countries). What is the limit to such centralization? In order to answer this question it is important to keep in mind that budgetary transfers should be used to cope only with *temporary* shocks (endogenous shocks), or, when shocks are permanent, these transfers should be used only temporarily. A country or a region that faces a permanent shock (e.g. a permanent decline in the demand for its output) should adjust by wage and price changes or by moving factors of production. Budgetary transfers can be used only temporarily to alleviate these adjustment problems.

The previous discussion suggests that the need to centralize the budget depends on the nature of the shocks. If these are primarily of the endogenous type, the need to have a centralized budget to deal with these shocks is strong. When asymmetric shocks occur as a result of unsynchronized business cycles, flexibility is not the answer. Instead, an insurance mechanism provided by a central budget is called for. By contrast, when the asymmetric shocks are exogenous, the focus should be on flexibility. Insurance can only be used as a temporary device to alleviate the cost of adjustment. We have given this view a graphical interpretation in Fig. 4.8 (see Chapter 4).

There is another problem with the centralization of national budgets. This has to do with moral hazard (again). The experience with regional budgetary transfers within nations (Italy, Belgium, and Germany, for example) is that it is very difficult to use these transfers in a temporary way. Quite often, when a region experiences a negative shock (the Mezzogiorno in Italy, Wallonia in Belgium, the eastern Länder (states) in Germany), the transfers through the centralized social security system tend to acquire a permanent character. The reason is that these social security transfers reduce the need to adjust. They tend to keep real wages in the depressed regions too high and they reduce the incentive for the population of the region to move out to more prosperous regions. As a result, these transfers tend to become self-perpetuating. This is illustrated by the fact that the Mezzogiorno has been a recipient of transfers (from the rest of Italy) representing 20–30% of the Mezzogiorno's regional output during most of the post-war period.[2] Similar regional transfers exist in other countries (e.g. Belgium, Germany).

These large and permanent regional transfers then create new political problems, when the inhabitants of the prosperous regions increasingly oppose paying for them. In some countries, these political problems can even lead to calling into question the unity of the nation. When the sense of national identity is weak, this can effectively lead to the break-up of the country.

It is important to bear in mind experience with regional transfers within European nations when considering the limits that should be imposed on the centralization of national budgets (including social security) in Europe. Centralization of the social security system at the European level risks creating Mezzogiorno problems involving whole countries. This could lead to quasi-permanent transfers from one group of countries to

---

[1] We assume here that wages are inflexible and that labour mobility is non-existent.

[2] See Micossi and Tullio (1991). The trends have not changed since 1991.

another. The sense of national identification being much less developed at the European level than at the country level, this would certainly lead to great political problems. These would in turn endanger the unity of the European Union. Thus, although Europe needs some further centralization of national budgets (including social security systems) to have a sustainable monetary union, the degree of centralization should stop far short of the level achieved within the present-day European nations. Some schemes of limited centralization of social security systems (in particular, the unemployment benefit systems) have been proposed and worked out by a number of economists (see Italianer and Vanheukelen 1992; EC Commission 1993; Hammond and von Hagen 1993; and Mélitz and Vori 1993). Other insurance mechanisms aiming at compensating for different growth rates of GDP have been proposed by Drèze and Durré (2012). In 2012, the President of the European Council, Herman Van Rompuy (2012), made a proposal for a limited unemployment insurance mechanism in his report to the European Council (the so-called Four Presidents Report). These proposals suggest that limited centralization can be quite effective in taking care of (temporary) asymmetric shocks. Unfortunately, in the follow-up to the Four Presidents Report, the Five Presidents Report,[3] this timid proposal for organizing an unemployment insurance mechanism at the Eurozone level was dropped. This suggests that in a few years time the willingness to go forward in a fiscal union may have declined.

This theory about how fiscal policies should be conducted in a monetary union has been heavily criticized. This criticism is not directed at the first conclusion, i.e. that it is desirable to centralize a significant part of national budgets in a monetary union. The criticism has been formulated against the second conclusion, which calls for flexibility and autonomy of national government budgets in monetary unions when the degree of budgetary centralization is limited. To this criticism we now turn.

10.2 Sustainability of government budget deficits

The major problem with the previous analysis is the underlying assumption that governments can create budget deficits to absorb negative shocks without leading to problems about the sustainability of these deficits. As many Western European countries found during the 1980s and the 1990s, however, government budget deficits can lead to such problems.

The sustainability problem can be formulated as follows. A budget deficit leads to an increase in government debt, which will have to be serviced in the future. If the interest rate on the government debt exceeds the growth rate of the economy, a debt dynamic is set in motion that leads to an ever-increasing government debt relative to GDP. This becomes unsustainable, requiring corrective action.

This debt dynamics problem can be analysed more formally starting from the definition of the government budget constraint (see Box 10.2 for more explanation):

$$G - T + rB = \frac{dB}{dt} + \frac{dM}{dt} \tag{10.1}$$

where G is the level of government spending (excluding interest payments on the government debt), T is the tax revenue, r is the interest rate on the government debt, B, and M is the level of high-powered money (monetary base).

---

[3] See Juncker et al. (2015).

The left-hand side of equation (10.1) is the government budget deficit. It consists of the primary budget deficit $(G - T)$ and the interest payment on the government debt (rB). The right-hand side is the financing side. The budget deficit can be financed by issuing debt (dB/dt) or by issuing high-powered money, (dM/dt). (In the following we represent the changes per unit of time by putting a dot above a variable, thus $dB/dt = \dot{B}$ and $dM/dt = \dot{M}$.)

As is shown in Box 10.2, the government budget constraint (10.1) can be rewritten as:

$$\dot{b} = (g - t) + (r - x)b - \dot{m} \tag{10.2}$$

where $g = G/Y$, $t = T/Y$, $x = \dot{Y}/Y$ (the growth rate of GDP), and $\dot{m} = \dot{M}/Y$.

Equation (10.2) can be interpreted as follows. When the interest rate on government debt exceeds the growth rate of GDP, the debt-to-GDP ratio will increase without bounds. The dynamics of debt accumulation can only be stopped if the primary budget deficit (as a percentage of GDP) turns into a surplus $((g - t)$ then becomes negative). Alternatively, the debt accumulation can be stopped by a sufficiently large revenue from money creation. The latter is also called 'seigniorage'. It is clear, however, that the systematic use of this source of finance will lead to inflation.

The nature of the government budget constraint can also be made clear as follows: one can ask under what condition the debt-to-GDP ratio will stabilize at a constant value. Equation (10.2) gives the answer. Set $\dot{b} = 0$. This yields:

$$(r - x)b = (t - g) + \dot{m} \tag{10.3}$$

Thus, if the nominal interest rate exceeds the nominal growth rate of the economy, it is necessary either for the primary budget to show a sufficiently high surplus $(t > g)$ or for money creation to be sufficiently high to stabilize the debt–GDP ratio. The latter option was chosen by many Latin American countries during the 1980s, and by some Eastern European countries during the early part of the 1990s. It has also led to hyperinflation in these countries.

The important message here is that, if a country has accumulated sizeable deficits in the past, it will now have to run correspondingly large primary budget surpluses in order to prevent the debt–GDP ratio from increasing automatically. This means that the country will have to reduce spending and/or increase taxes.

It may be interesting here to present a few case studies of the experience of European countries during the period 1980–2007. We select Belgium, the Netherlands, and Italy. We present data on government budget deficits of these countries during the years 1979–2007 (see Fig. 10.2).

It can be seen that these countries allowed their budget deficits to increase significantly during the early part of the 1980s. This increase in government budget deficits arose mainly as a response to the negative consequences of major recessions in these countries. The rest of the period was characterized by strenuous attempts to contain the explosive debt situation that followed from these earlier policies. We show the evolution of the debt–GDP ratios in these countries during the period 1980–2007 in Fig. 10.3.

At the end of the 1980s, after many years of budgetary restrictions, Belgium and the Netherlands had succeeded in stabilizing the debt–GDP ratio. They were able to do so by running substantial surpluses in the primary budget. These are shown in Fig. 10.4. The level at which Belgium achieved this stabilization of the debt–GDP ratio, however, was very high. As a result, when the next recession hit the country in 1992–3 it was quite difficult to use fiscal policies in a countercyclical way. On the contrary, Belgium was forced to clamp down

BOX 10.2 Debts and deficits

In this box we derive the relation between debts and deficits. Let us start from the government budget constraint

$$G - T + rB = \frac{dB}{dt} + \frac{dM}{dt} \tag{10.4}$$

where G is the level of government spending (excluding interest payments on the government debt), T is the tax revenue, r is the interest rate on the government debt, B, and M is the level of high-powered money (monetary base).

The left-hand side of the equation (10.4) is the government budget deficit. It consists of the primary budget deficit ($G-T$) and the interest payment on the government debt (rB). The right-hand side is the financing side. The budget deficit can be financed by issuing debt (dB/dt) or by issuing high-powered money, (dM/dt). We will assume, however, that the monetary financing constitutes such a small part of the financing of the government budget deficit in the European countries that it can safely be disregarded. (In the following we represent the changes per unit of time by putting a dot above a variable, thus: $dB/dt = \dot{B}$). It is convenient to express variables as ratios to GDP. Let us therefore define

$$b = \frac{B}{Y} \tag{10.5}$$

where Y is GDP, so that b is the debt–GDP ratio.

This allows us to write

$$\dot{b} = \frac{\dot{B}}{Y} - B\frac{\dot{Y}}{Y^2} \tag{10.6}$$

or using (10.5) and manipulating

$$\dot{B} = \dot{b}Y + b\dot{Y} \tag{10.7}$$

Substituting (10.7) into (10.4) yields

$$\dot{b} = (g - t) + (r - x)b \tag{10.8}$$

where $g = G/Y$, $t = T/Y$, $x = \dot{Y}/Y$ (the growth rate of GDP).

This equation defines the dynamics of debt. It says that in a world where the nominal interest rate, r, exceeds the nominal growth of the economy, x, the government must make sure that the primary budget ($g-t$) has a surplus. If not, the debt–GDP ratio will increase without limit. This must surely lead to a default on the government debt. We can therefore impose a necessary condition for solvency, i.e.

$$\dot{b} = 0 \quad or \quad (r - x)b = t - g$$

Note that this is a necessary condition. It may not always be sufficient. For example, the government debt ratio, b, may be stabilized at too high a level, so that when a large shock occurs the government may become unable (or unwilling) to continue to service the debt.

Another way to interpret this condition is as follows. Let us go back to equation (10.8). Assume that the primary budget balance is equal to zero ($g-t = 0$). In that case, one can say that the government uses its tax revenues to finance spending, excluding spending on interest. This means that interest spending is not covered by taxation. As a result, the government is financing its interest payments by issuing new debt. We can now see that this will be explosive if $r > g$. In the latter case the debt (the numerator) is increasing at the rate r, while GDP (the denominator) increases at the lower rate, g. Thus the debt-to-GDP ratio increases without bound. In order to stop this 'Ponzi game'[4] the government will have to produce a surplus on the primary balance so that at least part of interest payments are financed by taxes and not by issuing new debt.

---

[4] Ponzi game refers to a Mr Ponzi, who was operating in Boston in 1920 and attracted investors promising large rates of return. When these investors withdrew their money, Ponzi had to find new investors to finance these withdrawals because he did not make profitable investments himself. The scheme ultimately collapsed.

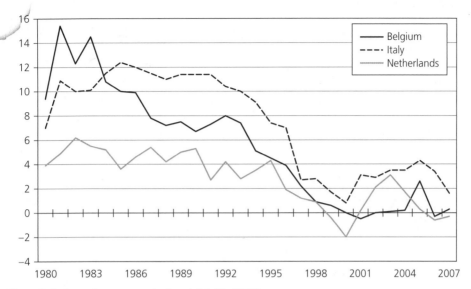

Figure 10.2 General government budget deficit (% of GDP).

Source: European Commission, *European Economy.*

on government spending and to increase taxes, thereby exacerbating the recession, without preventing the debt–GDP ratio from increasing again during 1992–3. Only during the second half of the 1990s did it succeed in reducing the debt–GDP ratio. However, at the start of EMU in 1999, it fell a long way short of the 60% benchmark mandated by the Maastricht Treaty.

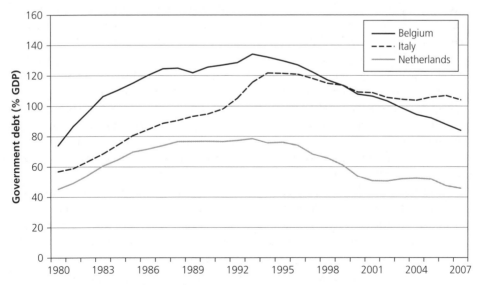

Figure 10.3 Gross public debt (% of GDP).

Source: European Commission, *European Economy.*

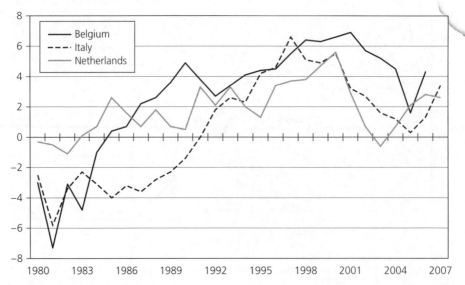

Figure 10.4 Government budget surplus, excluding interest payments (% of GDP).

Source: European Commission, *European Economy.*

Italy did not succeed in stabilizing its debt–GDP ratio during the 1980s because it failed to create the required primary budget surpluses. Only from 1992 did it manage to produce primary budget surpluses that led to a stabilization of the debt–GDP ratio in 1994–5. Note that this prevented the Italian government from using budgetary policies in a counter-cyclical way. As in the case of Belgium, Italy only managed to reduce the debt–GDP ratio during the second half of the 1990s but fell short of the 60% norm at the moment of entry into EMU.

These examples vividly demonstrate the limits to the use of fiscal policies in offsetting negative economic shocks. Such policies cannot be maintained for very long. The experience of these countries shows that large government budget deficits quickly lead to an unsustainable debt dynamics from which countries find it difficult to extricate themselves. The 'success' of Belgium and Italy during the late 1990s in reducing the debt–GDP ratio by running primary budget surpluses came about after many years of spending cuts and tax increases, and still left these countries with uncomfortably high debt levels at the start of EMU.

The preceding discussion also makes clear that fiscal policies are not the flexible instrument that the optimum currency theory has led us to believe. The systematic use of this instrument leads to problems of sustainability, which forces countries to run budget surpluses for a number of years. Put differently, having used them once, it will not be possible to use these fiscal policies again until many years later.

This analysis of the sustainability of fiscal policies has led to a completely different view of the desirable fiscal policies of member states in a monetary union. This view found its reflection in the Maastricht Treaty, which defines budgetary rules that countries have to satisfy in order to enter EMU (the 3% deficit and the 60% debt norms).[5] It also found expression in the

---

[5] The drafters of the Maastricht Treaty were very much influenced by the Delors Report, which was the first to express the need for strict rules on budgetary policies.

so-called 'Stability and Growth Pact' that the EU heads of state, at the insistence of Germany, agreed would have to be implemented after the start of EMU. This Pact is quite important as it is supposed to guide national budgetary policies in EMU. Its main principles are the following. (In Box 10.3 we describe the procedures of the Stability and Growth Pact in more detail.)

BOX 10.3 The Stability and Growth Pact: some institutional detail

The Stability and Growth Pact (SGP) consists of two parts: a surveillance part and a dissuasive part.[6]

The *surveillance* part lays down an early warning system, the objective of which is to prevent countries from producing excessive budget deficits. Its main features are the following:

- Members of the Eurozone have to submit Stability Programmes, which focus on public finance and which aim to bring about 'a budgetary position close to balance or in surplus and the adjustment path towards this objective'.

- These programmes are examined by the Council, which formulates its opinion (based on a recommendation of the Commission) on whether the countries' budgetary programmes have sufficient safety margins to avoid excessive deficits.

- These programmes are monitored by the Council, which can formulate a recommendation to take the necessary adjustment measures if a country's budgetary position deviates significantly from the medium-term objective.

The *dissuasive* part is triggered when the surveillance part does not produce results, or when excessive deficits emerge unexpectedly. The main aspects of the dissuasive part are the following:

- There is first the definition of the excessive deficit. This definition is based on Article 104 of the Maastricht Treaty, which defines a budget deficit as excessive if it exceeds the reference value of 3% of GDP 'except if it is exceptional and temporary and the deficit ratio remains close to the reference value'. The Treaty, however, does not define what is exceptional. The Pact gives content to the notion of exceptional deficit in the following way.

- A budget deficit in excess of 3% can be considered exceptional if: (i) it results from an unusual event outside the control of the member state (e.g. a natural disaster); or (ii) it results from a severe economic downturn. The latter is defined as an annual decline of GDP of at least 2%. In this case, the Council decides that there is no excessive deficit and the procedure is stopped. If the annual fall in real GDP is between 0.75% and 2%, the member state in question can present arguments justifying the excess deficit. If the decline in real GDP is less than 0.75% then the country involved should not invoke the exceptionality of the deficit.

- After a recommendation by the Commission, the Council decides whether or not there is an excessive deficit. If the Council decides that an excessive deficit exists it makes a recommendation to the member state to take effective action within four months to correct its deficit. If the member country fails to comply then the Council sends a notice giving another two months to comply. If this does not lead to corrective action then sanctions are imposed within two months. (The whole procedure is a lot more complicated than the summary given here. The interested reader can consult Cabral 2001.)

- If the Council decides to impose a sanction, the country involved will have to make a non-interest bearing deposit. The amount of this deposit (Dep) is given by the formula: $Dep = 0.2 + 0.1(Def-3)$, where Def is the deficit. All the variables are expressed as percentages of GDP. To give an example: if a country has a deficit of 4% then the deposit is: $Dep = 0.2 + 0.1(4-3) = 0.3$. It will have to make a deposit equal to 0.3% of GDP. The maximum amount of the deposit is set at 0.5%.

---

[6] The description of the Pact in this box is based mainly on Cabral (2001).

- If, within two years, the excessive deficit has not been corrected, then the deposit is turned into a fine. If, however, before these two years have elapsed, the Council considers that the excessive deficit has been corrected, the deposit is returned to the country in question.

Up to now, these sanctions have never been applied. The reader will be surprised at so much political *naïveté* from the drafters of the Stability and Growth Pact when they believed that such sanctions could ever be enforced.

Since the eruption of the sovereign debt crisis in the Eurozone, some of the provisions of the Stability and Growth Pact have been tightened. The aim is to prevent future unsustainable increases in government deficits and debts. The main new provisions are:

- The sanctioning procedure has been made more automatic by a change in the voting procedure. When the European Commission issues a warning or a sanction against a particular country this will be accepted automatically by the Council unless a qualified majority can be found to block it.

- National governments will have to present national budgets to the Commission before these are presented in national parliaments, giving the Commission a chance to make an assessment and formulate recommendations. This is called the 'European Semester'.

- The Commission will have more power to obtain information from national governments.

- A fine of 0.2% can be imposed on countries that are found to have falsified statistics on deficits and debts.

First, countries will have to aim to achieve balanced budgets over the medium run (i.e. over the business cycle). This is quite a formidable change compared to the Maastricht Treaty's 60% debt norm. It means that countries should not add new debt over the business cycle. Another way to interpret this balanced budget requirement is that the Pact forces countries to bring down their debt–GDP ratio to 0% (in the long run). Surprisingly, this fundamental change in the objectives of fiscal policy was little noticed at the time the Stability Pact was signed. Second, countries with a budget deficit exceeding 3% of GDP will be subject to fines. These fines can reach up to 0.5% of GDP.

The 3% norm was enshrined in the Maastricht Treaty; the novelty of the Stability Pact was to set up sanctions for those countries that do not abide by the 3% norm. The initial German proposal was to have fines that would be applied automatically when countries' budget deficits exceeded 3%. The other countries rejected this idea, however. As a result, the application of fines is the result of a long process during which countries are first warned by the European Commission and then given the chance to redress their budgetary situation. If all fails, fines can be imposed, but these fines can only be decided upon by a qualified majority of the Council of Ministers of Finance.

As a result of the sovereign debt crisis the voting procedure was changed. From now on a 'reverse majority voting' procedure will be used. This means that the Commission's proposals to apply fines will be accepted unless a qualified majority in the Council opposes it. This new voting procedure should make it easier to apply sanctions. In general, since the eruption of the sovereign debt crisis, the Stability and Growth Pact has been considerably tightened. For more detail see Box 10.3.

A third aspect of the Stability Pact is that the fines will not be applied if the countries in question experience exceptional circumstances, i.e. a natural disaster or a decline of their

GDP of more than 2% during one year. In cases where the drop in GDP is between 0.75% and 2%, the country involved can make its case before the Council of Ministers, invoking exceptional circumstances that justify the excess deficit. Countries that experience a drop in their GDP of less than 0.75% have agreed not to invoke exceptional circumstances. The presumption is that in this case they will have to pay a fine, although the imposition of the fine will still require a decision of the Council.[7]

The Maastricht Treaty and even more so the Stability and Growth Pact take the view that fiscal policies in a monetary union should be subjected to rules. Let us evaluate the arguments for rules on government budget deficits in a monetary union.

10.3 The argument for rules on government budget deficits

The basic insight of this view is that a country that finds itself on an unsustainable path of increasing government debt creates negative spillover effects for the rest of the monetary union. A country that allows its debt–GDP ratio to increase continuously will have increasing recourse to the capital markets of the union, thereby driving the union interest rate upwards. This increase in the union interest rate in turn increases the burden of the government debts of the other countries. If the governments of these countries choose to stabilize their debt–GDP ratios, they will be forced to follow more restrictive fiscal policies. Thus, the unsustainable increase in the debt of one country forces the other countries to follow more deflationary policies. It will therefore be in the interest of these other countries that a control mechanism should exist restricting the size of budget deficits in the member countries.

There is a second spillover that may appear here. The upward movement of the union interest rate, following the unsustainable fiscal policies of one member country, is likely to put pressure on the ECB. Countries that are hurt by the higher union interest rate may pressure the ECB to relax its monetary policy stance. Thus, unsustainable fiscal policies will interfere with the conduct of European monetary policy. Again, it may be in the interest of the members of the union to prevent such a negative spillover from occurring by imposing limits on the size of government budget deficits.

These arguments based on the spillover effects of fiscal policies appear reasonable. They have, however, been subjected to criticism.[8] The criticism has been twofold. One aspect is theoretical and concerns the role of capital markets. The second has to do with the enforceability of such rules.

1. *The efficiency of private capital markets.* Implicit in the spillover argument, there is an assumption that capital markets do not work properly. Let us now suppose that capital markets work efficiently, and ask what happens when one country, say Italy, is on an unsustainable debt path. Does it mean that the union interest rate must increase, i.e. that the interest rate to be paid by German, Dutch, or French borrowers equally increases?

---

[7] The original proposals of the German Minister of Finance implied the automatic application of fines. This, however, would have been in contradiction to the Maastricht Treaty, which stipulates that fines can only be imposed with a majority of two-thirds of the weighted votes in the Council. This implies that the implementation of the fines foreseen in the Stability Pact will in any case need a two-thirds majority independent of the question of whether or not the excessive deficit came about because of a drop in GDP, and whatever the size of that drop.

[8] See for example Buiter and Kletzer (1990); van der Ploeg (1991); von Hagen (1991a); and Wyplosz (1991).

The answer is negative. If capital markets in the monetary union work efficiently, investors recognize that the debt problem is an Italian problem. The market then attaches a risk premium to Italian government debt reflecting a higher risk of default. The German government is not affected by this. It is able to borrow at a lower interest rate, because the lenders recognize that the risk inherent in German government bonds is lower than the risk involved in buying Italian government debt instruments. Thus, if the capital markets work efficiently, there are no spillovers. Other governments in the union do not suffer from the existence of a high Italian government debt. In addition, it does not make sense to talk about *the* union interest rate. If capital markets are efficient there are different interest rates in the union, reflecting different risk premia on the government debt of the union members.

To what extent have financial markets been able to correctly price the different risks of the government bonds in the Eurozone? Fig. 10.5 allows us to obtain some insights into this question. It presents the spreads of 10-year government bonds of a number of Eurozone countries vis-à-vis Germany from 1991 to 2015. These spreads can be interpreted as additional risk premia for investing in these government bonds rather than in German government bonds. We observe that during the 1990s (the period prior to the Eurozone) these spreads were significant but declining. The most convincing explanation is that during this pre-Eurozone period the devaluation risk (vis-à-vis the German mark) was the most important source of the risk premium. As the start of the Eurozone came nearer the risk of devaluation declined and so did the risk premium.

At the start of the Eurozone in 1999 the devaluation risk disappeared; the spreads dropped to close to zero and remained in that position until 2008. Thus, during this period the financial markets considered that investing in, say, a Greek government bond carried the same risk as investing in a German government bond. This means that the markets perceived the default risk on Greek government bonds to be the same as on German government bonds. In 2008, perceptions dramatically changed, and spreads increased and reached levels that were higher than during the 1990s. Thus, suddenly, the markets perceived huge default risks on the government bonds of countries such as Ireland, Portugal, Greece (not shown), and Italy. Suddenly, these spreads declined dramatically again in 2012.

The evidence of Fig. 10.5 casts doubt on market efficiency. During almost ten years (1999–2008), financial markets did not perceive default risks on the government bonds of 'peripheral countries'. Thus, the markets did not see any sign of the fragility in the Eurozone that we have discussed in previous chapters. Then, suddenly, financial markets discovered this fragility and in a matter of a few weeks started to attach huge risk premia to government bonds of peripheral countries. Put differently, in 1999–2008 financial markets failed to see any differential risks in the Eurozone, and there was basically one long-term bond rate, despite the fact that government deficits and debt levels differed substantially between these countries. In 2008, the markets suddenly saw that the sovereign debt risks were dramatically different within the Eurozone. We analysed this phenomenon earlier and we came to the conclusion that financial markets were driven by sentiments of panic and fear during 2008–11. When the ECB announced its OMT programme in 2012 it took out the fear factor from the market, and, as a result, the spreads declined precipitously despite the fact that in most of the countries of the periphery the debt-to-GDP ratios continued to increase dramatically.

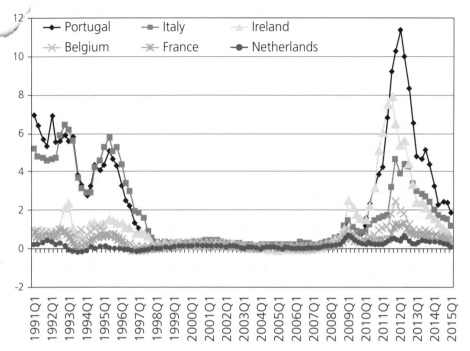

Figure 10.5 Spreads of 10-year government bond rates vis-à-vis Germany (1991–2015).

Source: Eurostat.

2. *The enforcement of fiscal policy rules.* A second problem with rules on the size of government budget deficits and debts has to do with the enforceability of these rules. Experience with such rules is that it is very difficult to enforce them. An example of such difficulties is the Gramm–Rudman legislation in the USA. In 1986, the US Congress approved a bill that set out explicit targets for the US Federal budget deficit. If these targets were not met, spending would automatically be cut across the board by a given percentage so as to meet the target. It can now be said that this approach with rules was not very successful. The US executive branch found all kinds of ways of circumventing this legislation. For example, some spending items were put 'off the budget'.

There is also evidence collected by von Hagen (1991*a*) for the American states pointing in the same direction. Von Hagen found that those states that had constitutional limits on their budget deficits or on the level of their debt had frequent recourse to the technique of 'off-budgeting'. As a result, he found that the existence of constitutional rules had very little impact on the size of the states' budget deficits.

Something very similar has been going on in Europe. The fiscal rules limiting the budget deficits to 3% have led governments to introduce 'off-budgeting' techniques or, as in the case of Greece, even outright misreporting of the numbers, so that what appeared to be budget deficits of less than 3% were in fact deficits exceeding 3% by a wide margin. In addition, other 'creative' accounting techniques have been used. A very popular one consists of selling government assets (buildings, railway carriages, etc.) and then leasing them back.

This allows governments to record the sales of the assets as current revenues, while disregarding the future payments for renting back the same assets. A variant of this technique has been used by France and Belgium. This has consisted of taking over the pension fund of the state-owned telephone company, selling the assets of the pension fund, and recording the proceeds of the sale as current revenue. This has had the effect of dramatically improving the budget deficit while burdening the future budgets of these countries. Thus, by focusing on a number such as 3%, countries are given strong incentives to engage in different practices that hide the true nature of the budget deficits. The outcome of this process is that the budget numbers have become less reliable.

To sum up, one can say that rules on the conduct of fiscal policies by the EMU members are necessary. Given the interdependence in the risk of bonds issued by different governments, financial markets may fail to price these risks correctly. As a result, some form of mutual control is necessary. The question arises, however, whether the Stability and Growth Pact may not have gone too far in stressing rigid numerical rules on the conduct of fiscal policies.

Before coming to a final verdict, it is important to analyse two issues. First, we study the extent to which monetary unions impose additional discipline on national budgetary authorities. If they do so, the need for additional rules is weakened. Second, we analyse the risk of defaults and bailouts in monetary unions. This risk is often considered to provide the major rationale for additional rules on fiscal policies in a monetary union.

10.4 Fiscal discipline in monetary unions

An important issue relating to the need for rules on fiscal policies has to do with the way a monetary union affects the fiscal discipline of national governments in such a union. Proponents of rules have generally argued that a monetary union is likely to reduce the fiscal discipline of national governments. Opponents of rules have argued the opposite.

In order to see clearly the different (and opposing) arguments, it is useful to ask how a monetary union may change the incentives of fiscal policy-makers and, in so doing, may affect budgetary discipline. The issue of whether a monetary union increases or reduces the degree of fiscal discipline of countries joining the union has been hotly debated in the literature.[9] Broadly speaking, there are two factors that are important here and that can lead to a change in the incentives of countries regarding the size of their budget deficits when they join the union. The first one leads to less discipline, the second to more discipline.

The phenomenon that leads to incentives for larger budget deficits can be phrased as follows.[10] When a sovereign country issues debt denominated in the domestic currency, the interest rate it will have to pay reflects a risk premium consisting of two components: the risk of default and the risk that the country will devalue its currency in the future. For most countries the risk of default is remote, while the risk of a currency depreciation is much less so. As a result, when the authorities of a sovereign country issue too much debt, the risk of

---

[9] For surveys, see Wyplosz (1991) and Wyplosz (2006).

[10] For a formal analysis, see Beetsma and Uhlig (1999) and Buti et al. (2002).

a future devaluation increases quickly so that the interest rate at which the authorities have to issue new debt also increases. Thus, the authorities are quickly penalized by the market, reducing their incentives to issue excessive debt. This devaluation channel does not exist in a monetary union.

The authorities of the member states of the union issue debt in a currency the price of which they can no longer affect by a devaluation. As a result, there is no longer any devaluation risk for the holder of this debt. There is still the default risk, which becomes more important and should increase when the country embarks on a path of excessive debt build-up. However, the implicit bailout guarantee that other members of the union may extend gives an incentive to member states to issue unsustainable amounts of debt. This is a moral hazard problem. A no-bailout provision may not solve this problem because it may not be credible. Even if the European authorities were solemnly to declare never to bail out member states, it is uncertain whether they would stick to this rule if a member country faced the prospect of being unable to service its debt. Thus, without mutual control the monetary union leads to excessive budget deficits and debts of the member states.

There is a second factor, however, which tends to reduce the incentive of member states of a monetary union to run excessive deficits. As we have stressed many times, countries that join the union issue debt in a currency they have no control over. This eliminates their ability to finance budget deficits by money creation. As a result, the governments of member states of a monetary union face a 'harder' budget constraint than sovereign nations that maintain their own currency. The latter are confronted with 'softer' budget constraints because they have access to the local national bank, which can be pressured to alleviate the burden of financing budget deficits. And even if in normal times the government of such a country may not use such pressure, it is more likely to do so in difficult times. The sheer fact that there is a national bank that can be pressured to finance budget deficits creates incentives for having larger budget deficits.[11]

Which one of the two effects—the moral hazard or the no-monetization one—prevails is essentially an empirical question in that it depends on institutional features and on the incentives governments face.[12] It is, therefore, useful to analyse the experience of member states in existing monetary unions and to compare this with the experience of sovereign nations. This is done in Table 10.1, where the average budget deficits of member states of existing monetary unions are presented together with the average of the budget deficits of the EC countries.

The most striking feature of Table 10.1 is the fact that the *average* budgetary deficit of the member states in monetary unions tends to be lower than the average deficit of independent countries in the EC.[13] This suggests that on average the existence of a union adds constraints to the size of the budget deficits of the member states. Thus, it appears that the no-monetization constraint is a powerful disincentive to running large budget deficits. It therefore seems that governments of member states of a monetary union face a 'harder' budget constraint

[11] For a formal statement of the incentives of governments in multi-party systems, see Alesina and Tabellini (1987) and Persson and Svensson (1989). A classic analysis is Buchanan and Tullock (1962).

[12] For an exciting analysis of the importance of institutions for making public finances sustainable, see von Hagen et al. (2002).

[13] This is also confirmed by Van Rompuy et al. (1991).

Table 10.1 Budget deficits of member states of unions and of EC member countries (as % of revenues)

	Weighted mean	Unweighted mean
USA (1985)	+ 10.9	+ 4.6
Australia (1986-7)	−10.1	−9.1
West Germany (1987)	−6.4	−8.2
Canada (1982)	−0.4	−1.4
Switzerland (1986)	−1.3	−0.7
European Community (1988)	−10.1	−11.4

than sovereign nations. The latter are confronted with 'softer' budget constraints and therefore have a stronger incentive to run deficits.

It should also be noted that, except in the case of West Germany, in none of the monetary unions analysed in Table 10.1 did the federal authority impose restrictions on the budget deficits of the member states. In the Federal Republic of Germany the federal government was able to limit the borrowing requirements of the *Länder* (states) with the consent of their representatives in the Bundesrat. This provision, however, was invoked only twice (in 1971 and 1973).[14]

Whereas federally imposed limits are rare, one frequently finds *self-imposed* constitutional limits on state and *Länder* budget deficits. In fact, in the USA the majority of the states have introduced such constitutional limitations. One possible interpretation for the frequency of self-imposed limits is that they may help to improve the reputation and the creditworthiness of the states in the capital markets, and therefore reduce the cost of borrowing.[15]

The evidence of Table 10.1 is of course not conclusive. More research should be carried out to find out whether the difference observed between the average deficits of member states of monetary unions and the average deficits of sovereign nations can be generalized to different time periods and a larger sample of countries. At the very least, the results of Table 10.1 suggest that the idea that in monetary unions member states have a strong incentive to create excessive levels of government debt is not corroborated by the facts of the 1980s.

Additional indirect evidence for the hypothesis that the size of deficits depends on the 'softness' of the budget constraint is provided by Moesen and Van Rompuy (1990). They classify industrial countries according to the degree of centralization of total government spending. The hypothesis tested is that governments that are more centralized may face less budget constraint than decentralized governments. This is so because in centralized countries a larger part of total government spending can potentially be financed by the issue of money. In decentralized countries, however, a larger part of government spending occurs through lower-level authorities that lack the access to monetary financing. Moesen and Van Rompuy find evidence for this hypothesis: during the period 1973–86 total government

[14] Van Rompuy et al. (1991).
[15] As discussed earlier, von Hagen (1991*a*) has argued that these constitutional limits on the budget deficits have been relatively ineffective. This would then suggest that, if perceived as ineffective in the capital markets, these constitutional restrictions should have a low effect on the risk premium.

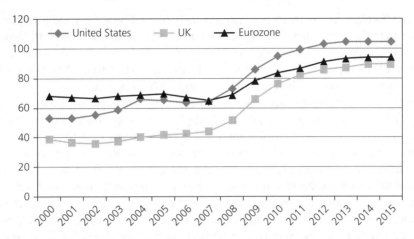

Figure 10.6 Government debt in the Eurozone, the USA, and the UK (% of GDP).

Source: European Commission, *AMECO*.

deficits increased faster in centralized countries than in decentralized ones. Put differently, during a period when government budgets were negatively affected by supply shocks and economic recession, the countries with more decentralized governments faced a stronger pressure to reduce spending and/or increase taxes than countries with more centralization of government functions.[16]

To conclude this section, it will also be useful to study the trends in government debt levels in the Eurozone and to compare these with those observed in major countries outside the Eurozone. We do this in Fig. 10.6, where we show the evolution of the government debt ratios in the Eurozone, the US, and the UK. We observe that there is no evidence of a faster increase in the Eurozone government debt ratio as compared with the US and the UK. On the contrary, since 2000 these ratios have increased significantly faster in the US and the UK than in the Eurozone. This can be seen from Table 10.2. We observe that while the debt to GDP ratios of the US and the UK doubled (US) or more than doubled (UK), the Eurozone's government debt to GDP ratio increased by only 38% during the existence of the monetary union. Thus, the second (no-monetization) effect seems to play a stronger role than the moral hazard effect. The fact that the members of the Eurozone have to issue

Table 10.2

Increase in debt to GDP ratio (2000–2015)	
US	98%
UK	130%
Eurozone	38%

Source: European Commission, AMECO

[16] Roubini and Sachs (1989) have identified other institutional features that have led to different trends in budget deficits, i.e. the degree of political cohesion of the governments in power.

debt in a 'foreign' currency severely restrains their possibilities of financing government debts. Because these member countries of the monetary union are cut off from the possibilities of monetary financing, they face a harder budget constraint than 'stand-alone' countries such as the US and the UK. This effect seems to be stronger than the moral hazard effect that has so much influenced the drafters of the Stability and Growth Pact.

The no-monetization effect also explains the intensity of the austerity programmes followed by many Eurozone countries during 2010–15. See also our discussion in Chapter 5, where we argued that the increasing government bond spreads in 2010 exerted a strong influence on policy-makers and led them to apply severe austerity measures. As the spreads increased due to market panic, these increases also gripped policy-makers. Panic in the financial markets led to panic in the world of policy-makers in Europe. As a result of this panic, rapid and intense austerity measures were imposed on countries experiencing these increases in spreads. Instead of being a machinery of budgetary indiscipline, the Eurozone became a vehicle imposing excessive discipline on member countries. This had everything to do with the fact that the member countries' governments were structurally weakened in that they had lost their natural ally, the local central bank as a lender of last resort.

10.5 Risks of default and bailout in a monetary union

The discussion in Section 10.4 allows us to shed some new light on the issue of whether a debt default is more likely in EMU, so that the risk of having to organize a costly bailout also increases. From our previous discussion one might conclude that since the member states of the EMU do not appear to behave in a less disciplined way than they did before joining EMU, the risk of default should not increase in EMU. There are other considerations, however, that one should add here to arrive at a correct appreciation of the risk of default in EMU. One has been stressed by McKinnon (1996). His analysis shows remarkable foresight of what was to come.

Sovereign nations can default on their debt in two ways. One is an outright default (e.g. stopping payment of interest on the outstanding debt). The other is an implicit default by creating surprise inflation and devaluation, which reduces the real value of the debt. Sovereign nations that control their own national banks can always resort to surprise inflation and devaluation to reduce the burden of their debt. They often do this to avoid outright default.

As soon as a country joins a monetary union it loses control over the central bank, and therefore can no longer create surprise inflation and devaluation to reduce the burden of its debt. As a result, pressure on the government to organize an outright default may actually increase in a monetary union. McKinnon (1996) argued that this would happen in EMU. The level of the debt of certain EU countries is so high that in the absence of implicit defaults by inflation and devaluation, the probability that outright default will occur increases. Thus, the default risk should increase in a monetary union.

One should add to this the analysis of McKinnon that, in a monetary union, liquidity crises can easily degenerate into solvency crises. We introduced this analysis in Chapter 1, where we stressed that in a monetary union the lack of a guarantee provided by the common central bank that government bonds will always be paid out can easily trigger liquidity crises. These can then raise interest rates to such high levels that governments find themselves unable to continue to service their debts. While the financial markets have ignored these risks for a long time, they have come back with a vengeance, as shown in Fig. 10.5.

The question that arises here is why some countries have seen the default risk increase significantly and others less so. It should be noted again that the increases of government debt ratios in the Eurozone have on average not been higher than in stand-alone countries such as Japan, the UK, and the US. However, for the reasons analysed earlier, Eurozone member countries are under greater scrutiny by financial markets than are stand-alone countries. The latter can afford higher increases in their government debt ratios (see Fig. 10.6) before the markets start seeing a default risk. This has to do with the fact that these countries provide an implicit guarantee that bondholders will always be paid out. Thus in this interpretation financial markets are less tolerant of debt levels of governments belonging to a monetary union than of stand-alone governments.

10.6 The Stability and Growth Pact: an evaluation

National fiscal policies in the EMU must find a balance between two conflicting concerns. The first one has to do with flexibility and is stressed in the theory of optimum currency areas: in the absence of the exchange rate instrument and a centralized European budget, national government budgets are the only available instruments for nation-states to confront asymmetric shocks. Thus, in the EMU, national budgets must continue to play some role as automatic stabilizers when the country is hit by a recession. This has been very clear with the recession that hit the Eurozone countries in 2008.

A second concern relates to the spillover effects of unsustainable national debts and deficits, which were described in previous sections. Unsustainable debts and deficits in particular countries may harm other member countries and may exert undue pressure on the ECB.

How does the Stability and Growth Pact strike a balance between these two concerns? It is clear that the Pact has been guided more by the fear of unsustainable government debts and deficits than by the need for flexibility. As a result, it is fair to say that the Pact is quite unbalanced in stressing the need for strict rules at the expense of flexibility. This creates a risk that the capacity of national budgets to function as automatic stabilizers during recessions will be hampered, thereby intensifying recessions.

The lack of budgetary flexibility to face recessions creates a potential for tensions between national governments and European institutions. When countries are hit by economic hardship, EU institutions are perceived as preventing the alleviation of the hardship of those hit by the recession. Worse, they are seen to be threatening to hand out fines and penalties when countries are struggling with economic problems. This certainly does not promote enthusiasm for European integration. On the contrary, it is likely to intensify Euro-scepticism.

We conclude that the Stability and Growth Pact has gone too far in imposing rules on national government budgets. The lack of flexibility of national budgetary policies in the EMU creates risks that may be larger than the risks of default and bailouts stressed by the proponents of rules. As we argued in the previous sections, there is very little evidence that a monetary union increases fiscal indiscipline or the risks of default and bailouts compared to a situation without a monetary union.

The flaws of the Stability and Growth Pact we have just described led to serious problems in 2002–4, when major Eurozone countries were hit by an economic downturn. This led to an increase of the budget deficits of France, Germany, Italy, and Portugal. In the name of the Pact, the European Commission insisted that these countries should return to budget balance even in the midst of a declining business cycle. A number of countries, in particular France and Germany, refused to submit their economies to such deflationary policies. The result was an inevitable clash with the European Commission, which, as the guardian of the Pact, felt obliged to start procedures against these countries. The result was very predictable. The Commission had to yield to the unwillingness of these countries to subject their policies and their commitments to the increasing number of unemployed to the rule of the mythical number 3. In November 2003, the Council of Ministers abrogated the procedure that the European Commission had started. For all practical purposes, the Pact had become a dead letter.

The recession that started in 2008 and the ensuing increase in government budget deficits and debts started a new phase in the application of the Stability and Growth Pact. The provisions of the Pact were tightened up again. We described the new provisions of the Pact in Box 10.3. Sanctions are to be made more automatic again, and the European Commission is to have a stronger monitoring power. Whether this tightened-up Stability Pact will be more successful in constraining government budget deficits and debts remains to be seen. In addition, under pressure from Germany, the members of the Eurozone agreed to introduce into their legislation the prohibition on running structural budget deficits of more than 0.5%. This has led to the 'Fiscal Pact' that should become law in all member states.

Our criticism of the Stability and Growth Pact should not be misinterpreted. We criticize it because we believe that centrally imposed sanctions and rigid rules are not a good idea. The underlying objective of the Pact, however, is a good one. This is that budget deficits and debt levels should be sustainable in the long run. As we stressed earlier, the Eurozone member countries have not done badly since the start of the Eurozone compared to 'stand-alone' countries.

Some economists, in particular Charles Wyplosz, have proposed the use of independent fiscal councils at the national level as an alternative to the Stability and Growth Pact. (See Wyplosz (2008) and Calmfors and Wren-Lewis (2011).) The idea is that independent fiscal councils are more effective because they create a bottom-up control system rather than a top-down one like the Stability and Growth Pact.[17]

10.7 A joint issue of common bonds

In Chapter 6, we sketched a proposal aimed at reducing the fragility of the Eurozone. This is the proposal to issue Eurobonds jointly. In this section we elaborate on this proposal.

By jointly issuing Eurobonds, the participating countries become jointly liable for the debt they have issued together. This is a very visible and constraining commitment that can convince the markets that member countries are serious about the future of the euro (see Verhofstadt 2009; Juncker and Tremonti 2010). In addition, by pooling the issue of government

---

[17] For more information on independent fiscal councils in the EU, see European Commission (2015).

bonds, the member countries protect themselves against the destabilizing liquidity crises that arise from their inability to control the currency in which their debt is issued. A common bond issue does not suffer from this problem.

A common Eurobond creates a number of serious problems that have to be addressed. In Chapter 6, we discussed the moral hazard risk implicit in this proposal. The common Eurobond issue contains an implicit insurance for the participating countries. Since countries are collectively responsible for the joint debt issue, an incentive is created for countries to rely on this implicit insurance and to issue too much debt. This creates a lot of resistance in the other countries that behave responsibly. It is unlikely that these countries will be willing to step into a common Eurobond issue unless this moral hazard risk is resolved.

A second problem (not unrelated to the previous one) arises because some countries such as Germany, Finland, and the Netherlands today (in 2016) profit from triple A ratings, allowing them to obtain the best possible borrowing conditions. The question arises what the benefits of common Eurobonds could be for these countries. Indeed, it is not inconceivable that by joining a common bond mechanism that will include other countries enjoying less favourable credit ratings, countries such as Germany, Finland, and the Netherlands may actually have to pay a higher interest rate on their debt.

These objections are serious. They can be addressed by a careful design of the common Eurobond mechanism, which must be such as to eliminate the moral hazard risk and must produce sufficient attractiveness for the countries with favourable credit ratings. This can be achieved by working on both the quantities and the pricing of the Eurobonds.

Proposals that incorporate these ideas have been made by De Grauwe and Moesen (2009) and by Bruegel (Delpla and von Weizsäcker 2010). It would work as follows. Countries would be able to participate in the joint Eurobond issue up to 60% of their GDP, thus creating 'blue bonds'. Anything above 60% would have to be issued in the national bond markets ('red bonds'). This would create a senior (blue) tranche that would enjoy the best possible rating. The junior (red) tranche would face a higher risk premium. The existence of this risk premium would create a powerful incentive for the governments to reduce their debt levels. In fact, it is likely that the interest rate that countries would have to pay on their red bonds would be higher than the interest rate they pay today on their total outstanding debt (see Gros 2010 on this). The reason is that the creation of a senior tranche means that the probability of default on the junior tranche may actually increase. This should increase the incentive for countries to limit the red component of their bond issues.

The Bruegel proposal can be criticized on the following grounds. To the extent that the underlying risk of the government bonds is unchanged, restructuring these bonds into different tranches does not affect its risk. Thus, if the blue bond carries a lower interest rate, the red bond will have a higher interest rate such that the average borrowing cost will be exactly the same as if there were only one type of bond (see Gros and Mayer 2011). This is an application of the Modigliani–Miller theorem, which says that the value of a firm is unaffected by the way the liabilities of that firm are structured.

All this is true to the extent that the underlying risk is unchanged. The point, however, is that the common bond issue is an instrument to shield countries from being pushed into a bad equilibrium (see Chapter 5). If the common bond issue succeeds in doing so, the underlying risk of the bonds of these countries does indeed decline. In that case, these countries are able to enjoy a lower average borrowing cost. At the same time, the marginal borrowing cost is likely to be higher than the average. This is exactly what one wants to have: a decline in the average debt cost, and an increase in the marginal cost of the debt. The former makes it easier to service the debt; the latter provides strong incentives towards reducing the level of the debt. This feature is important in reducing the moral hazard risk.

The second feature of a successful joint bond issue works on the pricing of the Eurobonds (see De Grauwe and Moesen 2009). This consists of using different fees for the countries participating in the blue bond issue. These fees would be related to the fiscal position of the participating countries. Thus, countries with high government debt levels would face a higher fee, and those with lower debt levels would pay a lower fee. In practical terms this means that the interest rate paid by each country in the blue bond tranche would be different: fiscally prudent countries would pay a lower interest rate than those fiscally less prudent. This would ensure that the blue bond issue would remain attractive for countries with the best credit rating, thereby giving them an incentive to join the Eurobond mechanism.

It should be noted that, if successful, such a common Eurobond issue would create a large new government bond market with a lot of liquidity. This in turn would attract outside investors, making the euro a reserve currency, and the euro would profit from an additional premium. It has been estimated that the combined liquidity and reserve currency premium enjoyed by the dollar amounts to approximately 50 basis points (Gourinchas and Rey 2007). A similar premium could be enjoyed by the euro, making it possible for the Eurozone members to lower the average cost of borrowing, very much as the US has been able to do.

10.8 Conclusion

According to the theory of optimum currency areas, a monetary union in Europe should be accompanied by some centralization of national budgets. Such centralization of the budgetary process allows for *automatic* transfers to regions and countries hit by negative shocks. It also makes it possible to consolidate part of the national government debt levels, thereby reducing the fragility of the monetary union.

Monetary unification in Europe has been realized, despite the fact that no significant central European budget exists. This poses the question of how national fiscal policies should be conducted in such an incomplete monetary union.

In this chapter, we discussed two views about this problem. The first one is based on the theory of optimum currency areas and suggests that national fiscal authorities should maintain a sufficient amount of flexibility and autonomy. The second one found its reflection in the Maastricht Treaty and the Stability and Growth Pact. According to this view, the conduct of fiscal policies in a monetary union has to be disciplined by explicit rules on the size of the national budget deficits.

We have evaluated these two views. The optimum currency area view is probably overoptimistic about the possibility of national budgetary authorities using budget deficits as instruments to absorb negative shocks. Although there are situations in which countries will need the freedom to allow the budget to accommodate for these negative shocks, the sustainability of these policies limits their effectiveness.

We also argued, however, that the case for strict numerical rules on the size of national government budget deficits is weak. There is little evidence that these rules are enforceable. In addition, the fact that national governments in a monetary union do not have the same access to monetary financing as most of them had before entry into the union 'hardens' the budget constraint and reduces the incentives to run large budget deficits. The fear that national authorities will be less disciplined in a monetary union than in other monetary regimes does not seem to be well founded. However, it is also true that financial markets have less patience with members of a monetary union than with 'stand-alone' countries, because the former cannot give a guarantee that the cash will always be available to pay out bondholders. As a result, members of a monetary union are punished more quickly by financial markets than 'stand-alone' countries and can quickly be pushed into a situation in which they face unbearably high interest rates that, in a self-fulfilling way, drive them into default.

All this has led us to criticize the Stability and Growth Pact for its excessive rigidity. It makes no economic sense to subject countries to a numerical limit (3%) that has no valid scientific basis. Similarly, it does not make sense to impose budget balance, i.e. to outlaw the issue of new debt, as a long-run constraint. Governments, like private companies, make investments that will profit future generations. It is desirable that these future generations share in the cost. This is achieved by issuing debt. What should be avoided is unsustainable debt levels, not debt per se.

As a result of the debt crisis that erupted in 2010, the Stability and Growth Pact has been strengthened again. Whether this new Pact will work better than the previous one remains to be seen.

The euro and financial markets

Introduction

The existence of the euro has important implications for financial markets in Europe and for international monetary relations in the world. In this chapter we analyse some of these issues.

11.1 EMU and financial market integration in Europe

The existence of the euro has the effect of speeding up financial market integration in Europe. The main reason is that the elimination of the exchange risk also eliminates an obstacle to the free flow of financial assets and services. As long as national moneys existed an exchange risk prevented full integration of financial markets. To give an example, consider the corporate bond market. Before the start of the Eurozone there were (small) corporate bond markets in France and Germany. An FF bond issued by Peugeot and a DM bond issued by Volkswagen were very different assets with different risks, not so much because the two companies were following different strategies, but mainly for macroeconomic reasons: the FF/DM rate could always be changed in the future. As a result, the differences in the risk–return composition of these two bonds were dominated by the risk of future exchange rate changes, upon which these two companies had no influence. Since the start of the Eurozone this has changed. When Peugeot and Volkswagen now issue bonds in the same euro, the market is able to price the inherent risks of these two bonds based on the pure corporate risk. When pricing the risk of these two bonds, the market does not have to take into account the risk of a change in the exchange rate between two national currencies any more. This facilitates the movement towards one unified bond market in the Eurozone.

The same can be said about equity markets, the government bond market, insurance markets, and other financial markets. The elimination of national currencies has removed an important obstacle to the complete integration of these financial markets.

Not all obstacles, however, were eliminated at the start of the Eurozone. There remain important differences in legal systems that create obstacles to the full integration of financial markets in the Eurozone. We will discuss the money market, the bond market, the equity market, and the banking sector in turn.

The integration of money markets

From 1999 to 2010, it can be said that money markets were fully integrated. The ECB applied the same interest rate for all its lending to the banks, and the latter translated this into the same interest rate when lending to other banks (interbank lending). The sovereign debt crisis that erupted in 2010 has ended this. The interbank market in the Eurozone has pretty much broken down, because banks do not trust each other any more. We analyse the reasons why this has happened when we discuss the integration of the banking sector.

The integration of bond markets

Government bond markets appeared to have been very much integrated since the start of the Eurozone in 1999. Bonds issued by the French and German governments, for example, were close substitutes, since the risk of these two bonds was almost indistinguishable. While, prior to 1999, the differentials in the bond rates could be as high as several hundred basis points, these differentials declined to less than 50 basis points from 1999 to 2008.

The government debt crisis has changed this, however. Since 2008, interest differentials on government bonds have increased sharply, as was documented in Fig. 10.5. The market now perceives government bonds to present a great diversity of risks, with bonds issued by Greece, Italy, and Ireland representing significantly more risk than bonds issued by Germany or France. Thus, it can be said that this represents a setback in the integration process in the government bond markets of the Eurozone. Government bonds in the portfolios of investors are not considered to be perfect substitutes any more.

What about corporate bond markets in the Eurozone? Although the introduction of the euro is a strong integrating force for the corporate bond market, the speed of integration has not been as fast as one could hope. The reason has to do with the differences in national legal systems. Accounting rules, corporate taxation, shareholders' rights, and laws governing takeovers continue to be very different across countries in the Eurozone. As a result, it will continue to be true that a Eurobond issued by Peugeot and one issued by Volkswagen will be different products. This could lead to divergent movements in the prices of these bonds, not because of exchange risks but because of unforeseen changes in national legislation on corporate taxes or changes in the rules governing takeover bids. In addition, the sovereign debt crisis has an influence on the corporate bond market. Quite often corporations cannot obtain a lower interest rate on their bond issues than the national government. As a result, corporations in countries with high government bond rates also issue bonds at higher interest rates. Only large multinationals with a worldwide diversification of their activities can escape the rule whereby the national government bond rate is a benchmark for their own bond issues.

The integration of equity markets

One of the main features of equity markets worldwide is the existence of a 'home bias'. This phenomenon has been widely observed in most countries, Domestic investors tend to buy mostly (i.e. 90% or more) domestic equities—even in those countries that allow the free movement of capital. One of the main factors explaining this home bias is the existence of national currencies. These create currency risks and have the effect of discouraging residents of a country from buying foreign-currency denominated equities. The creation of the euro provided an opportunity to reduce if not eliminate this home bias among investors in the Eurozone countries. The evidence seems to suggest that the euro is contributing to reducing the home bias within the Eurozone. This is especially visible with institutional investors (mutual funds, pension funds, insurance companies), which have increasingly allocated their equity portfolio on a Eurozone-wide basis.[1]

On the issuing side, the euro does not seem to have a strong integrating force. Most companies continue to list their shares on the national stock markets. There have been a few instances of cross-border listings, but these have remained scarce. The failure to integrate the issuing part of the equity market has much to do with obstacles arising from legal and regulatory differences between countries. Differences in accounting and taxation rules and differences in corporate governance practices prevent most companies from seeking listings in stock markets other than their own.

These differences in corporate taxation and accounting rules create difficulties in comparing the value of firms. More importantly, changes in these laws and regulations in one country will affect the value of the firms incorporated in these countries. As a result, there will continue to be a country risk attached to shares, despite the fact that the exchange risk (a typical country risk) has disappeared. The continuing existence of country risks slows down the full integration of equity markets in the Eurozone.

In order to boost capital market integration (bond and equity markets) the European Commission proposed in 2015 to launch a 'Capital Markets Union' (see European Commission (2015)). The main idea is that by removing the many legal and regulatory obstacles in the bond and equity markets, firms and households would face one large capital market very much like US households and firms do. It is still to early to tell whether this proposed Capital Markets Union will be successful.

The integration of banking sectors

While the euro led to a full integration of the interbank market within the Eurozone until 2010, when the sovereign debt crisis erupted, the retail part of the banking sector remained largely segmented throughout the period. Recently, some progress has been made in further integration. We show the evidence in Fig. 11.1. It presents the share of foreign establishments (branches and subsidiaries) in total domestic bank assets in the EU-15 in 2001 and 2006. We observe that foreign banks increased their market shares somewhat between 2001 and 2006, reaching close to 30% in 2006. Thus, there is progress in the integration of banking sectors but it is a slow process.

Why has the integration process of banking sectors at the retail level been so slow? The main reason undoubtedly is the continuing existence of national legislations that regulate banks in the national territories. In addition, there is the continuing existence of national regulators of the banking systems. An important step was taken towards a centralization of

---

[1] See Fidora et al. (2006) for evidence on the home bias. These authors find strong evidence that the home bias tends to decline when exchange rate variability is reduced.

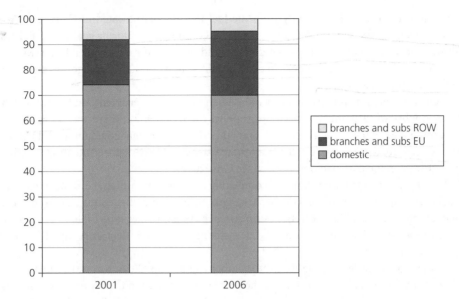

Figure 11.1 Average share of foreign establishments in total domestic bank assets in EU-15.

Source: European Commission, EMU@10, 2008.

the regulation and supervision of banks in 2014. The ECB has become the single supervisor of the systemic banks. We discussed this in Chapter 8. This should help in promoting the integration of the banking sectors at the retail level.[2]

Since the start of the sovereign debt crisis in the Eurozone, worrisome developments have come to the surface. The sovereign debt crisis in a number of countries (Greece, Ireland, Portugal, and Spain) has had the effect of putting a lot of pressure on local banks. These banks are the main holders of government debt for the country in which they operate. As a result, they have made large losses. In addition, as the government bond rates have increased, the interest rates at which the banks have to fund themselves increased significantly. Since banks are borrowing short and lending long, the borrowing rates increased faster than the lending rates. Many banks made large losses. These losses in turn created distrust about these banks. As a result, the banks of countries where the sovereign debt crisis was most intense lost their access to the interbank market. We have analysed this 'deadly embrace' between the sovereign and the domestic banks in previous chapters.

Thus, the sovereign debt crisis had the effect of closing the interbank market for banks in distressed countries. This was a step back in the integration process. It has forced the banks in these countries to obtain financing directly from the ECB.

One may ask why the sovereign debt crisis has disrupted the interbank market in the Eurozone, while a similar crisis in the US would not have this effect. If, for example, California were to experience a government debt crisis, this would not affect banks in California. Why is this? The answer is two-fold. Supervision and regulation are fully centralized in the US. Second, and even more importantly, the Federal government stands ready to help the

---

[2] See Section 8.6 for a discussion of this principle.

banks in California independently from the fact that they are located in California. The deposit insurance system is federal. As a result, when banks in California get into trouble the federal budget will be used to pay out deposit holders in Californian banks. It follows that the solidity of the Californian banks depends on the solidity of the Federal government, not of the Californian government.

Things are very different in the Eurozone. When the Irish government was hit by the debt crisis, doubts arose about its capacity to support the Irish banks. There was no European government to help out the Irish banks. Only the Irish government could do so. But the latter was weakened by excessive debt. As a result, distrust in the Irish government spilled over into distrust in the Irish banking system (see Gros 2012).

This shows again the importance of completing the monetary union, i.e. of having a central budget capable of sustaining the banking systems of the member countries. A European budget that sustains a European deposit insurance system makes it possible to protect the banks in a particular country from the devastating effects of a debt crisis involving that government.

As mentioned earlier, in June 2012 the member countries of the Eurozone decided to create a banking union aimed at resolving the problems discussed in the previous paragraphs. We discussed some features of this proposed banking union, in particular the creation of a single European supervisor. In November 2014, the ECB became the single supervisor of the systemic banks in the Eurozone. This is an important step forwards. Unfortunately, the other components of a banking union are less well developed. There is still no common deposit insurance mechanism and the resolution mechanism is insufficient, as we argued in Chapter 8.

Thus, the banking union in the Eurozone remains incomplete. As a result, when a national government experiences a debt crisis in the future it will again pull the domestic banks into a crisis also, shutting these banks out of the interbank market. Put differently, it appears that the integration of a key part of the financial system, i.e. the interbank market, can only be maintained if there is some form of budgetary union.

The disruption of the interbank market in the Eurozone has had another important effect. It has very much disrupted the payment system in the Eurozone. When, prior to the crisis, Country A made net payments to Country B (e.g. because it had a current account deficit), this appeared in the fact that banks of Country B accumulated claims on banks of Country A. And nobody noticed. When the sovereign debt crisis led to a breakdown of the interbank market in 2010 this was no longer the case. Instead, these payments led to an accumulation of claims by the national bank of Country B on the rest of the system. This follows from the operational rules of the Target2 system. Sinn and Wollmershäuser (2012) have criticized these rules and have argued that this leads to too large a risk for the German Bundesbank, which holds most of the claims (see also De Grauwe and Ji 2012 and Whelan 2012).

When the OMT programme was announced, fear and panic subsided and, as a result, some recovery of the interbank market occurred. This had the effect of reducing the Target2 balances (both the claims and the liabilities). This is shown in Fig. 11.2. We observe that in early 2010, with the eruption of the sovereign debt crisis, Target 2 balances exploded. Germany and the Netherlands accumulated large claims, while Spain and Italy accumulate large liabilities. From September 2012, these balances tended to decline strongly again. It is

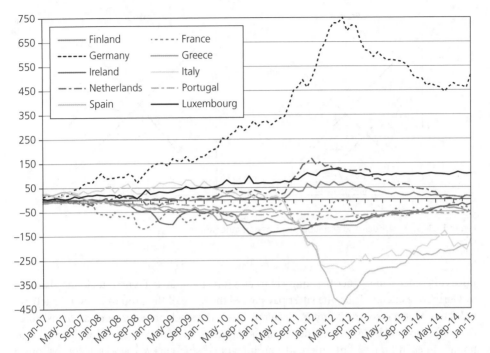

Figure 11.2 Target2 Balances (billion euros).

Note: Claims are positive, liabilities are negative numbers.

Source: Euro Crisis Monitor, Institute of Empirical Economic Research, Osnabrück University.

interesting to compare the Target2 balances and the spreads on ten-year government bonds (see Fig. 6.1). We then find that during the sovereign deb crisis, German Target2 balances and the spreads are highly correlated. Thus trust is key for a well-functioning interbank market.

11.2 Why financial market integration is important in a monetary union

Financial market integration is of great importance for the smooth functioning of EMU. The main reason is that it can function as an insurance mechanism facilitating adjustment to asymmetric shocks. We discussed the main principles of this market-based insurance mechanism in Chapter 1. Here we go into somewhat more detail. Let us return to the two-country model of Chapter 1, which we repeat here (see Fig. 11.3). We assume, as before, an asymmetric shock hitting France negatively and Germany positively. Suppose that the financial markets of France and Germany are completely integrated. Thus, there is one bond market and one equity market, and the banking sector is also completely integrated.

Let us concentrate first on how integrated bond and equity markets facilitate the adjustment. In France, as a result of the negative shock, firms make losses, pushing down the stock

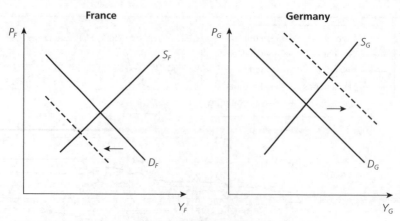

Figure 11.3 Aggregate demand and supply with asymmetric shocks.

prices of French firms. Since the equity market is fully integrated, French stocks are also held by German residents. Thus, the latter pay part of the price of the drop in economic activity in France. Conversely, the boom in Germany raises the stock prices of German firms. Since these are also held by French residents, the latter find some compensation for the hard economic times in France. Put differently, an integrated stock market works as an insurance system. The risk of a negative shock in one country is shared by all countries. As a result, the impact of the negative output shock in one country on the income of the residents of that country is mitigated.

A similar mechanism works through the integrated bond market. Firms in France make losses, and some also go bankrupt. This lowers the value of the outstanding French bonds. Some of these French bonds are held by German residents, so that they also pay the price of the economic duress in France.

An integrated mortgage market has similar effects on the degree of risk sharing. When, as a result of the negative shock in France, French real estate prices drop, this negatively affects the value of outstanding French mortgage-backed bonds. The opposite occurs in Germany. The positive shock there is likely to lead to a housing boom, increasing the value of German mortgage-backed bonds. Again, this will allow for risk sharing between France and Germany. The economically unfortunate French are compensated by the fact that they hold part of the German mortgage-backed bonds, while the economically fortunate Germans share in the French economic misfortunes by holding French mortgage-backed bonds.

Finally, the integration of the banking sector also facilitates risk sharing. Suppose the banking sector is fully integrated. This means that the banks operating in France and Germany are the same. Thus, Deutsche Bank has a large portfolio of French loans (to French firms, consumers, homeowners), and so does Credit Lyonnais of German loans. The negative shock in France has the effect of making a part of the French loans 'non-performing', i.e. some French firms and consumers fail to service their debt. As a result, Deutsche Bank loses revenue. It will be able to compensate for this by better revenues in Germany, where the boom boosts the value of the outstanding loans. Similarly, Credit Lyonnais will be compensated for its losses on its French loans by higher profits from its German activities.

We conclude that in a monetary union, financial market integration provides different channels of risk sharing. These make it possible for the residents of countries (regions) hit by a negative shock to keep their income at a relatively high level (compared to output). The counterpart of this risk sharing is that residents of the booming country see their income increase at a lower rate than their output.

Interesting empirical research has been undertaken to measure the importance of risk sharing among regions (countries) through financial markets. Asdrubali et al. (1996) have found that financial markets in the USA allow for considerable risk sharing among US regions. In fact, they come to the conclusion that this risk sharing through the market is about twice as important as the risk sharing provided by the US government budget. Research by Marinheiro (2002) compares the amount of risk sharing between the states in the USA with the risk sharing between the member states of the EU. The differences are striking. US capital markets redistribute 48% of asymmetric shocks in output that occur at the state level, while in the EU the private capital markets only redistribute 15% of the asymmetric shocks in GDP at the national level. Thus, when output in Massachusetts declines by 10% relative to the other US states, the US capital markets redistribute about 5% back to Massachusetts. In contrast, when, in the EU, the GDP of Italy declines by 10% relative to the rest of the EU, the European capital markets redistribute only 1.5% back to Italy. One may conclude that Europe has a long way to go to achieve the kind of financial market integration that will help to cope with asymmetric shocks in the monetary union.

There are other differences between the Eurozone and the USA that we have mentioned occasionally in this book. The US federal budget is an important instrument of regional redistribution: when the income of a US state declines by 10% the federal budget redistributes about 2.5% back to the state experiencing a negative shock. In the Eurozone, there is no similar inter-country risk-sharing mechanism in place. As a result, the whole burden of smoothing the effect of a negative output shock is placed on the national budget. Estimates by Marinheiro (2002) indicate that when output declines by 10% in a Eurozone country the national budget softens the blow by approximately 2.1%. Put differently, a decline in output of 10% leads to an increase in the national budget deficit of that country, so that 2.1% is redistributed from future generations to the present one.

From this evidence, it appears that the insurance system in the Eurozone is poorly organized at this moment. The financial markets and national governments are of little help in sharing the risk of asymmetric shocks across the Eurozone. The only risk-sharing mechanisms that are in place involve redistributions between different generations within the same countries.

From the previous discussion, one may conclude that, in the absence of budgetary unification in the Eurozone and assuming that countries follow the prescriptions of the Stability and Growth Pact, the main risk-sharing mechanism that will be available must come from the integration of financial markets. For this to happen, however, more progress towards financial market integration is essential. This is what the proposed Capital Markets Union that we discussed earlier aims to achieve. The example of the USA shows that the benefits in terms of risk sharing can be substantial.[3]

---

[3] See also Mélitz and Zumer (1999) on this issue.

11.3 Conditions for the euro to become an international currency

There is little doubt that if the Eurozone survives the debt crisis that erupted in 2010, the euro has the potential to become a major currency challenging the dollar, and the euro financial markets can become a pole of attraction for investors and borrowers very much in the way that the US financial markets are today. Since the start of the Eurozone some of this dynamics has already been going on. The share of the euro as a reserve currency held by foreign central banks has been increasing since the start of the Eurozone. We show the evidence in Fig. 11.4. We observe that the euro makes up more than 25% of all reserve holdings by central banks in 2013. However, the share of the dollar, although declining, remains more important. In 2013 it was still more than 60%.

A question that is often raised is whether the euro will overtake the dollar as an international currency. This question was recently analysed by Eichengreen (2012). In order to do so, it is important to study the factors that lead to the emergence of an international currency. We will distinguish between structural factors[4] that define the necessary conditions, and policy factors without which a currency cannot graduate to an international status even if the structural factors are met.

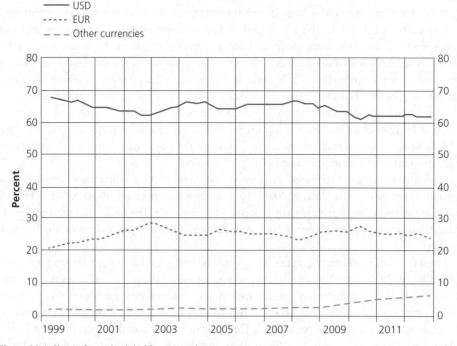

Figure 11.4 Share of euro in global foreign exchange reserves.

Source: European Central Bank, 'The International Role of the Euro' (July 2013).

[4] For a ground-breaking analysis, see Portes and Rey (1998).

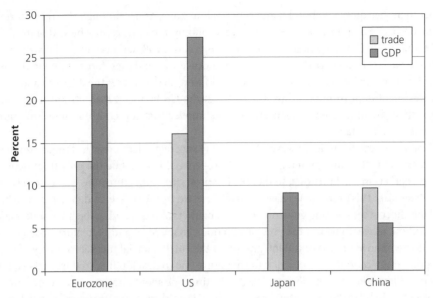

Figure 11.5 Share of output and trade in world totals, 2006.

Source: European Commission, EMU@10, 2008.

Structural factors

Size matters as a condition for a currency to graduate to international status. There is no denying that the Eurozone is big. In terms of output and trade (see Fig. 11.5), it is almost at par with the USA. In terms of the size of financial markets, however, the Eurozone has some way to go (see Fig. 11.6). We observe that the US equity and bond markets as a whole are about 70%

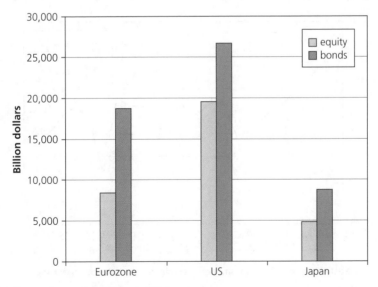

Figure 11.6 Outstanding equity and bonds, 2006.

Source: European Commission, EMU@10, 2008.

larger than the equity and bond markets of the Eurozone. Thus, although the 'real' economy of the Eurozone is almost as big as the US real economy, the same cannot be said of the financial economy. In terms of financial size, the USA is about 70% larger than the Eurozone.

Financial size influences the liquidity of financial assets, and therefore the ease with which large investors can adjust their portfolios. In addition, size increases the diversity and choice of investment opportunities. Thus, the fact that the US financial markets are significantly larger than the unified euro financial markets implies that the USA continues to enjoy a competitive advantage.

Economies are dynamic, however. Prior to the sovereign debt crisis in the Eurozone one could expect that monetary integration in Europe would accelerate the growth of debt and equity markets in the Eurozone, so that the financial size of the Eurozone would come closer to its 'real' size. This process may have been interrupted by the sovereign debt crisis, which has had the effect of segmenting government bond markets and disrupting the interbank market. In addition, as we argued in the previous sections, many legal and regulatory obstacles will have to be removed to make full integration of the euro financial markets a reality. This full integration is a *conditio sine qua non* for the Eurozone to develop financial markets equal in size to US financial markets. Since this will take time one should not expect that the euro will displace the dollar in the near future (see Galati and Wooldridge 2009 for a similar conclusion).

The policy environment

A currency can only graduate to an international role if there exists monetary and financial stability at home.[5] This stability in turn depends on the monetary and financial policies pursued at home. Where does the Eurozone stand here, as compared to the USA?

We look at some recent macroeconomic developments in both the EU and the USA. The foremost indicator of *monetary stability* is the rate of inflation (which measures the stability of the purchasing power of money). As far as inflation is concerned (see Fig. 11.7), we

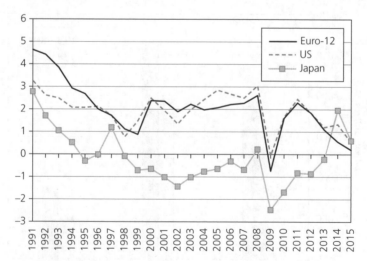

Figure 11.7 Price deflator private final consumption expenditure (yearly percentage change).

Source: European Commission, *AMECO.*

[5] See Hartmann and Issing (2002) on this.

observe a process of strong disinflation in both Europe and the USA during the 1990s. As a result, both countries entered the 21st century with low inflation. The average inflation rate in the US and in the Eurozone since 2000 has been very similar and close to 2% per year. In both countries inflation moved to the zero bound after 2010.

The low inflation experience of the last decade is to a large extent due to a significant change in the policy preferences of monetary authorities. In both Europe and the USA, price stability has become the major objective of policy-making. This is not likely to change much, so that one can expect considerable price stability in the future. This conclusion is reinforced in the case of Europe by the institutional design of the ECB. The ECB has a mandate for price stability, and has been made politically independent. This will boost the prospects for the euro to become an international currency.

Although necessary, price stability alone does not guarantee *financial stability*. This is very well illustrated by the case of Japan. As can be seen from Fig. 11.7, Japan was even more successful in maintaining price stability than Europe and the USA during the 1990s and most of the 2000s, and yet a financial crisis erupted that has led to a serious setback for the yen as an international currency. Put differently, if it was only price stability that mattered, the yen would now benefit from a large stability bonus, boosting its use as an international currency. This has not happened, because other conditions for financial stability must be satisfied. These have to do with government debts and deficits, and the stability of the financial system.

Concentrating on government debts, the Eurozone and the USA face similar problems. The USA was more successful than the Eurozone in reducing government debt level during the 1990s. However, from 2001 when the USA initiated a policy of deficit spending, the debt–GDP ratio started to increase faster than in the Eurozone, as Fig. 11.8 shows. This accelerated even further after the banking crisis of 2008, so that in 2015 the US had a significantly higher government debt level than the Eurozone. Thus, the emergence of the financial crisis in 2008 had a larger impact on US government debt than on the aggregated government debt of the Eurozone countries.

Despite a significantly worse public debt situation in the US than in the Eurozone, it was the Eurozone that was hit by a government debt crisis in 2010. We analysed the reasons why

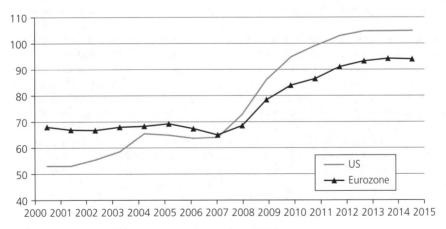

Figure 11.8 Government debt in the Eurozone and USA (% of GDP).

Source: European Commission, *AMECO*.

this was so in previous chapters. Clearly if the Eurozone does not manage to overcome that crisis, there is no chance that the euro will become a currency capable of challenging the dollar.

All this does not mean that the US does not face problems of its own. The fiscal crisis in the US, while unlikely to lead to the kind of liquidity squeezes and self-fulfilling default crises observed in the Eurozone, may trigger other problems. The temptation to solve the US debt crisis by inflation may be very strong;[6] in fact stronger than in the Eurozone, where the independence of the ECB is likely to make this option less likely. An inflationary burst in the US would do a lot to reduce the real burden of government debt, but would at the same time weaken the international position of the dollar (see Eichengreen 2012).

All this is going to create a lot of uncertainty about the future stability of the financial system. But since this uncertainty occurs on both sides of the Atlantic, it is difficult to know how it will affect the chances of the euro taking over part of the role of the dollar as an international currency (see Box 11.1).

BOX 11.1 Does an international currency have to be strong?

In the previous sections, we analysed the conditions under which the euro might become an international currency like the dollar. Does the euro have to be a strong currency (in the sense of appreciating vis-à-vis the dollar) in order to become an international currency?

It is important to realize that this second issue is very different from the first. The factors that determine whether a currency will be used internationally, both by investors and by issuers of debt and equity, have very little to do with the factors that determine whether a currency will appreciate or depreciate. During the post-war period the dollar developed as the major international currency, providing ample opportunities to investors in the world to buy dollar-denominated assets and to foreign firms and institutions to issue bonds and stocks. This happened while the dollar was sometimes appreciating and sometimes depreciating against other major currencies. These swings in the exchange value of the dollar were at times considerable, and yet the dollar remained the undisputed world currency.

We have identified in the previous sections the factors that determine whether a currency will become an international currency. These factors are: economic size and the size of financial markets; freedom to buy and to sell assets; a financial environment that is fully integrated; and reasonable financial and monetary stability.

With the exception of the last one, these factors are unrelated to those that affect the strength of a currency. Take, for example, the size of countries (economic and financial). This has nothing to do with the strength (or weakness) of a currency. Large and small countries can have strong or weak currencies. This point was often misunderstood during discussions prior to the start of EMU. Up to 1999, many observers believed that the euro would become a strong currency. This belief was based on a fallacious size argument. It went like this: the Eurozone would suddenly become a new and large economic and financial entity with its own currency. International investors would be very attracted by the new opportunities of a large bond and equity market in euros. As a result, investors from all over the world (both private and official) would start investing in euro assets. In order to do so they would have to sell dollars, yen, and other currencies in the foreign exchange market to buy euros. This would then inevitably increase the price of the euro. The euro was destined to become a strong currency.

(Continued...)

---

[6] See the impressive study by Reinhart and Rogoff (2009), who document how sovereign debt crises have often been 'solved' by creating inflation.

The argument is fallacious because it is only half of the story. With the start of the Eurozone, Eurobonds became attractive both for international investors wishing to hold more euro assets in their portfolios and for foreign institutions (firms, official institutions) wishing to issue bonds. While the investors buy euros, the issuers of bonds sell euros. An example will make the latter clear. Suppose a Brazilian company issues a bond denominated in euros. It will then use the proceeds of this Eurobond issue for its investments in Brazil, or possibly elsewhere. Thus, this company will sell the euros obtained by the bond issue to acquire the local currency, or possibly other currencies. This will put downward pressure on the euro.

The upshot of this is that when foreigners are attracted to use the euro either as investors or as issuers of debt, the effect on the value of the euro in terms of, say, the dollar cannot be determined a priori. It can go both ways. In fact, during the first year of the euro, 1999–2000 (when everybody expected a strong euro), the debt issue effect dominated the portfolio effect. Foreigners issued more Eurobonds than other foreigners were willing to acquire. The euro went down in the foreign exchange markets.

The price of a currency is determined by the present and expected future values of fundamental variables, such as interest rates, inflation rates, economic activity, the current account, etc. Thus, the euro may appreciate or depreciate in the future depending on how these variables evolve relative to how the same variables that affect the dollar evolve. It is generally very difficult to predict this. Since the future is so difficult to predict, forecasts are very much influenced by perceptions and beliefs. Thus, during the second half of the 1990s a very strong belief existed that the US economy was superior to the European economies. Tales of wondrous productivity miracles and a 'new economy' in the USA were being told and believed. These beliefs were only loosely related to reality, but they influenced how economic agents forecasted the future. All this led to a strong increase in the value of the dollar relative to the euro.

When recession hit the USA in 2001, it became clear to many observers that the US economy was not so very superior to the European economies, and that much of what had been said about the 'new economy' was based on fiction. This changed perceptions and beliefs again. As a result, market participants took a closer look at the current account of the US. During the euphoric years many of these participants had dismissed the bad news coming from the current account. Blinded by optimism, they failed to see that the current account was signalling that the economic boom in the US was unsustainable.

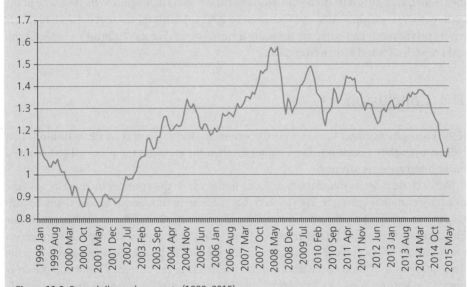

Figure 11.9 Euro-dollar exchange rate (1999–2015).

Source: European Central Bank.

After 2001, the mood about the dollar changed and pessimism set in. The US current account became the focus of attention again. And there was no good news there.

   At the same time, investors realized that their excessive pessimism about the euro was overdone. Moods and beliefs switched dramatically. The euro became the preferred currency in which to invest. This led to a dramatic increase in the value of the euro relative to the dollar (or, which is the same thing, a dramatic decline of the dollar). A classic bubble emerged, which led to a doubling of the value of the euro against the dollar (from $0.84 in 2001 to $1.6 in 2008: see Fig. 11.9. Few fundamentals could be invoked (apart from the US current account deficit) justifying this 'euro-bubble'. Not surprisingly, the euro crashed during the second half of 2008, as all bubbles do. Since then, the euro–dollar rate has moved up and down, gripped by shifting beliefs about the strengths and weaknesses of the US and the Eurozone. What remains perplexing is that despite the sovereign debt crisis in the Eurozone, the euro has remained relatively strong vis-à-vis the dollar. Since the second half of 2014 we observe a significant decline of the euro. This decline started as soon as the ECB announced it would start its QE programme, aiming at increasing the money base.

One last comment should be made here. Economic history teaches us that there is a lot of inertia in any change of the international position of a currency. This has to do with network externalities in the use of a currency; i.e. the utility of the use of a currency derives mainly from the fact that others use the same currency. And the more users there are of one particular currency, the greater the utility for all the users. This implies that when a particular currency, say the dollar, is the dominant one, this very fact makes it very useful. People will not easily switch to another currency under those conditions. This explains why the pound sterling remained the leading international currency until the Second World War even though the UK had already lost its dominant economic and financial position to the US early in the 20th century (see Cohen 2000 and Eichengreen 2005). All this means that the dollar is likely to remain the dominant currency for some time to come. (For a revisionist view see Chinn and Frankel 2005 and Eichengreen 2012.)

11.4 **Conclusion**

If the Eurozone manages to overcome the sovereign debt crisis and create institutions that reduce its fragility (as analysed in Chapter 6), then the euro has the potential to become a major international currency.

   In this chapter, we analysed the conditions under which the euro can increase its position as an international currency. We stressed that there are a number of factors that will help the euro to establish a firm position as a world currency. One is the economic size of the Eurozone, and the other is the existence of macro and monetary stability. These are necessary conditions for a currency to become widely used in the world. Another condition is the depth and sophistication of the financial markets backing the currency. Although the creation of the Eurozone led to a significant integration of Eurozone financial markets (mainly the money and bond markets), the sovereign debt crisis has had the effect of reducing the level of integration of these markets. In addition, the equity and banking markets are still considerably segmented, hampering the euro in its quest to become a world currency on a par with the dollar.

The further developments of the financial crisis add a lot of uncertainty about the future of the euro (and the dollar) as an international currency. Very much will depend on how successful the Eurozone authorities are in resolving this crisis.

We also argued that further financial market integration in the Eurozone should be pursued so as to provide an insurance mechanism against asymmetric shocks, thereby facilitating the smooth functioning of the monetary union. Such integration will require further steps towards integrating legal and regulatory systems. In other words it requires further political integration. In 2015 the European Commission announced proposals to integrate capital markets.

Finally, we argued that in order to avoid a disintegration of the money market (interbank market) in the Eurozone, it is essential that steps are undertaken towards a banking and budgetary union, which includes a common deposit insurance system.

References

Advisory Commission to Study the Consumer Price Index (Boskin Commission Report) (1996) 'Toward a More Accurate Measure of The Cost of Living', Final Report to the Senate Finance Committee, December.

Aiginger, K., and Leitner, W. (2002) *Regional Concentration in the US and Europe: Who Follows Whom?* Vienna: Austrian Institute of Economic Research.

Akerlof, G., Dickens, W., and Perry, G. (1996) 'The Macroeconomics of Low Inflation', *Brookings Papers on Economic Activity*, no. 1, 1–76.

Akerlof, G., Dickens, W., and Perry, G. (2000) 'Near Rational Wage and Price Setting and the Long Run Phillips Curve', *Brookings Papers on Economic Activity*, no. 1, 1–60.

Akerlof, G., and Shiller, R. (2009) *Animal Spirits: How Human Psychology Drives the Economy and Why it Matters for Global Capitalism*, Princeton: Princeton University Press.

Aksoy, Y., De Grauwe, P., and Dewachter, H. (2002) 'Do Asymmetries Matter for European Monetary Policies?', *European Economic Review*, 46: 443–69.

Alcidi, C., and Gros, D. (2010) 'The European Experience with Large Fiscal Adjustments', CEPS Policy Brief, available at: http://www.ceps.eu/book/european-experience-large-fiscal-adjustments.

Alesina, A. (1989) 'Politics and Business Cycles in Industrial Democracies', *Economic Policy*, 8: 55–98.

Alesina, A., and Grilli, V. (1993) 'On the Feasibility of a One- or Multi-Speed European Monetary Union', NBER Working Paper, no. 4350.

Alesina, A., and Spolaore, E. (2003) *The Size of Nations*, Cambridge, MA: MIT Press.

Alesina, A., and Summers, L. (1993) 'Central Bank Independence and Macroeconomic Performance: Some Comparative Evidence', *Journal of Money, Credit and Banking*, 25(2): 151–62.

Alesina, A., and Tabellini, G. (1987) 'A Positive Theory of Fiscal Deficits and Government Debt in a Democracy', NBER Working Paper, no. 2308.

Alesina, A., Angeloni, I., and Etro, F. (2001) 'The Political Economy of Unions', NBER Working Paper, Cambridge, MA.

Alesina, A., Blanchard, O., Gali, J., Giavazzi, F., and Uhlig, H. (2001) 'Defining a Macroeconomic Framework for the Euro Area', *Monitoring the European Central Bank*, 3, London: CEPR.

'All Saints' Day Manifesto' (1975) *The Economist*, 1 November.

Angeloni, I., and Ehrmann, M. (2003) 'Monetary Policy Transmission in the Euro Area: Early Evidence', *Economic Policy*, 18(37): 469–501.

Angeloni, I., Kashyap, A., Mojon, B., and Terlizzese, D. (2001) 'Monetary Transmission in the Euro Area: Where Do We Stand?', ECB Working Paper, no. 114, Frankfurt: ECB.

Arnold, I., and de Vries, C. (1997) 'The Euro, Prudent Coherence', unpublished manuscript, Tinbergen Institute, Erasmus University, Rotterdam.

Arnold, I., and de Vries, C. (1998) 'Endogenous Financial Structure and the Transmission of the ECB Policy', paper presented at the conference, Common Money, Uncommon Regions, organized by the ZEI, Bonn, 24–5 July.

Arnold, I., and de Vries, C. (1999) 'Endogenous Financial Structure and the Transmission of ECB Policy', unpublished manuscript, Tinbergen Institute, Erasmus University, Rotterdam.

Artis, M. J., and Zhang, W. (1997) 'International Business Cycles and the ERM: Is there a European Business Cycle?', *International Journal of Finance and Economics*, 2(1): 1–16.

Asdrubali, P., Sørensen, B., and Yosha, O. (1996) 'Channels of Interstate Risk-sharing: United States 1963–1990', *Quarterly Journal of Economics*, 3: 1081–110.

Bade, R., and Parkin, M. (1978) *Central Bank Laws and Monetary Policies—A Preliminary Investigation: The Australian Monetary System in the 1970s*, Clayton: Monash University.

Bagehot, W. (1873) *Lombard Street*, 14th edn, London: Henry S. King and Co., available at: http://www.econlib.org/library/Bagehot/bagLom1.html.

Balassa, B. (1961) *The Theory of Economic Integration*, London: Allen & Unwin.

Balassa, B. (1964) 'The Purchasing Power Parity Doctrine: A Reappraisal', *Journal of Political Economy*, 72: 584–96.

Baldwin, R. (1989) 'On the Growth Effects of 1992', *Economic Policy*, 9: 1–42.

Baldwin, R. (2006) 'The Euro's Trade Effects', ECB Working Paper, no. 594, European Central Bank, Frankfurt.

Baldwin, R., and Wyplosz, C. (2006) *The Economics of European Integration*, 2nd edn, New York: McGraw Hill.

Baldwin, R., Berglöf, E., Giavazzi, F., and Widgrén, M. (2001) 'Nice Try: Should the Treaty of Nice be Ratified?', *Monitoring European Integration*, 11, London: CEPR.

Baldwin, R., DiNino, V., Fontagné, L., De Santis, R. A., and Taglioni, D. (2008) 'Study on the Impact of the Euro on Trade and Foreign Direct Investment', Economic Papers 321, European Commission Directorate-General for Economic and Financial Affairs.

Barro, R., and Gordon, D. (1983) 'Rules, Discretion and Reputation in a Model of Monetary Policy', *Journal of Monetary Economics*, 12: 101–21.

Baye, M., Gatti, R., Kattuman, P., and Morgan, J. (2006) 'Did the Euro Foster Online Price Competition? Evidence from an International Price Comparison Site', mimeo, Indiana University.

Bayoumi, T., and Eichengreen, B. (1993) 'Shocking Aspects of European Monetary Integration', in F. Torres and F. Giavazzi (eds), *Adjustment and Growth in the European Monetary Union*, London: CEPR, Cambridge: Cambridge University Press.

Bayoumi, T., and Eichengreen, B. (1996) 'Operationalizing the Theory of Optimum Currency Areas', CEPR Discussion Paper, no. 1484.

Bayoumi, T., and Eichengreen, B. (1997) 'Ever Closer to Heaven: An Optimum Currency Area Index for European Countries', *European Economic Review*, 41(3–5): 761–70.

Bayoumi, T., and Eichengreen, B. (1999) 'Is Asia an Optimal Currency Area? Can It Become One?', in S. Collignon, J. Pisani-Ferry, and Y. C. Park (eds), *Exchange Rate Policies in Emerging Asian Countries*, London: Routledge, pp. 3–34.

Bayoumi, T., and Masson, P. (1994) 'Fiscal Flows in the United States and Canada: Lessons for Monetary Union in Europe', CEPR Discussion Paper, no. 1057.

Bayoumi, T., Eichengreen, B., and Prasad, E. (1995) 'Currency Unions, Economic Fluctuations and Adjustment: Some Empirical Evidence', CEPR Discussion Paper, no. 1172.

Beetsma, R., and Uhlig, H. (1999) 'An Analysis of the Stability and Growth Pact', *Economic Journal*, 109: 546–71.

Begg, D., Canova, F., De Grauwe, P., Fatás, A., and Lane, P. (2002) *Surviving the Slowdown (Monitoring the European Central Bank)*, London: CEPR.

Begg, D., Canova, F., De Grauwe, P., Fatás, A., and Lane, P. (2002) MECB update, '*Monitoring the European Central Bank*', London: CEPR.

Begg, D., Chiappori, P., Giavazzi, F., Mayer, C., Neven, D., Spaventa, L., Vives, X., and Wyplosz, C. (1991) *Monitoring European Integration: The Making of the Monetary Union*, London: CEPR.

Begg, D., De Grauwe, P., Giavazzi, F., Uhlig, H., and Wyplosz, C. (1998) *The ECB: Safe at Any Speed (Monitoring the European Central Bank 1)*, London: CEPR.

Begg, D., Giavazzi, F., von Hagen, J., and Wyplosz, C. (1997) *EMU: Getting the End-Game Right*, London: CEPR.

Beine, M., Candelon, B., and Sekkat, K. (2003) 'EMU Membership and Business Cycle Phases in Europe: Markov-Switching VAR Analysis', *Journal of Economic Integration*, 18: 214–42.

Belke, A., and Polleit, T. (2010) 'How Much Fiscal Backing Must the ECB Have? The Euro Area is Not (Yet) the Philippines', *International Economics*, 124(4) April.

Berger, H., and Nitsch, V. (2006) 'Zooming Out: The Trade Effect of the Euro in Historical Perspective', paper presented at the CESifo Conference, Euro Enlargement, Munich, 24 November.

Berger, H., and Nitsch, V. (2008) 'Zooming Out: The Trade Effect of the Euro in Historical Perspective', *Journal of International Money and Finance*, 2(8): 1244–60.

Bernanke, B., and Gertler, M. (2001) 'Should Central Banks Respond to Movement in Asset Prices?', *American Economic Review*, 2: 253–7.

Bernanke, B., and Mihov, I. (1997) 'What Does the Bundesbank Target?', *European Economic Review*, 41: 1025–52.

Bernanke, B., Laubach, T., Mishkin, F., and Posen, A. (1999) *Inflation Targeting: Lessons from the International Experience*, Princeton, NJ: Princeton University Press.

Bertola, C., and Svensson, L. (1993) 'Stochastic Devaluation Risk and the Empirical Fit of Target-Zone Models', *Review of Economic Studies*, 60: 689–712.

Bini-Smaghi, L. (2008) 'Financial Stability and Monetary Policy: Challenges in the Current Turmoil', speech by Lorenzo Bini-Smaghi, member of the Executive Board of the ECB, CEPS joint event with Harvard Law School on the EU-US financial system, New York, 4 April, available at: http://www.ecb.int/press/key/date/2008/html/sp080404.en.html.

Bini-Smaghi, L., and Gros, D. (2000) *Open Issues in European Central Banking*, London: Macmillan Press Ltd.

Bini-Smaghi, L., and Vori, S. (1993) 'Rating the EC as an Optimal Currency Area: Is it Worse than the US?', Banca d'Italia Discussion Paper, no. 187.

Bini-Smaghi, L., Padoa-Schioppa, T., and Papadia, F. (1993) 'The Policy History of the Maastricht Treaty: The Transition to the Final Stage of EMU', Banca d'Italia.

Bishop, G. (1999) 'New Capital Market Opportunities in Euroland', European Investment Bank Papers, 4(1).

Blanchard, O. (2008) Macroeconomics, 5th edn, London: Prentice Hall.

Blanchard, O., and Giavazzi, F. (2003) 'Macroeconomic Effects of Regulation in Goods and Labour Markets', Quarterly Journal of Economics, 118(3): 879–907.

Blanchard, O., and Muet, P.-A. (1993) 'Competitiveness through Disinflation: An Assessment of the French Macroeconomic Strategy', Economic Policy, 16: 11–56.

Blanchard, O., and Quah, D. (1989) 'The Dynamic Effects of Aggregate Demand and Supply Disturbances', American Economic Review, 79(4): 655–73.

Boeri, T., and Garibaldi, P. (2006) 'Are Labour Markets in the New Member States Sufficiently Flexible for EMU?', Journal for Banking and Finance, 30: 1393–407.

Boeri, T., Brugiavini, A., and Calmfors, L. (eds) (2001) The Role of Unions in the Twenty-first Century, Oxford: Oxford University Press.

Bofinger, P. (1999) 'The Conduct of Monetary Policy by the European Central Bank', Briefing Paper for the Monetary Subcommittee of the European Parliament, Brussels.

Boissay, F., Collard, F., and Smets, F., (2013), 'Booms and Systemic Banking Crises', ECB Working Paper Series No. 1514, February 2013.

Bordo, M., and Jeanne, O. (2002) 'Monetary Policy and Asset Prices: Does "Benign Neglect" Make Sense?', International Finance, 5(2): 139–64.

Borio, C. (2003) 'Towards a Macroprudential Framework for Financial Supervision and Regulation?', BIS Working Paper, no. 128.

Borio, C., and Lowe, P. (2002) 'Asset Prices, Financial and Monetary Stability: Exploring the Nexus', BIS Working Paper, no. 114.

Boskin Commission Report (1996) (Advisory Commission to Study the Consumer Price Index, 'Toward a More Accurate Measure of the Cost of Living', Final Report to the Senate Finance Committee, December).

Bruno, M., and Sachs, J. (1985) Economics of Worldwide Stagflation, Oxford: Basil Blackwell.

Buchanan, J., and Tullock, T. (1962) The Calculus of Consent, Ann Arbor, MI: University of Michigan Press.

Buiter, W. (1991) 'Reflections on the Fiscal Implications of a Common Currency', in A. Giovannini and C. Mayer (eds), European Financial Integration, Cambridge: Cambridge University Press.

Buiter, W. (1999) 'Alice in Euroland', CEPR Policy Paper, no. 1.

Buiter, W. (2000) 'Optimal Currency Areas: Why Does the Exchange Rate Regime Matter?', CEPR Discussion Paper, no. 2366.

Buiter, W. (2008) 'Can Central Banks Go Broke?' CEPR Policy Insight, No. 24, Centre for Economic Policy Research, London, May.

Buiter, W., and Kletzer, K. (1990) 'Reflections on the Fiscal Implications of a Common Currency', CEPR Discussion Paper, no. 418.

Buiter, W., Corsetti, G., and Roubini, N. (1993) 'Sense and Nonsense in the Treaty of Maastricht', Economic Policy, 8(16): 57–100.

Bun, M., and Klaassen, F. (2002) 'Has the Euro Increased Trade?', Tinbergen Institute Discussion Paper.

Bundesministerium der Finanzen (1996) Finanzbericht 1997, Bonn.

Bundesministerium der Finanzen (2006) Endgültige Abrechnungen des Länderfinanzausgleichs Finanzbericht 2006, Berlin.

Buti, M., and Sapir, A. (eds) (1998) Economic Policy in EMU, Oxford: Clarendon Press.

Buti, M., Roeger, W., and Veld, J. (2002) 'Monetary and Fiscal Policy Interactions Under a Stability Pact', in M. Buti, J. von Hagen, and C. Martinez-Mongay (eds), The Behaviour of Fiscal Authorities: Stabilisation, Growth and Institutions, New York: Palgrave.

Cabral, A. (2001) 'Main Aspects of the Working of the SGP', in A. Brunila, M. Buti, and D. Franco (eds), The Stability and Growth Pact, Basingstoke: Palgrave.

Calderón, C., Chong, A., and Stein, E. (2002) 'Does Trade Integration Generate Higher Business Cycle Synchronization?', mimeo, Central Bank of Chile.

Calmfors, L. (2001) 'Unemployment, Labour Market Reform and Monetary Union', Journal of Labour Economics, 19(2): 265–89.

Calmfors, L., and Driffill, J. (1988) 'Bargaining Structure, Corporatism and Macroeconomic Performance', Economic Policy, 6: 13–61.

Calmfors, L., and Wren-Lewis, S., (2011), What should fiscal councils do?, http://www.oecd.org/gov/budgeting/47741710.pdf.

Calvo, G. (1988) 'Servicing the Public Debt: The Role of Expectations', American Economic Review, 78(4): 647–61.

Calvo, G., and Reinhart, C. (2002) 'Fear of Floating', Quarterly Journal of Economics, 117(2): 379–408.

Canzoneri, M., Cumby, R., and Diba, B. (1996) 'Relative Labor Productivity and the Real Exchange Rate in the Long Run: Evidence for a Panel of OECD Countries', Discussion Paper, Department of Economics, Georgetown University.

Canzoneri, M., Valles, J., and Vinals, J. (1996) 'Do Exchange Rates Have to Address International Macroeconomic Imbalances?', CEPR Discussion Paper, no. 1498.

Carlin, W., and Soskice, D. (1990) *Macroeconomics and the Wage Bargain*, Oxford: Oxford University Press.

Carlin, W., and Soskice, D. (2005) *Macroeconomics: Imperfections, Institutions and Policies*, Oxford: Oxford University Press.

Cecchetti, S. G. (1999) 'Legal Structure, Financial Structure and Monetary Policy Transmission Mechanism', mimeo, Federal Reserve Bank of New York.

Cecchetti, S. G., Genberg, H., Lipsky, J., and Wadhwani, S. (2000) 'Asset Prices and Central Bank Policy', Geneva Report on the World Economy 2, CEPR and ICMB.

Chinn, M., and Frankel, J. (2005) 'Will the Euro Eventually Surpass the Dollar as Leading International Currency?', NBER Working Paper, no. 11510.

Clarida, R., and Gertler, M. (1996) 'How Does the Bundesbank Conduct Monetary Policy?', NBER Working Paper, no. 5581.

Clarida, R., Gali, J., and Gertler, M. (1999) 'The Science of Monetary Policy: A New Keynesian Perspective', CEPR Discussion Paper, no. 2139, May.

Clementi, F., Gallegati, M., and Palestrini, A. (2010) 'A Big Mac Test of Price Dynamics and Dispersion Across Euro Area', *Economics Bulletin*, 30(3), 2037–53.

Cohen, B. (2000) 'Life at the Top: International Currencies in the Twenty-first Century', *Essays in International Finance*, no. 221, Princeton.

Cohen, B., and Wyplosz, C. (1989) 'The European Monetary Union: An Agnostic Evaluation', unpublished typescript.

Collins, S. (1988) 'Inflation and the European Monetary System', in F. Giavazzi, S. Micossi, and M. Miller (eds), *The European Monetary System*, Cambridge: Cambridge University Press.

Connolly, B. (1995) *The Rotten Heart of Europe: The Dirty War for Europe's Money*, London: Faber & Faber.

Committee on the Study of Economic and Monetary Union (the Delors Committee) (1989) *Report on Economic and Monetary Union in the European Community* (*Delors Report*) (with collection of papers), Luxembourg: Office for Official Publications of the European Communities.

Corden, M. (1972) 'Monetary Integration', *Essays in International Finance*, no. 93, Princeton.

Costa, C. (1996) 'Exchange Rate Pass-through: The Case of the Portuguese Imports and Exports', Thesis, Master of Science in Economics, Catholic University of Leuven, Belgium.

Cukierman, A. (1992) *Central Bank Strategy, Credibility and Independence, Theory and Evidence*, Cambridge, MA: MIT Press.

Danthine, J. P., Giavazzi, F., Vives, X., and von Thadden, E. (1999) 'The Future of European Banking', *Monitoring European Integration*, 9, London: CEPR.

Davis, S., Haltiwanger, J., and Schuh, S. (1996) *Job Creation and Job Destruction*, Cambridge, MA: MIT Press.

De Cecco, M., and Giovannini, A. (eds) (1989) *A European Central Bank? Perspectives on Monetary Unification after Ten Years of the EMS*, Cambridge: Cambridge University Press.

De Grauwe, P. (1975) 'Conditions for Monetary Integration: A Geometric Interpretation', *Weltwirtschaftliches Archiv*, 111: 634–46.

De Grauwe, P. (1983) *Macroeconomic Theory for the Open Economy*, Aldershot: Gower.

De Grauwe, P. (1990) 'The Cost of Disinflation and the European Monetary System', *Open Economies Review*, 1: 147–73.

De Grauwe, P. (1991) 'Is the EMS a DM-Zone?', in A. Steinherr and D. Weiserbs (eds), *Evolution of the International and Regional Monetary Systems*, London: Macmillan.

De Grauwe, P. (1992) *The Economics of Monetary Integration*, 1st edn, Oxford: Oxford University Press.

De Grauwe, P. (1993) 'Is Europe an Optimum Currency Area? Evidence from Regional Data', in P. R. Masson and M. P. Taylor (eds), *Policy Issues in the Operation of Currency Unions*, Cambridge: Cambridge University Press.

De Grauwe, P. (2002) 'Challenges for Monetary Policy in Euroland', *Journal of Common Market Studies*, 40(4), November: 693–718.

De Grauwe, P. (2007) *Economics of Monetary Union*, 7th edn, Oxford: Oxford University Press.

De Grauwe, P. (2009) *Economics of Monetary Union*, 8th edn, Oxford: Oxford University Press.

De Grauwe, P. (2011) 'The Governance of a Fragile Eurozone', CEPS Working Documents, Economic Policy, May, available at: http://www.ceps.eu/book/governance-fragile-eurozone.

De Grauwe, P. (2012) *Lectures on Behavioural Macroeconomics*, Princeton, NJ: Princeton University Press.

De Grauwe, P. (2015) 'Secular Stagnation in the Eurozone', *VoxEU*, January, http://www.voxeu.org/article/secular-stagnation-eurozone.

De Grauwe, P., and Grimaldi, M. (2001) 'Exchange Rates, Prices and Money: A Long Run Perspective', *International Journal of Finance and Economics*, 6(4): 289–314.

De Grauwe, P., and Grimaldi, M. (2002) 'Exchange Rate Regimes and Financial Vulnerability', Papers of the European Investment Bank, 7(2).

De Grauwe, P., and Grimaldi, M. (2006) *The Exchange Rate in a Behavioural Financial Framework*, Princeton, NJ: Princeton University Press.

De Grauwe, P., and Heens, H. (1993) 'Real Exchange Rate Variability in Monetary Unions', *Recherches Économiques de Louvain*, 59(1–2): 105–17.

De Grauwe, P., and Ji, Y. (2012*a*) 'What Germany should Fear Most is its own Fear: An Analysis of Target-2 and Current Account Imbalances', available at: http://www.econ.kuleuven.be/ew/academic/intecon/Degrauwe/PDG-papers/Discussion_papers/Causes and consequences Target2 Imbalances-0910.pdf.

De Grauwe, P., and Ji, Y. (2012*b*) 'Target2 as a Scapegoat for German Errors', *VoxEU*, November, available at: http://www.voxeu.org/article/target2-scapegoat-german-errors.

De Grauwe, P. and Ji, Y. (2013*a*) 'Self-fulfilling Crises in the Eurozone: An Empirical Test', *Journal of International Money and Finance*, 34, April: 15–36, available at: http://www.sciencedirect.com/science/article/pii/S0261560612001829.

De Grauwe, P., and Ji, Y. (2013*b*) 'Panic-driven Austerity in the Eurozone and its Implications', *VoxEU*, 21 February, available at: http://www.voxeu.org/article/panic-driven-austerity-eurozone-and-its-implications.

De Grauwe, P., and Ji, Y. (2013*c*) 'Fiscal Implications of the ECB's Bond Buying Programme', *VoxEU*, June, available at: http://www.voxeu.org/article/fiscal-implications-ecb-s-bond-buying-programme.

De Grauwe, P., and Ji, Y., (2015) Quantitative easing in the Eurozone: It's possible without fiscal transfers, *VoxEU*, January, http://www.voxeu.org/article/quantitative-easing-eurozone-its-possible-without-fiscal-transfers.

De Grauwe, P., and Moesen, W. (2009) 'Gains for All: A Proposal for a Common Eurobond', *Intereconomics*, May/June.

De Grauwe, P., and Mongelli, F. (2005) 'Endogeneities of Optimum Currency Areas: What Brings Countries Sharing a Single Currency Closer Together', Working Paper, no. 468, European Central Bank, April.

De Grauwe, P., and Polan, M. (2005) 'Is Inflation Always and Everywhere a Monetary Phenomenon?', *Scandinavian Journal of Economics*, 107(2): 239–59.

De Grauwe, P., and Spaventa, L. (1997) 'Setting Conversion Rates for the Third Stage of EMU', CEPR Discussion Paper, no. 1638.

De Grauwe, P., and Vanhaverbeke, W. (1990) 'Exchange Rate Experiences of Small EMS Countries: The Cases of Belgium, Denmark and the Netherlands', in V. Argy and P. de Grauwe (eds), *Choosing an Exchange Rate Regime*, Washington, DC: International Monetary Fund.

De Grauwe, P., and Westermann, F. (2009) 'Financial Market Regulation in Europe', unpublished paper, CESifo, Munich.

De Grauwe, P., Dewachter, H., and Veestraeten, D. (1999) 'Explaining Recent Exchange Rate Stability', *International Finance*, 2(1): 1–31.

de Haan, J., and Eijffinger, S. (1994) 'De Politieke Economie van Centrale Bank Onafhankelijkheid', *Rotterdamse Monetaire Studies*, no. 2.

de Haan, J., Eijffinger, S., and Waller, S. (2005) *The European Central Bank: Credibility, Transparency and Centralization*, CESifo Book Series, Cambridge, MA: MIT University Press.

Delpla, J., and von Weizsäcker, J. (2010) 'The Blue Bond Proposal', *Bruegel Policy Brief*, May.

Demopoulos, C., Katsimbris, G., and Miller, S. (1987) 'Monetary Policy and Central Bank Financing of Government Budget Deficits: A Cross-Country Comparison', *European Economic Review*, 31: 1023–50.

De Nardis, S., and Vicarelli, C. (2003) 'The Impact of the Euro on Trade: The (Early) Effect is Not So Large', European Network of Economic Policy Research Institutes.

Dominguez, K., and Frankel, J. (1993) *Does Foreign Exchange Intervention Work?* Washington, DC: Institute for International Economics.

Dornbusch, R., Favero, C., and Giavazzi, F. (1998) 'Immediate Challenges for the European Central Bank', *Economic Policy*, 13(26): 15–64.

Drèze, J., and Durré, A. (2012) 'Fiscal Integration and Growth Stimulation in Europe', CORE Discussion Papers, CORE, Louvain-la-Neuve.

Driffill, J. (1988) 'The Stability and Sustainability of the European Monetary System with Perfect Capital Markets', in F. Giavazzi, S. Micossi, and M. Miller (eds), *The European Monetary System*, Cambridge: Cambridge University Press.

Dvir, E., and Strasser, G. (2013) 'Does Marketing Widen Borders? Cross-Country Price Dispersion in the European Car Market', unpublished paper, Boston College.

EC Commission (1977) 'Report of the Study Group on the Role of Public Finance in European Integration' (MacDougall Report), Brussels.

EC Commission (1990) 'One Market, One Money', *European Economy*, 44.

EC Commission (1993) 'Stable Money—Sound Finances, Community Public Finance in the Perspective of EMU', *European Economy*, 53.

Ehrmann, M., and Fratzscher, M. (2007) 'Explaining Monetary Policy in Press Conferences', ECB Working Paper, no. 767.

Eichengreen, B. (1990) 'Is Europe an Optimum Currency Area?', CEPR Discussion Paper, no. 478.

Eichengreen, B. (1992) 'Designing a Central Bank for Europe: A Cautionary Tale from the Early Years of the

Federal Reserve System', in M. Canzoneri, V. Grilli, and P. Masson (eds), *Establishing a Central Bank: Issues in Europe and Lessons from the US*, Cambridge: Cambridge University Press.

Eichengreen, B. (2005) 'Sterling's Past, Dollar's Future: Historical Perspective on Reserve Currency Competition', NBER Working Paper, no. 11336.

Eichengreen, B. (2012) *Exorbitant Privilege*, Oxford: Oxford University Press.

Eichengreen, B., and Schaling, E. (1995) 'The Ultimate Determinants of Central Bank Independence', in S. Eijffinger and H. Huizinga (eds), *Positive Political Economy: Theory and Evidence*, New York: Wiley & Sons.

Eichengreen, B., and Wyplosz, C. (1993) 'The Unstable EMS', CEPR Discussion Paper, no. 817.

Eichengreen, B., Hausmann, R., and Panizza, U. (2005) 'The Pain of Original Sin', in B. Eichengreen, and R. Hausmann (eds), *Other People's Money: Debt Denomination and Financial Instability in Emerging Market Economies*, Chicago: Chicago University Press.

Eijffinger, S., and de Haan, J. (2000) *European Money and Fiscal Policy*, Oxford: Oxford University Press.

Eijffinger, S., and Schaling, E. (1995) 'The Ultimate Determinants of Central Bank Independence', in S. Eijffinger and H. Huizinga (eds), *Positive Political Economy: Theory and Evidence*, New York: Wiley & Sons.

Engel, C., and Rogers, J. (1995) 'How Wide is the Border?', International Finance Discussion Paper, no. 498, Washington, DC: Board of Governors of the Federal Reserve System.

Engel, C., and Rogers, J. (2004) 'European Product Market Integration after the Euro', *Economic Policy*, CEPR and CESifo, July.

Enoch, C., and Gulde, A.-M. (1998) 'Are Currency Boards a Cure for All Monetary Problems?', *Finance and Development*, 35(4), International Monetary Fund, available at: http://www.imf.org/external/pubs/ft/fandd/1998/12/enoch.htm.

Erkel-Rousse, H., and Mélitz, J. (1995) 'New Empirical Evidence on the Costs of Monetary Union', CEPR Discussion Paper, no. 1169.

Eurispes (2003) *CARO, CIBO Indagine statistica dell'Eurispes sui prezzi dei prodotti alimentari in collaborazione con la Coalizione dei Consumatori*, Rome, June.

European Central Bank (1999) *Monthly Bulletin*, Frankfurt, January.

European Central Bank (2002) *The Single Monetary Policy in the Euro Area*, Frankfurt, April.

European Central Bank (2008a) *Single Euro Payments Area, Sixth Progress Report*, Frankfurt, November.

European Central Bank (2008b) *Financial Stability and Oversight, Monthly Bulletin (10 Year Anniversary Special Edition)*, Frankfurt.

European Central Bank (2011) *The International Role of the Euro*, Frankfurt, July.

European Central Bank (2013) *The International Role of the Euro*, Frankfurt, July.

European Commission (2004) *Preliminary Analysis of Price Data*, Directorate General Internal Market, Economic and Evaluation Unit B3, 13 July.

European Commission (2008) 'EMU@10: Successes and Challenges After 10 Years of Economic and Monetary Union', *European Economy*, 2.

European Commission (2010) *A Structured Framework to Prevent and Correct Macroeconomic Imbalances: Operationalizing the Alert Mechanism*, Brussels, November.

European Commission, (2015a) *Independent Fiscal Institutions*, Brussels, http://ec.europa.eu/economy_finance/db_indicators/fiscal_governance/independent_institutions/index_en.htm.

European Commission, (2015b) Green Paper, *Building a Capital Markets Union*, Brussels, http://ec.europa.eu/finance/consultations/2015/capital-markets-union/docs/green-paper_en.pdf.

European Commission (various years) *European Economy*, Brussels.

European Monetary Institute (1997) *The Single Monetary Policy in Stage Three*, Frankfurt, September.

Ferguson, R. W. (2002) 'Should Financial Stability be an Explicit Central Bank Objective?', IMF Conference on Challenges to Central Banking from Globalized Financial Systems, 16–7 September, Washington, DC.

Fidora, M., Fratzscher, M., and Thimann, C. (2006) *Home Bias in Global Bond and Equity Markets: The Role of Real Exchange Rate Volatility*, European Central Bank, Frankfurt, May.

Fidrmuc, J. (2003) 'Optimal Path into the EMU: Big Bang or Gradualism?' in K. Aiginger and G. Hutschenreitter (eds), *Economic Policy Issues for the Next Decade*, Boston, Kluwer.

Fidrmuc, J. (2004) 'The Endogeneity of the Optimum Currency Area Criteria and Intraindustry Trade: Implications for EMU Enlargement', in P. De Grauwe and J. Melitz (eds), *Monetary Unions After EMU*, Cambridge, MA: MIT Press.

Fischer, S. (1982) 'Seigniorage and the Case for a National Money', *Journal of Political Economy*, 90: 295–307.

Fitoussi, J., Malinvaud, E., Atkinson, A., Flemming, J., and Blanchard, O. (1992) *Competitive Disinflation: The Mark and Budgetary Politics in Europe*, Oxford: Oxford University Press.

REFERENCES

Flam, H., and Nordström, H. (2003) *Trade Volume Effects of the Euro: Aggregate and Sector Estimates*, Stockholm: Institute for International Economic Studies.

Flam, H., and Nordström, H. (2006) 'Euro Effects on the Intensive and Extensive Margins of Trade', CESIfo Working Paper, no. 1881, December.

Flood, R., and Garber, P. (1984) 'Collapsing Exchange Rate Regimes: Some Linear Examples', *Journal of International Economics*, 17(1–2): 1–13.

Frankel, J., and Rose, A. (1998) 'The Endogeneity of the Optimum Currency Area Criteria', *Economic Journal*, 108(441): 1009–25.

Frankel, J., and Rose, A. (2002) 'An Estimate of the Effect of Currency Unions on Trade and Output', *Quarterly Journal of Economics*, 117 (2): 437–466.

Fratianni, M. (1988) 'The European Monetary System: How Well has it Worked? Return to an Adjustable-Peg Arrangement', *Cato Journal*, 8: 477–501.

Fratianni, M., and Peeters, T. (eds) (1978) *One Money for Europe*, London: Macmillan.

Fratianni, M., and von Hagen, J. (1990) 'German Dominance in the EMS: The Empirical Evidence', *Open Economies Review*, 1: 86–7.

Fratianni, M., and von Hagen, J. (1992) *The European Monetary System and European Monetary Union*, Boulder, CO: Westview Press.

Fratianni, M., and Waller, C. (1992) 'The Maastricht Way to EMU', *Essays in International Finance*, no. 187, Princeton.

Frenkel, M., Nickel, C. H., and Schmidt, G. (2002) 'How Symmetric are the Shocks and the Shock Adjustment Dynamics Between the Euro Area and Central and Eastern European Countries?', The International Monetary Fund Working Paper, 02/222.

Froot, R., and Obstfeld, M. (1989) 'Exchange Rate Dynamics under Stochastic Regime Shifts', NBER Working Paper, no. 2835.

Friedman, M. (1968) 'The Role of Monetary Policy', *American Economic Review*, 58: 1–17.

Friedman, M. (1969 edn) 'The Optimum Quantity of Money', in M. Friedman, (ed.), *The Optimum Quantity of Money and Other Essays*, Chicago: Aldine.

Friedman, M. and Schwartz, A. (1963) *A Monetary History of the United States, 1867–1960*, Princeton, NJ: Princeton University Press.

Gaiotti, E., and Lippi, F. (2004) 'Pricing Behavior and the Euro Cash Changeover: Evidence from a Panel of Restaurants', Banca d'Italia, October.

Galati, G., and Wooldridge, P. (2009) 'The Euro as a Reserve Currency: A Challenge to the Pre-eminence of the US Dollar?' *International Journal of Finance and Economics*, 14: 1–23.

Genberg, H. (2006) 'Exchange-rate Arrangements and Financial Integration in East Asia: On a Collision Course?' Hong Kong Institute for Monetary Research, Working Paper, no. 15/2006, November.

Gerlach, S. (2002) 'The ECB's Two Pillars', mimeo, Hong Kong Institute of Monetary Research, October.

Gertler, M., Kioytaki N., and Queralto A. (2012) 'Financial Crises, Bank Risk Exposure, and Government Financial Policy' *Journal of Monetary Economics*, 59: pp. 517–34.

Giavazzi, F. (1985) 'Capital Controls and the European Monetary System', in Capital Controls and Foreign Exchange Legislation, Euromobiliare, Occasional Paper 1.

Giavazzi, F., and Giovannini, A. (1989) *Limiting Exchange Rate Flexibility: The European Monetary System*, Cambridge, MA: MIT Press.

Giavazzi, F., and Spaventa, L. (1990) 'The "New" EMS', in P. De Grauwe and L. Papademos (eds), *The European Monetary System in the 1990s*, London: Longman.

Giavazzi, F., Micossi, S., and Miller, M. (eds) (1988) *The European Monetary System*, Cambridge: Cambridge University Press.

Giersch, H. (1973) 'On the Desirable Degree of Flexibility of Exchange Rates', *Weltwirtschaftliches Archiv*, 109: 191–213.

Glick, R., and Rose, A. (2002) 'Does a Currency Union Reflect Trade?' The Times Series Evidence, *European Economic Review*, 46(6): 1125–51.

Glick, R., and Rose, A., (2015), Currency Unions and Trade: A Post-EMU Mea Culpa, CEPR Discussion Paper, No. DP10615, May

González-Páramo, J. M. (2008) 'Future of Banking Supervision in Europe', Speech by José Manuel González-Páramo, Member of the Executive Board of the ECB, IBF National Conference 2008, Beyond Financial Turmoil, Dublin, 22 October.

Goodfriend, M. (2011) 'Central Banking in the Credit Turmoil: An Assessment of Federal Reserve Practice', *Journal of Monetary Economics*, 58(1): 1–12.

Gordon, R. (1996) 'Problems in the Measurement and Performance of Service-Sector Productivity in the US', NBER Working Paper, no. 5519.

Gourinchas, P.-O., and Rey, H. (2007) 'From World Banker to World Venture Capitalist: The US External Adjustment and the Exorbitant Privilege', in R. Clarida (ed.), *G7 Current Account Imbalances: Sustainability and Adjustment*, Chicago: University of Chicago Press.

Greenspan, A. (2007) *The Age of Turbulence: Adventures in a New World*, London: Penguin Books.

Grilli, V. (1989) 'Seigniorage in Europe', in M. De Cecco and A. Giovannini (eds), *A European Central*

Bank? Perspectives on Monetary Unification after Ten Years of the EMS, Cambridge: Cambridge University Press.

Grilli, V., Masciandro, D., and Tabellini, C. (1991) 'Political and Monetary Institutions and Public Financial Policies in the Industrial Countries', *Economic Policy*, 13: 341–92.

Gros, D. (1990) 'Seigniorage and EMS Discipline', in P. De Grauwe and L. Papademos (eds), *The European Monetary System in the* 1990s, London: Longman.

Gros, D. (1995) *Towards a Credible Excessive Deficits Procedure*, Brussels: Centre for European Policy Studies.

Gros, D. (1996) *A Reconsideration of the Optimum Currency Approach: The Role of External Shocks and Labour Mobility*, Brussels: Centre for European Policy Studies.

Gros, D. (2010) 'The Seniority Conundrum: Bail Out Countries but Bail In Private Short-term Creditors', *CEPS Commentary*, 10 November.

Gros, D. (2012) 'Banking Union—Ireland versus Nevada: An Illustration of the Importance of an Integrated Banking System', CEPS Commentary, Brussels, available at: http://www.ceps.eu/book/banking-union-ireland-vs-nevada-illustration-importance-integrated-banking-system.

Gros, D., and Lannoo, K. (1996) *The Passage to the Euro*, CEPS Working Party Report, no. 16.

Gros, D., and Mayer, T. (2010) Towards a European Monetary Fund, CEPS Policy Brief, available at: http://www.ceps.eu/book/towards-european-monetary-fund.

Gros, D., and Mayer, T. (2011) Debt Reduction without Default? CEPS Policy Brief, available at: http://www.ceps.eu/book/debt-reduction-without-default.

Gros, D., and Tabellini, G. (1998) 'The Institutional Framework for Monetary Policy', CEPS Working Document, no. 126, Brussels.

Gros, D., and Thygesen, N. (1998) *European Monetary Integration: From the European Monetary System towards Monetary Union*, London: Longman.

Gros, D., Mayer, T., and Ubide, A. (2005) *The EMU at Risk*, 7th Annual Report of the CEPS Macroeconomic Policy Group, Brussels.

Grubb, D., Jackman, R., and Layard, R. (1983) 'Wage Rigidity and Unemployment in OECD Countries', *European Economic Review* 21(1–2): 11–39.

Hammond, G., and von Hagen, J. (1993) 'Regional Insurance against Asymmetric Shocks: An Empirical Study for the European Community', typescript, University of Mannheim.

Hancké, B. (2013) *Unions, Central Banks and EMU: Labour Market Institutions and Monetary Integration in Europe*, Oxford: Oxford University Press.

Hancké, B. (2014) 'Employment Regimes, Wage-Setting and Monetary Union in Continental Europe', in A. Wilkinson, G. Wood, and R. Deeg (eds), *The Oxford Handbook of Employment Relations: Comparative Employment Systems.* Oxford: Oxford University Press.

Hanke, S. (2002) 'On Dollarization and Currency Boards: Error and Deception', *Journal of Policy Reform*, 5(4): 203–22.

Harberger, A. (2008) 'Lessons from Monetary and Real Exchange Rate Economics', *Cato Journal*, 28(2): 225–35.

Hartmann, P., and Issing, O. (2002) 'The International Role of the Euro', Working Paper Series, European Central Bank, January.

Haskel, J., and Wolf, H. (2001) 'The Law of One Price: A Case Study', CESifo Working Paper, no. 428, March.

Hayek, F. (1978) *Denationalization of Money*, London: Institute of Economic Affairs.

Hayo, B. (1998) 'Inflation Culture, Central Bank Independence and Price Stability', *European Journal of Political Economy*, 14: 241–63.

Heinemann, F., and Hüfner, F. (2002) 'Is the View from the Eurotower Purely European? National Divergence and ECB Interest Rate Policy', Discussion Paper, no. 02–69, Centre for European Economic Research, University of Mannheim, October.

Hind, M. (2006) *Playing Monopoly with the Devil*, Yale: Yale University Press.

HM Treasury (1989) *An Evolutionary Approach to Economic and Monetary Union*, London: HMSO.

HM Treasury (2003) *UK Membership of the Single Currency: An Assessment of the Five Economic Tests*, June, Cm5776, London, available at: www.hm-treasury.gov.uk.

Hochreiter, E., Schmidt-Hebbel, K., and Winckler, G. (2002) 'Monetary Union: European Lessons, Latin American Prospects', Working Paper, no. 68, Austrian National Bank.

Holtfrerich, C.-L. (1989) 'The Monetary Unification Process in Nineteenth-Century Germany: Relevance and Lessons for Europe Today', in M. De Cecco and A. Giovannini (eds), *A European Central Bank? Perspectives on Monetary Unification after Ten Years of the EMS*, Cambridge: Cambridge University Press.

Houssa, R. (2008) 'Monetary Union in West-Africa and Asymmetric Shocks: A Dynamic Structural Factor Model Approach', *Journal of Development Economics*, 85(1–2): 319–47.

Ingram, J. (1959) 'State and Regional Payments Mechanisms', *Quarterly Journal of Economics*, 73: 619–32.

International Monetary Fund (1984) 'Exchange Rate Volatility and World Trade: A Study by the Research Department of the International Monetary Fund', Occasional Papers, no. 28.

International Monetary Fund (1997) *EMU and the International Monetary System*, Washington, DC.

International Monetary Fund (1998) *International Capital Markets*, Washington, DC: IMF.

International Monetary Fund (2001) *International Financial Statistics*, CD-ROM, August, Washington, DC: IMF.

International Monetary Fund (2002) *World Economic Outlook*, Washington, DC.

International Monetary Fund (2012) *World Economic Outlook*, October, Washington, DC: IMF, Chapter 3.

Ishiyama, Y. (1975) 'The Theory of Optimum Currency Areas: A Survey', *IMF Staff Papers*, 22: 344–83.

Issing, O. (2008) *The Birth of the Euro*, Cambridge: Cambridge University Press.

Issing, O. (2009) 'Why a Common Eurozone Bond isn't Such a Good Idea', *Europe's World*, summer, 77–9.

Italianer, A., and Vanheukelen, M. (1992) 'Proposals for Community Stabilization Mechanisms', in 'The Economics of Community Public Finances', *European Economy*, Special Issue.

Jozzo, A. (1989) 'The Use of the ECU as an Invoicing Currency', in P. De Grauwe and T. Peeters (eds), *The ECU and European Monetary Integration*, London: Macmillan.

Juncker, J.-C., and Tremonti, G. (2010) 'E-bonds Would End the Crisis', *Financial Times*, 5 December.

Juncker, J.-C., Tusk, D., Dijsselbloem, J., Draghi, M., Schulz, M., (2015), Completing Europe's Economic and Monetary Union, European Commission, Brussels.

Kaldor, N. (1966) *The Causes of the Slow Growth of the United Kingdom*, Cambridge: Cambridge University Press.

Kenen, P. (1969) 'The Theory of Optimum Currency Areas: An Eclectic View', in R. Mundell and A. Swoboda (eds), *Monetary Problems of the International Economy*, Chicago: University of Chicago Press.

Keynes, J. M. (1936) *The General Theory of Employment, Interest and Money*, London: Macmillan and Co.

Kindleberger, C. (2005) *Manias, Panics, and Crashes*, 5th edn, New York: Wiley.

Kopf, C. (2011) 'Restoring Financial Stability in the Euro Area', 15 March 2011, CEPS Policy Brief, Brussels.

Korhonen, I., and Fidrmuc, J. (2001) 'Similarity of Supply and Demand Shocks between the Euro Area and the Accession Countries', *Focus on Transition*, no. 2, Vienna: Austrian National Bank.

Krugman, P. (1979) 'A Model of Balance of Payment Crises', *Journal of Money, Credit and Banking*, 11(3): 311–25.

Krugman, P. (1987) 'Trigger Strategies and Price Dynamics in Equity and Foreign Exchange Markets', NBER Working Paper, no. 2459.

Krugman, P. (1989) 'Differences in Income Elasticities and Trends in Real Exchange Rates', *European Economic Review*, 33: 1031–47.

Krugman, P. (1990) 'Policy Problems of a Monetary Union', in P. De Grauwe and L. Papademos (eds), *The European Monetary System in the 1990s*, London: Longman.

Krugman, P. (1991) *Geography and Trade*, Cambridge, MA: MIT Press.

Krugman, P. (1993) 'Lessons of Massachusetts for EMU', in F. Torres and F. Giavazzi (eds), *Adjustment and Growth in the European Monetary Union*, London: CEPR, Cambridge: Cambridge University Press.

Krugman, P. (2010) 'Debt, Deleveraging, and the Liquidity Trap', *VoxEU*, available at: http://www.voxeu.org/article/debt-deleveraging-and-liquidity-trap-new-model.

Krugman, P., and Wells, R. (2005) *Macroeconomics*, New York: Worth Publishers.

Kydland, E., and Prescott, E. (1977) 'Rules Rather than Discretion: The Inconsistency of Optimal Plans', *Journal of Political Economy*, 85(3): 473–91.

Lamfalussy, A. (1989) 'Macro-coordination of Fiscal Policies in an Economic and Monetary Union', in Committee on the Study of Economic and Monetary Union, *Report on Economic and Monetary Union in the European Community*, Luxembourg: Office for Official Publications of the European Communities.

Lannoo, K. (1998) From 1992 to EMU: The Implications for Prudential Supervision, CEPS Research Report.

Lannoo, K. (2011) 'The EU's Response to the Financial Crisis: A Mid-Term Review', CEPS Policy Brief, available at: http://www.ceps.eu/book/eu's-response-financial-crisis-mid-term-review.

Lannoo, K., and Gros, D. (1998) *Capital Market, and EMU*, Report of a CEPS Working Party, Brussels: Centre for European Policy Studies.

Lares (1998) 'Estimation des échanges commerciaux entre le Bénin et le Nigéria: Bulletin Régional des échanges transfrontaliers', *L'Echo des Frontières*, no. 14.

Larosière, J. (2009) 'The High Level Group on Financial Supervision in the EU', Report, Brussels, April.

Larrain, F., Tavares, J., and Garcia, C. (2003) 'Regional Currencies versus Dollarization: Options for Asia and the Americas', Center for International Development, Harvard University, January.

Lomax, D. (1989) 'The ECU as an Investment Currency', in P. De Grauwe and T. Peeters (eds), *The ECU and European Monetary Integration*, London: Macmillan.

Lucas, R. E., Jr (1996) 'Nobel Lecture: Monetary Neutrality', *Journal of Political Economy*, 104: 661–82.

Ludlow, R. (1982) *The Making of the European Monetary System*, London: Butterworths.

Maastricht Treaty (Treaty on European Union) (1992) CONF-UP-UEM 2002/92, Brussels, 1 February.

McDonald, I., and Solow, R. (1981) 'Wage Bargaining and Employment', *American Economic Review*, 71: 896–08.

MacDougall Report (1977) (EC Commission, 'Report of the Study Group on the Role of Public Finance in European Integration', Brussels).

McKinnon, R. (1963) 'Optimum Currency Areas', *American Economic Review*, 53: 717–25.

McKinnon, R. (1996) *Default Risk in Monetary Unions*, Background Report for the Swedish Government Commission on EMU, Stockholm.

McKinnon, R. and Schnabl, G. (2002) 'Synchronized Business Cycles in East Asia: Fluctuations in the Yen/Dollar Exchange Rate and China's Stabilizing Role', Discussion Paper, Institute for Monetary and Economic Studies, Bank of Japan.

Maclennan, D., Muellbauer, J., and Stephens, M. (1999) 'Asymmetries in Housing and Financial Market Institutions and EMU', CEPR Discussion Paper, no. 2062.

Mankiw, G. (2006) *Macroeconomics*, 6th edn, New York: Worth Publishers.

Marinheiro, C. (2002) 'Output Smoothing and EMU: A View from the International Risk Sharing Literature with a Focus on the Stabilization Achieved via the Financial Markets', mimeo, University of Leuven, June.

Marini, G., Adriani, F., and Scaramozzino, P. (2004) 'The Inflationary Consequences of the Currency Changeover: Evidence from the Michelin Red Guide', CEIS Tor Vergata, Research Paper, no. 27.

Meade, E., and Sheets, N. (2002) 'Regional Influences on US Monetary Policy: Some Implications for Europe', *International Finance Discussion Papers*, no. 721, February, Washington, DC: Board of Governors of the Federal Reserve System.

Mélitz, J. (1985) 'The Welfare Cost of the European Monetary System', *Journal of International Money and Finance*, 4: 485–506.

Mélitz, J. (1988) 'Monetary Discipline, Germany and the European Monetary System: A Synthesis', in F. Giavazzi, S. Micossi, and M. Micossi (eds), *The European Monetary System*, Cambridge: Cambridge University Press.

Mélitz, J. (2004) 'Risk Sharing and EMU', *Journal of Common Market Studies*, Special Issue, 42(4): 815–40.

Mélitz, J., and Vori, S. (1993) 'National Insurance Against Unevenly Distributed Shocks in a European Monetary Union', *Recherches Économiques de Louvain*, 59: 1–2.

Mélitz, J., and Zumer, F. (1999) 'Interregional and International Risk Sharing and Lessons for EMU', CEPR Discussion Paper, no. 2154.

Micco, A., Ordoñez, G., and Stein, E. (2003) 'The Currency Union Effect on Trade: Early Evidence on Trade', *Euronomic Policy*, 18(37): 315–56.

Micossi, S., and Tullio, G. (1991) 'Fiscal Imbalances, Economic Distortions, and the Long Run Performance of the Italian Economy', OCSM Working Paper, no. 9, LUISS.

Mishkin, F. S., and Schmidt-Hebbel, K. (2001) 'One Decade of Inflation-Targeting: What Do We Know and What Do We Need to Know?', NBER Working Paper, no. W8397.

Moesen, W., and Van Rompuy, P. (1990) 'The Growth of Government Size and Fiscal Decentralization', paper prepared for the IIPF Congress, Brussels.

Mojon, B. (2000) 'Financial Structure and the Interest Rate Channel of ECB Monetary Policy', ECB Working Paper, no. 40.

Mongelli, F. (2002) '"New" Views on the Optimum Currency Area Theory: What is EMU Telling Us?', ECB Working Paper Series, no. 138, April.

Monticelli, C., and Papi, U. (1996) *European Integration, Monetary Co-ordination, and the Demand for Money*, Oxford: Oxford University Press.

Morales, A., and Padilla, A. J. (1994) 'Designing Institutions for International Monetary Cooperation', unpublished, Madrid: CEMFI.

Morandé, F., and Schmidt-Hebbel, K. (2000) 'Inflation Targets and Indexation in Chile', mimeo, Central Bank of Chile, August.

Morgan, J. P. (1997) *European Markets: The Next Three Years*, London: J. P. Morgan.

Morgan, J. P. (2000) *Global Outlook Update*, New York: J. P. Morgan Securities, September.

Mundell, R. (1961) 'A Theory of Optimal Currency Areas', *American Economic Review*, 51(4): 657–65.

Mundell, R. (1973) 'Uncommon Arguments for Common Currencies', in H. G. Johnson and A. K. Swoboda (eds), *The Economics of Common Currencies*, London: Allen and Unwin, 114–32.

Mussa, M. (1979) 'Empirical Regularities in the Behaviour of Exchange Rates and Theories of the Foreign Exchange Markets', in Carnegie Rochester Conference Series on Public Policy, *Journal of Monetary Economics*, 11(1): 9–57.

Myrdal, G. (1957) *Economic Theory and Underdeveloped Regions*, New York: Duckworth.

Neumann, M. (1990) 'Central Bank Independence as a Prerequisite of Price Stability', mimeo, University of Bonn.

Neumann, M., and von Hagen, J. (1991) 'Real Exchange Rates Within and Between Currency Areas: How Far Away is EMU?', Discussion Paper, Indiana University.

Nitsch, V. (2001) 'Honey, I Shrunk the Currency Union Effect on Trade', *World Economy*, 25(4): 457–74.

Nitsch, V., and Pisu, M. (2008) 'Scalpel, Please! Dissecting the Euro's Effect on Trade', ETH Zurich and National Bank of Belgium.

Obstfeld, M. (1986) 'Rational and Self-fulfilling Balance of Payments Crises', *American Economic Review*, 76: 72–81.

OECD (1990) *Economic Outlook*, Paris: OECD.

OECD (1999a) *EMU: Facts, Challenges and Policies*, Paris: OECD.

OECD (1999b) *Economic Surveys, Italy*, 1, Paris: OECD.

OECD (2000) *EMU One Year On*, Paris: OECD.

Orphanides, A. (2000) 'The Quest for Prosperity without Inflation', ECB Working Paper, no. 15, March.

Padoa-Schioppa, T. (2004) 'The Euro and its Central Bank: Getting United after the Union', Cambridge, MA: MIT Press.

Parkin, M., and Bade, R. (1988) *Modern Macroeconomics*, 2nd edn, Oxford: Philip Allan.

Parkin, M., Bade, R., Powell, M., and Matthews, K. (2000) *Economics*, 4th edn, Harlow: Addison Wesley.

Parsley, D.C., and Wei, S.-J. (2008) 'In Search of a Euro Effect: Big Lessons from a Big Mac Meal?' *Journal of International Money and Finance*, 27: 260–76.

Peersman, G., and Smets, F. (2001) 'The Monetary Transmission Mechanism in the Euro Area: More Evidence from VAR Analysis', mimeo, Frankfurt: ECB.

Persson, T. (2001) 'Currency Union and Trade: How Large is the Treatment Effect?', *Economic Policy*, 33: 335–48.

Persson, T., and Svensson, L. (1989) 'Why a Stubborn Conservative Would Run a Deficit: Policy with Time Inconsistent Preferences', *Quarterly Journal of Economics*, 104(2): 325–45.

Persson, T., and Tabellini, G. (1996) 'Monetary Cohabitation in Europe', NBER Working Paper, no. 5532.

Phelps, E. (1968) 'Money–Wage Dynamics and Labour Market Equilibrium', *Journal of Political Economy*, 76: 678–11.

Pisani-Ferry, J. (2002) 'Fiscal Discipline and Policy Coordination in the European: Assessment and Proposals', paper prepared for the Group of Economic Analysis of the European Commission, April.

Pisani-Ferry, J., Aghion, P., Belka, M., von Hagen, J., Heikensten, L., and Sapir, A. (2008) *Coming of Age: Report on the Euro Area*, Brussels: Bruegel.

Poole, W. (1970) 'Optimal Choice of Monetary Policy Instruments in a Simple Stochastic Macro Model', *Quarterly Journal of Economics*, 84(2): 197–216.

Portes, R., and Rey, H. (1998) 'The Emergence of the Euro as an International Currency', *Economic Policy*, Cambridge, MA: MIT Press.

Posen, A. (1994) 'Is Central Bank Independence the Result of Effective Opposition to Inflation? Evidence of Endogenous Monetary Policy Institutions', mimeo, Harvard University.

Prati, A., and Schinasi, G. (1998) 'The ECB and the Stability of the Financial System', IMF Working Paper, Washington, DC.

Reinhart, C., and Rogoff, K. (2009) *This Time is Different: Eight Centuries of Financial Folly*, Princeton, NJ: Princeton University Press.

Rogoff, K. (1985a) 'Can Exchange Rate Predictability be Achieved without Monetary Convergence? Evidence from the EMS', *European Economic Review*, 28: 93–115.

Rogoff, K. (1985b) 'The Optimal Degree of Commitment to an Intermediate Monetary Target', *Quarterly Journal of Economics*, 100: 1169–90.

Roll, E. (1993) 'Independent and Accountable: A New Mandate for the Bank of England', Report of an Independent Panel Chaired by Eric Roll, London: CEPR.

Romer, C. D., and Romer, D. H. (2010) 'The Macroeconomic Effects of Tax Changes: Estimates Based on a New Measure of Fiscal Shocks', *American Economic Review*, 100(3): 763–801.

Romer, P. (1986) 'Increasing Returns and Long-Term Growth', *Journal of Political Economy*, 94(5): 1002–37.

Rose, A. K. (2000) 'One Money, One Market: Estimating the Effect of Common Currencies on Trade', *Economic Policy*, 30: 9–45.

Rose, A. K. (2004) 'The Effect of Common Currencies on International Trade: A Meta-Analysis', in V. Alexander, J. Mélitz, and G. von Furstenberg (eds), *Monetary Unions and Hard Pegs*, Oxford: Oxford University Press.

Rose, A. K., and Engel, C. (2001) 'Currency Unions and International Integration', NBER Working Paper, no. 7872.

Rose, A. K., and Svensson, L. (1993) 'European Exchange Rate Credibility Before the Fall', NBER Working Paper, no. 4495.

Rose, A. K., and van Wincoop, E. (2001) 'National Money as a Barrier to Trade: The Real Case for Monetary Union', *American Economic Review*, 91(2): 386–90.

Roubini, N., and Sachs, J. (1989) 'Government Spending and Budget Deficits in the Industrial Countries', *Economic Policy*, 11: 100–32.

Russo, M., and Tullio, G. (1988) 'Monetary Policy Coordination within the European Monetary System: Is there a Rule?' in F. Giavazzi, S. Micossi, and M. Miller (eds), *The European Monetary System*, Cambridge: Cambridge University Press.

Sachs, J., and Sala-i-Martin, X. (1989) 'Federal Fiscal Policy and Optimum Currency Areas', Harvard University Working Paper, Cambridge, MA.

Sachs, J., and Wyplosz, C. (1986) 'The Economic Consequences of President Mitterrand', *Economic Policy*, 1(2): 261–322.

Sandbu, M., (2015) *Europe's Orphan: The Future of the Euro and the Politics of Debt*, Princeton, NJ and Oxford: Princeton University Press.

Sapir, A., (2015) 'Architecture Reform for an Heterogeneous EMU: National vs. European Institutions', paper presented at the Conference organized by the Bank of Portugal, Adjustment in European Economies in the Wake of the Economic Crisis, Lisbon, 9 May 2015.

Sato, K., and Zhang, Z. (2007) 'Real Output Co-movements in East Asia: Any Evidence for a Monetary Union?', *The World Economy*, 29(12): 1671–89.

Sauer, S. and Sturm, J.-E. (2007) 'Using Taylor Rules to Understand ECB Monetary Policy', *German Economic Review*, 8(3): 375–98.

Schadler, S. (2004) 'Adopting the Euro in Central Europe', International Monetary Fund, Washington, DC.

Schadler, S., Drummond, P., Kuijs, L., Murgasova, Z., and van Elken, R. (2005) 'Euro Adoption in the Accession Countries: Vulnerabilities and Strategies', in S. Schadler, (ed.), *Euro Adoption in Central and Eastern Europe*, International Monetary Fund, Washington, DC, pp. 147–80.

Shapiro, M., and Wilcox, D. (1996) 'Mismeasurement in the Consumer Price Index: An Evaluation', NBER Working Paper, no. 5590.

Shin, K., and Sohn, C.-H. (2007) 'Trade and Financial Integration in East Asia: Effects on Co-movements', *The World Economy*, 29(12): 1649–69.

Sibert, A. (2006) 'Central Banking by Committee', *International Finance*, 9(2): 145–68.

Sinn, H. W., and Reutter, M. (2001) 'The Minimum Inflation Rate for Euroland', NBER Working Paper, no. 8085.

Sinn, H.-W., and Wollmershäuser, T. (2012) 'Target Loans, Current Account Balances and Capital Flows: The ECB's Rescue Facility', *International Tax and Public Finance*, May, https://www.cesifo-group.de/portal/pls/portal/!PORTAL.wwpob_page.show?_docname=1216647.PDF.

Stark, J. (2008) 'Monetary, Fiscal and Financial Stability in Europe', speech by Jürgen Stark, Member of the Executive Board of the ECB, 11th Euro Finance Week in Frankfurt, 18 November, available at: http://www.ecb.int/press/key/date/2008/html/sp081118_1.en.html.

Stiglitz, J. E., and Weiss, A. M. (1981) 'Credit Rationing in Markets with Imperfect Information', *American Economic Review*, 3 (June): 393–410.

Sturm, J.-E., and de Haan, J. (2011) 'Does Central Bank Communication Really Lead to Better Forecasts of Policy Decisions? New Evidence Based on a Taylor Rule Model for the ECB', *Review of World Economics/Weltwirtschaftliches Archiv*, forthcoming.

Summers, L., (2014), Reflections on the New 'Secular Stagnation Hypothesis', *VoxEU*, October, http://www.voxeu.org/article/larry-summers-secular-stagnation.

Svensson, L. (1995) 'Optimal Inflation Targets, Conservative Central Banks, and Linear Inflation Contracts', CEPR Discussion Paper, no. 1249.

Svensson, L. (1997) 'Inflation Forecast Targeting: Implementing and Monitoring Inflation Targets', *European Economic Review*, 41: 111–46.

Svensson, L. (1998) 'Inflation Targeting as a Monetary Policy Rule', CEPR Discussion Paper, no. 1998.

Svensson, L. (2003) 'What is Wrong with Taylor Rules? Using Judgment in Monetary Policy through Targeting Rules', *Journal of Economic Literature*, 41(2): 426–77.

Tavlas, G. (1993) 'The "New" Theory of Optimum Currency Areas', *World Economy*, 33: 663–82.

Taylor, J. (1993) 'Discretion Versus Policy Rules in Practice', *Carnegie-Rochester Conference Series on Public Policy*, 39: 195–214.

Teulings, C., and Baldwin, R. (2014) Secular Stagnation. Facts, Causes and Cures. A new *Vox* ebook, October, http://www.voxeu.org/article/secular-stagnation-facts-causes-and-cures-new-vox-ebook.

Tower, E., and Willett, T. (1976) 'The Theory of Optimum Currency Areas and Exchange Rate Flexibility', Special Papers in International Finance, no. 11, Princeton, NJ: Princeton University.

Turnovsky, S. (1984) 'Exchange Market Intervention under Alternative Forms of Exogenous Disturbances', *Journal of International Economics*, 17: 279–97.

van der Ploeg, F. (1991) 'Macroeconomic Policy Coordination during the Various Phases of Economic and Monetary Integration in Europe', in European Commission, *European Economy*, Special Edition, P 1.

Van Neder, N., and Vanhaverbeke, W. (1990) 'The Causes of Price Differences in the European Car Markets', International Economics Discussion Paper, University of Leuven.

Van Rompuy, H., with Barroso, J.M., Juncker, J.C., and Draghi, M. (2012) 'Towards a Genuine Economic and Monetary Union', European Council, 5 December, Final Report.

Van Rompuy, P., Abraham, F., and Heremans, D. (1991) 'Economic Federalism and the EMU', in European Commission, *European Economy*, Special Edition, 1.

van Ypersele, J. (1985) *The European Monetary System*, Cambridge: Woodhead.

Verhofstadt, G. (2009) *De Weg uit de Crisis: Hoe Europa de wereld kan redden*, Amsterdam: De Bezige Bij.

von Hagen, J. (1991*a*) 'A Note on the Empirical Effectiveness of Formal Fiscal Restraints', *Journal of Public Economics*, 44: 199–210.

von Hagen, J. (1991*b*) 'Fiscal Arrangements in a Monetary Union: Evidence from the US', Working Paper, Indiana University.

von Hagen, J., and Fratianni, M. (1990) 'Asymmetries and Realignments in the EMS', in P. De Grauwe and L. Papademos (eds), *The European Monetary System in the 1990s*, London: Longman.

von Hagen, J., and Hammond, G. (1995) 'Regional Insurance against Asymmetric Shocks: An Empirical Study for the European Community', CEPR Discussion Paper, no. 1170.

von Hagen, J., and Lutz, S. (1996) 'Fiscal and Monetary Policy on the Way to EMU', *Open Economies Review*, 7: 299–325.

von Hagen, J., Hughes Hallett, A., and Strauch, R. (2002) 'Budgetary Institutions for Sustainable Public Finances', in M. Buti, J. von Hagen, and C. Martinez-Mongay (eds), *The Behaviour of Fiscal Authorities: Stabilisation, Growth and Institutions*, New York: Palgrave.

Wallace, H., and Wallace, W. (2000) *Policy-Making in the European Union*, Oxford: Oxford University Press.

Walsh, C. (1995) 'Optimal Contracts for Independent Central Banks', *American Economic Review*, 85: 150–67.

Walsh, C. (1998) *Monetary Theory and Policy*, Cambridge, MA: MIT Press.

Weber, A. (1990) 'European Economic and Monetary Union and Asymmetric and Adjustment Problems in the European Monetary System: Some Empirical Evidence', University of Siegen Discussion Paper, no. 9–90.

Whelan, K. (2012) 'TARGE T2: Not Why Germans should Fear a Euro Breakup', *Voxeu*, 29 April, http://www.voxeu.org/article/target2-germany-has-bigger-things-worry-about.

Wickens, M. (1993) 'The Sustainability of Fiscal Policy and the Maastricht Conditions', London Business School Discussion Paper, no. 10–93.

Winkler, A. (2011) 'The Joint Production of Confidence: Lessons from Nineteenth Century US Commercial Banks for Twenty First Century Eurozone Governments', mimeo, Frankfurt School of Finance and Management.

Wolf, M. (2012) 'Draghi Alone Cannot Save the Euro', *Financial Times*, 11 September.

Wolszczak-Derlacz, J. (2006) 'One Europe, One Product, Two Prices: The Price Disparity in the EU', Discussion Paper, 06.14, Center for Economic Studies, Catholic University of Leuven, August.

Wolszczak-Derlacz, J. (2008) 'Price Convergence in the EU—An Aggregate and Disaggregate Approach', *International Economics and Economic Policy*, 5(1): 25–47.

Woodford, M. (2006) 'How Important is Money in the Conduct of Monetary Policy?', paper presented at the Fourth ECB Central Banking Conference, 'The Role of Money: Money and Monetary Policy in the Twenty-First Century', Frankfurt, 9–10 November.

World Bank (2002) *World Development Indicators*, CD-ROM, Washington, DC.

Wyplosz, C. (1989) 'Asymmetry in the EMS: Intentional or Systemic?', *European Economic Review*, 33: 310–20.

Wyplosz, C. (1991) 'Monetary Union and Fiscal Policy Discipline', in European Commission, *European Economy*, Special Edition, 154.

Wyplosz, C. (2001) 'Do we Know How Low Should Inflation be?', in A. Herrero, V. Gaspar, L. Hoogduin, J. Morgan, and B. Winkler (eds), *Why Price Stability?*, First ECB Central Banking Conference, European Central Bank, pp. 15–33.

Wyplosz, C. (2002) 'Fiscal Rules or Institutions', paper prepared for the Group of Economic Analysis of the European Commission, April.

Wyplosz, C. (2006) 'European Monetary Union: The Dark Sides of a Major Success', *Economic Policy*, April: 207–61.

Wyplosz, C. (2008) 'Fiscal Policy Councils: Unlovable or just Unloved?', *Swedish Economic Policy Review*, 15: 173–92.

Wyplosz, C. (2012), 'The ECB's Trillion Euro Bet', *VoxEU*, February, available at: http://www.voxeu.org/article/ecb-s-trillion-euro-bet.

Xinpeng Xu (2004) 'An East Asian Monetary Union?', unpublished paper, The Hong Kong Polytechnic University.

Xu Ning (2004) 'Monetary Union in Asia', unpublished manuscript, University of Leuven.

Yin-Wong Cheung and Jude Yuen (2003) 'A Currency Union in Asia: An Output Perspective', paper presented at the CESifo Venice Summer Institute Workshop on 'Monetary Unions after EMU', July.

Zimmerman, H. (1989) 'Fiscal Equalization between States in West Germany', *Government and Policy*, 7: 385–93.

Index

Tables, figures, and boxes are indicated by an italic *t*, *f*, and *b* following the page number. Footnotes are indicated by 'n' following the page number.